2673
23.10

D1033416

The Story of Christian Music

Contents

Preface

Some of my earliest memories are of church music; my parents used to take my sister and me to the local country church at Wotton near Dorking, where at the age of six I was put in the choir, intrigued but totally mystified by the sounds and sights around me—the little bent man ringing the two bells before the service and the strict lady behind us, playing the harmonium with its big mirror like the one on my mother's dressing-table. My private schools developed in me a deep love for the music of the Church of England, but after countless sermons I still failed to understand what it was all for. My only memory of school confirmation was laying bets on how often the chaplain would have to relight his pipe during the classes.

At Cambridge, however, I was challenged spiritually, partly through the love and concern of Simon Barrington-Ward, then Chaplain of Magdalene College and now Bishop of Coventry. Later on, at York, I began to explore the musical implications of my new-found faith. During that time I moved back and forth from the splendour and formality of services at York Minster to the lively emotional commitment of a church just down the road.

It troubled me greatly at the time that this church's life and growth expressed itself with poor musical resources, while the aural and visual magnificence of the Minster seemed, from my naïve perspective, to be a façade concealing a spiritual void (see chapter 47 for further discussion). My tentative conclusion was that there is a need for bridges to be built between Christians. If only evangelicals, for instance, could feel happy singing Byrd and Gibbons as well as Graham Kendrick, and if only the great cathedrals in Britain could be stirred into deeper spiritual life . . .

Since then I have continued to try to work out ways to share my training with congregations anxious to use their musical gifts in God's service. Having turned my back on the cathedral world as a career, my involvement has mostly been with Christians with little or no musical education—though their expertise has sometimes surprised even them. A composer's inquisitive ear has led me to search for or to create music which can be an expression of faith and joy for a community, using all the skills available to them. Of necessity, this has meant crossing musical barriers set up by class and by denomination.

This book continues that process in another dimension. Of necessity, therefore, it deals as much as possible with music designed for or habitually used in Christian worship. I have used 'Christian music' as a shorthand for this restrictive concept, without any further implications concerning spirituality or superiority. Inevitably the field of Christian music is not always clearly fenced off, but I hope the reader will understand that I had to stop somewhere in so vast a topic, and trust that my chosen boundaries are not too arbitrary.

Writing the book has provided me with a glimpse of the fecundity of imagination with which humanity has responded to the creator God. I hope that that richness will greatly encourage the reader. But of more value still to me is the possibility that through a greater understanding of the diversity of Christian music each tradition may become more respectful and tolerant of the others. Best of all, we may rejoice in the endless variety of ways that Christians have chosen to worship, down the ages and across the world.

Introduction
The Power of Music

Now the Spirit of the Lord had left Saul and an evil spirit from God filled him with terror. Saul's servants said to him, 'Look, an evil spirit of God is the cause of your terror. Let our lord give the order, and your servants who wait on you will look for a skilled harpist; when the evil spirit of God troubles you, the harpist will play and you will recover.' Saul said to his servants, 'Find me a man who plays well and bring him to me'. One of the soldiers then spoke up... And so David came to Saul and entered his service... And whenever the spirit from God troubled Saul, David took the harp and played; then Saul grew calm, and recovered, and the evil spirit left him.[1]

This biblical narrative makes a dramatic claim. It suggests that music has a power to penetrate the mind where other forces fail, breaking down barriers directly and immediately. The mysterious nature of this process and its potency have never ceased to intrigue philosophers and creative artists.

That music can release prisoners of evil and bring them out into the light of sanity has resonances with the myth of Orpheus, the Greek god whose playing of the lyre could tame even the inhabitants of the underworld. Such powers foreshadow in legend those of Christ, who has been similarly depicted as a musician, particularly in the early days of Christianity. Legends from almost every culture and age have stories of the powers that music can 'raise or quell'. Even as late as 1621, Robert Burton in his book *The Anatomy of Melancholy* was prepared to take on trust ancient and picturesque stories about the effects of music:

In a word, [music] is so powerful a thing that it ravisheth the soul, the queen of the senses, by sweet pleasure... and corporeal tunes pacify our incorporeal soul... And 'tis not only men that are affected... Fish... as common experience evinceth, are much affected with music. All singing birds are much pleased with it, especially nightingales... and bees among the rest, though they be flying away, when they hear any tingling sound, will tarry behind. Harts, hinds, horses, dogs, bears are exceedingly delighted with it... and in Lydia in the midst of a lake there be certain floating islands (if ye will believe it) that after music will dance.[2]

The natural world demonstrates much unexpected truth in such folklore; how much more may sentient humanity be susceptible to music.

Recognition of music's Orphean powers is rare in the present rationalism of western culture. Here music is thought of as one of 'the arts' and thus relegated to areas of life regarded (like religion) as decorative, perhaps enhancing, but inessential.

In many non-Western societies, a different perspective puts an innate sense of the supernatural at the centre of life, together with its expression in music, dance, painting and sculpture. Eastern cultures, largely untouched by Western Christianity, have always thought this way. In Bali, for instance, there is no word for 'art', not because there is no music, theatre or sculpture (on the contrary, their traditions are among the richest in the world) but because these creative activities are inseparable from life.[3] To

Music therapy is not new. For centuries people have believed that music has the power to heal and restore. This sixteenth-century music school was located in the hospital of Nicholas Houe's House of Christian Charity in Paris. The viol players are patients on a recovery programme.

such peoples, music is known to have a unique control over the senses, and full advantage is taken of the fact.

Slowly, attitudes are changing in the West. Psychologists and psychiatrists, bound as they are by the scientific requirements of objective observation and deduction, are becoming more willing to acknowledge that religious awareness and artistic endeavour may be essential to mental well-being.

The neurologist Oliver Sacks is well aware of the ability of music to restore lucidity to those who have lost it or have never known it:

The power of music, narrative and drama is one of the greatest practical and theoretical importance ... We see how the retarded, unable to perform fairly simple tasks involving perhaps four or five movements or procedures in sequence, can do these perfectly if they work to music ... The same may be seen, very dramatically, in patients with severe frontal lobe damage and apraxia—an inability to *do* things, to retain the simplest motor sequences and programmes, even to walk, despite perfectly preserved intelligence in other ways. This procedural defect, or motor idiocy ... which completely defeats any ordinary system of rehabilitative instruction, vanishes at once if music is the instructor ...

What we see, fundamentally, is the power of music to organise—and to do this efficaciously (as well as joyfully!), when abstract or schematic forms of organisations fail ... Thus music, or any other form of narrative, is essential when working with the retarded or apraxic ...[4]

Sacks provides an example of this restorative power of music through one of his patients, Rebecca, who on one of her consultations summed up the way music worked for her: 'I'm like a sort of living carpet. I need a pattern, a design, like you have on that carpet. I come apart, I unravel, unless there's a design.'[5]

Significantly, one of Rebecca's patterns for life was that of worship:

... she loved the lighting of the Shabbath candles, the benisons and orisons which thread the Jewish day; she loved going to the synagogue, where she too was loved (and seen as a child of God, a sort of innocent, a holy fool); and she fully understood the liturgy, the chants, the prayers, rites and symbols ... All this was possible for her, accessible to her, loved by her, despite gross perceptual and spatio-temporal problems ...[6]

Music Therapy is a discipline developed in the

West over the past thirty years and is based on the premise that music has the capacity to heal. In a phrase that would also summarize perfectly the skills of David in the Old Testament, the modern therapist 'must be a highly skilled musician capable of musical creativity with clinically directed aims'.[7]

Sacks points out the similarity of the benefits offered by worship and music: in Rebecca's case both provided the design and order that she so clearly needed for her life.

The links between worship and music are deep-seated, for they both spring from a God-implanted desire to search for truth and order. Music is a manifestation of that search in the mental and physical realms, worship is its expression in the cosmic. What is more, God has ordered his creation in such a way that the unfolding of its truths is profoundly satisfying. As the Westminster Confession puts it: 'Man's chief and highest end is to glorify God, and fully to enjoy him for ever.'

Worship (literally 'worth-ship') is a fundamental human characteristic. It is, at best, the acknowledgment and celebration of God's utter perfection. Enjoyment of God begins with the privilege of discovering him. God has revealed himself in the way that humankind can best understand: through his son Jesus. But there is still much to be learnt about him through human creativity, which is at its most truthful when it reflects God's own creative nature. Paul, in his letter to the church at Rome, was sure that the evidence of that creativity was all around him:

Ever since the creation of the world his [God's] invisible nature, namely, his eternal power and deity, has been clearly perceived in the things he has made.[8]

Music, like other arts, is itself a response to the pattern and order of God's creation. The composer Vaughan Williams was therefore able to observe that 'music is the reaching out towards the utmost realities by means of ordered sound.'[9]

Music's power is diverse: it may merely entertain, but it can also excite, persuade, move and cure. It also acts upon its hearers in a number of ways: some react to it simply on an instinctive level, some search it for clues about their very existence, others listen for its messages about human behaviour. For music to satisfy three such differing expectations, it must be a versatile art. The romantic notion that it is a universal language accepted and understood by all is far too simple. On the contrary, music has often been the subject of fierce debate and has excited dissension and strife—especially among Christians. Because of this, a brief exploration of those three ways in which music can act on its hearers is highly relevant. They may be placed under three headings: *ecstasy, symbol* and *rhetoric.*

THE ECSTATIC DIMENSION OF MUSIC

Reaction to music can be immediate, even instinctive. Most people experience a compulsive physical response to the sensation of a regular pulse. The natural world (let alone the industrial) is full of noises that repeat—even the simple act of walking or running produces them. Synchronizing the mind and body with the beat that they produce can be pleasurable. Perhaps it is linked pre-natally to the sound of the mother's heartbeat and its associations with security. Whatever the reason, it is then but a small step to re-create the sensation for enjoyment, perhaps by clicking sticks or bones together, or by hitting a drum.

Ecstasy may seem far too strong a word for subliminal reactions that merely set feet tapping

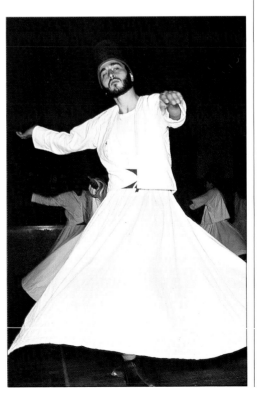

The Mevlevi, whirling dervishes from Konya, Turkey, spin round and round to achieve a trance-like state of ecstasy. The power let loose in ecstatic states forms a key element of worship in some of the world's religions. Does ecstasy have a place in Christian worship? And is music a legitimate means to induce it?

and hands clapping rhythmically during a song. But if the beat becomes insistent and compelling then the state induced may rightly be called ecstasy, since the word means 'put out of one's senses'. Some music can overtake the mind until it is oblivious to all else:

> **... the rhythm literally forces us into physical movement. Our magical impulses stir once again into wakefulness, and indeed we sometimes enter a kind of trance-state that is completely foreign to our normal consciousness.**[10]

Trances are deliberately induced in some religions, often by means of rhythm and its physical expression. The primal forces summoned up by the music of ecstasy clearly have great strength.

THE SYMBOLIC DIMENSION

In direct contrast to the ability of music to possess or control is its capacity to act as a signpost for an idea which lies outside or beyond it. The most potent symbol was expressed by early Christian writers, who imagined that integrated patterns of music (and of other arts, too) were part of a great symphony of order, initiated and sustained by God, the 'greatest of all composers, who has composed the universe of universes'.[11]

In the second century after Christ, Clement of Alexandria wrote:

> **[God's creative song] ordered the universe concordantly and tuned the discord of the elements in an harmonious arrangement, so that the entire cosmos might become through its agency a consonance.**[12]

So the music composed and played by human beings became a symbol for the infinitely grander patterns and synchronies of God's creation. Accepting that music possesses a mystical dimension has important consequences for Christians. In particular, it allows music to be understood in terms of beauty, for, according to St Thomas Aquinas, 'beauty is the splendour of order'.[13]

This in turn permits music to be judged true or false according to the accuracy with which it reflects the nature of God's creation. For some artists, like the poet Ezra Pound, this provides a yardstick for the assessment of good and bad art:

> **Bad art is inaccurate art. It is art that makes false reports ... If an artist falsifies his report as to the nature of ... god ... of good and evil ... of the force with which he believes or disbelieves this, that or the other ... if the artist falsifies his reports on these matters ... then that artist lies. By good art I mean art that bears true witness, I mean art that is most precise ...**[14]

Here, in music's attempt to address fundamental issues, is a further link with worship. It is hardly surprising that one is to be found at the service of the other in almost every religion in the world.

RHETORIC—THE MUSIC OF FEELING

Music's third ability is to communicate emotion. Like ecstatic music, this expressive quality springs from deep wells in human consciousness. Consider, for example, the fact that children are able to express their feelings by sounds, some of which could be called melodic, long before they learn to speak. Some linguists suggest that is evidence that vocal music came before language in the developing skills of humanity.

Even when language has been established, melody can be a more potent means of conveying feeling, a fact most remarkably demonstrated in the realm of Christian music.

In the North American states of Georgia and South Carolina, eighteenth-century traditions of life and worship are still preserved. In the intense

Two children join in the music during worship at the Corrymeela Community in Northern Ireland. Here Protestants and Catholics are drawn together across the country's fierce divisions. In its essence, music's place in worship is to unite—each person to the whole congregation, and the whole congregation to God.

spiritual atmosphere of remote and isolated Baptist congregations, the high point of the service is the sermon, which the preacher delivers on an upward curve of emotion. His voice begins in relaxed and natural tones, but as the intensity of the message gathers force the pitch of his voice rises and falls through a widening range, individual notes emerging ever more clearly until he has made the transition to impassioned singing. At this point the congregation are drawn in and begin to sing with the preacher.[15]

As the great nineteenth-century man of letters, Thomas Carlyle, noted:

All passionate language does of itself become musical—with a finer music than mere accent; the speech of a man even in zealous anger becomes a chant, a song.[16]

The art of persuasion by speech was highly developed in the age of classical antiquity. The ancient Greek system of education in the skill of language, the *trivium,* was three-way, consisting of *grammar, dialectic* and *rhetoric.* Rhetoric was not at all the dismissive term it can be today, but a highly organized armoury of techniques by which an orator might win over his audience.

Musicians have long believed that their art, too, has rhetorical powers. By the seventeenth century they were attempting to exploit the classical techniques of rhetoric in order to make their music emotionally persuasive. The history of Western classical music from that time on is the evidence of their success, and music which strives to express emotion has remained the dominant force in Western classical and popular music.

THE WESTERN CLASSICAL TRADITION

From a broad perspective, this tradition of rhetorical music is relatively short-lived and geographically confined, but Westerners have tended to imagine that it is the only framework for organizing music purposefully and truthfully. This assumption explains the West's dismissal of the music of other cultures as barbaric or outlandish. A *History of Modern Music* published in 1871 typifies this view:

The history of music is altogether European. Not that the orientals have, or have had, no music of their own...

but that ... their music has no charm, nor indeed meaning, for us ... The modern European system is nearer the truth than any other.[17]

Nowadays such an attitude would be deplored, but its consequences still linger on, especially in areas of Christian music cloistered by tradition. A perspective limited to the view from one particular culture can lead to misunderstandings: an audience listening out for rhetoric may be left cold by music which is primarily symbolic, or horrified, even revolted, by the music of ecstasy.

In Christian circles, such misunderstandings can be compounded by denominational tunnel vision. Christian music today springs from an extraordinary diversity of traditions: it may be ecstatic, symbolic or rhetorical depending on its origins. Each strand of Christianity has its musical signature. Hugo Cole, the critic and composer, has noted the relationship of

the musics of the various faiths, denominations and congregations to the faiths themselves... The connection is very close, and expresses itself unambiguously to one alert to musical tones of voice.[18]

It is fatally easy to perceive these distinct tones of voice merely as signposts signifying potentially threatening differences. But God's view of this diversity, according to the Bible, is inclusive. Twice the New Testament book of Revelation stresses that representatives of 'every race, language and nation' will be privileged to worship at the great and final gathering before the throne of God.[19] In the searching light of this apocalyptic vision it is evident that God not only accepts but rejoices in the varieties of race, culture and language of the people that have committed themselves to him.

God's kingdom can only continue to be built among humanity as this process of mutual acceptance goes forward. It is the intention of this book not only to point out the varieties of human experience embodied in Christian music but also to enjoy its richness and diversity. My hope is to encourage readers, not only in a better understanding of their own Christian heritage, but also in the discovery of a deeper sympathy with Christians of other cultures and with their unique styles of worship.

The Birth of Christian Music

From Old Testament times to AD 1400

Chapter 1

Music in the Old Testament

Christianity began in the midst of Jewish society. Its sensational message of salvation was first proclaimed there by a Jew whose family history linked him to King David, the greatest hero of Israel's history. Early Christian converts respected Jewish customs and continued to live and worship in the community of their families and forbears. The roots of their new faith were embedded in ancient custom, and they referred constantly in their writings to the Hebrew scriptures whose prophecies they believed were fulfilled in the coming of Jesus, the Messiah. The place that music occupied in Jewish life thus forms an important backdrop to this study, the continuity in liturgical music from Judaism to Christianity being one of the vital spans in the 'sacred bridge' that links the two faiths.

The biblical Old Testament is a wonderfully detailed documentary of a people's mythology, history and philosophy. But it is primarily a collection of sacred writings and was never intended to chronicle every facet of Jewish life. The incompleteness of the picture it paints is sometimes tantalizing.

There are, on the one hand, passages of fine detail where Bible characters come to life, fully rounded, recognizable in their humanity. But in other places the writers fall silent: they fail to tell us what to them was obvious, for they could not be expected to predict the requirements of a readership 3,000 years on. As a source of information about music in Jewish society the Old Testament is characteristic: occasional vivid detail and frustrating gaps which may never be bridged. Music is one of the areas where the Bible does not readily yield its secrets.

The Old Testament covers a long period—some 2,000 years—and during this time Hebrew culture changed greatly. Its earliest history is nomadic and tribal, a dramatic contrast with the high civilization which had developed by the time Solomon's temple was built (in about 900BC). The musical details of the Old Testament books become gradually more plentiful as we read on.

The earliest music

Early references to music in the Bible are indirect, such as the following snatch of song recorded in the book of Numbers. 'Israel', God's people, are journeying to the land promised to them. Then it was that Israel sang this song:

> '... *Sing out for the well*
> *that was sunk by the princes*
> *and dug by the leaders of the people*
> *with the sceptre, with their staves.'*[1]

This song refers to a particular situation but probably became a time-honoured ritual at a tribe's approach to a watering-place. There is, however, no clue to how the music sounded.

The study of musical cultures across the world suggests that remote and isolated settlements may preserve musical traditions intact for millenia. It is no surprise, then, to find that the Bedouin Arabs of today share aspects of their music with the nomadic Jews of the Old Testament. Bertram Thomas, an inveterate traveller of the Middle East, recorded the final morning of a long desert journey across southern Arabia with the Bedouins earlier this century:

We were arriving. The Bedawin moved at

This painting on the wall of an Etruscan tomb of the Tarquin dynasty shows musicians in a funeral procession. Their instruments—double pipes and lyre—were common to the Mediterranean world of the seventh century BC. At this time Josiah was king in Jerusalem, looking to reform the temple worship.

a sharp pace, chanting the water chants. Our thirsty camels pricked up their ears with eager knowingness. The last sandhill was left behind. After the next undulation we saw in the dip of the stony plain before us Na'aija, where we had planned a final watering, and beyond it the towers of Doha silhouetted against the waters of the Persian Gulf.[2]

The characteristic Bedouin 'shouts'—set formulae identifying a particular tribe—are probably paralleled in biblical phrases such as 'a hand upon the banner of the Lord'.[3] The ark of the covenant almost certainly began and ended its journeys with musical shouts of this kind, recorded in the book of Numbers:

And as the ark set out, Moses would say, 'Arise, Yahweh, may your enemies be scattered
and those who hate you
run for their lives before you!'
And as it came to rest, he would say,
'Come back, Yahweh,
to the thronging hosts of Israel.'[4]

One or two early songs are more vividly drawn, particularly the Song of Miriam in Exodus. It is particularly interesting that here the song is led by a woman:

Miriam the prophetess, Aaron's sister,

took up a timbrel, and all the women followed her with timbrels, dancing. And Miriam led them in the refrain:
    'Sing of Yahweh: he has covered himself in glory,
horse and rider he has thrown into the sea.'[5]

The impression is of a wild, vigorous and noisy music, inseparable from physical movement. The short lines and simple text indicate plenty of repetition, perhaps simple stepwise melodies constantly returning to a few central pitches. Together with an infectious beat, it probably led to the ecstatic state which such music can readily induce.

Singing has been, and still is, accompanied by instruments in the folk-music of the Near East. The Hebrew names for two families of stringed instruments mentioned in the books of Chronicles and Kings make the connection: *kle shir* (translated as 'lyre') means 'the tools of singing' and *lsharim* (translated as 'harp') means 'for the singers'. What are nowadays called lyre and harp are among a number of instruments mentioned extensively in books concerned with the settlement of the Jews in the Holy Land.

In common with many cultures except those of the developed world, music seemed to have a place in almost every activity and at almost every event in Jewish life. Songs of war, in victory and in defeat, are recorded in several places. One of the most striking is the song of the women who greeted David after his conquest of the Philistines, recorded in the first book of Samuel:

[They] came out to meet King Saul from all the towns of Israel, singing and dancing to the sound of tambourine and lyre and cries of joy; and as they danced the women sang [the word used here is *anah,* **'to answer' or 'to respond']:**
   'Saul has killed his thousands, and David his tens of thousands.'[6]

The constant repetition of this refrain must have taken the singers on an upward curve of ecstatic joy, though at the same time it must have fed Saul's cancerous jealousy.

David's later triumphs were the scene of even wilder rejoicing as he led the ark to Jerusalem:

On this relief found in an Assyrian palace at Nineveh, Elamite musicians play after a battle. Their instruments are vertical and horizontal harps, and the performance appears to incorporate a dance step. The whole scene echoes a number of significant Old Testament occasions.

David and all the House of Israel danced before Yahweh with all their might, singing to the accompaniment of lyres, harps, tambourines, sistrums and cymbals.[7]

The variety of instruments, with percussion and dance, was evidently a potent mixture; the traditions of many oriental cultures suggest that they would have utilized the simplest and most direct music. Such release and catharsis demands that the partakers are wholly at one with what is being celebrated, abandoning themselves

willingly. Once again the women seem to have been fully involved in the celebrations.

The result was striking. David's emotional demonstration of commitment highlighted division and dissent. Michal, David's wife, whose relationship with him must have become an uneasy one by this time, found such histrionics distasteful; she 'despised him in her heart' and later rebuked and scorned him.

Temple music

Up to this point, the music described has not been the property of the professional musician, but of people in general—the 'House of Israel'. But in a second description of the arrival of the ark of the covenant in Jerusalem[8] there is the earliest reference to the formation of a trained and official body of musicians to lead worship (hereditarily the privilege of the House of Levi). All manner of musical instruments are mentioned, together with the text of a song of thanksgiving more extensive than any recorded up to this point.[9]

After the building of the temple of Solomon (about 900BC), the liturgy becomes sumptuous and spectacular. The Bible describes the opening ceremonies and the part that music played in them in some detail:

The entire body of levitical cantors, Asaph, Heman and Jeduthun with their sons and brothers, was stationed to the east of the altar, robed in fine linen and playing cymbals, harps and lyres. A hundred and twenty priests accompanied them on the trumpet. All those who played the trumpet, or who sang, united in giving praise and glory to Yahweh. Lifting their voices to the sound of the trumpet and cymbal and instruments of music, they gave praise to Yahweh, 'for he is good, for his love is everlasting'.[10]

Such ceremonial splendour was by no means unique in the ancient world. There are detailed descriptions from Egypt and Sumeria of temple-worship earlier than 2000BC. Babylon, too, had a similar and long-established tradition, with guilds of singers, players and artists of all kinds forming part of a 'learned community, a kind of college, which studied and edited the official liturgical literature'.[11]

The temple at Jerusalem had a chequered

history. It was destroyed in 586BC, rebuilt from 520BC and further desecrated in 168BC when Antiochus used it to house a heathen altar. Through all this the traditions of temple worship were preserved, some graphic accounts of them being recorded during the latter period, particularly in sources outside the canonical books of the Old Testament.

The apocryphal book Ecclesiasticus (about 200BC) contains a vivid description of the service for the Day of Atonement[12] which is paralleled in the Talmud—a large collection of Jewish teaching—which also contains this description of the final part of the daily services of offering:

They gave him the wine for the drink-offering, and the Prefect stood by each horn of the altar with a towel in his hand, and two priests stood at the table of the fat pieces with two silver trumpets in their hands. They blew a prolonged, a quavering (?) and a prolonged blast. Then they came and stood by Ben Arza, the one on his right and the other on his left. When he stooped and poured out the drink-offering the Prefect waved the towel and Ben Arza clashed the cymbals and the Levites broke forth into singing. When they reached a break in the singing they blew upon the trumpet and at every blowing of the trumpet a prostration. This was the rite of the Daily Whole-offering... This was the singing which the Levites used to sing in the temple.[13]

This source also mentions that the choir had at least twelve singers, all men, with supplementary boys 'to add sweetness', and that the instruments consisted of nine or more lyres *(kinnor)*, kithara *(nebel*—though usually translated as 'harps' or 'lyres'), between two and twelve cane pipes *(balil)* and cymbals *(mezaltaim)*. The pipes (often called 'flutes' in translation) were in reality twin-bodied reed instruments, very like the *auloi* depicted in Greek iconography. They were played at certain times of year—at Passover and during the eight days of the Feast of Tabernacles.[14]

From the same period, the Roman *Letter of Aristeas* gives a vivid eye-witness account of temple sacrifice, of which this is only a short extract:

[During the sacrificial service] the deepest silence prevails, so that one would suppose that there was not a single person in the place, although the ministers in attendance number some 700, not to mention the large multitude of those who await their sacrifices to be offered; everything is performed with reverence and in a manner worthy of the Divine Majesty.[15]

The Dead Sea Scrolls of the Essenes (a Jewish sect) were discovered at Qumran in 1947, but have not yet been dated with certainty. Whether or not they are contemporary with biblical writings, they write about music and instruments in very similar terms:

...I raised a bitter lament
and made a doleful moan and groan
and plied my harp [kinnor] in
mournful dirge...
But suddenly I perceived
that there was no more affliction
to rack me with pain.
Then did I ply my harp
with music of salvation,
and my lyre [nebel] to the tune of joy;
yea, I plied the pipe [balil]...
in ceaseless praise.[16]

Worship—impulsive or formal?

The function of music in worship changed in the thousand years or so from the time when David danced in triumph before the ark of the covenant to the time of Christ, in response to changes in society.

The early descriptions are often of music being created impulsively, as a response to events (such as David's triumphs) and enabling the release of emotions amongst a people willing to express them openly. Such scenes of abandon are recalled nowadays in the practices of a number of Christian communities around the world—above all in the music of the Ethiopian Orthodox Church which maintains remarkable links with the distant past.

Music therapists today are quite certain that, under the right conditions, such open expression of feeling is beneficial and healthy:

Music therapy permits what the analyst

This bronze sistrum, a percussion instrument from Egypt in the ninth century BC, is of a kind still used nearly three thousand years later in Ethiopian Orthodox worship.

The Psalms in Temple Worship

T hough they were not the only texts sung in the temple, the biblical psalms occupied a central place in its liturgy and numerous references give some insight into how they sounded. The Talmud gives a list of psalms appropriate for each day of the week:[1]

◆ On the first day:
Psalm 24

◆ On the second day:
Psalm 48

◆ On the third day:
Psalm 82

◆ On the fourth day:
Psalm 94

◆ On the fifth day:
Psalm 81

◆ On the sixth day:
Psalm 93

◆ On the Sabbath:
Psalm 92

The book of all 150 psalms was compiled over a long period, its present form being established well after the exile and the re-building of the temple. Some of the titles, such as 'a psalm of Asaph' or 'of the sons of Korah', indicate the repertoire of a particular hereditary guild of musicians; others indicate the occasions on which the psalms were used, still others giving the name of the melodic formula used to accompany them (similar to Indian *rags* or Arabic *maqamât* which also bear evocative names).

Both the Talmud and many of the psalm-headings show that the Levites sang accompanied, often by plucked stringed instruments. The musical structure was governed by the liturgical sections into which psalms were divided ('. . . when they reached a break in the singing they blew upon the trumpet'). These breaks are sometimes indicated by the word *Selah*, often translated as 'pause'.

Left: In this illumination from the eleventh-century Winchester Psalter, King David plays on the 'kle shir', or lyre. David was the greatest patron of music and psalmody in Israel, and therefore greatly loved by Christian and Jewish musicians alike.

Right: Jerusalem's 'Wailing Wall' remains a focus of Jewish devotion because it was part of Herod's temple, and thus a link with thousands of years of worship. Christians also have a link with Old Testament praise through their use of the Psalms, the hymnbook of both the Bible's testaments.

The precise musical setting of the psalms will always be a matter for speculation, but the structure of the verses offers some clues. Firstly, the familiar parallelism of the Hebrew poetry readily suggests musical equivalents:

I am up before dawn to call for help,
I put my hope in your word.
I lie awake throughout the night,
*   to meditate on your promise.*[2]

A number of musical responses to the poetic structure developed in Jewish worship. The word *anah,* meaning 'to respond', is important here. It was used in describing the music at David's victory celebrations and is still found today in connection with Jewish antiphonal singing.

The Talmud elaborates considerably on the concept of 'response'. It describes a number of possibilities: for instance, how a soloist may sing the entire melody of a verse, the other singers answering with a repeat of the same first half-verse; or how the soloist and singers may take

alternating half-verses; or perhaps all may sing a refrain after each verse;[3] finally, for teaching purposes, the soloist's half-verses might be repeated by the rest. But in few of these schemes does there appear to be room for participation by the people; the temple choir, it seems, sang on their behalf.

Hebrew poetry does not rhyme, nor does it have a consistent metre like a modern hymn-tune or classical poetry. It has pronounced weak and strong stresses, but their number is free. (A number of modern translations, such as the *Jerusalem Bible,* attempt to convey something of these qualities.) The musical rhythm was therefore probably dictated by the text and not confined to a steady beat, while the melodic scheme would have to be able to accommodate irregular verse-lengths.

The names of tunes which head some of the psalms probably consisted of a pair of short melodic ideas, one for the first half-verse and one for the second, not at all unlike Gregorian chant. Harmonization would have been most unlikely, but drones of unisons, fourths

and fifths have been suggested.[4]

Even in translation, the nature of the psalms have produced remarkably consistent patterns of musical setting over a period of nearly 3,000 years. Plainsong, Anglican chant, or the more recent settings of Joseph Gélineau all echo the patterns of the original Hebrew. In spite of what one writer has called the 'rash and apparently uncontrollable innovations' in modern psalm-singing,[5] this suggests that the structure and beauty of the Hebrew psalms are too strong to be neglected by musicians and will continue to enrich both Jewish and Christian music.

Music in the Synagogue

The Bible provides ample evidence of the gradual development of synagogue worship, with its origins in the period of Babylonian captivity known as the exile. But although the distinction between synagogue (the institution) and synagogue (a building) is an important one, the word itself simply means 'place of assembly'.

The book of Nehemiah, which marks the beginning of the Jews' return from exile in the early sixth century BC, gives a moving and vivid account of such an assembly, where, in the open air, 'Ezra the scribe stood on a wooden pulpit which they had made for the purpose' to read from the Book of the Law.[1]

Meetings for civil matters, for worship and particularly for religious instruction became commonplace, the New Testament providing plenty of examples of the latter.[2] The earliest buildings in which such meetings were held date from the middle of the third century BC, the time of the dispersed Jews in Egypt.

The style of worship in synagogues was based on the practices of the temple, though moderated by omitting the sacrificial acts and rituals (these were replaced in the synagogue by prayers or readings referring to sacrifice, there being no altar). A Levite, Joshua ben Chananiah, writing shortly after the time of Christ, noted that

the [temple] choristers used to go in a body to the synagogue from the orchestra by the altar, and so participated in both services.[3]

He was writing at a time of tension between temple and synagogue, which serves to highlight the difference between the two institutions. In *The Sacred Bridge,* Werner notes that

The temple had developed a type of liturgy which, with its hierarchy, its sacrificial cult, and its rigid organization, engendered a sharp distinction between the officers of the ritual and the community of the faithful, the latter being almost passive bystanders.[4]

Synagogue worship, on the other hand, was organised and conducted by lay people and not by a hereditary priesthood. Services consisted of readings from the Law and from the Prophets, of psalmody, teaching, prayer and final blessing.

The psalms, prayers and readings would be cantillated, that is, recited in a heightened speech resembling simple song. Its basis was the chanting of the text on a single note, but with simple melodic alterations to indicate the grammatical structure. The Christian liturgy of the East still uses the technique extensively—scholars of Byzantine music call it *ekphonesis*. The principles behind cantillation are elaborated in chapter 4. Synagogue music needed the skilled leadership of a cantor, whose sole responsibility it became in later times.

These trumpet-like instruments, from an ancient Jewish manuscript, include the curved ram's horn, or 'shofar', the national trumpet of Israel.

discourages: the acting out of the emotions. But with music this is done with some control through the guilt-free medium of non-verbal sound.[17]

In this respect music therapy is still out of step with the received wisdom of Western society, for many Europeans fear and discourage the expression of deeply-felt emotion. The problem of coping with grief provides a very clear example.

Western funerals are designed to keep expressions of anguish and sorrow out of sight; grief publicly expressed is an embarrassment, even when it would seem to be justified and understandable. In other parts of the world relatives and friends of departed loved ones demonstrate their feelings freely and physically, rocking their bodies, wringing their hands, weeping and wailing. Their singing is a highly emotional outpouring from depths of feeling.

It is this elemental side of music which is at work in many scenes in the history of ancient Israel; it accompanies (or makes possible) the expression of strong emotion, which in turn is often the cause of dramatic events such as the collapse of the walls of Jericho[18] or a prophecy.[19]

Yet, unlike the lone dissent of Michal at David's dance before the ark, there have been countless objections from Christians when music has been given the freedom to wield this power. In the Old Testament there is a gradual move away from this ecstatic dimension to liturgical music of a more contemplative kind, formal, symbolic and ritualized. The change, in keeping with the style of worship to which it belonged, coincided with the move from open-air ceremonies to a liturgy celebrated in the cavernous acoustics of a large building.

Worship in the temple must have been thrilling and colourful to eye and ear, but in its latter days the music became part of a ritual which seems to have left little room for spontaneity. Instead, it acted more as symbol. Trumpets, for example, represented God's power, authority and majesty, while the cantillation of scripture was a potent reminder of the sanctity of the scriptures, setting the word of God apart from the unsanctified conversations of daily life. This won the chant a central place in Hebrew worship.

While the startling power of ecstatic music may be sacrified in their favour, musical symbols are nonetheless valuable tools in the search for truth, above all in their ability to summarize or to enclose a complex thought in one simple and striking image.[20]

These two abilities of music, to possess and to symbolize, have profoundly affected the quality and nature of Christian worship whenever music makes an appearance. Unhappily, those convinced of the efficacy of one have tended vigorously to deny the value of the other, and the divisions thereby created have been deep and damaging.

Chapter 2

Music in the Early Church

This synagogue in
Capernaum was described
by Egeria, a Spanish nun,
in about AD381, but beneath
it lies an older building in
which Jesus often preached
(Luke 4:31; John 6:59).
Scholars continue to
speculate on the music that
resonated in such places.

Connections between Jewish and early Christian worship are well documented and new links are still being discovered. Even the temple worship is relevant here, not so much as a direct influence— Jesus and his disciples were generally antagonistic to what went on in the temple,[1] but through the synagogue— which had adapted the ceremony of the temple to its own use. Surprising though it may seem, Christianity did not require an entirely new set of principles to guide its worship.

These links may provide one of the reasons for the relative scarcity of musical reference in the New Testament, for there would be no need to record the detail of established worship. Because Christians saw their faith as a completion of

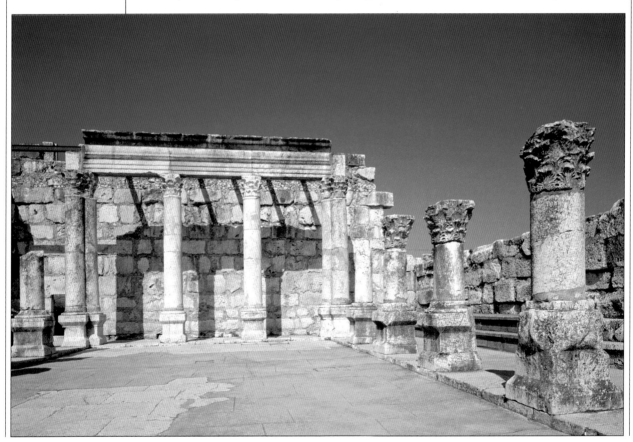

Judaism, they were able to continue to use many parts of Jewish liturgy, but to see them in a new light.[2]

The traditions of the synagogue continued to be absorbed into Christian worship for some time, in spite of the persecutions of AD44 and the Council of Jerusalem, which in AD49 ruled that pagan converts to Christianity need not keep the Law of Moses.[3] Cantors, trained to lead the singing in the synagogue and then converted to the Christian faith, continued to put their skills to use in their new church.

Church and synagogue

Not only did the early Christians speak Aramaic—the language of Jesus himself—as did their fellow Jews in Palestine, but they shared with them a similar 'church year'. The Jewish New Year begins in the autumn, which is when the earliest Christians celebrated the birth of Christ[4]—Christmas has only been celebrated on 25 December since the fourth century. The Christian Easter Eve coincided exactly with the time of Passover, a fact fundamental to an understanding of the significance of the Eucharist.

Both church and synagogue had (and still have) in common: the idea of baptism, the 'Liturgy of the Word' (which for the Christian is the first part of the Eucharist—readings, the singing of psalms and hymns, teaching and prayers), fasting and the encouragement to develop a personal life of prayer. Furthermore, the scriptural content of synagogue and early Christian worship has been shown to correspond in some remarkable ways.[5]

These points of comparison are well documented, but to compare the music of the early church with that of the synagogue is more difficult. Neither Jews nor Christians are known to have noted down any of the music they used for worship until at least the sixth or seventh century AD. The best and perhaps only means of investigation is indirect—by comparing the oldest written musical sources of the Christian church with the present-day singing of those Jewish communities which have preserved their traditions over two millenia. The isolated and highly orthodox Yemenite Jews form one society whose music shows some remarkable correspondences with the earliest known Christian sources.

But Christians were also composing new

La - me-na-tze-ach al ha-gi-ttit   mi - ze-mor le-a ssaf.

Je-ru-sa-lem, Je - ru-sa-lem, conver-te-re ad Do-mi-num De-um tu - um.

songs in celebration of the faith:

> **... be filled with the Spirit. Sing the words and tunes of the psalms and hymns when you are together, and go on singing and chanting to the Lord in your hearts...[6]**

Although some translations only stress 'making melody in your hearts', there is every reason to believe that Paul's exhortation to sing was literal. The terminology of some translations is not very helpful, since 'hymn' (and 'spiritual song' in many other versions) has a great diversity of meanings to present-day readers of differing traditions.

At the time of Paul's letters, the hymn, in rhyming verses, did not exist. Later, Augustine (354-430) gave a definition of the word 'hymn':

> **A hymn is a song containing praise of God. If you praise God, but without song, you do not have a hymn. If you praise anything, which does not pertain to the glory of God, even if you sing it, you do not have a hymn. Hence, a hymn contains the three elements:** *song* **and** *praise* **of** *God.*[7]

Paul also probably means to include spontaneous praise in song under the influence of the Holy Spirit, which many Christians today call 'singing in tongues'. The literal meaning of 'spiritual songs' is 'odes'—'spiritual' as opposed to secular.

The words of some early hymns are recorded in the New Testament, a number of them in the book of Revelation,[8] such as this fragment:

> **And I seemed to hear the voices of a huge crowd, like the sound of the ocean or the great roar of thunder, answering, 'Alleluia! The reign of the Lord our God**

The similarity of these two chant formulae for the Lamentations of Jeremiah suggest a common origin. The upper one was transcribed in the late nineteenth century from Yemenite singing and represents a pre-Christian Jewish tradition; the lower is medieval Gregorian chant. Such musical links between Judaism and Christianity form what Eric Werner's remarkable book has called 'the Sacred Bridge'.

The Spread of Christianity

*F*irst, then, those of the sect were arrested who confessed; next, on their disclosures, vast numbers were convicted... And ridicule accompanied their end: they were covered with wild beasts' skins and torn to death by dogs; or they were fastened on crosses, and, when daylight failed, were burned to serve as torches by night. Nero had offered his gardens for the spectacle.[1]

Thus wrote Tacitus, the Roman imperial historian and vehement Christian-hater, recording events of Nero's reign from AD54–68. The story was to be repeated again and again, with horrific variations, over the next two centuries.

Why were the Christians such a menace? They were reputedly not criminals but pacifists, honest and trustworthy, as some contemporaries, such as Pliny, had recorded. But they bore the marks of conspiracy: followers of a man executed for treason and obstinately refusing to acknowledge or sacrifice to the gods by which Roman civilization swore and which gave the emperor his divinity. In short, they were members of an illegal society which had to be stamped out.

Apart from the physical threat of torture and death, Christians also faced the spiritual threat of heresy. As the faith spread rapidly to nations outside Palestine—to Greece, to Gaul, to Egypt, to Syria and Rome—the resident philosophies and religious beliefs of these nations had their effect.

The great diversity of doctrine that could be called 'Christian' caused deep concern to the leaders of the early church. The Gnostics, for instance, could not have been called Christians by the standards of most of today's denominations, and the urgent need for conformity was already being voiced by the end of the first century.

Clement of Rome recommended in his *Letter to the Corinthians* (written about AD95) that the laity should obey the clergy, even on pain of death, shifting the balance of power very much in favour of the ecclesiastical leadership. Later, Bishop Irenaeus (about AD130–200) insisted that salvation was only possible through the one church, and that outside it 'there can be no salvation'. By about AD200, Christian leaders were working urgently to create and to strengthen a catholic, or universal, church.

Their efforts were assisted by the unstable political circumstances in which Christians had to live:

Pressed by their common danger, members of scattered Christian groups throughout the world increasingly exchanged letters and travelled from one church to another. Accounts of the martyrs, often taken from records of their trials and from eyewitnesses, circulated among the churches in Asia, Africa, Rome, Greece, Gaul and Egypt. By such communication, members of the diversified earlier churches became aware of regional differences as obstacles to their claim to participate in one catholic church.[2]

Far from scattering and confusing the early church, persecution and heresy worked to strengthen it. The early church fathers strove to define the faith in order to excommunicate heretics (later on they were to use more brutal methods) by establishing agreements on forms of worship, selecting and canonizing the writings of the New Testament and by proposing a creed which all Christians could confess.

It was the Emperor Constantine (about AD274–337) who brought about a fundamental change in the political status of Christians. A legend tells that, before joining battle with Maxentius for the leadership of the Roman Empire, Constantine saw a cross blazing in the sky with the words *in hoc signo vinces*—'in this sign you will conquer'.

Constantine took his subsequent resounding victory to be a sure sign of God's favour and his conversion to the Christian faith reversed the fortunes of Christendom at a stroke. Through the Edict of Milan in 313 he not only granted Christians freedom of worship throughout the Empire, but also put many in positions of public authority and allowed the church to own property.

In 328 Constantine created a great new city in the East bearing his name—Constantinople. It was to become a bastion of Christian culture and learning, a formidable rival to the other Christian Patriarchies around the Mediterranean—Antioch, Jerusalem, Alexandria and Rome. Worship in these centres was conducted in splendid new buildings and with great ceremony, in keeping with Christianity's new image as a state religion.

What is more, Christians in different countries began to worship in different languages, rather than in the Greek which had become the common language of earlier times. A number of different liturgical traditions arose, defined by geographical area and sometimes by the language adopted. The Western churches (including such areas as Spain, the Celtic countries and Gaul) adopted Latin for worship, Eastern countries tending to use the vernacular—Arabic in Syria, Greek in Byzantia, Coptic in Egypt. The effects of these ancient languages on Christian worship is still evident, as a number of the traditions laid down at this period are alive to this day. The story of these Eastern traditions is continued in Part 5.

The cithara seen on this Greek vase from the fifth century BC is being played by Apollo. Music was a central part of Greek cultural life. It was Pythagoras who discovered the relationship between numbers and musical scales, and stories about Orpheus were seminal myths for the Greeks. Little is known of how their music sounded, but it seems likely that Christian singing followed Greek as well as Jewish example.

the Almighty has begun; let us be glad and joyful and give praise to God, because this is the time for the marriage of the Lamb...'[9]

The acclamation 'Alleluia' suggests a refrain, following traditional practice in Jewish psalmody. The Gospel of Luke includes some songs which were perhaps already established in the worship of the early church by the time he recorded them. They are the song of Mary (the Latin version begins *Magnificat)*, the song of Zechariah *(Benedictus)* and the song of Simeon *(Nunc Dimittis)*.[10] By translating these songs back from the Greek of the Gospels to the original Aramaic, the characteristic rhythms and structure of Hebrew psalms are revealed, suggesting that they were chanted in the same way. The words of other early Christian hymns are quoted by Peter and Paul in their letters.[11]

Beyond these tantalizing glimpses of the earliest Christian worship in the first century, other evidence in the New Testament is circumstantial. The author of the book of Revelation, for instance, seems to base his visions of worship in the heavenly Jerusalem in chapters 4 and 5 on the words of the *Sanctus,* ('Holy, holy, holy') still used in the Eucharist. A similar text must therefore have been part of Christian worship in his own day.

Christian worship

In about AD111 Pliny the Younger, Roman governor of Bithynia and Pontus, wrote to the Emperor Trajan for guidance on the attitude he should take to Christians. Writing as an unbeliever, he describes them in this way:

> They affirmed, however, that this was the extent of their fault or error, that they were wont to assemble on a set day before dawn and to sing a hymn among themselves to the Christ, as to a god, and that they pledged themselves by vow not to some crime, but that they would commit neither fraud, nor theft, nor adultery, nor betray their word, nor deny a trust when summoned; after which it was their custom to separate and to come together again to take food—ordinary and harmless food, however.[12]

Dancing and instrumental music were almost universally shunned, because of their powerful associations with debauchery and immorality. For example, this commentary on Isaiah dating from the fourth century clearly associates lyre-playing with prostitution:

> You place a lyre ornamented with gold and ivory upon a high pedestal as if it were a...devilish idol, and some miserable woman, rather than being taught to place her hands upon a spindle, is taught by

you... to stretch them out on the lyre. Perhaps you pay her wages or perhaps you turn her over to some female pimp, who, exhausting the licentious potential of her own body, presides over young women as the teacher of similar deeds.[13]

There are many similar examples in contemporary writing. This vitriolic attack on both instrumental music and dancing dates from the fourth century:

> ... in blowing on the tibia [pipes] they puff out their cheeks... they lead obscene songs... they raise a great din with the clapping of scabella [a type of foot percussion]; under the influence of which a multitude of other lascivious souls abandon themselves to bizarre movements of the body.[14]

The vehemence of these comments indicates the church's desire to distance itself as far as possible from instrumental music or dancing. Christians were warned not to practise either, even outside the hours of formal worship.

Chapter 3

The Beginning of the Western Middle Ages

The name 'Middle Ages' was coined in the fifteenth century by European thinkers—artists and musicians among them—who turned their attention with renewed intensity to the world of classical antiquity as a model for their own age.

The bridge between their new classical age and the original one was the *medium aevum,*

the medieval or Middle Ages, whose beginnings are usually reckoned from the fall of imperial Rome and the time of Pope Leo the Great. Though the Renaissance represented an important turning-point in European thought, the medieval culture it gradually replaced had itself been influenced by certain classical writers

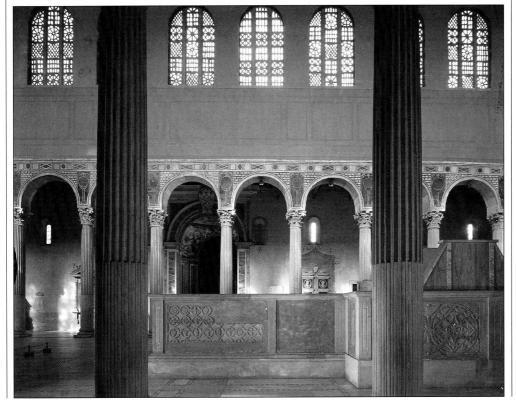

The basilica of Santa Sabina in Rome preserves remarkably clearly the setting in which Christians would once have worshipped. It dates from the times when Christianity became the official religion of the Roman Empire.

Worship in Fifth-Century Jerusalem

Egeria, a Spanish nun, made a pilgrimage to Jerusalem at the beginning of the fifth century, and subsequently described her experience. This rare account is vivid and fascinating. Here she describes Sunday morning worship, perhaps at Easter.

First of all she observes the large crowd collecting in front of the church doors—they arrived early to be sure of getting in (she calls this a vigil):

Before cockcrow the whole crowd collects, as many as the place will hold. For, as they are afraid that they may not be there at cockcrow, they come beforehand and sit there. And hymns and antiphons are sung; and after each hymn or antiphon a prayer is offered. For the priests and deacons are always there for vigils, on account of the crowd...

She then describes the service of Matins, the first of the day:

But when the first cock has crowed, the bishop descends and enters... All the doors are opened and the whole crowd streams into the sanctuary. Here innumerable lights are shining; and when the people have entered, one of the priests recites a psalm, and they all respond; then prayer is offered.

[Two more psalms and prayers follow, then] ...censers are brought into the sanctuary, so that the whole basilica is filled with odours. Then where the bishop stands inside the rails, he takes the Gospel and advances to the door and himself reads of the Lord's resurrection.

And when he has begun to read this, there is such a moaning and groaning of all the people, and such weeping...for that the Lord endured such grievous things for us. Then the Gospel having been read, the bishop comes forth and is led to the Cross with hymns, and all the people with him. There again one psalm is recited and prayer offered. Again he blesses the faithful, and the dismissal is given.

As the bishop comes forth they all approach to kiss his hand; and presently the bishop betakes himself to his own house. From that hour all the monks return to the sanctuary and psalms and antiphons are sung till daylight...

If any of the laity, either men or women, wish it, they stay there till it is light; but if they do not wish to do so, they return to their houses and go to sleep again.

At dawn Egeria moves to the Great Church of Constantine, built on Golgotha, where first of all she hears many sermons from a number of priests during a service lasting till about ten in the morning. After this:

the monks escort the bishop with hymns from the Great Church to the sanctuary. And when the bishop arrives with hymns, all the doors of the sanctuary basilica are opened; and all the people enter (that is, the faithful; for the catechumens [converts under instruction but not yet baptised] enter not).

Then the baptised Christians all take Communion together. Finally she adds:

Among all these details this is very plain, that psalms or antiphons are always sung; those at night, those in the morning, and those through the day, whether at the sixth hour [mid-day] or ninth hour [mid-afternoon] or vespers [early evening], being always suitable and intelligible as pertaining to the matter at hand.[1]

These final comments suggest that the traditional daily round of services (the Daily or Divine Office) was already established by the fifth century and a comparison of Egeria's experience with the fuller details of the liturgy in the following chapters will show some interesting common ground.

Egeria stresses the importance of music, particularly the thread of psalm-singing which runs through all she describes. There are plenty of opportunities for the congregation to participate in the music: 'everyone responds' in the psalms. This suggests one of the traditional Jewish practices, that of cantor and congregation singing alternate verses. The reference to hymns here may mean a distinct type of music somewhat different from psalms—such as the hymns of Ambrose of Milan. An antiphon is a short sentence in song (see box).

In Egeria's time the two parts of the Eucharist—the Liturgy of the Word and the Communion—were geographically separated by being held in different buildings (the Christians returned to the basilica for the Communion where they had earlier heard Matins) and only baptised Christians were permitted to attend the latter.

These two sections of the service are still identifiable in many denominations today. The liturgy was clearly ceremonial, but this did not preclude emotional involvement on the people's part, particularly at the reading of the Gospel. The women, too, seem to have been given equal rights amongst the congregation, a state of affairs which was to change in harsher times to come.

Pope Gregory the Great, seen dictating a manuscript in this imagined portrait some two hundred years later than he lived, saw a need to unify the different forms of worship then in use. This harmonization inevitably included the music used in liturgy, hence Gregory's longstanding connection with church music, and particularly chant.

and their philosophy, with important consequences for Christian music.

During the fifth century the church hierarchy increased its power yet further. Pope Leo the Great, (Leo I, 440–461) showed himself to be an impressive diplomat, negotiating the retreat of Attila the Hun across Europe in 452 and later dissuading the conquering Ostrogoths from pillaging Rome. So it was by default that the church authorities found themselves taking up the reins of international politics as Roman imperial power collapsed around them.

Gregory the Great

A number of popes built on this power-base, none more impressively than Gregory the Great, who was born in about 540 and pope from 589 to 604. Gregory was a highly intelligent man, with considerable abilities of leadership.

With immense energy, he set about re-establishing Roman authority, both civil and ecclesiastical. He worked in international and local politics, rebuilding the fabric of the city (the aqueducts, for instance). He developed a welfare system of charities and hospitals and revised and tightened a tax system to pay for the administration of the city and its surroundings— all of which was put into effect by the clergy. Law and the penal code were redrawn in detail under his supervision.

Yet he also preached and wrote voluminously concerning faith and doctrine, aware of the need for a clear and unequivocal voice in Christian matters. Pope Gregory's double success in law and faith was of prime importance for the

In this tenth-century mosaic over the south door of Hagia Sophia in Istanbul, Emperor Constantine, who founded Constantinople as the focus of the Eastern Empire, presents a model of the city to the Virgin Mary. Justinian, the Byzantine emperor responsible for building Hagia Sophia, presents a symbolic model of the church. In medieval times, church and state were to form a complex web of authority and influence over people's lives.

missionaries sent to the remoter corners of Europe. They needed to be able both to present an authoritative gospel and to offer an efficient network of administration to the barbarian kings. In 597, for instance, Gregory's mission to England landed in Kent and within twenty years not only was the Kentish king converted to Christianity, but he had also accepted a workable legal system along with it.

As part of the process of increasing the authority of the Church of Rome, Gregory strongly encouraged conformity in styles of worship. The differing Latin liturgies (Mozarabic, Gallican, Ambrosian, Celtic) were gradually absorbed into the Roman, with an inevitable effect on the melodies that characterized them.

Music was still not being written down, so it is difficult to tell what those changes were, but by the time music was widely notated (around the tenth century) there was near universal agreement on the shape of worship—the church year was established in fine detail, along with its liturgical structure and its music. One or two centres held out against change and, as a result of past dispensations, the Mozarabic liturgy can still be heard today in the Spanish cathedral of Toledo,[1] as can the Ambrosian in the northern Italian cathedral of Milan.

But Pope Gregory, a great diplomat, administrator and theologian, would probably be surprised to know that he is most widely remembered for the changes to the music for the Roman liturgy which took place during his papacy. This enduring attribution is the result of the apocryphal musical deeds that medieval scholars later invented for him. It is therefore an inaccurate though long-standing tradition which gives the name *Gregorian* chant to the richest collection of Christian music in the world.

Chapter 4

The Monastic Tradition

For some believers the new opulence of Christianity's status as an imperial religion was inappropriate, even repugnant. Antony (about 251–356) is believed to have been the first to propose extreme asceticism and worldly deprivation as an essential foundation for Christian living. The means of this deprivation were prayer, fasting, celibacy and isolated contemplation in the most inhospitable place on earth—the Egyptian desert. Antony's example was followed by many others who established communities all over Europe and the Middle East in pursuance of lives lived wholly in the service of God.

One of the early Christians most influential in shaping monastic tradition was Benedict of Nursia (about 480–about 530), the abbot and founder of the monasteries of Subiaco and Monte Cassino in Italy. He proposed a Rule for his Order, a 'school of the Lord's service, in which we hope to order nothing harsh or rigorous'. The Rule divided the day into six hours of prayer, five of manual work and four of the study of Scripture.

Many other fraternities came into existence later, but the example of Benedict was the most important. Even the worship of the Protestant Church has inherited parts of his Rule, such as the addition of a doxology (the 'gloria') to the ending of psalms.

The monks' day

The Rule's six hours of prayer are divided up into a daily round of services, consisting of the Mass (the Lord's Supper or Eucharist) and the Divine Office:

◆ *Matins ('morning') before daybreak*

◆ *Lauds ('praises') at dawn*

◆ *Prime (at the first hour) 6 am*

◆ *Terce (third hour) 9 am*

◆ *Sext (sixth hour) mid-day*

◆ *None (ninth hour) 3 pm*

◆ *Vespers ('evening') about 6pm*

◆ *Compline ('completion') end of the day*

These services are linked together by their common basis in the biblical psalms, in such a way that the whole cycle of 150 psalms is sung every week. The Lesser Hours (that is, Prime, Terce, Sext and None) are simple and unadorned, lasting perhaps twenty minutes each. They all have a similar pattern and begin with a greeting, probably sung, such as

Priest: *Dominus vobiscum* [**The Lord be with you**]
Congregation: *Et cum spiritu tuo* [**And with your spirit**]

After this, a hymn is sung, followed by three psalms. A passage from scripture is then chanted by a reader, followed by a short response from

These monks are plainly singing a 'lauda', folk music for a festival procession. The monastery was the setting above all others, where Christian music was sustained and developed through the Dark Ages.

everyone. A brief dismissal concludes the worship.

Modes

There was no concept in medieval times of 'key'. To present-day musicians there is a significant difference between the keys, say, of F and A. The contrast between them may be deliberately exploited by changing from one to another during a piece. The collisions and tensions that can then result are one of the chief ways of building longer pieces of music without them becoming wearisome to the modern ear.

Most popular Western music today uses only two modes, major and minor. Like all modes, they are defined by the characteristic intervals that make them up. The major mode—what is now called the major scale—starts with two intervals of a tone (in C major, C to D, then D to E) but the distinct quality of the minor mode is created by the second interval only being a semitone (D to E flat). Thus modes are identified not by the names of notes, but by their unique sequences of intervals.

The musical sensitivities and expectations of a medieval cleric were quite different from those of musicians using the major/minor scale system. Contrasts generated to sustain interest and to build narrative structures on a large scale played no part in his thinking. His music was built on a system of eight modes: eight different arrangements of tones and semitones.

Medieval musicians were fascinated to read ancient Greek writers who described their own music in much the same way. Theorists enthusiastically but incorrectly applied the names of the Greek modes to their own music, even though few details of ancient Greek music were known to them. In reality, the medieval tradition owed more to the synagogue.

Almost all Gregorian chant, no matter how ornate, conforms to one of the eight modes. For psalm-singing there are eight 'tones' corresponding to the eight modes. So it is that the aural character of different chants owes a great deal to the interval-patterns on which the modes are built.

Hymns

Another type of music in the Divine Office is the hymn. In New Testament times and even up to the fifth century, Augustine's definition of hymn held good, that it was simply a 'song in praise of God'. Gradually a new type of liturgical song became popular. It was different from other types of chant in that it did not use the words of scripture (though it might have been closely based on them) but was freely composed in words and music.

The use of this type of hymn began with Eastern Christians and became an important part of the Byzantine liturgy. It was Ambrose (Bishop of Milan from 374) who encouraged their use in the Western church. Augustine records in his autobiographical *Confessions*:

... the church at Milan had begun to seek comfort and spiritual strength in the practice of singing of hymns, in which the faithful fervently united with heart and voice ... Ever since then the custom has been retained, and the example of Milan has been followed in many other places, in fact in almost every church

This pigmented stone figure is thought to represent Ambrose of Milan, often called the father of hymnody in the Western church.

Antiphons

The antiphon was a particular feature of the psalm-singing of the Lesser Hours. A number of psalms have a short refrain placed between each verse; Psalm 136 ('his love endures for ever') is an example, as are the 'Hallel' psalms which are punctuated by shouts of *Hallelujah*—('praise the Lord').

Thousands of such short refrains were freely composed in medieval times, to be interlaced between psalm-verses in order to make a spiritual comment or to emphasize a theme of worship. The words might be drawn from one of the psalm verses themselves, or from another passage of scripture. Whatever the case, since the refrain alternated with the psalm verses, it was called an *antiphon*, from the Greek 'sounding against'.

To sing even this short refrain between every psalm-verse (and in Matins there are nine psalms to be sung) would extend worship beyond human endurance, so the convention was established that, in most cases, the antiphon is only sung at the beginning and end.

Pueri Hebraeorum, * vestimenta prosternebant in vi-a, et clamabant

dicentes : Hosanna filio David : benedictus qui venit in nomine Domini.

An antiphon for Palm Sunday, freely composed to a text closely based on Matthew's Gospel, chapter 21 verses 8 and 9. It is typical of Christian chant that its word-setting should be contemplative and not dramatic.

throughout the world.[1]

Ambrose himself wrote a number of hymns and was not unaware of his talent:

They also say that the people are led astray by the charms of my hymns. Certainly; I do not deny it. This is a mighty charm, more powerful than any other. For what avails more than the confession of the Trinity, which is proclaimed daily in the mouth of all the people?[2]

Many hymns are attributed to Ambrose; four hymns reckoned to be authentically his are *Aeterne rerum conditor, Deus Creator omnium, Iam surgit hora tertia* and *Veni redemptor gentium.*

These hymns are composed in metrical stanzas, quite unlike biblical poetry, and it is interesting for modern hymn-writers to note that Ambrose does not feel obliged to provide rhyme.

Cantillation

The Lesser Hours, services for Prime, Terce, Sext and None, contain some of the most straightforward types of chant, based on a relationship between words and music of great simplicity. A great deal of the chant has its origin in cantillation, a kind of heightened speech used in the Jewish worship of the synagogue. At its simplest, it translates into musical shapes which follow the natural rise and fall of the voice when reading. Evidently, the degree of inflexion was sometimes a matter of taste, for Augustine complained rather disparagingly, that Athanasius 'used to oblige the readers to recite the psalms with such slight modulation of the voice that they seemed to be speaking rather than chanting'.[1]

The modulation of the speaking voice is of fundamental importance to Gregorian chant. In prayers or readings, for instance, the cantor or priest will chant on one note, which he may alter to make a very simple and brief melodic inflexion at points of punctuation.

In many languages a question is conveyed by raising the pitch of the voice at the end of a sentence, and this becomes part of the grammar of Gregorian chant. A full stop is be

conveyed by a fall in the voice, and likewise a comma. There are many different formulae, but all aim to make the chant respond to the grammar of the text. Worship in the early Middle Ages did not permit instrumental accompaniment, so the voice was entirely unaccompanied.

The chanting of psalms follows the same principle. The Hebrew verses of the psalms are structured in complementary halves, so the music of the chant follows this fundamental grammatical outline. Each verse is sung to a reciting note called the tenor (from the Latin *tenere,* 'to hold'). The half-way point of the verse is marked by a simple melodic bend called the mediant (meaning 'half-way') and the end is marked by a slightly more elaborate melodic shape called the termination.

The principle and the pattern holds good for any psalm-verse, whether the words are describing 'war arrows hardened over red-hot charcoal' or 'I call to the Lord and he answers me'. In short, the music does not attempt to describe the meaning of the text, but rather adorns or clothes the words in song.

The rising scale at the very beginning of the psalm (called the intonation and

sung by the cantor or priest alone) assists the main body of singers to tune in to the musical scale being used. The cantor's task is to select a vocal range comfortable for the congregation.

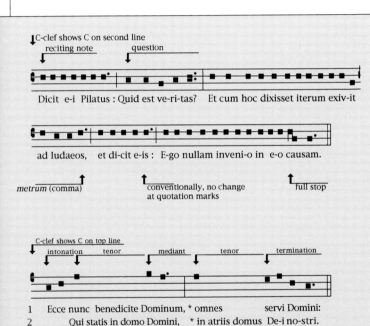

C-clef shows C on second line

reciting note   question

Dicit e-i Pilatus : Quid est ve-ri-tas?   Et cum hoc dixisset iterum exiv-it

ad Iudaeos, et di-cit e-is : E-go nullam inveni-o in e-o causam.

metrum (comma)   conventionally, no change   full stop
                    at quotation marks

This tone for cantillation of the Gospel highlights the grammatical shape rather than the emotional implications of the reading (the text is from John chapter 18 verse 38). As in the many other tones, there are set formulae for a comma or pause, question and full-stop which mimic the natural inflexions of the voice. The notation used here, sometimes called Gothic or square, was commonplace in the thirteenth century and is still used in modern chant books. In spite of the four-line staff, it can be read like modern music.

C-clef shows C on top line

intonation   tenor   mediant   tenor   termination

1 Ecce nunc benedicite Dominum, * omnes   servi Domini:
2 Qui statis in domo Domini,   * in atriis domus De-i no-stri.

The first two verses of Psalm 133 set to the eighth psalm-tone, whose final (last note) and tenor correspond to mode 8 on the modes chart. In monastic tradition the first half-verse is sung by the cantor, the rest taken by alternate sides of the choir, verse by verse.

C-clef shows C on second line

authentic: mode 1   mode 3   mode 5   mode 7

          final D   final E   final F   final G

plagal: mode 2   mode 4   mode 6   mode 8

          final D   final E   final F   final G

F-clef shows F on second line

This chart shows the eight modes (scale-systems) around which Western music was built in the Middle Ages. The ascending scales show the approximate range of melodies in that particular mode. The finals are the key-notes on which the tunes finish and the white notes are the tenors used for recitation.

Chapter 5

Music of the Spheres: the Medieval World-View

Almost all Gregorian chant, no matter how involved or decorated, has its origins in one of three types of music: cantillation (prayers, readings, psalms), free composition (antiphons) and new poems set to music (hymns). From these simple beginnings, the liturgies of both West and East gradually became more ornate. By about the eleventh century the complexity of some of them was remarkable, as the musical techniques of adornment created sounds far from the experience of the early Christians.

The cynical explanation for this ever-increasing elaboration of the liturgy and of its music is that it reflected the image that the church intended to present: all-powerful, authoritarian, blessed with spiritual and material riches. But its driving force lies elsewhere, in the medieval Christians' understanding of the world. Their first and fundamental desire was to see God in all things. Paul's letter to the Romans says:

Ever since God created the world his everlasting power and deity ... have been

there for the mind to see in the things he has made.[1]

The people of the Middle Ages were certain of God's existence and of supernatural powers at work around them: it was truly an 'age of faith'. The church cited the Bible as the final written authority for all points of doctrine, but the nature and diversity of God's creation was also minutely scrutinized, for it was believed that its every detail bore a message for mankind.

Hidden messages

One of the most charming examples of this can be found in bestiaries. A medieval bestiary is a kind of natural history book, a compilation by a monastic scribe of everything there was to be known about the animal kingdom. They are fascinating documents, with the most entertaining illustrations, for a Yorkshire monk was unlikely to have seen, for example, an elephant, and his second- or third-hand sources of information left much to his imagination.

Without the opportunity to travel the author had no sure way of telling what was fable and what was fact. Thus the bestiaries unwittingly mix real animals (many like horse and dog being accurately and lovingly described) with mythical creatures like the phoenix, the manticore or the basilisk. All are treated with equal respect.

But the real purpose of the book is to bring out the meaning that lies behind creation. What, for instance, has God to teach us through the basilisk?

The monk who drew this elephant was plainly working from second-hand information. Medieval scholars were interested in everything but had close knowledge of only a very restricted world. Yet they saw the whole scheme of things as working together under the scrutiny of God.

The Basilisk... is the king of serpents. People who see it run for their lives, because it can kill them merely by its smell. Even if it looks at a man, it destroys him. Nevertheless, Basilisks are conquered by weasels... God never makes anything without a remedy.[2]

Thus every phenomenon of nature, whether real or imagined, was a sermon on the nature of God, once the church had unlocked the door to its meaning.

Numerology

While the authors of the bestiaries rejoiced in the wonder of living things and their lessons for mankind, the most powerful sermon of all lay in the numbers and proportions that ordered the natural world. The medieval preoccupation with number amounted to an obsession. Biblical commentators were so preoccupied with the hidden meaning of number that they neglected the straightforward message. For example, a verse from Psalm 33 invites everyone to: 'Give thanks to the Lord on the harp; with the ten-stringed psaltery chant his praises.'

The difficulty the church authorities had with the literal use of musical instruments for praise (see Chapter 3: Music in the Early Church) led a third-century writer to an allegorical interpretation:

The musical instruments of the Old Testament are not unsuitable for us if understood spiritually... The harp is the active soul; the psaltery is pure mind. The ten strings can be taken as ten nerves, for a nerve is a string. Therefore, the psaltery

The angels on the rib-vaulting in Gloucester cathedral's fourteenth-century choir make up a heavenly orchestra. Yet they are using secular instruments. It took a long time for instruments to be accepted as part of medieval worship.

is taken to be a body having five senses and five faculties...[3]

The significance of number led the church to construct great edifices of learning around the significance of the Holy Trinity, the twelve apostles, the 24 elders of the book of Revelation, the proportions of the ark[4] or the number of the beast.[5]

This picture from an eleventh-century Italian choirbook illustrates the theme of the antiphon below it: 'Behold the wood of the cross, on which hangs the well-being of the world. Come, let us adore.' Signs (neumes) above the text give information only as a reminder of what the singers have already learned. These unheighted neumes give invaluable information to scholars about the development of chant.

The idea of a universe synchronized in every detail by numbers and their proportions is classical and pagan, but through the works of Pythagoras and Plato[6] it was readily accepted by Christians. By marrying their study of astronomy with biblical references to heaven, they built up a picture of a universe created and sustained by God, whose planets created a cosmic music through their harmonious movement. Like the Greeks before them, Christians understood astronomy and music to be inextricably bound together by their common basis in number. The Roman philosopher Boethius wrote in the sixth century:

There are three types of music. The first type is the music of the universe (*musica mundana*), the second, that of the

human being *(musica humana)*, and the third type is that which is created by certain instruments *(musica instrumentis constituta)* such as the kithara, or tibia or other instruments which produce melodies.

Now the first type, that is the music of the universe, is best observed in those things which one perceives in heaven itself, or in the structure of the elements, or in the diversity of the seasons. How could it possibly be that such a swift heavenly machine should move silently in its course?... it is impossible that such a fast motion should produce absolutely no sound, especially since the orbits of the stars are joined by such a harmony that nothing so perfectly structured can be imagined... Thus there must be some fixed order of musical modulation in this celestial motion.[7]

Thus even the humble *musica instrumentalis constituta* was linked through the music of the human soul ultimately to the music of the spheres, for all three were part of the same divinely controlled system. Mankind had therefore to strive to make music which synchronized with this harmoniously vibrating universe and which would therefore form a worthy part of God's great symphony of proportions.

This cosmological picture gradually blurred and faded as faith in scientific discovery replaced belief in the unknown and unseen. But this was not to happen for at least another thousand years.[8]

The Eleventh-Century Mass

This plan outlines a Mass as it might have been celebrated in the eleventh century. The Ordinary of the Mass (indicated here with bold text) is the term given to the texts that never change; the *Proper* (in italic) are those texts which vary with the church's calendar and therefore are 'proper' or appropriate for the occasion.

The Liturgy of the Word:

◆ *Introit*
Antiphon, psalm-verse and repeat of antiphon
Sung by the choir as the priest and ministers process to the altar

◆ **Kyrie**
Often a three-fold repetition of 'Lord, have mercy' and 'Christ, have mercy'
Everyone sings

◆ **Prayers**
The priest offers prayers of confession and forgiveness

◆ **Gloria**
Free composition
A song of thanks and praise (see Luke chapter 2 verse 14)

◆ **Versicle & response**
'The Lord be with you'—'And also with you'
Exchanged between priest and congregation

◆ **Collects**
Cantillation
Prayers for the day

◆ **Epistle**
Cantillation
New Testament reading

◆ *Gradual*
Antiphon, psalm-verse, antiphon
Highly elaborate music for the choir

◆ *Alleluia*
'Alleluia', psalm-verse, 'Alleluia'

For the choir

◆ *Sequence*
Free composition
For the choir

◆ **Gospel**
Cantillation
The service book is carried to the rood-loft with great ceremony

◆ **Credo**
Free composition
A statement of faith for all to say or sing

Eucharistic feast:

◆ *Offertorium*
Antiphon only
For the choir

◆ **Prayers**
Including *Sursum corda*—'Lift up your hearts'—and the Proper Preface for the day
Preparation for the Communion

◆ **Sanctus and Benedictus**
Free composition. The Sanctus is repeated again after the Benedictus
Everyone sings

◆ **The Canon of the Mass**
Consecration of the bread and wine

◆ **Pater Noster**—The Lord's Prayer
Free composition
Recitation by the priest

◆ **Agnus Dei**
Free composition in three parts, each beginning *Agnus Dei*—'Lamb of God'
Everyone sings

◆ **The Communion**
The bread and wine are received with great ceremony

◆ *Communion*
Antiphon only
For the choir

◆ **Versicle and response**

◆ **Postcommunion**
Cantillation

◆ *Ite, Missa Est*—
Versicle of dismissal to which everyone responds *Deo gratias*—'thanks be to God'

The two parts of the Mass, the Liturgy of the Word and the Eucharistic feast, were in earlier times two separate services. Although they were merged in the later Middle Ages, their distinct characters can still be sensed in Eucharistic celebrations today, one being a preparation for the other.

Chapter 6

Music for the Liturgy

At the foundations of Gregorian chant lay two simple concepts: the heightened speech of cantillation and the free composition of songs setting scripture or sacred poetry. By a process of glacier-like evolution, these fundamental principles came to be housed in a highly adorned liturgy, itself part of a church year which prescribed every aspect of worship down to the minutest details. The immeasurably increased solemnity of the worship of the Middle Ages was a product of both temporal and spiritual forces. Not only did the church wish its sacrifices of praise to reflect the majesty and glory of the God whose ambassador it was, but it also needed a ritual of splendour to suit its status as a powerful political force.

The services in which liturgical elaboration was most evident were Mass and its two preparatory vigils, Vespers and Matins.

Vespers

Vespers, for instance, begins with a versicle and response from verse 1 of Psalm 70, and continues with five psalms, each with its own antiphon (see boxed article on *Antiphon*). A reading is then followed by a hymn, which in turn leads to the high point of the service, the singing of the *Magnificat*. Like the psalms, the *Magnificat* begins and ends with an antiphon (a so-called Marian antiphon, the *Magnificat* being the song of Mary). The importance of the occasion—especially on solemn feasts in the church year—is symbolized by the more involved melodies.

More antiphons (interestingly, now separated from their parent psalms) continue Vespers with prayers, and the service finishes with the closing versicles and responses. Such elaborate music, particularly its melismas (several notes to one syllable) by now made it impossible for a lay congregation to sing, and so it became the property of the trained choirs of monasteries, cathedrals and college chapels.

Matins

Matins, if anything more ornate than Vespers, is built round the singing of nine psalms. These psalms are grouped in three 'Nocturns' (night-watches) and alternate with readings which in turn are followed by elaborate responsories.

These responsories show another step in the elaboration of the chant. As their name suggests, they are intended as a response of praise and adoration to the scripture which has just been

---

This complex responsory for Matins at the feast of Corpus Christi was intended for expert musicians. It consists of a central verse sandwiched between an antiphon. The psalm-tone for the verse is highly decorated—the original tenor is marked with crosses.

the cantor sings as far as *   quilisma, a vocal embellishment   the rest of the choir join in

Immolabit hae-   dum * multitudo fi-li-o-rum Is-ra-   el ad

ve-   speram Paschae: * Et e-   dent carnes,   et a-

verse, sung by a few voices only

zy-   mos   pa-   nes. ℣. Pascha   nostrum immola-

tus est Christus: i-   taque e-pu-le-mur in azymis sin-ce-ri- ta- tis

et   ve-ri-ta-tis.   * Et edent...panes. [repeat]

final D of mode 1

read. Many consist of an antiphon (the freely-composed refrain), a psalm-verse, and a repetition of the antiphon. The whole is so decorated that the original long reciting note or 'tenor' is hard to recognize.

Mass

The celebration of the Eucharist is, of course, at the centre of Christian worship. There is clear evidence in the New Testament that Jesus' disciples took seriously his command to 'do this as a memorial of me', recorded in Luke's Gospel, and there are many later references to the holding of Eucharistic feasts.

Its importance is not simply a remembrance of the person of Jesus, but a celebration of what, after the first Eucharist (the Last Supper), became his sacrifice once-and-for-all and on behalf of everyone. As Paul said in his first letter to the Corinthians:

As often as you eat this bread and drink this cup, you proclaim the Lord's death until he comes.[1]

The depth of meaning of the Eucharistic feast encouraged Christians to celebrate it with particular solemnity even in the early days of the church. As a result, special musical traditions have accompanied it from the earliest times.

By the eleventh century Mass was often celebrated with sufficient ceremony to justify it being termed ritual theatre. Its many striking visual symbols went hand-in-hand with elaborate music.[2]

The celebration of the Lord's Supper or Eucharistic Feast was known in the first few centuries of Christianity as *dominicum,* meaning 'the Lord's'. It is not understood why this name should have been replaced by 'Mass' sometime after the fifth century. The word 'mass' is a reference to the last words of the service: *Ite, missa est,* literally 'Go, it is the dismissal'. 'Mass' is an anglicization of *missa.* Eastern Orthodox Christians call the service 'Divine Liturgy'.

Within its basic shape, the relative solemnity of Mass varied according to the place and circumstances of its celebration. At Easter, Christmas or Pentecost, for instance, the ceremony and its music would be especially elaborate. Dispensations allowed local variations in liturgical detail, such as the distinctive 'Sarum' Rite which became widely used in England from

This beautifully decorated page is from a missal used at Lesnes Abbey in France from about 1200. The text is of the Sursum Corda: 'Lift up your hearts. We lift them to thee.'

the thirteenth century till the Reformation. There were also dramatic differences in the human and financial resources available from place to place, but the structure of the service would remain essentially the same, whether celebrated in a village church, Cluny Abbey in France or Salisbury Cathedral in England.

The unchanging texts of the Mass *Ordinary* are familiar for listeners to classical music, as many composers of the last 600 years have used them for their Mass settings. In the first few hundred years of Christianity, however, these were the words intended for the whole congregation to utter with the help of simple chants. The *Proper* was then more appropriately sung by members of the choir (the *schola cantorum)* or perhaps by a small group of expert cantors. The musical creativity of the *schola* gradually changed the *Proper* into a complex art-music, its unique elaboration by polyphony laying the foundations for the future development of Western music.

The Development of Notation

Guido D'Arezzo (about 995–1050), an Italian monk, did much to develop the miraculous new possibilities of notation, which allowed the choristers in his charge to sing new chants without having heard them first; in other words, to sight-read. He wrote to a friend:

Pope John [XIX, 1024–33], who governs the Roman Church, heard of our song-school's reputation. He heard in particular of how, by means of our antiphoners [books of antiphons] boys could learn songs they had never heard. He was greatly astonished, and sent three messengers to bring me to him... The Pope was most glad to see me... and asked a great many questions. He turned over the pages of the antiphoner as if it were some great prodigy... He did not move from the place where he sat... until he had learned to sing one versicle that he had never heard. What more is there to say? I had to leave Rome soon—the summer fevers in those wet and swampy places were death to me. We agreed, however, that when the winter returned I would return with it, to explain our work to the Pope... and to his clergy.[1]

Other methods of writing down music had been used for at least a century before this, but by signs placed above the words, they could only serve as a reminder of what the singer already knew. Guido's idea was to put the signs (the neumes) on parallel lines representing certain notes of the mode, the signs then standing for actual notes. Sometimes for additional help the lines were colour-coded; yellow or green for the note C, red for F.

There was no indication of the relative duration of the notes (there are therefore widely differing schools of thought on the performance of the chant), but even so, the basis of modern notation had been laid down.

Guido also invented the first solmization method (a sol-fa system) to help his choirboys to distinguish the tones and semitones of which the modes are constructed. The key to his method was a hymn in praise of St John, *Ut queant laxis,* which by good fortune began each line on a new note of an ascending scale. The syllables sung at the beginnings of the lines could be separated from the hymn and made to represent each note of the scale:

UT queant laxis
REsonare fibris
MIra gestorum
FAmuli tuorum
SOlve pollutes
LAbii reates, Sancti Johannes.

Once musical notes had begun to be written down instead of having to be memorized, the choristers had to be trained in new skills, those of reading music and sight-reading.

Chapter 7

From the Ear to the Page

Over a period of nearly a thousand years, Christian music was sung and passed on to the following generation entirely by memory, an extraordinary feat by any standards. Isidore of Seville (about 560–636) wrote a definition of music which included the statement:

Unless sounds are held in the memory by man they perish, because they cannot be written down.[1]

At a time when books were rare and when only a small proportion of the population could read, the memorizing of vast amounts of scripture was necessary and commonplace.[2] Occasionally today people with highly trained memories can still demonstrate these mental skills, usually as no more than a party trick, of little use in an age of sophisticated data banks. However, worshipping Christians of all ages have found that the combination of words and music is of immense help in committing the Word of God to memory and to the mind.

The Alleluia and the Sequence

The cantors' capacity for the retention and recall of the chant was eventually stretched beyond its limits. Significantly enough, the breakdown occurred in the one area where words were not available to assist the memory—in the final syllable of the Alleluia.

One of the gifts of the Spirit mentioned by Paul in his letters to the churches is the gift of 'tongues'.[3] This gift has been exercised and enjoyed down the ages as a free expression of praise. Sometimes the gift of tongues extends to song, perhaps to an unknown language, perhaps to a simple word like 'Alleluia', or without any words at all. The Alleluia of the Proper may be evidence of this gift having been used during Mass.

The Alleluia is a psalm-verse with an antiphon set to the word 'alleluia'. Its origin could lie in a spontaneous musical expression of praise in an outpouring of the power of God's Spirit. At a later stage, perhaps, the music became more formalized. Whatever their origin, Alleluias became characterized by their remarkable

the jubilus, 'rejoicing'

Al-le-lu- ia.

musical extension of the final syllable.

By this time music was no longer the humble servant of the words, as in the simple chants of the Lesser Hours, but an expression of praise in an abstract medium, without the aid of text. Not for nothing did Augustine refer to this unique type of chant as *jubilus*—'rejoicing':

One who rejoices (*jubilat*) does not speak words, but it is rather a sort of sound of joy without words, since it is the voice of a soul poured out in joy and expressing, as best it can, the feeling, though not grasping the sense ... Filled with too much joy, he cannot explain in words what it is in which he delights ... and whom does jubilation benefit but the ineffable God?[4]

Alleluias are among the most highly ornamented chants. In this Alleluia for Easter Sunday there are forty-five notes to the final syllable. The difficulties of committing these chants to memory prompted the addition of words to the 'jubilus'.

Such spontaneous musical praise did not make special demands on the memory, but the traditional melodies with long melismas (passages of several notes on one syllable) caused serious difficulties.

A characteristic solution was described by Notker Balbulus ('the stammerer'), a ninth-century monk at the monastery of St Gall in Switzerland. He wrote:

When I was still young, and very long melodies (longissimae melodiae)—

repeatedly entrusted to memory— escaped from my poor little head, I began to reason with myself how I could bind them fast.[5]

He related how a monk from Jumièges near Rouen sought sanctuary with him as his own monastery had been sacked by the Normans (in 862). The French monk had brought with him some verses which he had set to the textless *jubilus* of the Alleluia. Realizing that the additional text was the solution to his memory

Rich Church: Poor People

The evolution of chant into a complex art-form continues to fascinate musicians, not just on account of the music's inherent beauties but also because it lays the foundations for western art-music. But this same evolution put most Christian music far beyond the grasp of the common people of its time. Their own musical expression of faith was only to be heard outside the walls of church and cathedral. Feast-days, for instance, gave opportunities for great processions accompanied by rough-hewn music, such as the immensely popular *laude spirituale* (spiritual praises) of the later Middle Ages. Such colourful events have their close parallels in Italy, Spain and South America today.

Folk music like the *laude* was the chief Christian expression of a people barely able to find the basic necessities of life. The masses also desperately lacked education and spiritual guidance to rescue them from a faith riddled with superstition. In these fundamental needs of body and soul they were largely disregarded by the church.

Even provisions to educate the local parish priest were almost non-existent. Complaints were heard from all quarters: the Bishop of Angers wrote in 1222 that his priests included:

innumerable contemptible persons of abject life, utterly unworthy in learning and morals... from whose execrable lives and pernicious ignorance infinite scandals arise. The church sacraments are despised by the laity, and in many districts the lay-folk hold the priests as vile and... despicable.[1]

But the church hierarchy was sufficiently élitist for the bishops themselves to be far above contradiction. The institution's enormous wealth was confined to a minority of powerful prelates, who were not ashamed to make their position in society clear by parading their affluence in public. Bishops travelled with mounted retinues of dozens. A maximum of such facilities was laid down by Walter, Archbishop of Canterbury in the mid-thirteenth century: an archbishop could have no more than fifty men and horses; bishops thirty; archdeacons seven, and no hounds or hawks. His edict was not adhered to.[2]

The church began to establish the tradition that forgiveness of sins could be bought. Friars would be permitted to sell 'indulgences' so that those who could afford them were given the reassurance that their journey to heaven would be made easier.

The Benedictine order became a travesty of its origins. Benedict's Rule of silence, of work on the land, of humble devotion with the minimum of material support was left far behind, far enough for the Cistercian order to be founded at the end of the eleventh century to re-establish these principles.

In 1338 there were ninety monks in the Benedictine monastery of Mont St Michel in Normandy. Of the monastic income of £9,000 a year £1,700 was spent on food, £500 on clothing, £460 on repairs, £500 on taxes, £300 on lawsuits, £120 on fuel and £2,200 on wine.[3]

Worship in the great cathedrals and abbeys took place in the choir, a 'church within a church', sealed off by screens from the greater building. Ordinary people were generally only allowed into the nave, which was often used for trade, like an indoor market. The townsfolk had no place in the spiritual life of these great buildings, except that the acquisition of money lay behind many of the services held there. For those who were rich enough, a fee would pay for a commemorative Mass for a departed loved one or for a Mass for the benefit of one's own soul.

problem, Balbulus then set about composing his own improved texts. Now he had words which, when put to the former melismas, 'bound them fast' in his memory. The story is undoubtedly over-simplified, but what is certain is that Balbulus' lively artistic imagination turned textless chant into a new musical genre.

These so-called Sequences became immensely popular in the Middle Ages for the creation of long meditative songs. Some of the most beautiful were written by the Abbess Hildegard of Bingen (1098–1179) in a collection known as the *Symphonia*. It was not until the reforms of the Council of Trent in 1562 that the huge numbers of sequences permitted in medieval liturgy were reduced. In the Gregorian chant-books of the Roman Catholic Church today only a handful are listed of the thousands once sung.

Troping

The term used for the addition of music or text (or both) to an already existing vocal piece is

Pieter Brueghel the Elder's paintings of country life, though dating from the time of the Renaissance, portray a village world that was quite remote from the wealth of cathedrals, monasteries and court chapels. The church and its elaborate liturgy and music made little impact at this level of society.

'troping'. Apart from the obvious possibilities of adding melodic embellishments to a chant such as melismas, troping was one of the most favoured ways of adorning Christian music and of heightening its solemnity. As an example, the words *Christe Eleison* ('Christ, have mercy') on a solemn occasion might become: *Christe, rex unice, Patris almi Nate co-aeterne, eleison* ('Christ, the only king, eternally begotten of the beloved Father, have mercy').[6]

At the great feasts of Easter and Christmas, a liturgical drama might be placed as a prelude to Mass before the Introit, troping, or adding to, the Mass itself. The *Quem Quaeritis* ('whom do you seek') dialogue, for instance, could either be a re-enactment of the Easter morning scene with Mary at the tomb of Jesus, or of the shepherds seeking the crib of Jesus on Christmas night, according to the season.

The *Play of Herod* is another such liturgical drama, much more extensive. All these were sung to music in the Gregorian tradition and, incidentally, provide some important clues in understanding how musicians of the Middle Ages intended to portray human emotion through music.[7]

NOTATION—A REVOLUTION?

The importance of the development of notation cannot be stressed too strongly, for it allowed new types of music to be created which would have been quite out of the reach of traditions where music was passed on by ear.

Up to this time, Christian music was, like a folk tradition, bound to change as it was passed on and interpreted afresh by a new generation. But music written down was music fixed, locked, as it were, into a certain shape. Finally, the composer could put his name to the manuscript and become associated with it, even long after his death.

Until notation arrived, only a few composers of Christian music were known, but very gradually from that time on, more individuals were to become identified with their music and today, 900 years on, they are extolled as 'artists', as spokespeople for their culture, expecting recognition and dues from society.

The process of this change was slow, but it gradually created in the West a unique musical tradition. It brought rich blessings to Christian worship and later created the art-form now called 'classical music', but at the same time it has been controversial and divisive.

A few people have realized that the invention of musical notation brings curses as well as blessings. For example, composers over the centuries have become more and more precise in their requirements, first finding ways to indicate the length of notes, then specifying their medium (voice or various instruments), then their loudness and speed of execution, and most recently the phrasing and articulation. But performers have in turn been given less and less room to be creative and to make their own decisions in these areas.

Similarly, Balbulus' addition of words to the *jubilus* in the Alleluia allowed him to regain control of his memory, but only at the expense of altering the very nature of the *jubilus* itself.

Thus for every gain, which the present post-industrial society usually regards as an 'improvement', there is usually a loss. What Socrates was once reported to have said about the invention of the alphabet might equally well apply to the adoption of musical notation:

This discovery... will create forgetfulness in the learner's souls, because they will not use their memories; they will trust to the external written characters and not remember of themselves. The specific which you have discovered is an aid not to memory but to recollection, and gives...only the semblance of truth; they will hear much and learn nothing; they will appear to know much and will generally know nothing; they will be tiresome company, for they will seem wise without being wise.[8]

Chapter 8

From Gregorian Chant to Polyphony

For the first eight hundred years of Christian worship the musical vehicle for the liturgy was melody. It might take the form of a cantillated prayer of extreme simplicity or of an ornate Gradual for a solemn occasion. But whatever its complexity, monody—the single line of melody untainted by any accompaniment—was the most perfect and satisfying symbol for the unity of Christian believers. It was the advent of notation that allowed polyphony—many melodies together—to develop, in directions that have since made Western music unique.

When buildings are constructed on land which is plentiful, the area they occupy is not a critical factor in their design, and conurbations can be made up of low-storey houses spreading outwards from a centre. But as soon as space becomes restricted, then the cost of land rises and economics dictate that buildings must become taller if housing expansion is to continue. So it was with Gregorian chant. The limits of human endurance meant that solemn chant had developed to its greatest practical length. But a continuing desire for its adornment on special occasions led musicians to consider embellishing the chant in another way altogether: by singing different melodies simultaneously.

The first steps towards a new concept of singing, known as *organum,* came mostly from France. For a long time France had favoured a special quality of ceremony in worship. The choir at the Abbey of St Martial at Limoges for instance, gradually took to singing certain items of the Mass by splitting the choir into parts, one group singing the original chant and others (perhaps the basses) singing four or five or eight notes below. The idea (called *organum)* was a simple method of introducing a further degree of decoration into the chant, but one which nonetheless needed no writing down.

Other possibilities were explored too, especially those which allowed the two parts to become more independent. This freer type of *organum* required one part to sing the original chant and a second line to supply a more florid part against it. One of the most valuable collections of these two-part pieces, the Winchester Troper, was compiled during the tenth and eleventh centuries at Winchester Cathedral in southern England. This precious manuscript contains all the different sorts of troping (interpolations and additions to the chant) as well as the two-part 'florid' *organum.*

The beginnings of polyphony

The great Cathedral of Notre Dame is perhaps the best known of all Gothic cathedrals. Considering its immense size and complexity, it was built with considerable speed between 1163 and 1250, the bulk of it being complete by 1200.

The creation of such a magnificent structure is evidence that France was beginning to enjoy a period of stability and affluence, a country in whose towns culture and learning could flourish as never before. During the building of the new cathedral, composers working at its music school were notating a type of *organum* more lavishly decorated than anything yet heard.

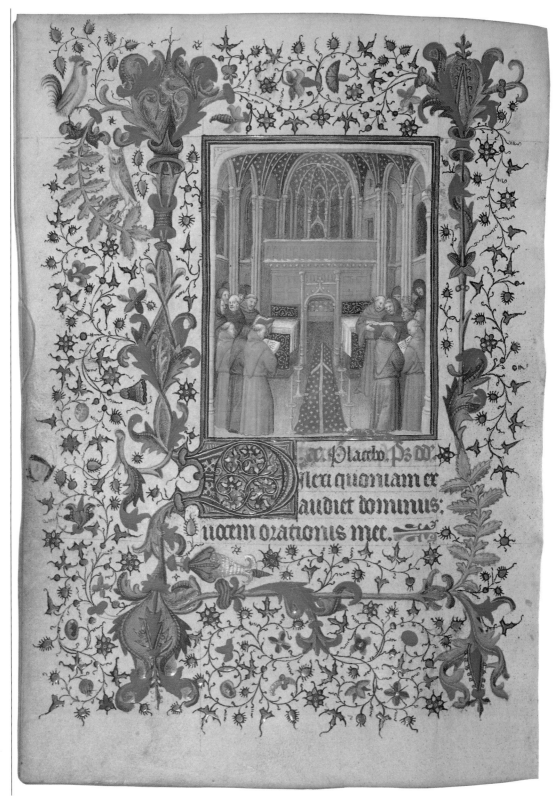

An anonymous treatise reveals the names of two famous composers from Notre Dame at this period, both canons at the cathedral:

Léonin was the best composer of *organum.* **He wrote the** *Great Book of Organum,* **for Mass and Office, to augment the Divine Service. This book was used until the time of the great Perotin, who shortened it and rewrote many sections in a better way ... with the most ample embellishments of harmonic art.[1]**

This once again draws attention to the continuing delight of Christians in elaborating the liturgy, and luckily the Great Book itself survives. Corroborative evidence shows that the florid *vox organalis* added to the chant was sometimes improvised from a number of stock musical phrases. Certainly the special expertise of the musicians was rewarded accordingly:

And to each clerk of the choir who will attend Mass, two deniers, and to the four clerks who will sing the Alleluia in *organum,* **six deniers ...[2]**

As in the music of the Winchester Troper, Léonin's pieces (compiled between about 1150 and 1170) supplied an extra vocal line. This was added to sections of chants which in themselves were already decorative—such as Graduals or Alleluias at Mass or Responsorial chants at Matins.

The extra line that Léonin added (called the *duplum* or second part) needed considerable singing skill. It had to be sung quite fast, not least because as many as forty notes of the *duplum* fitted to just one of the original chant. As a result, some parts of the chant became greatly stretched out, with its singers spending perhaps twenty seconds or half a minute on a single note. The words, of course, progressed even more slowly.

No wonder then that Perotin, Léonin's successor, shortened parts of these compositions. At the same time he enriched the harmony still further by adding new voice-parts: a *triplum* (third part) and sometimes even a *quadruplum* (fourth part). The independence of the vocal lines can now properly be called polyphony.

Another feature of this remarkable music was the presence of a regular pulse in triple time. The 'perfection' of the number three was inherent in the medieval world-view. As the theorist Jean de Muris wrote in 1319:

That all perfection lies in the ternary number is clear from a hundred comparisons. In God, who is perfection itself, there is singleness in substance, but threeness in persons; He is three in one and one in three. Moreover: [there

Facing page: **These singing monks are shown on a beautifully illuminated manuscript of the Offices of the Dead.**

The magnificent Gothic cathedral of Notre Dame in Paris. While it was being built, music for its liturgy began to be composed, not just as a single melodic line, but in the polyphonic style which has since come to dominate Western music.

are]...in individuals generation, corruption and substance; in finite time-spans beginning, middle and end; in every curable disease onset, crisis and decline. Three is the first odd number and the first prime number. It is not two lines but three that can enclose a surface. The triangle is the first regular polygon...[3]

The rhythm of this early polyphony soon resolved itself into the quick triple time so characteristic of medieval music of this period. Until this time there had been little need for written guidance to the singers concerning rhythm, but the complexity of the Notre Dame *organum* for the first time necessitated a system for notating rhythm as well as pitch.[4]

The startling effect of the choir suddenly changing from the lone and sinuous melody of the chant to three- or even four-part music did not please everyone. There are records of an increasing number of complaints from churchmen of this elaborate music. John of Salisbury, a contemporary of Perotin, wrote a particularly vitriolic criticism:

Music sullies the Divine Service, for in the very sight of God, in the sacred recesses of the sanctuary itself, the singers attempt, with the lewdness of a

The words of this early 'conductus' suggest that their purpose was to introduce a scripture reading. They would have been sung as the reader was 'conducted' to the lectern. The last verse *(below)* reads: 'Clean and pure therefore let this gathering be that hears and perceives what the lesson says.' This 'conductus', dating from the mid-twelfth century, is hymn-like, tuneful and fairly straightforward. Over the next hundred years more complex 'conducti' in two or three parts became popular, eventually giving way to the motet.

Munda sit, pu-ra sit   hec er - go   con-ci - o

au- di-at, sen-ti - at,   quid di-cat lec-ti- o.

lascivious singing voice and a singularly foppish manner, to feminise all their spellbound little followers with the girlish way they render the notes and end the phrases.[5]

But such criticism cannot have represented the majority in the liturgical corridors of power, as the practice quickly spread to a number of monasteries and cathedral churches across Europe.

The motet

Where the original plainsong melody had a melisma—a number of notes sung to one syllable—the composers of Notre Dame felt it appropriate in their *organum* settings to make the chant move along faster and in rhythm. Strange though it may seem, they took to writing these sections (called *clausulae*) separately from the main piece, so that one could be substituted for another, like engine spare parts.

Before long, these sections were soon being performed as separate pieces in their own right. What is more, composers started to add completely new sets of words to the upper parts (yet another example of troping), creating what they called a 'motet', that is, a piece with words to the added lines (from the French *mot,* meaning 'word').

The result is the most sophisticated musical form known to the Middle Ages, a piece in two, three or even four parts, whose foundation (the so-called *tenor*) is a fragment of chant, snipped out, as it were, from the middle of a traditional melody. The tenor had a regular pulse imposed on it, while around it were added between one and three freely-composed voice-parts with new texts. By this means it was perfectly possible for up to four different sets of words to be sung together.

Motet technique was developed in a number of ways in the thirteenth century, which were not by any means always pleasing to the church. Such pieces became popular for secular ceremonies (at banquets for instance) and popular tunes would be incorporated in them. Some of these found their way back into church motets, and Pope John XXII in 1323 was compelled to issue a Papal bull, in which he made some very significant complaints:

Certain disciples of the new school... prefer to devise new methods of their own rather than to singing in the old way. Therefore the music of the Divine Office is disturbed with these notes of quick duration. Moreover, they... deprave it with discants and sometimes pad out the music with upper parts made out of profane songs. The result is that they often seem to be losing sight of the fundamental sources of our melodies in the Antiphoner and Gradual...The consequence of all this is that devotion,

the true aim of all worship, is neglected, and wantonness, which ought to be shunned, increases. We hasten to forbid these methods...[6]

The conductus

Not all medieval part-music had the complex structure of the motet, for the Church initiated another type of polyphony in its continuing pursuit of the 'embellishment of harmonic art'. During the twelfth century it became customary in services of solemnity to lead the lesson-reader to the lectern with a short song called a *conductus* (from the Latin *conducere,* to lead).

Once again, more complex and lengthy chants of this processional type developed, as musicians delighted in the addition of as many as three extra parts against the original. The result was a piece of music newly composed in all parts (not usually based on traditional chant or other tunes) and with all voices singing the same text.

Franco of Cologne, a composer and theorist of the later thirteenth century, described how such pieces were written:

He who wants to write a *conductus* should first invent as beautiful a melody as he can, then using it as a *tenor* is used in writing discant [in other words, writing another melody against it, the *tenor* being the original 'beautiful melody']. He who wishes to construct a third part *[triplum]* ought to have the other two in mind, so that when the *triplum* is discordant with the *tenor,* it will not be discordant with the discant, and vice versa.[7]

This method of composition is very different from classical music of the last few hundred years. If a choir sings a four-part hymn or anthem, for instance, all voices fill in a particular harmony. If one is missing, or breaks down, the effect on the composer's intentions is probably fatal. But in medieval times polyphonic music was perceived as a number of layers. The composing process began with the *tenor,* then the *discant* or *duplum,* then the *triplum,* then the *quadruplum*—as many layers as circumstances required.

A composer (like Perotin) would feel quite at liberty to add another layer to pre-existing music, or to perform a piece with one of the upper layers missing. Such methods would produce truly appalling results if applied to classical music, but

make good sense in the field of Western popular music today. In jazz especially, the 'tenor', in the form of popular song 'standards', is common property, to be surrounded by other musical lines depending on the occasion.

Like the motets, medieval songs in *conductus* style became fashionable outside the Church as

The Old Hall Manuscript, a set of polyphonic mass settings and motets, was compiled and written in the reign of King Henry IV of England. It was possibly intended for the Chapel Royal in the early fifteenth century.

well as within it and courtly musicians used the idiom to create part-songs about the crusades, about politics and about love.

The Ordinary of the Mass

In the late thirteenth century, polyphonic settings during the celebration of Mass extended for the first time to the Ordinary, those unchanging texts which had at one time been opportunities for the expression of faith of the whole Christian community. In well-endowed cathedrals and monasteries the Ordinary texts were left more and more to the choir, who sang on behalf of those present (and perhaps even of those absent). It is a poignant irony that much of the outstanding Christian music of the Middle Ages, and the superb cathedrals that echoed to it, can be understood as monuments to the vaingloriousness of the church during this period.

The life of Guillaume de Machaut illustrates well the blend of secular and sacred that was common in this period. Born in about 1300, after taking holy orders—joining the clergy—he was made a canon of Rheims and of St Quentin, attached to the cathedral. He had also, from 1323, been secretary to John of Luxembourg, King of Bohemia, who had taken him on his military campaigns all over Europe before Machaut became canon. King John was killed at Crecy in 1346 and from that time Machaut was patronized by the Kings of France, Cyprus and Normandy, his fame as a poet and musician spreading throughout the European courts.

In spite of his holy orders and with a few notable exceptions, his creative energies were devoted to writing long, elegant and sophisticated love-poems, some of which he set to music. Some of the love-lyrics he wrote in his sixties were inspired by his relationship with a nineteen-year-old girl. The poetry of this 'jolly and worldly ecclesiastic' was known and admired by a younger contemporary of his, Geoffrey Chaucer (1340–1400).

Apart from some motets with sacred texts, Machaut's outstanding music for the church was his *Messe de Notre Dame,* a comprehensive setting of the Ordinary of the Mass for four voices. Settings of the Ordinary already existed by this time, but they seem to be compilations of pieces from various sources and not always complete. His setting is ornate and written with extreme care and great creative energy—it was probably created for some special occasion, though whether it was for Mass at the coronation of Charles V of France in 1364 is now disputed.

Machaut's Mass is the first setting of the type that countless composers have written since, consisting of a *Kyrie, Gloria, Credo, Sanctus, Agnus Dei* and a final *Ite, Missa Est.* Machaut uses the composing techniques of both motet and conductus, moving from music of intellectual sophistication and artistry (such as the *Amen* to the *Credo)* to a simpler style that suggests that he may have taken some heed of Pope John XXII's Bull of a few years earlier. As a monument to the Middle Ages' expression of spiritual truth, it is outstanding.

England's great late-medieval poet, Geoffrey Chaucer, knew and admired the work of Guillaume de Machaut. Both poets moved easily between sacred and secular subjects. This is so also of Machaut's music.

Chapter 9

Wycliffe's Challenge to the Church

Behind the Christian music of the Middle Ages lie spiritual and musical developments in sharp contrast. The musical changes were creative, stimulating and positive, but they occurred alongside a depressing and shameful spiritual decline.

On the one hand, elaboration of the liturgy led Christian music to a unique exploration of the rich and exciting world of polyphony, culminating in the splendour of Machaut's Mass. The contrasting spiritual deterioration on the other hand was brought into sharpest focus by Machaut's contemporary, John Wycliffe, an Oxford scholar and theologian who offered the most vigorous challenge to the abuses of the Roman Church.

Considering the breadth of Wycliffe's criticism, it seems surprising that he died in his own parish of Lutterworth in Leicestershire with his head still on his shoulders (in 1384). He condemned at every opportunity the church's temporal riches, which he saw as an effective stumbling-block to any return to Christ-like humility. He continually pointed out that the Gospels provided no justification for the church's pride and materialism and that it was the duty of the secular powers to take ecclesiastical reform into their own hands.

He condemned the sale of indulgences, scorned the doctrine of transubstantiation (by which the church taught that at the Eucharist the real nature or 'substance' of the bread and wine changed into Christ's body and blood, though their outward appearance remained the same) and held that the doctrine of papal supremacy

was to be doubted. The popes' position on the latter point was already undermined by the presence, for most of that century, of two rival popes, at Rome and Avignon.

Above all, Wycliffe believed that everyone had a right to read and hear the Bible in his or her native tongue and he duly translated the Bible into English for the purpose. From Wycliffe's few

John Wycliffe, contemporary of Chaucer and Machaut, criticised the church both for its wealth and for its doctrinal errors. His teaching prefigured the Reformation a century and a half later.

words about Christian music, it is clear that he thought of its elaborate traditions as divisive and vainglorious:

> **In the old days, men sang songs of mourning when they were in prison, in order to teach the Gospel, to put away idleness, and to be occupied in a useful way for the time. But those songs and ours do not agree, for ours invite jollity and pride, and theirs lead to mourning and to dwelling longer on God's Law. A short time later vain tricks began to be employed—*discant, contre* notes, *organum* and *boquetus*[1] ...which stimulate vain men more to dancing than to mourning....When there are forty or fifty in a choir [sic!], three or four proud and lecherous rascals perform the most devout service with flourishes so that no-one can hear the words, and all the others are dumb and watch them like fools.[2]**

With his observation that the music is too complex for the words to be heard, Wycliffe strikes at the heart of the musical dilemma, a problem which he saw as part of the wider issue of the travesty of the Christian gospel. For the first time the questions which re-echo down to the present day are firmly raised: Can art-music have a place in Christian music? Is ornate choral music inherently unhelpful to Christian worship, or did Wycliffe only condemn it through its association with a distorted gospel? Can high-art music enhance the church's offering of praise to God, or must music always remain the servant of the ordinary worshipper? Within 150 years, the Western Church was to be split to its foundations over these issues.

PART 2

Renaissance and Reformation

1400 – 1600

Chapter 10

Luther and the Reformation

The seeds of the Reformation lay in the Renaissance. The latter term refers to a rebirth of the ideals, the philosophy and cultural riches of the Greek and Roman Empires, a rebirth which challenged and undermined the cosmology of the Middle Ages. The shift in perspective had implications for everyone, not merely for theologians and scholars. For by the sixteenth century a Christian Reformation affecting the whole of Europe had begun. The church, its music and liturgy, was on the brink of profound transformation.

The seeds of dissent

Wycliffe's bitter complaints were followed by others after his death in 1384. But the church was still powerful enough to exercise an effective control over doctrine and forms of worship. There were regional differences of style and emphasis, but they were more like differing dialects than distinct languages. All in all, there was a megalithic unity to Western Christendom which was to remain intact for some time to come.

A reformation in Bohemia (now part of Czechoslovakia) led by Jan Hus and directly inspired by Wycliffe's writings was crushed by the execution of Hus himself in 1415. Nevertheless, there is evidence of the Lollards, an English Wycliffian sect, throughout the fifteenth century.

Meanwhile, the renaissance of classical learning enabled Christians such as Erasmus to produce new and authoritative translations into English of early Christian writings, particularly the New Testament. These and other reforming movements throughout the fifteenth century

increased the number of intellectuals among the secular authorities, eager and ready for reform.

Rebellion by the peasantry, on the other hand, was not the way forward. The violence with which both the English Peasants' Revolt and the German Peasants' March were crushed proved that both church and secular authorities were united against them. Reform of the church had to come from within.

The dissension which had been simmering for so long finally erupted with the Reformation of the early sixteenth century in which the Christian faith was split into a number of strands. In spite of some genuine desire to maintain unity, Christianity suffered its second fundamental schism, this time into several fragments, as opposed to the earlier division into the two great strands of East and West (see chapter 28).

Martin Luther

Luther, an Augustinian monk of Wittenburg, had the dogged determination and the conviction to challenge the Roman Church head on. His attack initially took the form of the famous ninety-five theses, which he posted on the door of the church at Wittenburg Castle on 31 October 1517. This might have been of merely local interest had it not been for the invention of printing. Printed pamphlets allowed news to spread with lightning speed. By this means Luther's public protest travelled the whole of Europe within a month and found widespread support. He followed up his theses with the printing and distribution of hundreds of tracts over the next three years.

He was protected from being burned as a heretic by Frederick the Wise, founder of the

The Renaissance

In fifteenth-century Italy scholars and educated people were increasingly fascinated by the ancient civilizations of Greece and Rome. More ancient manuscripts of literature and philosophy of the 'classical' era were discovered, translated and circulated. An awareness grew that before the invasions of the Goths in the fifth century, Rome had been a centre of a civilization unparalleled in the world.

By comparison, the art and culture of medieval Italy was seen to be undistinguished. Now there was a desire to restore the cultural centres of Italy to their former glory.

Artists, sculptors and architects developed an increasing respect for the achievements of the classical age, whose work was still to be seen all around them. The perfection of the human form in Greek sculpture, for instance, demonstrated an impressive knowledge of anatomy which artists were determined to rediscover.

Architects not only made detailed mathematical studies of classical buildings, but became fascinated by the theory and philosophy behind their design. The ancient Roman architect Vitruvius, for instance, had proposed that the proportions of the human frame should act as the basis of proportioning buildings. This idea was seized upon by Renaissance architects.

Painters sought ways of becoming more persuasive in their biblical story-telling, abandoning the two-dimensional and symbolic style of the Middle Ages for a new realism, and conveying as compellingly as possible the human drama of the scene and the movements and emotions of the characters. A true understanding of perspective became a vital technique.

In short, humankind—the body, the mind and the soul—became the centre of enquiry. This was not yet an arrogant humanism usurping God's 'everlasting power and deity', but an awareness that humankind was the prime evidence of God's creativity, even his greatest creation. As Psalm 8 puts it:

You have made him little less than a god,
you have crowned him with glory and splendour,
made him lord over the works of your hands,
set all things under his feet.

The ceiling of the Sistine Chapel in the Vatican, Michelangelo's great labour. The theme is God creating humankind, and in the true spirit of the Renaissance human beings and celestial beings bear equal weight in the whole composition.

Unlike painting, sculpture and architecture, changes in musical outlook were not as obvious or as rapidly adopted. Perhaps it was because musicians were unable to enjoy first-hand experience of the music of the ancient Greeks. Commentaries and theoretical treatises were their only contact with the music of the classical world.

Nonetheless, medieval principles of composition gradually changed and polyphonic music became more integrated. Layers of parts could not be added or subtracted at will. Very gradually, too, a sense of harmonic progression developed which was the means for music to become a persuasive and rhetorical art, influencing the emotions as much as the mind.

university at which Luther was professor of theology, but in 1521 the Emperor Charles V summoned him to justify himself. In a letter Luther described the proceedings succinctly:

All they said was: 'Are these books yours?' 'Yes.' 'Will you recant?' 'No.' 'Then get out.'[1]

After the excommunication which followed, Luther was given further protection by Frederick and took the opportunity to write more pamphlets, to begin a German translation of the New Testament (a task for which he was well qualified) and to consider new forms of worship. An increasing number of German states were prepared to allow their churches to adopt his reforms and the movement was expanding rapidly.

Luther's challenges to the church included all those of Wycliffe—the moral need for the church to put its own house in order; the right of every person to read the Bible for themselves; the condemnation of the sale of indulgences—but hinged on one vital point. His reading of the apostle Paul and of Augustine of Hippo, and above all, his own personal experience, convinced him utterly that no one could earn righteousness in God's sight; faith in Christ and repentance were the only route. Therefore indulgences, pilgrimages, monastic orders, as ways of buying or earning one's way into God's favour, were utterly unacceptable, spurious inventions of the church to line its coffers.

Such a message earned him support from the secular powers, for it would inevitably lead to a transfer of wealth from church to state. But Luther's desire for change was not motivated by politics but by sincere Christian conviction and the consequence of a balanced spiritual and family life.

Luther's background as an Augustinian monk had taught him the value of a devotional life of prayer and also gave him a deep love of music. Not only was he profoundly familiar with the traditional Gregorian chant but his training as a singer and lutenist enabled him to compose adequately in the polyphonic style of the times. In common with the ancient Greeks, he knew the power of music, for good and ill:

Next to the Word of God, music deserves the highest praise. She is a mistress and governess of those human emotions...

which control men or more often overwhelm them ... Whether you wish to comfort the sad, to subdue frivolity, to encourage the despairing, to humble the proud, to calm the passionate, or to appease those full of hate ... what more effective means than music could you find?[2]

Here he appears to be stressing less the symbolic aspect of music, characteristic of the Middle Ages, and more the human aspects of the art and its effects, good and bad, on the emotions. In this respect Luther was a product of the Renaissance.

Luther's fundamental desire that Christians should worship God in sincerity and with understanding did not mean that he wished to abandon the Latin Mass. On the contrary, he suggested a double solution to the problem of congregational involvement, through the Formula Missae of 1523 and the German Mass of 1526.

The Latin Mass, he suggested, should be for the use of cathedrals and abbeys where such solemnity was appropriate and where the majority of the participants understood the language. The German Mass, on the other hand, was for the benefit of the local parish church, where songs, readings and prayers should be in a language that everyone could understand. In practice and after some years of experiment, many services were conducted in a mixture of both languages, with musical settings in one or the other, even alternating verses of hymns in Latin and German. Scripture readings might be in one tongue and repeated immediately in the other.

The more formal type of Lutheran Mass was not at all unlike the Roman Mass in the outline given in chapter 6. Its musical basis was still that of Gregorian chant. Luther suggested that polyphonic music could adorn certain parts of the liturgy as well as much of the ceremonial, including the vestments, the candles, even the elevation of the host—showing the bread and wine to the people just before Communion.

But there was a vital difference: this was a corporate act, shared by the congregation. No Christians were barred from entering, and both bread and wine were offered to everyone. Luther emphasized congregational participation in the music, too. He suggested including German songs at certain points. He also encouraged the use of the Daily Office—particularly the Greater Hours of Vespers, Compline and Matins, and that all 150 psalms be 'preserved in the ears of the church'.[3]

Reacting against centuries of tradition, Luther did not insist that a rigid liturgical rule had to be followed:

'It is not necessary . . . that ceremonies, instituted by men, should be observed uniformly in all places.'[4]

He was anxious and insistent that his ideas should not become sectarian; his desire was for reform, not schism. Unfortunately, as a study of

In Cranach's great triptych in the Church of St Marien, Wittenberg, Martin Luther is given great emphasis. In the left panel Luther helps Philipp Melanchthon with a baptism; in the centre he is among the apostles at a last supper; in the right he makes his confession. In the lower panel Luther preaches on his central theme, the death of Christ on the cross for us.

J.S. Bach will show, this lack of firm edicts allowed the Lutheran movement later to lose its clear sense of direction.

Luther's musical ideas were most striking in the *Deutsche Messe,* which includes musical examples of the kind of German singing he hoped to encourage. Once more his starting-point was the church's long-standing musical traditions. He and his helpers set about translating the Latin texts into German while carefully and sensitively re-moulding the tunes so that they could fit the different stress-patterns of the German language. Usually this meant simplifying the chant and making it more direct and strong. Latin hymns in the Ambrosian style were the easiest to transform, but chants for the Ordinary of the Mass were adapted to German, the greater flexibility of chant and Latin text

Lutheran Song

For the Reformers, it was vital for the Bible to be available in the language of the people. There was also a ready market for Christian songs in everyday language, even though books would have been too expensive for many parishioners to own.

Luther insisted that the songs should be learned by heart if at all possible. For this purpose, schools attached to the Lutheran churches taught their boys (girls were not part of the educational system!) to lead the congregational singing, at the same time giving the young people a deep familiarity with these new Christian songs.

For the first five years after the Ninety-five Theses there was no music written specifically for the Protestant movement. But with the appearance of Luther's liturgical reforms there began a steady stream of books—the *Etlich Christlich Lieder* (published in Nuremberg, 1524), *Enchiridion geistlicher Gesenge* (Leipzig, 1529), *Geistliche Lieder* (Wittenberg, 1533), *Geystliche Lieder* (Babst in Leipzig, 1545) and many more.[1]

The continuing links with Gregorian chant are the key to understanding how this music was sung. In spite of ornate polyphonic pieces for choir, the basis for the Roman liturgy was still unison singing, emphatically without accompaniment. Organs were being built into many churches for the first time in the fifteenth century, but they made a different contribution to the liturgy from what most people expect today.

There was certainly no feeling that congregations needed the support of an organ in singing of any kind. They and the choir were perfectly capable of enjoying a first-rate tune without the help of any supporting harmony, so most of the early song-collections simply print the melody.

It may appear puzzling that Luther's very first publication of songs (the *Neue geistliche Gesänge* of 1523) is in four-part harmony. The explanation for this lies in its presentation, not as a modern hymn-book, with all the harmony parts conveniently laid out for the organist, but as a set of four part-books, each for the use of one voice or group of voices. This book was therefore probably to popularize Luther's music among students and people with a reasonable education.

Musical skills and theory were part of a good education no matter what profession one might enter; some musical accomplishment was an assumed part of a good upbringing. These days with passive television-watching it may be hard to imagine how in Luther's time students would gather round a table to sing in harmony from part-books just for amusement. The subject matter of these songs was not much more sophisticated than those of the pop world today, so this was another important area where Christian praise could do battle with more worldly pursuits.

In church, the congregation would sing their songs in unison and unaccompanied. The choir, however, might well have been capable of singing in four parts, in which case it often took the responsibility of giving the people a rest and singing every other verse for them. The song would therefore be changing from harmony to unison and back again and alternating between congregation and choir.

The organ (and maybe other instruments if available) was used to support the choir, doubling the voice-parts for security, but it would have been considered quite illogical for the instrument to play parts against the firm unison line of congregational singing. This modern usage only became accepted during the seventeenth century.

making the task rather more involved.

Luther also used simple melodies familiar to ordinary people—Latin or German devotional songs, school songs, children's songs, folk-songs or carols. A number of these melodies have since spread widely through the Christian world—*Resonet in Laudibus (Joseph lieber, Joseph mein)*, *Quem Pastores Laudavere* and *In Dulci Jubilo* are three examples. Words were sometimes slightly altered (as in the latter, to remove an unacceptable emphasis on the Virgin Mary) or completely rewritten. For example the tune to the love-song *Innsbruck ich muss dich lassen*—'Innsbruck I must leave you'—was used for countless hymns, the earliest being *O Welt, ich muss dich lassen*—'O world, I must leave you'. This melody can be found at several points in J.S. Bach's *St Matthew Passion*.

Luther also wrote a number of hymns himself, both words and melody. The most famous must be *Ein' feste Burg*—'A safe stronghold'. Its original rhythmic scheme makes it more subtle and lively than the version usually sung today.

Not only did Luther recognize the power of music as an aid to devotion, to enhance and to elevate worship, but he was also keenly aware of the need to educate the younger generations into Christian ways. Music had a part to play here too. Young people, he believed, could be encouraged to turn away from music with bad associations by acquaintance with music of a more wholesome kind.

And you, my young friend, let this noble, wholesome and cheerful creation of God [ie music] be commended to you. By it you may escape shameful desires and bad company. At the same time you may by this creation accustom yourself to recognise and praise the Creator. Take special care to shun perverted minds who prostitute this lovely gift of nature and of art with their erotic rantings...[5]

This did not necessarily mean that the two musics, sacred and profane, had to be entirely separate (as they were for most of the Roman Church's history) but that the profane could be made sacred by encouraging new and wholesome associations. Some four-part Christian songs published in 1571 had very secular origins:

Street songs, knightly and miners' songs,

changed in a Christian, moral and ethical manner, in order that the evil, vexatious melodies, the useless and shameful songs to be sung in the streets, fields, houses, and elsewhere, may lose their bad effects if they can have good, useful Christian texts and words.[6]

Martin Luther wrote both the words and music of this famous hymn around 1528. By the eighteenth century the lively and unpredictable rhythms of early versions (this one dates from 1581) had been ironed out, and it is a smoother but blander melody that is found in modern hymnbooks.

Chapter 11

The Swiss Reformers—the Calvinist Tradition

The Lutheran reforms spread quickly across Europe, east and north. Lutheran songbooks were published in Bohemia and in Holland, Denmark and Sweden only a few years after their first appearance in Germany. From the seventeenth century onwards, Lutheran immigrants took their faith even further, to the New World. The characteristic musical developments of these communities are discussed in Part 7.

Ulrich Zwingli

The other great force in the Reformation of Europe came from Switzerland, firstly from Zürich, where in 1518 Zwingli was made people's priest at the Cathedral, and then from Geneva through Calvin.

One of the great tragedies of this period of turmoil and questioning is that the great visionaries of Christian reform could not agree on essential matters of doctrine. Instead, they created distinct sects, constantly vilifying and even slaughtering each other. The spirit of the Reformation certainly encouraged a large number of lunatic factions to spring up—Munzerites, Adamists, Devillers and Libertines, to name but a few. Some European towns viewed with alarm the presence of as many as twelve such sects in their midst. But much more regrettable was the fact that Luther and Zwingli met in 1530 and failed to agree on points of doctrine.

Were the bread and wine of the Eucharist literally changed into flesh and blood? Both found the idea abhorrent. But Luther was unable to accept Zwingli's (and later Calvin's) position that the sacraments were only memorials—symbols of a greater truth. Both Luther and Calvin used the Bible as their authority and refused to give ground. The divisions went deeper, though. Luther believed that the society of which he was a part was still a Christian one. It certainly needed to experience repentance and to know justification by faith; it certainly needed a return to the true ways of Christ, but he saw himself as a reforming spirit within a unified world. So he was happy for the folk-melodies of that world to be reformed and redeemed for use in worship. Zwingli and Calvin held a different position. They understood the true church, defined by the most literal interpretation of the Bible, as being separate from the world. For them, that true church was the only church, and thus an entirely new beginning was needed.

The fact that Zwingli was a highly educated musician (apparently a talented instrumentalist) did not, as in Luther's case, lead to any kind of emphasis on music in worship. On the contrary, his musical experience concerned the sophisticated art-world of polyphony and he had little interest in the simpler fare of congregational singing. In any case, his sensitivity to music was overridden by other more pressing concerns. Eventually, the Christians of the Swiss cantons who adopted Zwingli's reforms and those staying loyal to Rome took to settling their differences by force; Zwingli died in a sectarian battle in 1531.

Calvin

What Zwingli began in German-speaking Switzerland was developed in the French-speaking communities by the most imposing figure of reform, Jean Calvin. He was a French refugee who arrived in Geneva in 1536, the same year in which the city adopted Zwingli's reformed faith. Calvin, like Zwingli, saw the world divided into those destined to be saved and those destined for damnation. The Calvinists were therefore exclusive—they and only they were able to offer salvation.

Calvin, a highly-trained lawyer, established a comprehensive system of state government based on a number of biblical tenets. It was an enigmatic blend of compassion, democracy and harsh discipline.

In Calvin's rule, the church leadership was elected by and from its congregations, without, of course, any reference to Rome. The pastorate was required to take its duties seriously, however, and church members would be visited periodically. If irregularities were noted—lapses of morals, superstitious practice, the use of Latin prayers, the visiting of taverns, dancing—then those concerned would be reprimanded in front of their congregation. Depending on the severity of the lapse, they might be banned from receiving communion or driven out of the church. In extreme cases they might be executed, on the authority of the Old Testament Books of the Law.

The austerity of Calvinism

Calvin's deep suspicion of society at large led to an austerity in worship which excluded any possibility that art or artefacts could distract the people's attention. A Calvinist church was completely devoid of decoration; there were no pictures, vestments, candles or images of any kind. The pulpit, the source of God's Word and the only recognized authority for the elect, was placed at the centre.

In such surroundings the presence of music caused some misgivings. It was, of course, tainted by association with the unacceptable practices of the Roman Church or linked with singing and dancing. In the first case, one's soul was at risk; in the second, one's morals. None of Luther's redeeming of folk-melody would do—music had to be kept on the tightest rein.

As Calvin saw it, the New Testament scriptures only recognized psalms as material suitable for Christian song. Accordingly, the Calvinists absolutely forbade any texts to be sung in church except the Book of Psalms and one or two canticles. Furthermore, Calvin insisted on:

... simple and pure singing of the divine praises, forasmuch as where there is no meaning there is no edification. Let them come from heart and mouth, and in the vulgar tongue. Instrumental music was only tolerated in the time of the Law [the Old Testament] because of the people's infancy.[1]

Singing in harmony and the use of instruments of any kind were therefore expressly forbidden.

The north rose window of the cathedral at Sens in France shows the exalted Christ surrounded by a concert of angels; the atmosphere is one of colour, beauty and imagination. The window was made at about the time Calvin moved from France to lead the reform in Geneva, where the style of worship was to be in complete contrast: austere, and centred on a considered response to the preaching of the word.

The Genevan Psalter

About 1550 Theodore de Beza (1519–1605) had finished translating all 150 psalms into French. A professional musician, Louis Bourgeois (about 1523–1600), was commissioned to set them to music. The result was the Genevan Psalter, completed in 1562.

Such a task might appear a simple one and the results of little interest. In reality, the Genevan Psalter had a profound influence on the Christian world. Paradoxically, the crippling musical restrictions under which Bourgeois had to work were beneficial. The very simplicity and directness of the tunes makes them strong and memorable. They do not have the rhythmic variety of the Lutheran melodies, nor do they ever set more than one note to a syllable (the more decorative elements of Gregorian chant can still be sensed in Lutheran song).

Almost all the tunes use only two types of note, long and short. Dotted notes are very rare and lines inevitably begin and end with long notes. All this, with the complete lack of harmonic support, suggests the musical equivalent of bread and water. But if music has to be this restricted, then the Genevan Psalter, like early Gregorian chant, cannot be bettered.

The tunes were a compilation from a number of sources, as were those of the Lutheran tradition. Some had their origins in Gregorian chant, a few from folk-melodies and some from Lutheran tunes, in spite of the fact that the Calvinists hated the Lutherans as much as they hated the Roman Catholics. Though the musical borrowings are not as easy to spot as those of Luther, it is encouraging to note that music can cross the highest barriers erected by human failings.

Calvin wanted first-rate melodies for his congregations. Music had the capacity *'d'esmouvoir et enflamber le coeur des hommes'* [to move and inflame the heart of humanity][1] and therefore it should be used to praise God with the

qualities of 'weight', 'modesty' and 'majesty' appropriate to such a task.

The impact of the Genevan Psalter in and even beyond the Reformed Christian world was immense. A great many polyphonic arrangements were made of it, many by the finest composers of the day. The composer Claude Goudimel (died 1572), on the title page of his psalm-collection of 1565 explained that the songs were:

non pas pour induire à les chanter en l'Eglise, mais pour s'esiouir en Dieu particulièrement ès maisons [not for leading the singing of the church, but for the glorifying of God specifically in the home].

It was common practice for such vocal pieces to be played on instruments, or with instruments and voices mixed. They were also arranged for the popular combination of voice and lute, again for private devotions and therefore still within the realm of music for worship. Outstanding composers continued to make choral arrangements of the Genevan Psalter (Claude le Jeune, for instance) and the Psalter was translated into many languages, including Dutch, German and English before the end of the century. The Genevan Psalter has inspired countless other metrical settings and its melodies have invaded psalters and hymn-books all over the world.

Qui au con-seil des malings n'a 'es - té. Qui n'est au trac des pe-cheurs ar-re-sté, Qui des moqueurs au banc pla-ce n'a-pri-se: Mais nuict & iour la Loy contemple,& pri - se De l'E-ter-nel, & en est de - si - reux, Cer-tai - ne - ment ce - lui là est heu - reux.

The majesty simplicity of this psalm from a precursor (1542) of the Genevan Psalter is typical of Calvinist music. The music is more straightforward than Lutheran tunes of the time, mostly requiring only two lengths of note. These easy and memorable melodies have proved to be a lasting influence on the Christian world.

Chapter 12

The Reformation in England

It would be a mistake to imagine that the common people of the sixteenth century had any freedom of choice in matters of religion. On the continent of Europe that freedom could only be exercised by the rulers of the many small kingdoms into which much of it was divided. Whatever brand of Christianity the rulers adopted, their subjects had to follow, to the point of fighting in the sectarian battles with neighbouring states that happened to choose a different path. Even the aristocracy were by no means protected from trouble if they chose to swim against the tide.

The Anabaptists, members of the one reformed sect which consistently and quietly preached freedom of conscience in religion, were cruelly and inhumanly persecuted from all sides. Only the nobility of Poland made any significant efforts to keep the sectarian arguments peaceful.

Henry VIII and the break with Rome

The Reformation in the British Isles (not Scotland, since it was a separate kingdom) was not so much due to its ruler exercising his freedom of conscience, but rather precipitated by political necessity.

Henry VIII's divorce from Catharine of Aragon could only be achieved at the cost of a break with Rome. At first Henry simply envisaged that he himself would replace the pope as head of the church in England; he was not attracted by the Lutheran ideas of reform. A pile of Lutheran books was burnt outside Great St Mary's Church in Cambridge in 1520 and well after the Act of Supremacy of 1536, when Miles Coverdale published his *Goostly* [Spiritual] *Psalms and Spiritual Songs* in English, they were still being banned.

Possibly the most drastic effect on Christian music during Henry VIII's reign was caused by the dissolution of the monasteries, some of which had maintained the Roman traditions of liturgy and music in splendour. A number of centres of Christian culture were spared, including cathedrals (thirteen of which had schools attached), the Chapel Royal at Windsor and the college foundations at Oxford, Cambridge, Winchester and Eton. Liturgical reforms did not entirely extinguish their medieval traditions, with the result that the style of worship in English cathedrals today has links with a much earlier past.

The reign of Edward VI (1547–52) began with

King Henry VIII of England with his fool. The king is seen here as a musician, which he certainly was. The Reformation in England, beginning under Henry, took a form which preserved the link with earlier centuries of Christian music.

further dissolutions of churches that supported 'vain opinions of purgatory and masses... to be done for them which be departed'.[1] Many of these churches had made considerable provision for music.[2]

All cathedrals received a Royal Visitation during the first years of Edward VI's reign. The Visitors made sweeping recommendations concerning the liturgy, reducing its great complexity, simplifying the visual spectacle and forbidding the use of the organ, the singing of Latin antiphons, responsories or sequences and sometimes reducing the numbers in the choir. The recommendations were sometimes drastic and must have caused the musicians considerable dismay.

At Lincoln Cathedral the Visitors commanded that

> **[The choir] shall from henceforth sing or say no anthems of our Lady or other Saints, but only of our Lord, and them not in Latin; but choosing out the best and most sounding to Christian religion they shall turn the same into English, setting thereunto a plain and distinct note for every syllable one: they shall sing them and none other.[3]**

Edward's reign also gave Archbishop Cranmer his greatest opportunities for reform. He had already approved the publication of Coverdale's *Great Bible* in 1539 (though at the price of ten shillings its circulation could not be very wide) and within two years of Edward's accession had produced the first of his two versions of the *Book of Common Prayer.*

The Book of Common Prayer

In 1549 the Act of Uniformity under Edward made the *Book of Common Prayer* compulsory in all places of worship in England, Wales and Ireland. Unlike the sophisticated sets of service-books required for the Roman liturgy and its local variants, this book was all in English, gave little guidance concerning the use of music and was relatively straightforward and simple.

In the 1549 *Book of Common Prayer,* the structure of the Mass, renamed Holy Communion, was maintained in a simplified form, though omitting the Gradual. In a further revision of 1552, however, the other items of the Proper were also cut. Musicians were therefore left with none of the texts that had received the most lavish musical attention. The Daily Office was ingeniously compressed into two services— Matins and Evensong.

Matins was based on the Roman Matins of Salisbury Cathedral—the Sarum rite. Its canticles

The Eton Choirbook

The beginning of the sixteenth century produced impressive collections of music such as the *Eton Choirbook* which illustrate a peak of sumptuousness for Roman liturgy. The circumstances that created these *Magnificats* and Marian antiphons may have completely lost touch with the simple and direct world of the New Testament, but as works of art they are breathtaking. The Latin text is clearly only a vehicle for the music, which is of unprecedented richness and sonority. Sections of choral writing with as many as nine independent voice-parts (the voices ranging from the deep bass to the highest treble) alternate with passages for a few highly-skilled soloists.

Breathtakingly beautiful though this music is, it was in the medieval tradition, old-fashioned even for its time. It was an adornment and elaboration of the liturgy—a mirror of divine order perhaps, but beyond the congregation's understanding. No wonder that Erasmus said of it:

> *Modern music is so constructed that the congregation cannot hear one distinct word. The choristers themselves do not understand what they are singing, yet according to priests and monks it constitutes the whole of religion... In college or monastery it is still the same: music, nothing but music...[1]*

The choirbook from the chapel of Eton College is beautifully illuminated. The page shown is from Walter Lambe's 'Salve Regina'.

were the *Venite*—Psalm 95—and the *Te Deum* ('We praise you, O God') with a reduced number of readings, the canticle sung at Lauds (the *Benedictus*—Zechariah's song found in Luke's Gospel, chapter 1) and sometimes the *Quicumque vult* (the Athanasian Creed) which was a part of Prime. Terce, Sext and None were cut altogether. Evensong married Vespers (with its psalms and *Magnificat)* to Compline (whose canticle is the *Nunc Dimittis*, the song of Simeon in Luke's Gospel, chapter 2). These changes were by no means taken up with enthusiasm and many establishments, proud of their time-honoured liturgical traditions, dragged their feet for some time.

Merbecke

In 1550 John Merbecke, a student of the work of Calvin and a keen reformer, published his *booke of Common praier noted*. He intended it as a solution to the difficulties that cathedral churches faced, as Merbecke provided simple music for the Ordinary texts for Communion and for the versicles and responses, psalms, canticles and prayers of Matins and Evensong.

Following those of Luther and Calvin, many of his settings use traditional music as their basis, but he chose to keep to the free rhythm of the words and to use a method of notation reminiscent of Gregorian chant.

But Merbecke's music made little headway as further liturgical changes, not to mention storms, rendered his settings unusable. His music is still familiar to Anglicans today because of its revival in the nineteenth century, ironically enough by a group of Anglo-Catholics with motives totally at variance with his own.

During the five years of Queen Mary's bloody attempts to restore the Catholic faith after Edward's death in 1552, many reformers fled to Lutheran Germany or to Geneva. The publication of metrical psalters in English continued in Geneva, such as Sternhold and Hopkins' *One and fiftie Psalms of David* of 1556. These were very much in the Calvinist tradition, with simple and strong tunes and no harmonization.

Elizabeth's reign

Queen Elizabeth, on her accession in 1558, once more reversed the religious decrees of Mary and restored the position roughly to that of 1552 and the second version of the *Book of Common*

Prayer. While this step led swiftly to her excommunication by Pope Pius V, the Queen determined to avoid further bloodshed and to tread a middle path. The more radical reformists were no more happy with this position than were the Catholics. Both parties found quite different reasons to object to the *Book of Common Prayer,* but both knew relative safety in her realm.

Elizabeth herself enjoyed the ceremonial side of worship and the Chapel Royal continued to employ the services of the finest musicians in the land (though there is plenty of evidence that it did not pay them enough). Reformed clergy were uneasy at the theatrical splendour with which the Queen celebrated St George's Day, 1562, as recorded by a contemporary:

At Whitehall the Queen's grace went from her Chapel with twelve Knights of the Garter in robes with collars of gold with garters, twenty of her Chapel in copes of cloth of gold . . . singing the English procession from the Chapel, round the Hall and back again . . . [the Dean of] her Chapel bore a book and a robe, and Master Norres bore the black rod, in a robe, and Master Garter, all three in crimson satin; the Bishop of Winchester wore his robe of red . . .[4]

On the other hand, an early seventeenth-century writer recalled that

. . . not so fewe as an 100 paires organs were pulled down (and many of them sold or imploide to make pewter dishes). And commands were given for short playinge, or none at all, for shortenings or alteringe their songs and service to give place for preachinge, and casting service as it were quite out of doors.[5]

Along with this, ardent reformers attempted to do away with candles, vestments, crucifixes, the practice of kneeling to receive communion and other 'popish' practices. But in spite of this pressure, a Royal Injunction permitted that

. . . for the comforting of such that delight in music . . . an Hymn, or suchlike song to the praise of Almighty God [might be sung at such times] in the best sort of melody and music that may conveniently

be devised, having respect that the sentence [that is, the meaning] of the Hymn may be understood and perceived.[6]

It is this tolerance that allowed the Church of England to benefit from a golden age of music.

The golden age

The finest musical talent in the country was to be found at the Chapel Royal. Christopher Tye, Thomas Tallis and John Sheppard were all of a generation that experienced dramatic changes in the liturgy, their careers spanning the reigns of Edward VI and Mary. Tallis lived and worked well into the time of Elizabeth. As a result, they were able to create superbly worked masses, motets, antiphons and responsories with Latin texts.

Tallis and Tye made a special contribution to the simpler and more austere requirements of reformed English texts, including a number of anthems and canticles. Other later composers (such as Peter Phillips, Richard Dering and Tallis' famous pupil William Byrd) wrote both Latin and English texts because they were Catholics. If anything, the richness of this productive period grows into the next century, many canticles and anthems in English being set by Orlando Gibbons, Adrian Batten, Thomas Weelkes and Thomas Tomkins, in spite of the increasingly vocal Puritan camp.

Significantly, the vast majority of these (and many more) composers wrote with equal facility for other purposes—dance-music for the nobility; songs for devotion or entertainment; instrumental music for recreation. Unlike today, there was no need for a violent change in musical style from the secular to the sacred. It was sufficient, as Thomas Morley wrote, to be aware that for the liturgy the music should have an appropriate solemnity:

you must cause your harmony to carry a majesty ... but let it be in long notes, for the nature of it will not bear short notes and quick motions, which denote a kind of wantonness.[7]

According to Thomas Tudway, albeit writing a hundred years later, the results were admirable:

...the Air so solemn, the fugues and & other embellishments so just, & naturally taken, as must warm the Heart of anyone, who is endu'd with a Soul fitted for devine raptures.[8]

Humble parish churches were unlikely to have boasted an organ or choir and psalm-singing was the chief musical content of services which centred on the reading and expounding of the Bible. Sternhold and Hopkins produced a psalter of all 150 psalms (published by John Day in 1563) followed over the years by many others. Psalm-singing at church became very popular as the century progressed. The Bishop of Salisbury, writing from London in 1560, noted:

Religion is now somewhat more established than it was. The practice of joining in church music has very much helped this ... You may now sometimes see at St Paul's Cross, after the service, six thousand persons, old and young, of both sexes, all singing together and praising God.[9]

Chapter 13

The Catholic Reformation

The effects of the Renaissance penetrated the Roman Church's music only slowly. The Church was a benevolent employer of the most brilliant composers, allowing them gradually to transform medieval styles to Renaissance ideals without restricting their creative freedom. When serious change was finally imposed on musicians—well into the sixteenth century—the result of the pruning (some say) was a leaner and stronger Christian music, to which the Roman Catholic Church still refers as its musical 'golden age'.

Even before Luther's time there was a desire for reform from within the Roman Catholic Church. The reforming zeal was at first mainly evident in Spain under Cardinal Ximenes, a prelate whose power sprang from both the Church and the united Spanish crowns of Aragon and Castile. Under his leadership the Spanish church became disciplined and confident, seeking out and persecuting Moors, Jews and Protestant Christians through the operations of the Inquisition.

Over the same period the Portuguese exploration of the East (Vasco de Gama travelled round the African Cape to India) and the Spanish exploration of the West not only brought wealth and glamour to their countries but also vastly expanded the numbers of converts to the Roman Catholic faith. Their motives for this fresh wave of the crusading spirit were the familiar mixture of altruism and greed:

. . . to serve God and His Majesty, to give light to those who were in darkness, and to grow rich, as all men desire to do.[1]

The Roman Church's puritan movement gathered particularly around Ignatius Loyola (1491–1556) who adopted an ascetic and disciplined life, regulated by a rigorous course of 'Spiritual Exercises'. Those inspired to follow him called themselves the Society of Jesus, or Jesuits, and became a significant power for reform.

Unlike the Protestants, however, Jesuits pledged themselves with unswerving loyalty to Rome; indeed, they believed that this loyalty was the source of their salvation, rather than the Protestants' justification by faith. Under the influence of this reforming spirit and with the leadership of Pope Pius V, a new and vigorous inquisition was set up against Protestant sects, the celibacy of the priesthood was re-affirmed (the Protestants encouraged their priests to marry) and the Vatican's sculptures and paintings of the human form were adorned with carefully-placed fig-leaves.

Music written for the well-endowed Roman monasteries and cathedral churches around this time is undoubtedly a high point in the history of Christian music. It deserves some attention not just because musicians today respect it so deeply but because, in spite of its artistic excellence, it was the very opposite of what Catholic reformers believed Christian music should be.

This fifteenth-century melody was probably first sung in a crusade against the Turks. The words, 'the man-at-arms fills everyone with fear', are aggressive, but the melody became very popular among church composers. There were more than two dozen settings of the Ordinary of the Mass made, based on the tune. One of the last of these is by Palestrina and was published in the late sixteenth century.

L'hom - me, l'hom - me, l'homme ar - mé,

L'homme ar - mé, l'homme ar - mé doibt on doub

ter, doibt on doub - ter. [etc...]

The beginnings of counterpoint

During the fifteenth century the Ordinary of the Mass (the unchanging texts of the *Kyrie, Gloria, Credo, Sanctus* and *Agnus Dei)* became more and more the focus of musical attention. Guillaume Dufay (1400–74) for instance, set the Ordinary of the Mass at least eight times. His music (especially the music he wrote later in life) sounds different from the medieval music described earlier. The motet style of composition still governed Dufay's settings—that is, they were based on a fragment of traditional chant, two or more voices then weaving an inventive web around it. But it became common practice to use the same chant as the basis for all the sections of the Mass setting.

One of Dufay's Mass settings called *Missa Caput,* for instance, uses the melody of an antiphon *Venit ad Petrum* ('He came to Peter') as the basis for all five sections. The chant basis (called *cantus firmus)* of this type of Mass setting might have some connection with the occasion for which the Mass music was written, but would not have been sung in the service in its original form. What is more, these melodies were so heavily concealed by their musical surroundings that they might very well go unrecognized by the congregation.

Since the best composers of the time were equally occupied with writing music for the glittering and indolent life at court, it was perhaps a small step for Dufay to choose a secular tune as the basis for a Mass setting. So in his *Missa 'Se la Face ay Pale'* Dufay took the melody of one of his own love-songs and used it as a *cantus firmus.* In another, he used the battle-song *L'homme Armé.* This tune was very well-known in the French-speaking world; many other composers used it in Mass settings and its characteristic sound could scarcely fail to be recognized.

Many other composers (Busnois, Ockhegem, Taverner) followed Dufay's example in writing *cantus firmus* or 'parody' Masses. The *cantus firmus* (the melody of the love-song, for example) was distributed from time to time among all the voice-parts and the medieval technique of composing layer upon layer gave way to a greater blend of all parts, each carrying a fair share of responsibility for the overall sense of the music.

Perhaps the greatest composer of them all, Josquin des Prez (1440–1521) created a deeper

integration still by requiring the voices to copy each other melodically.

The melodic ideas that begin new sections of the music came to be called *puncta*—'points'. When voices imitate, the points are set against each other, the technique called counterpoint. Sometimes (as in a so-called 'canon' Mass) long stretches of music in one voice-part were made to be identical but out of step with another. In short, Renaissance composers had developed music of such profound creativity and ingenuity that few (and not always the singers themselves)

were able to appreciate all its subtleties.

By the end of the century choirs singing in this tradition had become skilled in the part-music required of them. The whole choir was expected to be able to take part in these complex pieces rather than the solo voices of the time of Machaut. Instruments were sometimes used to double with some or all of the choir to keep the music secure.

Guillaume Dufay stands with a portative organ and Binchois carries a harp in this miniature from 'Le Champion des Dames' by Martin le Franc.

The Council of Trent

The Council of Trent (Trento is an Italian town near the borders of Austria and Switzerland) met intermittently from 1545 to 1563 to discuss and to recommend all manner of reforms in the Roman Church.

One of its original intentions was to see if any reconciliation with the Protestants was possible. But by the time the Council started its meetings, it was far too late for that. There were many other issues before it, however, and although music was not high on the list of priorities

practices, and were deaf to the more recent complaints of reformers like Erasmus. And yet the Mass music by Isaak, Obrecht and Josquin is recognized as unsurpassed in the history of Western Christian music.

Christian worship on the one hand and artistic creativity on the other were, in some people's minds, directly incompatible, a situation more

The Council of Trent continued its work, with intervals, for eighteen years from 1545. The intention was to meet the Protestant Reformation with a reformed and renewed Catholic Church.

(recommendations did not appear till 1562) the Council eventually announced:

In the case of those Masses which are celebrated with singing and with organ, let nothing profane be intermingled, but only hymns and divine praises. The whole plan of singing... should be constituted not to give empty pleasure to the ear but in such a way that the words may be clearly understood by all... and thus the hearts of the listeners may be drawn to the desire of heavenly harmonies, in the contemplation of the joy of the blessed.[2]

The comments about mingling 'profane', 'lascivious' or 'impure' music with the Mass indicate that musicians and clerics had long forgotten the Papal Bull of 1323 forbidding such

anomalous and tragic when it is remembered that the composers without doubt believed that God himself was the source of their creative gifts.

Palestrina

It was Giovanni Pierluigi da Palestrina (about 1525–94) whose talents supposedly dissuaded the Council of Trent from taking its revisionist recommendations to extremes. The legends concerning his relationship with the Council centre on one of the best-known of his 104 Mass settings, the *Missa Papae Marcelli*.

Unlike almost any other composer of Christian music, Palestrina has been held in high esteem continuously since his death. Such adulation has not served him entirely well, since over the years his admirers have been tempted to glamorize the slender facts about his life and work.

Palestrina lived and worked throughout his

life as organist, singer and composer for the Church in Rome. He was deeply involved in the musical traditions of the city's three most venerated churches: San Giovanni in Laterano (where he was *maestro di capella* from 1555 to 1560), Santa Maria Maggiore (he was *maestro di capella* from 1561 to 1566 and had been a choirboy there) and St Peter's in the Vatican.

In 1555 Palestrina was invited by Pope Julius to join the Sistine Chapel choir. The official mechanism for appointment was brushed aside, including the entrance examination and the regulation that choir members had to be unmarried. But reform was in the air. Within a matter of months, almost immediately after his own election, Pope Paul IV learned of the irregularities of Palestrina's appointment, dismissing him and two other married singers from his choir. However, Palestrina's reputation ensured that within a month he had been appointed to San Giovanni, where the previous *maestro di capella* had been the young Netherlands composer Orlande de Lasso.

About five years earlier, in 1549, the Roman Bishop Bernardino Cirillo had written an extended letter about church music to a colleague. In it he deplored the inclusion of secular melodies in Mass settings:

They say, 'Oh, what a fine Mass was sung in chapel!' And what is it, if you please? It is *L'Homme Armé,* **or** *Hercules Dux Ferrariae* **or** *Philomena.* **What the devil has the Mass to do with the armed man, or with Philomena, or with the Duke of Ferrara?**[3]

Having observed that Michelangelo's nude figures on the Sistine Chapel roof were more suitable for the 'loggia of some garden', he complains that composers in the modern style of counterpoint

...have put all their industry and effort into the writing of imitative passages, so that while one says 'Sanctus', another says 'Sabaoth', [and] still another says 'Gloria tua,' with howling, bellowing and stammering...

Ten years later the Council of Trent made its brief pronouncement on music and in April 1565 a significant entry in the Sistine Chapel diary was made:

At the request of the most Reverend Cardinal Vitellozzi we were assembled in his residence to sing some Masses and to test whether the words could be understood, as their Eminences desire...[4]

The story goes that Palestrina's *Missa Papae Marcelli* was one of the works heard on this occasion, though no evidence has yet been found

Giovanni Pierluigi da Palestrina, a sixteenth-century Italian composer of church music whose popularity has never waned.

to prove it. The music may have been written in 1555, when Marcellus was Pope for only three weeks, or as a test case for Cardinal Vitellozzi.

Whatever its background, the *Missa Papae Marcelli* is distinctive. When Palestrina published the music in 1567 along with six other Mass settings in the Second Book of Masses, he explained that his intention was 'to adorn the holy sacrifice of the Mass in a new manner'.[5] The technique of counterpoint is suppressed where there is any danger that the text might be obscured. Thus the *Gloria* and *Credo* are writen with almost no imitation between the voices and the most important words are repeated for emphasis and clarity. Even in the opening *Kyrie* long melismas (many notes to one syllable) are avoided, the interplay of the parts and the frequent repetition of the words conveying the text with unfailing clarity. Musical variety is preserved by ingenious use of every possible combination of the six available voice-parts.

It seems that Palestrina regarded this type of

setting as a particular genre and did not by any means adhere slavishly to the new principles. In a letter to the Duke of Mantua, who had commissioned a Mass from him, Palestrina asks whether it should be rewritten:

I beg you to inform me how you prefer it—whether short, or long, or written so that the words can be understood.[6]

The later sets of Masses published by Palestrina contain settings in both the new and the old styles (the 1570 collection contains yet another based on *L'Homme Armé*), suggesting that the Council of Trent's pronouncements were by no means universally upheld.

Palestrina was also heavily involved in the revision of Gregorian chant, which the Council found to be full of 'barbarisms, obscurities, contrarities and superfluities'. He was given the task of 'purging, correcting and reforming', the results of Palestrina's work alongside many

Organ Music

No instrument seems to have had so much of its history invented for it as the organ. The common association of the instrument with Christian worship has led to all kinds of claims for its ancient use in church for which there now seems little evidence. Organs had their uses in a Christian context in earlier medieval times, but not usually in the liturgy. Pope John VIII (872–882) wrote of an instrument installed as a teaching aid in the science of musical proportions, other organs were used processionally (outdoors) and may even have served the purpose of summoning people to church as bells do now.

Indisputable evidence of the use of organs in the liturgy appears in about the twelfth century and by the fifteenth century organ music was a widely accepted dimension of worship.

The Roman Catholic tradition

The organ was, for a long time, not used to accompany congregational singing, but had its own voice, of equal status to and independent of the singers. What did this mean in practice? Early organ manuscripts (of which there are not very many) are varied, but their most usual purpose was to substitute for a sung part of the service.

If a hymn was to be sung on a solemn occasion, then the choir might sing verses alternating with the organ, when the organist would play a verse on the congregation's behalf. This concept of

These monks, their organ and its bellows, were painted on an Italian earthenware dish in or around 1515.

others being published in 1614 as the so-called Medicean edition of the chant. Large numbers of chants which used tropes (additional and probably unscriptural texts) were pruned away. Of hundreds of sequences, for instance, only a handful were left.

Three hundred years later scholars—such as the monks of Solesmes described in chapter 24—would be hard at work undoing Palestrina's efforts and attempting to restore the chant to its earliest known state.

substitution extended to many different parts of the liturgy—antiphons, psalms, canticles or the Ordinary of the Mass. At various points in any of these the organ might take the place of choir or congregation, with a piece (called a *verset)* based on the melody.

This gave the organ a central role in worship, on an equal footing with the choir. For this purpose an organ was installed at Notre Dame in Paris at the beginning of the fourteenth century, where its use impressed a contemporary writer:

> *We see many clerics who, owing to a certain miraculous prodigy of their innate musical talent, improvise and perform on the organ the most difficult musical melodies, which the human voice would scarcely have presumed to undertake.[1]*

This substitution for and elaboration of the chant by the organ is yet another dimension to the medieval delight in beautifying the liturgy. It persisted in certain traditions, in spite of doubts and adverse criticism, until quite recent times.

Calvinist attitudes

The objections to organ music which led to the Calvinists stripping the Genevan churches of their organs were therefore nothing to do with the organ's secular associations (as was certainly the case with instruments associated with

dancing—shawms, crumhorns, viols and the like). Rather it was the 'popish' habit of taking away from the congregation words which were rightly theirs to utter. Of course, the melody of a hymn can bring its associated words to mind, but for many reformers, this was not enough. They drove the organ out of the liturgy because it prevented the congregation from active participation in worship.

The use of the organ was confined to the musical adornment of joyful and public occasions, and therefore excluded for a long time from funeral rites, litanies and the burning of heretics. There was also resistance, at least in France, to the use of the organ for the *Credo* and for the office of Matins.

The Lutherans

The Lutherans were ambivalent about the organ. No hard and fast rules were drawn up and many large city churches had a fine instrument which they were happy to use in alternation with congregation or choir in canticles and hymn-singing—primarily on the special feast-days of Easter and Christmas.

The organ was for a time specifically excluded from some parts of the services, though by the end of the sixteenth century its use in providing continuity and moments of meditation was accepted. From then on the status of organists in the Lutheran church rose; they were permitted to play preludes on hymn-tunes, either between the congregation's verses or elsewhere, and to play during Communion and maybe at

the 'elevation of the host' (the point before Communion where the priest held the bread up high for the congregation to see). There is plenty of evidence that Lutherans came to accept other instruments in worship as well.

The organ in Britain

In village churches the chances of hearing any organ music at all was remote, especially in Britain, where there was little tradition of church organ-building compared with that of the rest of Europe.

Organ music was therefore confined to the larger and wealthier churches. It was excluded entirely from Scotland, which had won its way to a whole-hearted Calvinism under John Knox in 1561.

The use of the organ in England was a continual source of controversy, but the manuscript collection called the Mulliner Book,[2] written at least partially for use in St Paul's Cathedral, well illustrates the role of the organ as a solo instrument in worship. The book contains music by several organists of the Chapel Royal (Redford, Blitheman, Tallis) and contains music dating from before and after the Reformation.

The Golden Age of Spanish Music

The discovery by Christopher Columbus in 1492 of a 'New World' far to the west of Spain and Portugal opened the route for undreamed-of riches to be brought back to Europe within fifty years. The plundering of the civilizations of Mexican Indians and the Incas of Peru helped to make Portugal and the Habsburg Empire the most powerful political forces in Europe.

By 1535 the two branches of the Habsburg dynasty, Austrian and Spanish, controlled not only the whole of Spain (Granada in the south and Navarre in the north having ceded in 1492 and 1512 respectively) but also Milan, southern Italy, Sicily, Sardinia, Tunis, the Netherlands and parts of Germany and Austria. One key to ruling successfully on such a scale was to display the wealth that lay behind the throne.

The Spanish Habsburgs, Charles V (king of Spain 1516–56) and his son Philip II (reigned 1556–98) were particularly generous patrons of the arts. They fostered and employed the outstanding talent of their country and made sure that Spain's creative excellence was widely known. Spanish musicians and composers accordingly became renowned throughout Europe and the Roman Catholic Church did not hesitate to benefit from their talents.

Toledo Cathedral, where by a special dispensation the ancient Mozarabic liturgy is still used today.

Cristóbal de Morales

When Cristóbal de Morales (about 1500–53) was being trained as a choirboy in Seville, the capital of Andalusia, he would soon have become aware that he was living in one of the most cultured cities in the world. Under the influence of the rich musical life of Seville he became one of Spain's most expert church musicians. His baritone voice and compositional

talent caught the attention of Pope Paul III and he was invited to join a number of other Spanish singers among the two dozen or more voices of the Sistine Chapel choir in Rome.

Between 1536 and 1543 Morales travelled the cities of Western Europe with the Pope's retinue, enjoying the use of his own horse and servant—perks that went with a job of such high standing. The papal tours gave Morales the chance to introduce his music to the great cathedrals, whose musicians were ready to acknowledge that his church compositions were the finest of their time.

Morales returned in 1545 to take up the post of *maestro de capilla* (choirmaster) at the Spanish cathedral of Toledo. His last few years in his native country were unhappy, marred by disagreements with his superiors. In Toledo Cathedral the musical tradition

focussed on organ music, whereas Morales had built his reputation on the composition of a more austere unaccompanied music for Mass. Perhaps he was consoled by the fact that two of his pupils, Francisco Guerrero (1528–99) and Juan Navarro (about 1530–80) were becoming known as the finest Christian composers of their generation.

Antonio de Cabezón

While Morales' fame spread throughout Europe as the result of his patronage by the Pope, the blind keyboard-player Antonio de Cabezón (1510–66) became the most favoured musician of the Spanish King Philip II. His post as organist of the King's private chapel took him in the King's company to Italy, Germany, the Netherlands and England. His talents as a player and composer excited a great deal of interest, for the compelling expressiveness of his keyboard music suggested all kinds of new creative possibilities to the musicians who had the chance of hearing him.

Cabezón made a profound contribution to organ music in worship through pieces of great variety. Some of these wove contrapuntal ingenuity around a known melody such as a hymn, others presented embellished and ornamented versions of such tunes. Still others, the *tientos,* were colourful and free fantasies. Most of this music was printed by Cabezón's son Hernando in a collection called *Obras de música para tecla, arpa y vihuela.*[1]

Tomás Luis de Victoria

Victoria (1548–1611) came from a family with strong Jesuit connections. He was trained from an early age by the *Maestros de capilla* at Avila Cathedral near Madrid. After a period at a Jesuit school in the area, at the age of about eighteen he went to a college in Rome (again run by Jesuits) with official duties as a singer. In 1569 he became an organist and chorister at the church of Santa Maria di Monserrato in Rome, later joining a community of lay-priests (who were not in a religious order) and entering the lower ranks of the clergy.

Victoria's increasing wealth during this extended Italian stay and his developing reputation as a composer of unaccompanied choral pieces allowed him to publish several sumptuous volumes of his music. In about 1587 he decided to return to Spain, when Philip II offered him the post of chaplain to the Empress María who was living in retirement in a convent in Madrid.

For the next fourteen years or so, Victoria was able to enjoy writing for and directing the expert convent choir of men and boys (separated from the nuns by a grille). He was offered the most prestigious musical posts of the great Spanish cathedrals, but in vain—the convent of *las Descalzas de Santa Clara* had too much to offer his musical talents.

Almost all Victoria's music was vocal

music for the liturgy, like that of Morales, Guerrero and Navarro before him. Of his twenty settings of the Ordinary of the Mass, seven are parody Masses—all but one built round music from sacred motets by Guerrero, Morales, Palestrina

A musical detail from the central panel of the altarpiece dedicated to St Vincent the Martyr at Saragossa.

or Victoria himself. His style is direct, however, and the ideals of the Catholic Reformation are expressed in its simplicity of purpose, albeit controlled by an incomparable intellect.

Some of his most solemn and dramatic works were published in Rome. The 1585 collection contains settings of the Lamentations of Jeremiah and two versions of the Passion story, according to Matthew and John. This was traditionally required to be sung with other penitential music during Holy Week (leading up to Easter Sunday). Victoria's sonorous *Lamentations* and his dramatic telling in music of the trial and crucifixion of Jesus are as profoundly moving as his better-known motets.

Victoria's hymns also deserve more attention, though *Jesu dulcis memoria,*

which is probably sung more than any other, was not his composition. Victoria's true hymns (of which there are dozens) followed the common practice of setting the even-numbered stanzas in polyphony, the alternate verses being sung to the traditional chant.

Villancicos

One of the intentions of the Catholic Reformation was to introduce a simpler and more populist music into worship with which the common people could identify. In the Spanish-speaking world it was *villancicos* which best fulfilled that need.

Villancico (the word literally means 'peasant') was the name given to a popular song with a refrain. It had early connections with the music of the Arab invaders of Andalusia. By the fifteenth century *villancicos* were being written and performed for the entertainment of aristocratic audiences: they were courtly love-songs under a rustic disguise.

The reformers encouraged the introduction into worship of *villancicos* on important feast-days. Well-known tunes were given newly-fashioned texts in Spanish, or wholly new sacred songs were written in the same popular style. In either case, their presence in worship caused consternation to the old guard.

Villancicos continued to be permitted in worship for another 200 years, until their operatic style became too much of an embarrassment to conscientious churchmen.

The Hispanic New World

From the very beginnings of the Spanish conquest of the Americas, music was understood to be an essential part of the expression of Christianity among the thousands of new converts. Not only were the Mexican Indians taught plainchant, but the same splendid forms of music from Spain were soon established in the New World. The unaccompanied choral music and *villancico* tradition of Mexico City Cathedral quickly became the equal of any in Spain, even under its first *maestro de capilla* Canon Juan Xuáres (appointed in 1539). Especially sumptuous music developed in the early seventeenth century in Puebla Cathedral

with the encouragement of talented composers: Juan Gutiérrez de Padilla (about 1590–1664) and Francisco López Capillas (about 1615–73) among many others.

In Peru, the administrative centre for the Spanish Americas, Christian music of high quality (such as Morales' Masses) could be heard in the cathedral at Cuzco in the mid-sixteenth century. A rich tradition of liturgical music developed in Lima Cathedral (which was consecrated in 1572).

Ignatius Loyola is seen receiving the bull from Pope Paul III which authorized the founding of the Order of Jesus, the Jesuits. Ignatius was Spanish, and his order did much to give effect to the renewal set in motion by the Council of Trent.

Chapter 14

The Power of Music

Many events of the Reformation and Counter-Reformation, especially the sectarian violence, were deep offences to the Christian gospel. This is not the place to reflect at length on that tragedy. But while music was low on the list of critical issues in the violent debate, it nonetheless provides a microcosm of the problems then facing the Christian world.

As far as their music was concerned, the three great Churches of Europe—Catholic, Lutheran and Calvinist—demonstrated a triangle of dissension of which there are still echoes in every argument concerning the liturgy and its music:

The Catholic, in church, listens without singing; the Calvinist sings without listening; the Lutheran both listens and sings—simultaneously![1]

In other words, for many Roman Catholic worshippers, participation in Christian music was not possible. As in so many other aspects of faith, the church took it upon itself to act as an intermediary between God and his people.

The Calvinists, believing that the Christian church on earth had to be begun again, went back to what they could learn of the early church; Christian music had to conform, with everything else, to what they read there.

The Lutherans managed to hold a precarious balance between the congregational singing characteristic of the early Church and an expression of faith through the art-music of experts.

The blending of participation and listening might occur even during one hymn, as happened in a special celebratory service in 1659, described by a contemporary:

... the first verse is sung by the congregation, the second is sung as a solo by the cantor, the third is performed by four girls unaccompanied, the fifth is sung by the congregation, the sixth by the schoolboys in the choir, and the last is taken by the congregation, the organ and all the singers.[2]

Such a scenario would be a challenge to any musical director and potentially a recipe for musical chaos. Spiritually, however, it has the attractive possibility of being the outward evidence of a church working as the Body of Christ, with its many parts making up a single unit.

The majority of Christian denominations today have found that this middle course can reflect the unity of Christ in the diversity of talent which makes up the church.

The Christian approach to the unredeemed world is the other painful issue raised during the years of the Reformation. Church leaders of all persuasions were agreed in their deep suspicion of the ecstatic and physical dimension of music. Luther wrote of the 'erotic rantings' of the secular world and the Council of Trent similarly objected to musical 'things that are lascivious', 'outcries and uproars' and 'seductive and impure melodies'.

The humanist tendencies of the Renaissance led musicians to be more aware of the control that music can exercise over the emotions, that is, its rhetorical power. Luther observed music's capacity to comfort, to terrify, to encourage, to humble, and so on. By doing so he emphasized the rhetorical rather than the symbolic property of music, revealing himself as a man of the

When Galileo and others discovered that the age-old view of the earth at the centre of the universe might be wrong, accepted ideas of the harmony of the spheres seemed under threat.

Renaissance rather than of the Middle Ages.

Calvin also acknowledged music's 'well-nigh incredible power to move us whither it will' but saw in it a serious threat to Christians who wished to keep on the narrow path to eternal life. Not long after, Galileo's suggestion that the sun, not the earth, was at the centre of the galaxy threatened to topple once and for all the church's cosmology and its long-held theories about the God-sustained harmony of the spheres.

At just the same time a new humanism seemed to be putting mankind at the centre of his universe. Both were threats to the church's established order and the complaints about a secular element in Christian music were attempts to resist those changes.

The beginning of the seventeenth century heralded an acknowledgement that the rhetorical power of music was of prime importance. The new music it created forms the foundations for present-day Western musical practice. The Churches of the time accommodated those changes, but as usual not without difficulty.

PART 3

The Flowering of Christian Music

1600–1800

Chapter 15

The Development of Oratorio

In Venice... I heard the best musicke that ever I did in all my life both in the morning and in the afternoon, so good that I would willingly goe an hundred miles afoote at any time to heare the like... This feast consisted principally of Musicke, which was both vocall and instrumental, so good, so delectable, so rare, so admirable, so super-excellent, that it did even ravishe and stupefie all those strangers that never heard the like... Sometimes there stand sixteen or twenty men together... and when they sung, the instrumentall musitians played also. Sometimes sixteene played together upon their instruments, ten Sagbuts, foure Cornets, and two Violdegambaes of an extraordinary greatness... At every time that every severall musicke played, the Organs... plaied with them.[1]

In this way Thomas Coryat recorded his impressions of worship in the Basilica of St Mark's in Venice at the height of its musical fame. Musicians all over Europe knew something of the splendours created by the line of illustrious composers employed there, from Adrian Willaert of the mid-sixteenth century, through Claudio Merulo, Andrea and Giovanni Gabrieli (uncle and nephew) to the great Claudio Monteverdi (1567–1643).

The design of the building itself profoundly affected the music of these composers. Following the example of Willaert, they developed music which explored the cavernous acoustics of the building, usually placing musicians in the huge wooden *pulpitum magnum cantorum* (great pulpit of the singers) known familiarly as the tub—*bigonzo.*

Occasionally, even larger groups might be spread further afield, the music of opposing groups being made to shift its ground, coming first from one choir, then from another, then creating illusory echo-effects, and finally (in the words of another observer):

> ...at the Gloria Patri, all ten choirs resumed singing together. I must confess to you that I have never experienced such rapture...[2]

The ecstatic words of visitors to such showcase churches of the Catholic faith testify to its continual patronage of the finest musicians of the day.[3] Just as people visit King's College Chapel, Cambridge today for a musical feast, so musicians came as pilgrims to St Mark's, Venice. They also made their way to Rome to hear such artists as Girolamo Frescobaldi play at St Peter's. A contemporary account records how he could be heard improvising instrumental fantasies in alternation with the choir, and 'displaying a thousand kinds of inventions on his harpsichord while the organ stuck to the main tune'.[4]

Such musical splendours were, in general, welcomed by the Roman Church and had a profound effect on the musical taste of educated people in the seventeenth century. The Roman Church also absorbed some startlingly new developments from the secular world of courtly entertainment.

Music and emotion

Prompted by the Renaissance rediscovery and emulation of the classical tradition, the rhetorical power of music, extolled so much by the ancient Greeks, became a deepening fascination for composers. Through their music they aimed to exercise that emotional power over their audiences of which Calvin so solemnly warned.

A group of Florentine intellectuals (they called themselves the *Camerata)* set about a modern re-creation of the long-held ideals of ancient Greek theatre, tragedy in particular. Because the documents and records they had to work from were so incomplete their results were very little like the dramas of classical antiquity, but through the interest of singers like Giulio Caccini and composers like Claudio Monteverdi, the new musical style they created had a profound impact on Western art-music.

Caccini described in great detail (in *Le nuove musiche* of 1602) the technique and theory of the 'new music'. The intention was 'to move the passion of the mind'. The means was the simplicity of a single human voice, the opposite of the massed choirs of St Mark's. Accompanied by the gentlest of instruments (lute, theorbo, or small keyboard instruments) whose harmonies were governed by the nature of the words being sung, a new kind of intimacy was created.

Music could now draw the audience into a dramatic world of human emotion. The new dramatic medium which used these musical means came to be called *opera*. Naturally enough, the first operas most often and most appropriately drew on the stories of Orpheus, whose legendary musical powers extended even beyond the emotional world to the physical.

The Roman Church welcomed this *stile rappresentativo* (a style representing human emotions) into its worship along with other aspects of new music, in spite of its secular origins and associations. The ornate splendours of a work like Monteverdi's *Vespers* combine the polychoral (using many choirs) style of the Gabrielis with *stile rappresentativo* to create a vivid demonstration of the emotional excitement and colour of the Christian music of the period.

Of the new musical styles that invaded Christian music in the seventeenth century (the Venetian polychoral music described above, dance-music and opera) it was the latter that had the most profound effect. After all, churchmen had been complaining for generations that music

had an exasperating tendency to distract from and obscure the text. Here at last was a type of music whose very purpose was to put across words and their emotional content as clearly as possible. And now the outstanding composers patronized by the church looked again at the dramatic events of the Bible, seeking to bring them to life through these new operatic means.

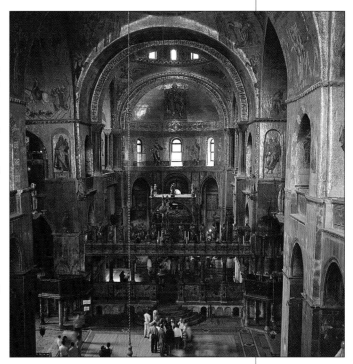

ORATORIO

The dramatic treatment of biblical narrative found its place, not so much in the liturgy, but in special occasions such as the *Congregazione dell'Oratorio* (the gathering of the prayer-hall). This was a meeting of aristocratic laymen for prayer, to hear the Bible read and commented upon, and for singing. There could be no better place for music to make Bible readings more persuasive.

Giacomo Carissimi (1605–74) has become justly famous for his dramatizations of Latin biblical texts. They became known as oratorios because of their first appearance at the *Oratorio* (prayer-hall). Biblical stories about characters such as Daniel, Jonah and Jephthah were dramatized, as well as episodes such as the Judgement of Solomon and the Deluge. The Old Testament provided plenty of human interest

The interior of St Mark's, Venice. The side galleries, at clerestory level, gave an ideal setting for the polychoral ('many-choired') music of such composers as Giovanni Gabrieli. The different choirs would sometimes take up position in different galleries, and the music would echo between them.

from which simple lessons could be drawn.

Some of the more vivid scenes used a chorus and the oratorio was held together by a *testo* (a narrator). André Maugars heard this music in the exclusive setting of the Oratory of San Marcello in Rome in 1639:

> **This admirable and delightful music is presented only on Fridays in Lent, from three to six o'clock. The church ... has a spacial rood-loft at the end with an organ of moderate size, quite mellow in sound and suitable for voices. On the sides of the church, there are two other small galleries, where the best instrumentalists are placed. The singers begin with a psalm motet, and then the players of instruments furnish a very good symphony. Then is sung a story from the Old Testament, in the form of a religious drama ... Each soloist represents a character in the story and gives perfect expression to the force of the words. Next one of the most famous preachers delivers a sermon, after which is sung the gospel of the day, such as the story of the Good Samaritan ... I cannot praise enough this recitative music.[5]**

These Lenten meetings were attended by the high aristocracy of Rome, but oratorio found a much wider following later on in the century when presented in Italian. Legrenze and Stradella were two composers who wrote a dozen such oratorios between them. The high drama of pieces such as Stradella's *St John-the-Baptist* was known to Handel in the next century and helped him in his turn to see how music could bring the Bible to life.

Oratorio is a form of music which has continued to be created down to the present day, even though it may not always be known by that name. Some might argue that it is not music for Christian worship. But it can be a means of teaching Christian truth and can therefore fulfill a vital function in proclaiming Christianity.

The Splendours of Monteverdi

Monteverdi's *Vespers* consists of musical settings of the psalms, a hymn, a Sonata and the *Magnificat* for the Feast of the Blessed Virgin Mary. The psalms surround the traditional Gregorian chant with complex and sonorous music for two choirs best positioned some distance from each other in the Venetian style.

Each verse of the hymn *(Ave Maris Stella)* is presented by a different combination of musicians, from many voices in a rich eight-part texture to a solo voice and keyboard. Here, in the Sonata and in the *Magnificat* there are interludes of dance music for instruments alone, perhaps the nearest the church had yet approached to the physical and ecstatic enjoyment of music in Old Testament times. The psalms were interlaced with music for solo voices in the new operatic style, highly emotive evocations of texts from the Song of Songs.

The *Magnificat* is the most complex and extensive piece of all. Each short phrase of the canticle generates a musical movement with its own character, using sharply contrasted combinations of voices and instruments and evoking a wide emotional range.

The piece abounds in magical echo effects, particularly in the final *Gloria Patri,* where they are combined with remarkable vocal virtuosity in the new *stile rappresentativo.*

Chapter 16

The Music of the Lutheran Church

While the Roman Church was enjoying the glories of highly sophisticated polychoral music and the emotionally charged 'new music' of oratorio, the Lutheran Church was benefitting from its own group of brilliantly inventive composers. From the beginning of the seventeenth century the number of outstanding composers is legion: names such as Melchior Vulpius, Michael Praetorius and Johann Crüger appear in present-day hymn-books, but this does no justice to the quantity and quality of their music.

Michael Praetorius (1571–1621) was particularly prolific: he wrote more than 1,200 liturgical pieces, many of them hymns and motets. In some of this music he shows a keen awareness of the Venetian polychoral style, but he made it relevant to German congregations by using familiar Lutheran melodies as a base, in much the same way as earlier composers had used Gregorian chant.

Lutheran organ music

Lutheran composers for the organ were inspired particularly by the Dutchman Jan Sweelinck (1562–1621). He lived and worked in a country riven with the tensions between Calvinism and Catholicism, but nevertheless acquired such a reputation as organist at the Oude Kirk in Amsterdam that his pupils came to him from all corners of Europe.

Although the Calvinist traditions of the Netherlands did not allow accompanied congregational singing, the organ was too highly respected there to be eliminated entirely from worship (the reputation of Dutch organ-builders is still among the highest in the world). Thirteen of Sweelinck's organ pieces are devotional meditations on Calvinist and Lutheran hymn melodies. These would have found a place at the opening or close of a service, perhaps occasionally introducing or following the sermon. Their serene detachment and the precision and perfection of their invention conveys a meditative intensity quite unlike the heady excitement of Frescobaldi's keyboard fantasies in Rome.

Sweelinck's influence was carried to Germany by his pupil Samuel Scheidt (1587–1654), chiefly known for his great collection of organ music called *Tablatura Nova*. Like Sweelinck, many of the pieces in the collection clothe Lutheran hymn-tunes with an intellectual music, a symbolic offering back to God of the composer's creative gift, reminiscent of the attitudes of medieval times.

Later organist/composers such as Franz Tunder, Johann Pachelbel, Dietrich Buxtehude and Johann Kuhnau used a variety of ways to decorate and adorn melodies familiar to their congregations, such pieces being known as chorale preludes. J.S.Bach (who followed Kuhnau as organist at Leipzig) had the greatest talent of all for writing these devotional fantasies around congregational melodies.

The musicians' duties

While the Lutheran Church boasted many

brilliant organists and composers, it was also able to draw on the talents of well-trained singers and instrumentalists. These were employed by the town council and the imperial power of the area to provide music for worship, for political ceremonies, for conferences, for weddings and funerals.

Towns and cities would employ a cantor (whose duties included the organizing and teaching of music at local schools), a town organist and a number of singers and players. In Hamburg in 1642 new regulations stated that the cantor had, as part of his duties

to provide good, suitable music on feast days as well as for every Sunday, for all the town churches.[1]

Although the cantor had a fairly free hand in deciding what music should be provided, there was artistic as well as financial control. He had to

adhere to the modern, fashionable *stilo modulandi* [operatic style], so that congregations would be able to hear both the old and the new, and both tastes would be pleased. In addition, most people understand the words better in a harmonic rather than a motet setting.[2]

This statement may be compared with the situation that church musicians face today. 'Old'

meant the 'point counter point' of the sixteenth century, the learned style of fifty or more years before. The 'new' was the persuasive and emotional music of early opera.

Dead tradition in worship, presenting only a museum of past practice, tends to fear and reject the new. But the Lutheran Church of the seventeenth and eighteenth centuries was living and growing, dynamic rather than static, capable of absorbing new musical ideas and changes of attitude without time-honoured elements being threatened:

In the view of his [the cantor's] employers and the congregation which was his audience there was no more point in repeating music, apart from the familiar hymns, than there would have been in repeating sermons. The cantor was under attack if he did not produce new music in an up-to-date style ...[3]

Furthermore, Hamburg expected its cantor to create worship-offerings of a high standard:

The solo singers are to be experienced and good; more mediocre singers can assist by singing in the full choir.[4]

But 'slovenly, lazy, bad performances' were not permitted; excellence as well as modernity was part of the contract.

Christmas 1659 in the Nikolaikirche, Berlin

In the times that followed the Thirty Years' War the musicians in the Lutheran Church were many—and varied. Paul Gerhardt, deacon at the Nikolaikirche in Berlin wrote a vivid description of the Christmas morning service held there in 1659:

The church is cold. Candles are being lighted. The people are coming and taking their places. A group of schoolboys is at one side of the gallery and a choir of mixed voices at the other side. Below the pulpit we see a Collegium Musicum, a voluntary musical society composed of tradesmen and craftsmen, who perform on violins and wood-wind instruments, gathered around a small movable organ. Then there is a male quartet, also a military band with trumpets, kettledrums and drums.

After the organ prelude a chorale [Lutheran hymn] is sung....Now three clergymen with white clergymen's bands and black robes have appeared at the altar. The entire liturgy is sung in Latin [the use of Latin or German varied from place to place] by the choirs and the schoolchildren. Next a college student, dressed as an angel with large white wings, sings from the pulpit an Old Testament prophecy, accompanied by the Collegium Musicum below.

More chanting from the altar, and then the principal door of the church opens, and in comes a procession of girls, headed by the teacher, all dressed as angels. They proceed to the high altar, where the teacher sings the first verse of 'Vom Himmel hoch' and the second verse is sung by the girls

in two-part counterpoint. The third verse is taken by the organ and the choir in the gallery as a beautiful five-part motet. While the procession has been marching down the aisle, one of the ministers chants a 'Gloria' answered by the electoral court-and-field trumpeters with fanfares and drumrolls.

After the sermon there is more chanting by the liturgist, and the instrumentalists play a boisterous 'Te Deum'. Then follows another Latin anthem by the school-children.

Things now begin to happen in the organ loft: over the railing is raised a cradle with a doll, while some boys with incessant mooing imitate the animals in the Bethlehem stable. The choir and congregation sing a hymn, and at this point high up on the organ façade a Bethlehem star, illuminated and supplied with small bells, is turned round and round, operated by an organ stop.[1] Three wooden images, representing the three Wise Men, with their traditional attributes, solemnly move forward and bow before the doll in the cradle. At the same time we notice two puppets, representing Moors, standing on each side of the central group. One blows a trumpet, and the other beats a drum. Throughout this scene on the gallery railing the Collegium Musicum plays a ritornello [an instrumental refrain].

A boy soprano intones 'In Dulci Jubilo', which is continued by male voices, accompanied by shawms and bombards. The song is scarcely over before a sight exceedingly beloved of the children appears in

the centre aisle. It is old Father Christmas himself in his white beard, with pointed cap on his head and a large sack on his back, soon surrounded by 'angels' and children, who vie with each other for the good things that are to be given out. When the large sack is empty and Old Father Christmas has disappeared behind the sacristy door, then is sung as the closing chorale 'Puer natus est Bethlehem'.

Chapter 17

Heinrich Schütz

During the Thirty Years War (1618–48), musicians of the time seem to have had a healthy disregard for the sectarianism which caused such bloodshed and turmoil. Heinrich Schütz (1585–1672), for instance, was given permission and financial support by his first employer, the Landgrave of Marburg, to study music in Venice (1609–12) under the then aged Giovanni Gabrieli.

Nearly twenty years later, after much persuasion, the more tight-fisted Elector of Saxony allowed Schütz to visit Venice again, this time to experience the new operatic style of Monteverdi which could by then be heard as much in church as out of it. So it was that a Protestant employed by a Protestant court studied for at least five years under Roman Catholic musicians, absorbing from them the latest in musical fashion and turning it to compelling and brilliant use in his own Christian music.

Schütz' enthusiasm for the latest Italian style in music enabled him to create the greatest music of the century, but the textual foundation for almost all his surviving music is the Bible. He seems to have had little interest in writing instrumental music. Instead, he seems to have been driven by the challenge of bringing the Bible to life.

Schütz' use of the Bible narrative is not so much in its formal liturgical context, but in its ability to instruct on a personal level concerning human and divine relationships. In his motets he frequently uses operatic means to intensify the human drama of God's intervention in the world. Many of these settings are of the psalms and are typified by his first publication, the *Psalms of David,* a striking result of his first Venetian visit.

The twenty-six large-scale settings use all the spectacular techniques of his teacher Gabrieli (as many as four separate choirs are needed for some) but individual vocal lines are designed to convey the psalmist's expression of feeling as strongly as possible. Only on hearing these settings can Schütz' balance of the universal and personal dimensions of the psalms be appreciated fully.

Just before his second Venetian visit (in 1627) he produced another set of psalms. This time they were simpler four-part settings of metrical translations by Cornelius Becker. Their popularity for congregational use lasted at least until the end of the century, but perhaps proved a little too involved rhythmically and harmonically for singers of modest talent. Some of these settings have reappeared in German hymn-books this century and are once more becoming better known.

Sometimes artistic inspiration and sheer necessity come together to produce something exceptional. To suggest that composers need a free rein to create what their inspiration dictates is a romantic fiction. On the contrary, practical restrictions are absolutely necessary to provide a framework for creativity.

In Schütz' age of patronage the restrictions were those of circumstance and necessity rather than of choice—those who paid the piper definitely called the tune. And there were two driving forces behind the motets that Schütz composed after his second visit to Venice. Firstly, he was deeply impressed with the new music he heard there (particularly that of Monteverdi) and he sought to put that highly expressive and emotional style to good use in his Biblical settings. But secondly, as the preface to his

Kleine geistliche Konzerte (Little Sacred Concertos[1]) makes clear:

> ... honourable music ... has not only decreased as a result of the persistent dangers of war around us ... but in many places has been completely subdued [by] other general ruins and violent disorders.[2]

There was a clear necessity to write music for small forces for the depleted choirs of war-torn Germany, reasonably straightforward to sing and using sometimes as few as one or two voices accompanied only by a bass instrument and small organ. Yet this necessary reduction in scale was just what was needed to make the new style work best; it created intimacy, it could draw the listener into the biblical world, such as Mary's meeting with Jesus outside the tomb on the first Easter Sunday morning.

Schütz' interest in the Bible extended beyond the countless motet-settings of the *Cantiones Sacrae* (Sacred Songs), *Symphoniae Sacrae* (Sacred Symphonies[3]) or *Geistliche Chormusik* (Sacred Choral Music). He also found opportunities to set dramatic biblical scenes on a much larger canvas. This was nothing new: musical settings of the drama of Jesus' trial and crucifixion (his 'Passion') or of the Easter or Christmas stories were traditional in the Roman and Lutheran Churches. But Schütz takes a particular interest in these stories, setting first the narrative of Jesus' resurrection *(Resurrection Story)*, then the Seven Words of Jesus on the Cross, the Christmas story *(Christmas Oratorio)* and finally three settings of the Passion according to Luke, John and Matthew.

The variety of approach in these dramas is an object-lesson for composers today who may consider setting biblical texts. In the *Resurrection Story* the narrative is given to an evangelist who sings in a kind of recitation which lends drama and intimacy to the words, at the same time surrounded by a halo of sound from four viols. Unusually, some characters such as Mary or Jesus are sung by two voices in harmony.

The *Christmas Story* uses instrumental forces to intensify characters in the drama. Herod, for instance, is accompanied by clarini (high-sounding trumpets) and four scribes are complemented by two trombones.

In complete contrast the settings of the Passion use no instruments at all, but return to the comparatively austere world of the sixteenth century—the evangelist and the characters in the story sing by themselves, unsupported by any harmony. But the whole choir takes the part of the crowd in short but incisive outcries. Characteristically, Schütz avoids any commentary or elaboration in the form of hymns or songs. In these last works he penetrated to the heart of the Christian faith simply by turning to the Bible.

The simple expressiveness of Schütz's biblical dramas is a marvel. Here, in the 'Resurrection Story', Jesus' words to Mary on the first Easter morning are sung by two voices, accompanied by a bass instrument (perhaps a viola da gamba) and keyboard (perhaps an organ). The figures under the 'continuo' stave instruct the keyboard-player which chords to play. The words set are Jesus' 'Woman, why do you weep? Whom do you seek?'

Patronage

Church musicians, of whatever tradition, have for the most part lived (at least until recently) under patronage. This meant that they depended wholly on church or state for their livelihood. They were treated as servants, relying on their own musical reputation and the honesty and charity of their patrons to keep body and soul together. In a truly Christian society, such patronage should be a guarantee of security and fair dealing. When the patronage failed in its Christian principles, as it often did, the personal results were disastrous.

The horrors of the Thirty Years' War which began in 1618 caused serious disruption to church life in Germany. During its course, sectarian warfare between German states and the consequent famines and plagues decimated the population of Germany—by the mid-century it had been nearly halved.

No church musician escaped the effects of such devastation, either in family losses or in the reduction of talented singers and players. Heinrich Schütz (arguably the greatest composer of the seventeenth century) suffered along with the rest. In Dresden, where he was employed as *Hofkapellmeister* (Musical Director) of the Chapel Royal, the court went through periods of being unable or unwilling to pay him or his musicians. Schütz constantly had to write begging letters on behalf of the singers and players in his charge:

I hear that he [Kaiser, a bass in his choir] is lying like a pig in a sty, without a bed and sleeping on straw, and he has already pawned his coat and doublet. His wife came to me yesterday, pleading with me to take them under my paternal wing and help them in their plight... I find it neither laudable nor Christian that in such

estimable great lands one cannot or will not support twenty musicians, and I live in the humblest hope that Your Electoral Majesty will reconsider this.[1]

A performance of German church music in Bach's time, the frontispiece of a Musikalisches Lexikon.

Chapter 18

J.S. Bach

The great stream of outstanding composers in the Lutheran tradition of the seventeenth and early eighteenth centuries finds its final and most complete expression in Johann Sebastian Bach. Here the three dimensions of Christian music discussed in the introduction—symbolic, rhetorical and ecstatic—are uniquely integrated.

The Lutheran Church's continuing demands for an extensive musical contribution to worship, as well as the developing possibilities of the Baroque[1] style, created music of superb quality. The current interest in early music is encouraging both church choirs and professional groups to explore the rich creativity of this period. The work of Johann Pachelbel (which extends far beyond the beautiful *Canon in D*), Johann Krieger, Franz Tunder, Dietrich Buxtehude, his pupil Nickolaus Bruhns, Johann Kuhnau, Georg Telemann and many others marks a period of excellence in Christian music which has probably never been surpassed.

At the end of an era and at the head of them all stands J.S. Bach (1685–1750), the greatest composer that Western culture has produced. Strong words perhaps, but many of the greatest figures of Western music—Haydn, Mozart, Beethoven, Wagner, Schoenberg, Stravinsky—have all said as much and have freely acknowledged their indebtedness to his music.

Bach the craftsman

Yet Bach's contemporaries saw him from a very different perspective. He was known only locally as a composer, but more widely as a performer. As an organist he was clearly

phenomenal. Plenty of anecdotes have survived which typify reactions to his playing:

When he was called from Leipzig to Cassel to pronounce an organ properly restored [a task he was frequently called to perform], he ran over the pedals with the same facility as if his feet had wings, making the organ resound with such fullness, and so penetrate the ears of those present like a thunderbolt, that Frederick... Prince of Cassel, admired him with such astonishment that he drew a ring with a precious stone from his finger and gave it to Bach as soon as the sound had died away.[2]

Such descriptions project the uneasy feeling that Bach was admired less for his artistry and creativity than for his mental and physical agility, but he certainly was very much admired as a

A double canon by Bach headed 'A Canon for J.G.Fulde'.

player and improvisor by organists throughout Europe. His music, however, was not universally welcomed:

When in a large town [Bach's] Passion Music was done for the first time, with 12 violins, many oboes, bassoons, and other instruments, many people were astonished and did not know what to make of it. In the pew of a noble family in

Haussmann's contemporary portrait of Johann Sebastian Bach. The greatest of Western composers devoted much of his prodigious output to music for performance in worship.

church, many Ministers and Noble Ladies were present, who sang the first Passion Chorale out of their books with great devotion. But when this theatrical music began, all these people were thrown into the greatest bewilderment, looked at each other and said: 'What will come of this?' An old widow of the nobility said: 'God save us, my children! it's just as if one were at an Opera Comedy.' But everyone was genuinely displeased by it and voiced just complaints against it. There are, it is true, some people who take pleasure in such idle things...[3]

Bach did not always have an easy relationship with the church that employed him. At the age of twenty, he was given his first full-time post as organist at the New Church in Arnstadt. In 1706

members of the church Consistory (an ecclesiastical court) firstly reproved him for visiting Lübeck for sixteen weeks where he had only been given permission to go for four (he had gone to visit Buxtehude). Then they went on to

... reprove him for having hitherto made many curious variations in the chorale, and mingled many strange tones in it, and for the fact the Congregation has been confused by it.

and later observed:

... the organist Bach had previously played rather too long, but after his attention had been called to it by the Superintendant, he had at once fallen into the other extreme and had made it too short.[4]

Any organist is aware that the post includes a measure of tedium; Bach seems only too human in this youthful clash with authority. His later disputes with the town council of Leipzig concerned a continuing problem of lack of funds and inadequate support for his choirs and musicians.

The overall picture is certainly not one of a creative artist fêted for his prodigious talent. Instead, Bach was regarded as he regarded himself: as a craftsman following in a long family tradition. His task was to glorify God by the composition of music, working to the best of his ability and for a reasonable wage.

Unlike Handel and many other better-known musicians of his day, he never travelled far from home, was only once given well-publicized attention by the nobility (when as an old man he visited Frederick the Great's Prussian Court in Potsdam) and published very little of his music.

Bach was therefore known and appreciated chiefly in the small area of Germany where he lived and worked. He expected his fate as a composer to be that of any other in the same position—he would hear his music performed on the occasions for which he wrote it, to be supplanted in due course by the music of his successor. His position was akin to that of many musicians of the Middle Ages, content in relative anonymity and satisfied in the exercising of a God-given craft.

It would be a great mistake to imagine that the craftsman-like attitude of Bach, or others in his position, inevitably created well-meaning but arid music. On the contrary, one of Bach's most remarkable talents was his ability to shed new light on a time-worn formula. He was well acquainted with all the fashionable musical styles of the day and did not hesitate to adopt them. But his remarkable mind enabled him to go far beyond his contemporaries, breathing new life into a conventional task.

The six Brandenburg Concertos, for instance, are an incomparable summary of everything a composer could possibly do (and rather more) within the confines of a Baroque concerto. The imagination which he brought to bear on even the smallest task did not endear him to those who wished music (especially Christian music) to be straightforward and without too much intellectual or emotional challenge. This was undoubtedly the cause of the adverse reactions to his Passion music.

Bach and symbolism

The recurring tensions between Bach and his employers and congregations might suggest that he was frustrated by the lack of appreciation due to him as an outstanding artist. But there are many signs in the few scattered records of Bach's own words that he was driven to artistic creativity by stronger forces than a need for fame or even for a decent wage. In his letter of resignation to his employers at Mühlhausen in

Bach's Cantatas

Nowhere is Bach's music more obviously expressive of his personal faith than in his cantatas. The word 'cantata' was first used in the context of Lutheran church music by the pastor and poet Erdmann Neumeister (1671–1756), whose texts Bach set in abundance.

Neumeister explained his intentions in his foreword to a collection of cantata texts that he wrote for all the Sundays and feast-days of the church year:

Having properly performed my official duties on Sundays in the church, I attempted to transform the most significant thoughts that were treated in the sermon into poetic language for my private devotional use.[1]

Neumeister then produced these poems specifically for setting to music, probably with the guidance of the composer Johann Krieger (1649–1725) who also first set them to music. The cantata was strategically placed between the Gospel reading and the sermon, to have the greatest chance of reinforcing the message of both.

The musical methods of opera were the natural choice for giving expression to the spiritual content. Church ethics would not have allowed cantatas to be staged, but with such emotionally vivid music this was no great loss. Another composer of the time wrote:

These ... 'cantatas' have completely replaced the former German songs. Their invention, however, originated in opera. As I became aware of the pleasantness of their mixed styles, namely recitative and aria, which are at one moment happy, the next sad, one moment in this mood, the next in that, I turned from the old type of long ode with many verses ... to a poem that mixes recitatives and arias.[2]

These cantatas are therefore a significant departure from earlier Lutheran music like that of Schütz, whose texts were almost always directly biblical. A move away from God's word might be seen as a move for the worse, but the use Bach makes of his cantata-texts is so compelling that they remain unsurpassed as musical expression of Christian truth.

Bach's use of familiar words and melodies from the great heritage of Lutheran chorales reinforced the congregation's awareness of the cantata as worship, even if they were not expected to participate.[3]

Bach put more of his creative energy into his cantatas than into any other form. During his lifetime he may have completed five year-cycles of cantatas, one cantata for each Sunday and holy day. Out of these 300 or so, about 200 survive today. Altogether they are a unique legacy in Christian music, created by the requirements of orthodox Lutheranism, but expressing a Pietist's faith in God and testifying to the joy of a personal relationship with Jesus Christ.[4]

1708 he expressed the simple desire:

... to work towards the goal, namely, a well-regulated church music, to the Glory of God.[5]

This could easily be taken as rather uninspiring diplomacy were it not in reality a rebuke to his employers (one of many) for the lack of support he received for such a task, for the sentence begins: 'I should have liked...' Then in a commentary to a short book on musical theory, he stated that

The aim and final reason, as of all music... should be none else but the Glory of God and recreation of the mind. Where this is not observed, there will be no real music but only a devilish hubbub.[6]

The 'Crucifixus' from Bach's Mass in B minor holds symbol, rhetoric and ecstasy in perfect balance. The 'unlucky thirteen' repetitions of the ground bass (this extract gives two of them) symbolize the temporary triumph of evil when Jesus 'was crucified also for us under Pontius Pilate'; the mournful rhetoric of the exceptionally poignant harmony is unique for its time, and yet the whole piece dances with the gentle ecstasy of a 'saraband'.

As an orthodox Lutheran Bach here echoes Luther's own views on the edifying power of music and makes no distinction between secular and sacred. God sees and hears all: humankind must therefore strive to please him in all. Bach strove to 'make a well-sounding harmony to the Glory of God' by an unceasing exploration of the possibilities of traditional musical grammar that for him represented order.

His collection of keyboard pieces under the general title of 'Clavier-übung' ('keyboard practice') is a perfect example of highly persuasive music under a forbiddingly intellectual exterior. The third volume is a collection of organ works which contains, as the title-page reads: 'various preludes on the Catechism and other hymns for the organ, for music lovers and especially for connoisseurs of such work, to refresh their spirits...'

The pieces are based on traditional Lutheran melodies (some of them are Gregorian chant) and are presented in a cycle reflecting the themes of the church year. To symbolize the Greater and Lesser Catechism (Luther's essentials of the Christian faith for adults and children) Bach presents two settings of each traditional melody, one on a grand scale and one in simple form and without pedals.

There is also a Trinitarian symbolism in the three massive settings of the traditional *Kyrie*—one addressed to the Father, one to the Son and one to the Holy Spirit. Furthermore, the whole collection is framed by an opening prelude and closing fugue, both in the key of E flat (requiring three flats in the signature), the fugue having three sections with three melodies, much of it in triple time. These are impressive symbols, but a sympathetic hearing is all that is needed to convince a listener that they are far more than mere intellectual games.

But there is something symbolic in the very nature of Bach's music, built as it is from layers of melodies which copy and confront each other in a ceaseless web of counterpoint. Marco Pallis likens the interactions of these voices to human relationships:

To speak of a world is to speak of contrast and opposition, for the distinction of one being from another inevitably imposes this condition... These beings may either converge or diverge or, for a brief space, move parallel with one another... and this will from time to time bring the

beings into contact or even collision . . . What does this picture suggest but a counterpoint which, by its continual interplay of tensions and releases, expresses that unity out of which all its constituent elements have arisen and which they are all for ever seeking to regain . . . The musical parallel is self-evident and it is this, in fact, which confers on contrapuntal music its strange power to move the soul.[7]

Is it therefore too fanciful to suggest that Bach's music invites an emotional response because horizontal diversity (the many voices) is brought into vertical unity (the 'well-ordered harmony') in a way that symbolizes the waywardness of human relationships and a longing for the stability and unity of the kingdom of God?

BACH AND RHETORIC

Bach's music was not merely symbolic, but also intended as a powerful expression of feelings. In common with his contemporaries, Bach had a firm belief in the power of music to move its hearers. Music had the capacity to be expressive, not just of pain and joy, but also of anger, love, jealousy and hate. These emotional states were called *Affekten* ('affects' or moods) and each was associated with a specific musical idea:

Since *joy* is an expansion of our vital spirits, it follows that this affect is best expressed by large and expanded intervals. *Sadness,* on the other hand, is a contraction of those same subtle parts of our bodies. It is, therefore, easy to see that the narrowest intervals are most suitable.[8]

Bach, like every other musician of his day, adopted these theories wholeheartedly. The difference is that he used them with more imagination and subtlety than others, not only providing vocal arias with the accompaniment that exactly complemented the 'affect' of the words (as other composers did in opera) but also using these same methods to resonate with the words of a particular hymn which would be in the mind of the congregation for whom he played it. The prelude on *Durch Adams Fall* (Through Adam's Fall) in his *Orgelbüchlein* (Little Organ Book) surrounds the hymn melody with heavy and dissonant descending intervals in the bass, not only a standard gesture for the affect of despair, but also symbolic of falling and of fear.

Pietism

Bach found himself at odds with some sectors of his congregation, who objected to his rhetorical methods—the powerful emotional effects of his music. They also objected to his setting non-biblical texts to music. The trouble sprang from increasing divisions within the Lutheran Church itself. Orthodoxy had for some time been failing to satisfy the emotional needs of Lutheran Christians and a powerful evangelical movement developed during the eighteenth century, initiated by P.J.Spener (1635–1705). This movement was known as Pietism.

Spener suggested that spiritual rebirth and the beginnings of a personal relationship with Jesus Christ were the prerequisite for church membership, and furthermore, that the church's priesthood was not and should not be specially privileged. On the contrary, all true believers were themselves the priesthood. This idea was particularly threatening to orthodox Lutherans. Spener instituted Sunday afternoon meetings for Bible study and prayer first of all in Frankfurt and then further afield. These groups he called *collegia pietatis,* fellowships of the saved.

The Pietists had much in their favour: a new sense of the 'priesthood of all believers', a renewed appreciation of the Bible, a sensitivity to the needs of the poor and a missionary zeal. But they had a negative side. In their rejection of orthodox Lutheranism they also set their face against much that could be wholesome, including the creative instincts of which Luther approved. Luther himself had said:

I would like to see all arts in the service of Him who made them.[9]

This the Pietists firmly rejected and, as a result, sought to curb the activities of musicians like Bach. Pietism certainly lay behind some of the church authorities' reluctance to support Bach in his repeated requests for a reasonable number of skilled players and singers. And yet Bach himself had strong Pietist sympathies, to judge from items in the inventory of his personal library made at his death:

> ... in *Octavo*
> ... **Rambach's** *Reflection on the Tears of Jesus*
> **Müller's** *Flame of Love*
> **His** *Hours of Refreshment*...
> **Gerhard's** *School of Piety,* **5 vols.**
> **Neumeister's** *Table of the Lord*
> **Spener's** *Zeal against Popery*...[10]

Further evidence of Bach's Pietist leanings can be found in the texts that he set to music so persuasively. These concern the individual's relationship with Jesus, the personal response of the believer. The texts he set were often highly emotive and his musical response to them was equally strong. Had the Pietists penetrated beyond their prejudices and listened attentively to Bach they would have found much to edify them in their spiritual lives.

The ecstatic dimension in Bach's music

The dire warnings and deep suspicions of the Church Fathers concerning the ecstatic dimension of music—its ability to bypass the intellect and evoke a physical response, such as dance—are repeated constantly across the history of Christianity. Nevertheless, the many celebrations of strongly rhythmic music and dance described in the Old Testament suggest that an ecstatic dimension is a central part of musical experience. Outside the Christian church and in other cultures this has been celebrated and accepted freely.

The sophisticated world of Baroque music, of fugues and figured basses, does not seem a likely place to find ecstatic music. But Wilfrid Mellers, a twentieth-century expert on Bach, suggests that Bach's Christian music is capable of precisely that:

The Moravian Brethren

The most far-reaching effects of Pietism, the movement in the Lutheran Church started by P.J. Spener (1635–1705), were felt through the spiritual revival of the Moravian Church, whose history could be traced back to the early reformation of the Bohemian Church under Jan Hus, a contemporary of Wycliffe.

Count Nicolaus of Zinzendorf (1700–60), Spener's godson, encouraged the hymn-singing traditions of the Moravians in what he called 'hours of song' which were first introduced in the town of Herrnhut[1] in the 1720s. Zinzendorf described this song-centred worship in a letter to the King of Prussia:

The cantor takes up the subject of the sermons that have just been given and chooses whole and half verses from 20 or 30 songs that illustrate the subject in a clear and orderly fashion: and cantor, organist, teacher, and audience are so practised that no one is permitted to hesitate, nobody may consult a book... During public prayers, however, I first have a familiar song recited before [the sermon]. After it, however, if I do not find a song in the hymnal that I would like to have sung to emphasize the subject matter of my sermon to the audience and to offer it to the Saviour as a prayer, I invent a new song of which I knew nothing before and which will be forgotten as soon as it has served its purpose.[2]

Over about thirty years, the Moravians published thousands of hymns and songs, many of them the result of spontaneous singing, some no doubt by the prompting of the Holy Spirit. The quality of many of the songs reflected their ephemeral and transitory nature, like many Christian songs today, but some became very influential.

John Wesley met some Moravians while on a boat crossing to America and was much impressed by the spiritual power of their singing; the experience awoke him to the efficacy of hymn-singing.[3] Zinzendorf's hymns may occasionally be found in evangelical hymn-books today.[4] They are often concerned with personal salvation and with self-examination before God. The English translations are usually by John Wesley.

The Moravian Brethren established themselves in the British Isles, the New World and elsewhere, their constantly renewed repertoire of hymns becoming known in many languages.

It's an apotheosis of the dance if ever there was one; and this despite the fact that Protestantism, far more oppressively than Catholicism, had banished dance from worship in accord with its denial of the flesh; certainly his music, whatever dogma he intellectually subscribed to, reinstates dance as 'a play of Powers made visible' (Langer) ... In this sense sensual dance is a sacral act, and Bach's blood, nerves and sinews were wiser than his Church. In this chorus [*Cum Sancto Spiritu* from the B Minor Mass] he responds to an older rhythm, which Bernard of Clairvaux referred to when he wrote:

Jesus the dancers' master is,
A great skill at the dance he is,
He turns to the right, he turns to the left,
All must follow his teaching deft.

In order adequately to perform the 'Cum Sancto' and the many comparable passages in Bach, we must learn to swing no less than do, in our own day and world, black and brown North and South Americans as they worship God in the corybantic revel of gospel song and dance. It's worth noting that Gesner, rector of St Thomas's School and sometime critic of Bach's management of his academic duties there, remarked of Bach's direction of a rehearsal that 'the rhythm takes possession of all his limbs. I believe that my friend Bach must have many men like Orpheus within him!'

... For those who have ears to hear and limbs to cavort Bach's Gloria is a present excitation far more powerful than anything our jaded world can offer.[11]

The debt that much modern Christian music owes to Baroque composers has many dimensions. But one outstanding feature is the preference, then and now, for music with a strong pulse. Underpinning the music of Bach, for instance, is a beat, to be sensed most strongly in the commonplace 'walking' or 'running' bass, a restriction of the bass line to notes of equal value.

Bach's interest in the music of Vivaldi and Corelli undoubtedly sharpened this quality in his music. The theory of affects, discussed earlier, encouraged a strong pulse to be firmly established for a substantial period, contributing to and sustaining the affect, or mood, of the piece.[12]

The technique is akin to jazz and its very similar treatment of double-bass or bass guitar. What is more, both Baroque music and jazz have important roots in dance. From the humble

tavern to the theatre, from the village hall to the aristocrat's palace, dance was an essential social grace in eighteenth-century Europe.

Art-music—music for performance—was by no means set apart from dance-music; on the contrary, many suites of dances (not least by Bach himself) were written for the harpsichord, for stringed instruments and for orchestra.

Calvinists may have protested against dance-music in church worship, but on the whole they readily accepted its place in the secular world. It

A famous baroque organ at Amorbach in Germany. Bach stood in a great tradition of German organist-composers.

is worth noting that between 1717 and 1723 Bach was employed by Prince Leopold at the Calvinist court of Cöthen. Consequently, during that time Bach had practically no church-music duties whatever, but he wrote much instrumental music—extensive collections of dance-movements (Allemandes, Sarabandes, Gigues, Minuets) and countless other pieces which are dances in all but name.

When he returned to writing music for the church, he did not hesitate to borrow material for his cantatas from the instrumental concertos he had originally written years before. Just as dance was present in courtly music, it was equally evident in Bach's music for the church.

The eternal truths

In its embodiment of every facet of musical experience—the symbolic, the rhetorical or emotional and the ecstatic or physical—Bach's music finds a response with almost anyone. It can resonate with those who are sensitive to music on almost any level. It is compelling to the casual listener who expects immediate musical satisfaction. But equally it reveals unfathomable depths to those prepared to study its symbolic nature.

Cultural change gradually alters the perspective of succeeding generations on music of the past, but since Bach's music inhabits such a broad area it cannot fail to continue to delight its hearers with revelations of beauty, whatever their expectations. That beauty is of eternal and abiding truths: created order and human relationships, the perfection of God's universe and the agonies and joys of mankind's struggle to find its place within it.

If Bach was in many ways a typical product of his generation, what has been said of him can also apply to many other composers of that time. But it is significant that those who looked for wide recognition did not spend so much of their time writing Christian music. Telemann (1681–1767), although a church musical director in Hamburg for many years, made a bigger reputation from his forty operas than from his church music. Handel (1685–1759), also from Hamburg, built his personal and financial success in the world of secular music, again chiefly through opera.

Bach was perhaps the last truly great musician who owed his living almost entirely to the church. Many others have since been employed by it, but the opportunities and expectations of musicians in this position have on the whole gradually declined since Bach's time. Indeed, Lutheran church music suffered a particularly rapid and painful collapse at the end of the eighteenth century, revival having to wait until the twentieth and a renewed interest in its Baroque heritage.

Chapter 19

Turmoil in England: Commonwealth and Restoration

The time when, was in the year 1644, the Place where, was in the stately Cathedral Church of the Loyal City York. The occasion of it was, the great and close Seige which was then laid to that City, and strictly maintain'd for eleven weeks space... By this Occasion, there was shut up within the City abundance of People... who all or most of them came constantly every Sunday, to hear Publicke Prayers and Sermon in that spacious Church. And indeed their Number was so exceeding great, that the Church was even cramming or squeezing full.

They had a custom in that Church... that always before the Sermon, the whole Congregation sang a Psalm, together with the Quire and the Organ; And you must know, that there was then a most Excellent-large-plump-lusty-full-speaking Organ, which cost (as I am credibly informed) a thousand Pounds.

This organ... being let out, into all its fulness of Stops, together with the Quire, began the Psalm. But when the Vast-Conchording-Unity of the whole Congregation came thundering in, even so, as it made the very ground shake under us; (Oh the unutterable ravishing Soul's delight!) In the which I was

so transported, and wrapt up into High Contemplations, that there was no room left in my whole Man for anything below divine and heavenly Raptures; Nor could there possibly be any Thing in Earth to which That very Singing might be truly compared except That glorious and miraculous Quire, recorded in the Scriptures, at the Dedication of the Temple... where at their Singing of Psalms, Praises or Thanksgivings, the Glory of the Lord came down amongst them.[1]

This eyewitness account by Thomas Mace, a committed Christian and a staunch Royalist, gives an idea of the spiritual intensity that metrical psalm-singing could generate. Yet Mace had political as well as musical reasons for recording his experiences at York. He was in a city loyal to the Crown and under siege from Cromwell's armies. He was probably not aware that this was one of the last occasions that York Minster was to be used for worship for years.

That same year, Parliament issued

Two Ordinances of the Lords and Commons assembled in Parliament for the speedy demolishing of all organs, images and all matters of superstitious monuments in all Cathedralls, and Collegiate or Parish-Churches and

Chapels, throughout the Kingdom of England and the Dominion of Wales; the better to accomplish the blessed reformation so happily begun, and to remove all offences and things illegal in the worship of God...[2]

Worship during the Commonwealth

Already the Puritans had dissolved the traditional hierarchy of the Church of England and within three years cathedrals became redundant, turned

The era of Oliver Cromwell and the Commonwealth brought the only attempt in the history of the church in England to sever the links with the past—those traditions of liturgy and music which reach back to early medieval days.

instead into ammunition dumps and staging posts for the army. In addition, Christian feasts (including Christmas) were no longer to be celebrated; marriage ceremonies in church were forbidden. Mace, in common with many, saw all this as a compound tragedy: political, social and religious.

Use of the *Book of Common Prayer* was made illegal in 1645 and about one-third of the ten thousand or so parish priests felt forced to resign. They were replaced by Presbyterian ministers in tune with the Puritan cause. The organization of the church was supposedly democratized through new provincial and national assemblies, but the poet and political commentator John

Milton noted the reality: 'New Presbyter is but old Priest writ large.'

Forms of service were very straightforward, stripped of any adornment, spectacle, ritual or set prayers:

◆ *introductory prayer*

◆ *readings*

◆ *psalm*

◆ *prayers*

◆ *sermon*

◆ *prayers*

◆ *(optional) psalm*

◆ *blessing[3]*

This simple structure will be familiar to many non-conformist worshippers today. In Cromwell's Commonwealth, Anglicanism and Roman Catholicism were abhorred to the same degree that non-conformists were encouraged, the latter including the Baptists, Congregationalists and Quakers, and also the Jews.

The Puritans were highly suspicious of music and its trappings. Psalm-singing was the only form of Christian music which was approved, Psalms were sung metrically, very much in the manner of the European Calvinists, to verses often little more than doggerel, as this doxology shows:

All glory to the Trinity,
that is mightes most,
The living father and the Sonne,
and eke the holy ghost.
As it hath bene in all the time,
that hath bene heretofore:
As it is now and so shalbe,
henceforth for evermore.

The century-old translations of the psalms by Sternhold and Hopkins remained very popular in spite of other recommended versions. Scotland had an official psalter imposed in 1650.

'Lining out'

The Puritans took a number of measures to try to ensure that the form and content of services was understood by the most humble parishioner, even when it meant overturning valued traditions. In 1644 one recommendation had a startling and widespread effect on the singing of psalms:

> **In singing of psalms, the voice is to be tunably and gravely ordered; but the chief care must be to sing with understanding, and with grace in the heart, making melody unto the Lord ... Every one that can read is to have a psalm-book ... but for the present, where many in the congregation cannot read, it is convenient that the minister, or some other fit person ... do read the psalm, line by line, before the singing thereof.**[4]

The results of this injunction were simple but bizarre. Each line of the psalm verse was recited—and often sung—by the leading voice, which the congregation would then follow. However, there was little or no musical expertise in the leadership: the minister received no musical training and in all probability neither did his clerk. The result, which came to be called 'lining out', was wayward to say the least.

Both leader and individual members of the congregation tended to take their own time (and a very long time indeed it was—perhaps half a minute for each line!). Where harmonization was attempted it was unsupported by any organ or instruments, probably improvised and most unlikely to conform to the four parts of a printed book.

Later on the slow pace of the singing allowed the possibility of decoration and ornamentation of the melody by extra notes, though these might be spontaneously and simultaneously created by several singers at once. The result was a kind of semi-improvised chaos, undoubtedly very remote from what trained musicians could tolerate, but with the heady excitement of the musically ecstatic.

For a time it became a significant folk tradition, persisting in England into the eighteenth century. Remarkably, the tradition is still just alive today and can be heard in remote Gaelic-speaking areas of Scotland (in the Isle of Lewis, for example) and in about 200 small Baptist churches in the Southern States of North America.

The Restoration—crisis in parish church and cathedral

With the defeat of Cromwell and the restoration of Charles II to the throne in 1660 the Church of England was reinstated. The Act of Uniformity of 1662, together with severe punishments for dissenters, required the revised *Book of Common Prayer* to be used once more throughout the Church of England.

Nonetheless, the Puritans' demolition of worshipping traditions, of organs, and most of all,

the destruction of the irreplaceable contents of church and cathedral choir-libraries, were body-blows to Christian music from which recovery was very slow. Indeed, the annihilation or dispersal of choir-books meant that musicians have remained ignorant of much pre-Restoration church music right up until the research of twentieth-century scholars. Music in the parish church fell to a very low standard. Because the landed gentry and other educated people no longer supported the country parishes with their resources, the churches became places of worship where music was uniquely the province of ordinary people.

In spite of the fact that metrical psalms had no official place in the Anglican liturgy, they were forced upon the local parish priest by their popularity—it was the only kind of music the congregations knew and in which they could

The puritan era, a time of great seriousness in morals and religion, also saw terrible destructiveness. The image-breakers shattered many irreplaceable wall paintings and statues. But it was harder to touch music.

join. The parish priest himself probably did not sing these psalms. Indeed, most educated people found such primitive music excruciating. The contemporary Thomas Mace again remarks:

For when we Sing unto God, we ought to Sing chearfully, and with a loud voice, and heartily to rejoyce ... 'Tis Sad to hear what whining, toting, yelling, or Screeking there is in many Country Congregations, as if the people were affrighted, or distracted.[5]

Meanwhile, the cathedrals were suffering very serious financial troubles and good musicians could not be found for the fees they offered, made paltry by inflation. As Thomas Tudway noted, in 1716:

Deans & Chapters, since the Reformation, tyeing their Clerks down to the same allowance now, when money is not a 5th part in value to what it was then, have brought generall neglect of the service & a very mean and lame way of performing it, for want of encouragement ... This insufficient provision, I take to be, the sourse of the decay of Cathedrall Service with us; and what makes this yet more evident is that where there is encouragement, or a maintenance, as at the Royall Chappell, St Pauls, Westminster Abby &c, they abound in good voices, and the service is perform'd with decency & solemnity that God is truely worship'd, as of old, in the beauty of Holines ...[6]

According to Roger North, another contemporary musical observer:

The Cathedral Churches in the North ... have the ordinary wind instruments in the Quires, as the cornett, sackbutte, double curtaile and others, which supply the want of voices ...[7]

These instruments were those associated with the town bands, the city waits, and presumably were allowed to participate in Christian worship only under these desperate circumstances.

Parish churches and Independent chapels fared even more badly in their musical provision, with no organ or other musical talent to lead them. Their musical fare was extraordinarily limited, no more than a universal adherence to the metrical psalms—either the old way of Sternhold and Hopkins, or the new of the Tate and Brady Psalter first published in 1696.

Chapter 20

The Glory of the Chapel Royal

The enthusiastic support of Charles II for music at the Chapel Royal created the sharpest contrast with Christian music in the rest of the country. The contemporary Thomas Tudway, Professor of Music at Oxford, and later Composer and Organist Extraordinary to Queen Anne, noted:

The King took great delight in the Service of his Chappell, & was very intent upon Establishing his Choir ... as allmost to double the number of Gentlemen, & Children of the Chappell which it consisted of before the Rebellion.

His Majesty who was a brisk, & Airy Prince, comeing to the Crown in the Flow'r & Vigour of his Age, was soon ... tyr'd with the Grave and Solemn way, And Order'd the Composers of his Chappell, to add symphonys &c with Instruments to their Anthems ...

In about 4 or 5 years time, some of the forwardest, & brightest Children of the Chappell, as Mr Humfrey, Mr Blow, &c began to be Masters of a faculty in Composing; This, his Majesty greatly encourag'd, by indulging their youthful fancys, so that every month at least ... they produc'd something New, of this kind ... Thus the secular way was first introduced into the service of the Chappell ...

This however did not Oblige the Cathedrals throughout England, to follow such an Example; for indeed such an Example was very improper for their

imitation; because they had none of the fine voices, which his Majesty had in his Chappell.[1]

The great diarist John Evelyn attended the Chapel Royal's services from time to time and recorded his impressions, with mixed feelings:

Instead of the antient grave and solemn wind musicke accompanying the organ, was introduced a Consort of 24 Violins betweene every pause, after the French phantastical light way, better suited to a Tavern or Play-house than a Church.[2]

The unfamiliar French style clearly caused the musicians some difficulty, as another diarist, Samuel Pepys, noted:

An anthem, ill sung, which made the King laugh ...[3]

Charles II was perceptive enough to see that English composers needed experience and training in the continental styles with which he wished to be surrounded. Accordingly, in 1664 he sent Pelham Humfrey (1647–74) abroad with a considerable sum of money to improve his musical education.

The exact details of his travels are not known, but he returned in 1667 'an absolute Monsieur'. His anthems use the rhetoric—the emotional effects of well-matched music and words—of the Baroque style to involve the congregation (or should one say 'audience'?). In a number of anthems violin solos alternate or interweave with dramatic solos for voices *(By the Waters of Babylon,* for example). Humfrey's music displays a wonderful sensitivity to the English language through the Monteverdian technique of recitative *(Hear, O Heavens)*.

Humfrey died at the early age of 27, but John Blow lived well into the eighteenth century and composed such quantities of music that one is right to suspect that quality was sacrificed to speed. His anthems are either of the verse-anthem type, with orchestral *ritornelli* (refrains or interludes) or so-called 'full' anthems, written solely for choirs of up to eight voice-parts.

That the Chapel Royal was happy to hear occasional anthems in Latin is indicated by a dozen or so by Blow (as opposed to the hundred he wrote in English) of which *Salvator Mundi*

The Music of the Chapel Royal

The Chapel Royal (or Royal Chapel) has been in existence as a musical organization since the thirteenth century. It still exists today, as it did then, to provide the sovereign of the time with the facilities for worship—vestments, utensils, service books and particularly music. The Chapel moved from place to place as required, adorning the liturgy with a rich tapestry of music.

After the Reformation, though English was substituted for most of the Latin, music continued to play a vital part in the Chapel's worship; readings and prayers (including the Creed) were intoned on a single note; responses and psalms were sung to chants. These were the traditional plainsong formulae of medieval times, often richly and imaginatively harmonized with three or four added parts.

Anglican chant

Tallis had supplied such settings for psalms and responses as far back as the mid-sixteenth century. They appear, along with others, in an invaluable compilation of cathedral music made by John Barnard, a minor canon of St Paul's Cathedral, in 1641, just before the Puritan purges. Gradually the plainsong melodies were forgotten and replaced by newly composed chants, sung to each half of the psalm-verse. This could be called the beginnings of Anglican chant.

The choir stalls traditionally divided the choir into two, called *decani* (the south, the Dean's side) and *cantoris* (the north and 'cantor's', or Precentor's side) and the psalm-verses were taken alternately by the two sides following the long-established Roman tradition.[1]

Over the next hundred years or so the so-called 'single' chants were replaced by double ones, where a musical sentence in two phrases fits to a whole verse of the psalm.

Canticles

A minor canon of St Paul's, James Clifford, published in 1633 some 'brief directions' concerning the practice at St. Paul's Cathedral:

The first Service in the morning

After the Psalms a Voluntary on the organ alone. After the first lesson is sung Te Deum laudamus... *After the second lesson* Benedictus... *or* Jubilate. *After the third Collect is sung the first Anthem. After that the Litany. After the Blessing... a Voluntary alone on the Organ.*

At Evening Service

After the Psalms a Voluntary alone by the Organ. After the first lesson Magnificat. *After the second lesson*

Nunc Dimittis or Deus misereatur... After the third Collect is sung the first Anthem. After the Sermon is sung the last Anthem.[2]

The Canticles (marked in italics) are

(Saviour of the world) is deservedly the best known. Waves of harmonic tension and relaxation are created between voices to express as powerfully as possible the plea to Christ the Saviour of the world. His English setting of Jesus' words on the cross 'My God, my God, look upon me, why hast thou forsaken me?' is equally intense and compelling.

The lavish scale of Charles II's musical requirements is no more evident than in a special commission from Matthew Locke (about 1621–77) in 1666. Locke was a court composer already well known for his anthems and Latin motets when the King asked for a 'Song of Thanksgiving for His Majesty's Victory over the Dutch'.

In response Locke wrote *Be thou exalted, Lord* for three four-part choirs, larger forces than required by any other English composer of the

straightforward. The voice-parts tended to move through the text together (homophonically) while alternating between *decani* and *cantoris*.

Some of the grander settings (so-called 'verse' Services) use the further contrasts possible between the full choir and solo voices. Settings by Byrd, Mundy, Orlando Gibbons, Child, Tomkins and Batten continued to be used throughout the seventeenth century—long after their composers' deaths. The prominent place of solo organ music after the psalm is noteworthy; it continued as a long-standing tradition, but was abandoned during the nineteenth century.

Anthems

Anthems were the central 'sacrifice of praise' at the Chapel Royal, even overshadowing the sermon. Clifford shows us that the 'first' service contained one, the following Eucharist contained another and that a further two were sung at Evensong.

Anthems permitted the greatest artistry and invention of which the musicians of the Chapel were capable; they were usually of a complexity that made them impossible to perform elsewhere.

The choir of Westminster's Chapel Royal, an illustration from an account of the coronation of James II. The original caption ran: 'Gentlemen of the Chapel Royal, in number 32.'

Henry Purcell

It was Henry Purcell (1659–95), however, who made the most remarkable contribution of all to this period of sumptuous music at the Chapel Royal. For him it was something of a family affair, for he and his brother were accepted as choristers with his father and uncle already in the choir. His musical training enabled him to tune and repair organs and earned him the post of 'composer for the King's violins' at the age of eighteen. Before he was twenty-one he became one of the organists both of the Chapel Royal and at Westminster Abbey.

Through Pelham Humfrey and others Purcell came to understand the latest French and Italian styles of composition and drew on both for his church music, some of which is extravagantly expressive.

The operatic techniques and dance rhythms that can be heard in Humfrey and Blow are very evident in Purcell—particularly in his verse anthems, which have solo passages for one or two voices alternating with the 'full' choir. What is most remarkable is his inventiveness, which he poured into situations over which other composers might not have wished to labour too long.

The full and verse anthems are rarely routine and often contain moments of unforgettable genius, even though most of his church music was written early on in his short career.

Brilliant though his church music is, it was the semi-operas such as *King Arthur* or *The Fairy Queen* and the songs for dozens of theatre plays that reached the wider public and which led Roger North to observe that 'a greater musicall genius England never had'.[1]

At that time, there was, alas, no cause or opportunity for Purcell to write any Christian music for the worshipping public. His Christian music remains, like so much of the music for the Chapel Royal, on a higher level than can be reached by any but the very best choirs and soloists. Indeed, his anthems have been reckoned to be sufficiently long, difficult or controversial for past editors to mutilate them with cuts and alterations of all kinds.

'My Beloved Spake' is one of Purcell's best known verse-anthems. The sensuous imagery of the Song of Songs inspired some striking musical ideas, such as these angular lines which begin the first verse (solo) section.

Henry Purcell, seen in this portrait from the year of his death, was first a chorister then organist at the Chapel Royal. He wrote anthems for performance by the choir.

time and approaching the Italian splendours enjoyed in St Mark's, Venice, in the sixteenth century. In addition, the voices were accompanied by strings, including a consort of viols playing 'in the Gallery'.

It is no surprise that seventeenth-century styles of worship should reflect the hierarchical nature of a class-based society. Attitudes to the new and the adventurous were also sharply differentiated by class.

At one extreme, traditions of worship in the country areas, once established by the reformers, changed very slowly and with great reluctance. The Old Version of the psalter existed side by side with the New Version of Tate and Brady for years; indeed, the New never wholly replaced the Old, which clung on in places till the mid-nineteenth century. On the other hand, the Chapel Royal encouraged, for a time at least, the production of several new anthems a month in the latest continental styles.

Does a slow rate of change indicate sterility? Do congregations cling to tradition for the illusion of safety it may bring? Or does the excitement of the new and the colourful blur a sense of the enduring truths of the Christian faith?

These questions are still relevant today, for English cathedrals cling to the old ways while patterns of parish worship, together with their musical content, are changing with bewildering rapidity. Perhaps resistance to such change and a desperate need for it are both signs of a faith under threat—for the coming eighteenth century was an Age of Reason not unlike the present.

Chapter 21

English Congregational Music:
The Birth of the Hymn

The period from the Restoration to the end of the eighteenth century in England was one of extremes. Music of the Chapel Royal flourished most impressively at a time when the spiritual and musical life of the Christian community at large was slipping to a very low ebb.

The Anglican Church was guilty of providing the outward image of worship, without being too concerned about the spiritual welfare of its congregations. The abject poverty and the pitiful quality of life for the masses were matters of no consequence for the very wealthy; sharply differentiated musical styles in worship typified the two extremes.

Not until the arrival of the Methodists and Evangelicals in the mid-eighteenth century did compassion seem once more to return to Christianity, and with it came a renewed awareness of the need and the possibility of redemption, expressed in a great surge of hymns. With them returned the corporate expression of faith in God which lies at the heart of Christian worship.

EARLY HYMNS

In the seventeenth century hymns did not at first exist as an expression of worship for everyone, for the public singing of texts not directly from the Bible was still regarded by many as an 'error of popery'. Instead, they were written for the aristocracy and performed in their private chapels by professional musicians. Some of the most beautiful hymn-tunes from the earlier seventeenth century and now commonplace in English hymn-books were created under these circumstances.

One of the earliest moves towards congregational hymn-singing came from a minister of the Particular Baptists, Benjamin Keach, who in about 1673 persuaded the majority of his congregation in Southwark, outside London, to sing a hymn at the end of Communion, remembering the Gospel account of the Last Supper: 'And when they had sung an hymn, they went out into the Mount of Olives . . .'

The practice caused much controversy and threatened the Particular Baptists with schism. Twenty years later Keach published the decisive *The Breach Repaired in God's Worship; or, Singing of Psalms, Hymns, and Spiritual Songs, proved to be an Holy Ordinance of Jesus Christ* and in 1697 he published a collection of thirty-seven hymns.[1] Hymns also began to appear in supplements to collections of psalms, such as the *Divine Companion* published by Henry Playford in 1701.

What did Keach and his contemporaries mean by 'hymn', as opposed to psalm or spiritual song? A hymn was considered to be a devotional poem 'of human composure', intended for corporate worship. The writer who began the new era of the Christian hymn was Isaac Watts (1674–1748) whose hymns are still sung by every denomination today. (It is encouraging to know that this non-conformist minister is represented by six hymns in the 'New Catholic Hymnal' of 1971).

One of the reasons for the very widespread use of Watts' hymns down the ages was his ability to summarize universal Christian experience—sentiments with which all worshippers could identify. Since he composed his hymns in the standard metres of the psalms (short, common and long) they were easily married to any number of familiar tunes.[2]

Watts wrote well over 400 hymns and psalm paraphrases, but he stood only at the start of a veritable explosion of hymn-writing. More than 450 different metrical psalters and at least 250 different hymn-books were published during the eighteenth century. The very nature of the hymn makes it impossible to count the number of poems or tunes these figures might represent. For it is a mistake to regard a hymn as a fixed and final creation. Like the church buildings they are sung in, they are subject to continual alteration.

Firstly, the tunes to which the words were matched were constantly changing from one publication to another. Secondly, both words and tunes were frequently altered from the first time they appeared. Perhaps those who baulk at present-day revisions would do well to consider how many changes their favourite hymns may already have suffered before reaching the pages of a modern hymn-book.

This apparent lack of respect for the original or the 'authentic' gives an important clue to the true nature of hymn-writing. With few exceptions, it is best understood as a folk-art. Even sophisticated thinkers like Isaac Watts or John Wesley were aware that hymns could not be poetry fully-fledged. Isaac Watts said of himself:

I make no pretences to the name of poet or polite writer . . . I am ambitious to be a servant to the churches and a helper to the joy of the meanest Christian.[3]

Watts was certain of the need to be simple and straightforward, to avoid the expression of sentiments more involved than a singing congregation could grasp:

. . . I would neither indulge any bold metaphors, nor admit of hard words, nor tempt the ignorant worshipper to sing without his understanding.[4]

This would be a challenge to any writer and Watts admitted its difficulties:

It was hard to sink every line to the level of a whole congregation, and yet to keep it above [critical] contempt.[5]

Some of the best-known English hymns of the Christian church stem from Watts' desire to interpret the psalms afresh in the light of the New Testament. *Jesus shall reign where'er the sun* (part of Psalm 72) and *O God, our help in ages past* (Psalm 90) are outstanding examples, which, however, only became very widely known in the later nineteenth century and in considerably altered form. They are sung nowadays much shortened, and John Wesley changed the original *Our God, our help* to *O God . . .*

The melodies to which such hymns were sung were published in a great variety of ways, reflecting the great variety of situations in which they were sung. The simplest (and for a long time the commonest) congregational singing was without any accompaniment or harmonization at all. The older psalm-tunes have a simplicity and strength that is imposing without harmony. But such tunes would often have been profusely decorated by the singers, and in a country church probably 'lined out' with the help of the parish clerk, who would say or sing each line in turn with the people echoing him.

Music in the town

In the eighteenth century Anglican churches in towns and cities began to aspire to a more refined style of music. Efforts were made for the first time to find groups of singers that might be trained to assist the congregation to sing better. The Society for the Promotion of Christian Knowledge was founded in 1698 to campaign for the establishment of religious societies and charity schools. The schools existed to give free education to the poor of the parish, but the inmates in their turn began to receive some musical training in order to assist in parish worship.

Some of the more well-to-do town parishes might have boasted a choir of charity children and a recently installed organ. The money for these facilities had to be raised locally and the school-children were instructed to be grateful:

At Chelsea a charity school was founded in 1707 by William Petyt, and the school building included a special 'cloister' or covered arcade, three arches in length, facing the street. Here the scholars were to stand after service twice each Sunday 'with their caps off... until the congregation passed by', and were to 'be given to understand who are their benefactors and instructed that as often as they pass by any of them they pull off their caps and make them a bow.'[6]

For those who could afford them, the presence of choir and organ transformed the musical content of the worship, though not to everyone's pleasure. It was not always accepted that the choir should sing anything by itself, nor that it should sit apart from the congregation. The organist often took the opportunity to play over the tune in a highly decorated way and then to provide interludes between verses and even between lines.

The practice of organ improvisations ('voluntaries') after the morning psalm was practised for many years in urban areas. For the benefit of the organist, hymns were printed with a bass line, perhaps with figures to indicate the harmonies that the organist should play.

Other books added a middle line for those who might be able to harmonize—Playford's *The whole book of psalms...compos'd in three parts* (1677) was particularly successful. Although tunes did appear in the familiar four-part layout of present-day hymn-books, it was at least a century before a significant number of choirs were capable of leading congregations in this way.

Some Anglican churches in towns and cities even aspired to imitate the cathedral style on special occasions. The charity children might be encouraged to sing on their own (perhaps at the annual 'charity sermon') and anthems were composed for treble voices and organ in the tuneful Italian style that owed something to Purcell and later to Handel.

But at St Thomas' Church in Southwark (where there was no choir and no organ till 1879[7]) and in many churches:

... the cause was almost hopeless. The clerk commences his stave, and goes through it almost wholly unaccompanied, or perhaps joined towards the close, by the feeble efforts of a single voice or two.[8]

Music in the country

The countryside in the eighteenth century did not have the easy accessibility that car-owners now expect of it. Villagers could rarely afford to travel and their life was largely isolated from the rapidly developing world of urban commerce and industry. Worship in country churches therefore tended to develop in distinctive ways, often very different from town churches. There was no money to build organs, and there were few educated people in the congregation able or willing to raise musical standards.

The old way of psalm-singing remained popular and the parish clerk continued to have his way. Gradually it was accepted that a choir could help to improve matters. The choir usually won for itself a place in the old west galleries of Gothic parish churches. In other places they sometimes had a gallery provided for them. Such choirs sometimes became very keen, spending nights during the week practising together. They received a rudimentary musical training from travelling singing-teachers, who found some sort of living by offering instruction to anyone who could pay for it:

There are men who travel, and style themselves professors of, and instructors in, psalmody; they are furnished with books of their own selection which are seldom correct, and these are disposed of in every place where they go. While such measures are countenanced, it is impossible to expect that their disciples should ever arrive at any degree of perfection.[9]

A uniquely primitive kind of music developed under these circumstances. As west-gallery choirs became more confident, they attempted to sing in harmony, usually with the hymn-tune taken by the tenor voices and with up to three more voices added around them. They even embarked on anthems circulated by the singing teachers, written in a vivid and ungrammatical style by composers such as William Tans'ur (1706–83) and George FFitch.[10] Unfortunately, the musical results were sometimes distressing, and not very edifying for the congregation which was excluded from taking part in such pieces.

In the latter half of the eighteenth century musical instruments became accepted as a means of reinforcing the choristers in the gallery. Churches even bought instruments for their use. The bass was the part that most obviously needed bolstering and the most lowly choirs might use a vamphorn—simply a long megaphone—to amplify the voice! Otherwise bassoon and cello were found to be the most useful. Other treble instruments (wind instruments tended to carry better) played along with the upper voices to create some kind of harmony.

had begun... The interior of Hayslope Church... was free from the modern blemish of galleries. The choir had two narrow pews to themselves in the middle of the right-hand row, so that it was a short process for Roshua Rann [the parish clerk] to take his place among them as principle bass, and return to his desk when the singing was over... None of the old people held books—why should they? not one of them could read. But they knew a few 'good words' by

This nineteenth-century painting of an English village choir shows singers and instrumentalists, men and women, adults and children. The atmosphere is miles away from the robed professionalism of the cathedral.

A number of printed books were produced with music to help such players, but mostly the instrumentalists played from the voice-parts or by ear. George Eliot's novel *Adam Bede* contains a detailed and sympathetic evocation of worship in a country parish church, of which this can only be a glimpse:

Presently the sound of the bassoon and the key-bugles burst forth; the evening hymn, which always opened the service,

heart, and their withered lips now and then moved silently, following the service without any clear comprehension indeed, but with a simple faith in its efficacy to ward off harm and bring blessing.

The isolation of some country parish churches and especially of non-conformist chapels encouraged congregations to develop their own music. The Baptists at Lumb, in the moors and forests of Rossendale north of Manchester, built up an enthusiastic tradition of hymn-singing and composition under their minister, John Nuttall. These 'Larks of Dean' were Lancashire farmers and gradually

... developed into a strong local society of musical composers, of whom John Nuttall's two sons James (1745–1806) and Henry (1747–1810) both excelled in composing hymn tunes. James's tunes bore such names as Bocking Warp,

Friendship, Lark, Sampson, Spanking Rodger and Temple ... Like many late eighteenth-century composers elsewhere throughout England, they revelled in Handel's oratorios and so far as their resources allowed tried imitating his style. Their tunes invariably go with a swing, teem with runs and repetitions, and often finish with a few bars of rousing chorus. Dauntless enthusiasm and robust joyousness were the keynotes of their religion ... [11]

Handel and *Messiah*

For the congregations of most country churches, the music for which the eighteenth century is now remembered was almost unknown. But not altogether. Following his arrival in England in 1710, Handel had increasingly dominated the art-music of Britain: his Italian operas became highly fashionable in London till about 1728 and he wrote the most splendid church music for state occasions, as Purcell had done before him *(Zadok the Priest* and the *Utrecht* and *Dettingen* settings of the *Te Deum* for instance).

For the London opera audiences he provided biblical oratorios to be performed during the Lenten closed season. These were operas in all but name—performed in the manner of opera, by opera singers and in their theatres. Only the staging was missing.

All this did have some effect on Christian music, albeit indirectly. Firstly, a number of English composers of the time (Maurice Greene, John Stanley, William Boyce) admired Handel and his achievements and were able to transmit something of his style to the more humble musical surroundings of Christian worship. Secondly, the work that he wrote in 1741 called *A Sacred Oratorio, Messiah* had an effect eventually reaching far beyond the circumstances of its first performances.

Messiah was originally written for a charity concert at the New Music Hall, Fishamble Street in Dublin, on 13 April 1742. The idea of presenting it in a London theatre caused some initial unease. As *The Universal Spectator* put it, on the date of its first performance in London, on 23 March 1743:

How will this appear to After-Ages, when it shall be read in History, that in such an Age the People of England were arriv'd to such a Height of Impiety and Prophaneness that the most sacred Things were suffer'd to be us'd as publick Diversions, and that in a Place, and by Persons, appropriate to the Performance not only of light and vain, but all too often prophane and dissolute pieces?

Clearly, the secular and sacred had to be kept strictly apart. What is more, *Messiah* was unlike any of Handel's other oratorios. Not only was it contemplative of its theme rather than vividly dramatic, but the subject was Christ himself, unlike the other oratorios based almost exclusively on Old Testament figures. For some liberal thinkers, its serious Christian message was an uncomfortable intrusion into worldly and high-class

entertainment.

Messiah in its entirety had no place in church worship. Nonetheless, its effect on Christian music (albeit delayed) was profound, for local choirs and their instrumentalists, particularly in the north of England, began to join together to perform oratorios, *Messiah* in particular. The Ellenbrook Monthly Meeting was one such society, made up largely of handloom weavers, who, in the early nineteenth century

... became good performers, and had a large experience and knowledge of Handel's music, Dr. Croft's, Dr. Greene's, Dr. Boyce's ... and other anthems. At the quarterly meetings the proceeds were divided between the four choirs, with which they generally bought a score copy of some oratorio ... and from this the instrumental parts were copied. [1]

This was an early stage of the widespread development of choral societies in the nineteenth century, many of which are still thriving today. More importantly, contact with music of high professional excellence gave the choirs involved an idea of what might be achieved in the music of their local churches.

Cathedral musicians, who felt this

Recently, interest in this rough-hewn Christian music has intensified, particularly around the parish church of St Mary in Puddletown, Dorset, where the family of the novelist Thomas Hardy worshipped for many years. In September 1990 the traditions of west-gallery music were revived for a BBC television broadcast of *Songs of Praise* from the church, since when a number of other churches have considered recreating their own forgotten west-gallery traditions, evidently far more widespread than previously supposed. There is now evidence of such bands in a number of Welsh churches, one (at the Baptist church in Upper Rhymney) surviving up to the Second World War.[12]

John and Charles Wesley

For the Wesleys, questions of decorum in worship were a distraction from the fundamental aim, which was to proclaim that, through Christ, everyone, and not simply the Calvinist elect, had the right to salvation and eternal life. To proclaim that message, both John and Charles Wesley

idea of what might be achieved in the music of their local churches.

Cathedral musicians, who felt this sophisticated music to be their province, were not all happy with this development:

These [village practitioners], since the rage of oratorios has spread from the capital to every market town in the kingdom, can by no means be satisfied unless they introduce chants, services, and anthems, into their parish churches, and accompany them with ... scolding fiddles, squalling hautboys, false-stopped violoncellos, buzzing bassoons ... in place of an organ.[2]

Handel's 'Messiah' performed by a massed choir and orchestra in 1785 in Westminster Abbey to commemorate the composer's death in 1759. It still remains the one piece of sacred music for the concert hall which most British people would recognize.

made a unique contribution to Christian hymnody, in words and music, that severed denominational boundaries.

In 1735 John Wesley, already involved with developing the spiritual life of Oxford undergraduates (the 'Oxford Methodists'), accepted an invitation to travel with his brother

John Wesley, seen here preaching from his father's tomb in Epworth churchyard, England, wrote the words to many hymns which his brother Charles set to music. Their hymns were intended to be clear and simple enough to be sung by everyone, and they have been so ever since.

Charles as a missionary to Georgia on behalf of the Society for the Propagation of the Gospel.

They found themselves travelling with some Moravian Christians (see Box: *The Moravian Brethren* in Chapter 18) whose expression of faith through their hymn-singing made a deep impression. The Wesley brothers' experiences in Georgia were traumatic, but for John they especially helped him to understand

...what I least of all suspected, that I,

who went to America to convert others, was never converted myself...[13]

In 1738, partly through the study of Luther, both he and Charles experienced true conversion profoundly and personally, finding themselves 'at peace with God'. In the words of Charles' journal: 'I saw that by faith I stood.'

John Wesley then visited the Moravians at their Herrnhut community to experience their Christian living for himself. His love for their music led him to translate a number of their hymns and to encourage the use of a number of German melodies then unknown in England.

Apart from preaching, Charles Wesley's special gift was to encompass his Christian experience in hymns. They are

... songs of individual experience, marking the successive stages of penitence, conversion, justification, pardon and sanctification in the life of the Christian pilgrim...[14]

The impact on countless lives of many of Charles Wesley's 6500 hymns need not be re-emphasised here. His hymns were a challenge to musicians, too, for they were cast in a far greater variety of metres than those of Isaac Watts. Clearly, their music often needed to be composed specially, allowing the possibility of a more intimate relationship between words and music. In the late 1740s Handel wrote three melodies for texts by Charles Wesley ('Sinners, obey the gospel word', 'O love divine' and 'Rejoice, the Lord is King'). Another composer of the time, J.F.Lampe, provided many more.

The Wesleys had very clear ideas of the role of music in worship. John Wesley closely supervised the content of the dozens of Methodist hymn-books published during his lifetime, to be set down exactly as they were sung by their congregations. In the preface to *Sacred Melody* (1761) he wrote:

I have been endeavouring for more than 20 years to procure such a book as this. But in vain: Masters of music were above following any direction but their own. And I was determined, whoever should compile this, should follow my direction. Not mending our tunes, but setting them down, neither better nor worse than they were ...

The Methodists insisted that the music to their hymns should be accessible to all and where possible sung by all. Gone (or almost gone) were the old metrical psalms, gone also was the involved part-singing of some country churches, gone was the separation of choir from congregation. Like Luther, John Wesley was happy to adapt popular tunes from any source (much to the disapprobation of high churchmen).

Above all, strenuous efforts were made to educate congregations into singing well, as the Methodist Conference Minutes of 1765 testify:

Teach them to sing by note, and to sing our tunes first: take care they do not sing too slow. Exhort all that can in every congregation to sing. Set them right that sing wrong. Be patient herein.

Accordingly, some hymn-books included sections on how to read music and to 'tune the Voice'.

When the whole congregation had developed the capacity to sing with heart and soul (in a way that is rarely experienced nowadays) then a number of musical elaborations were possible. Women and men occupied different parts of the chapel and could therefore be asked to sing antiphonally—taking turns to sing. The whole congregation was often capable of singing in full harmony, obviating the need for any instrumental accompaniment. Hymns developed with repetitions of text and independence of parts which are still well known today.

Instrumentalists in Anglican churches also attacked these tunes with relish. Hardy's *The Return of the Native* recounts:

One Sunday I can well mind—a bass viol day—and Yeobright had brought his own. 'Twas the hundred and thirty-third to Lydia, and when they'd come to

Ran down his beard and o'er his robes Its costly moisture shed,

neighbour Yeobright, who had just warmed to his work, drove his bow into them strings that glorious grand that he e'en a'most sawed the bass viol into two pieces.

This chorus, here depicted by Hogarth, is attempting to sing a popular 'ORATORIO or SACRED DRAMA' by Handel's contemporary, William De Fesch. Although the piece was revived at least once after its performance in 1733, the music is now lost.

Wales: Land of Song

The Welsh have a respect for the art of singing which the English delight to caricature. It shows itself in all sorts of ways: the roaring song of the rugby crowds at Cardiff Arms Park, the continuing excellence of some male-voice choirs... On another level comes the bardic tradition of *Cerdd Dant,* in which exacting poetic and melodic structures must be improvised against a folk-tune. In all this there is perhaps a distant race memory of the role music used to play in an isolated and agrarian society—a memory which has faded more quickly and completely in England.

Like Italian, the Welsh language is a wonderful vehicle for song: its strong stresses and lilting quality are already half-way to music. The exceptional hymnody of Wales has benefitted from it as much as the folk-song: tunes such as *Olwen* or *Crugybar* have repetitive rhythmic patterns related to the language.

The advent of Methodism had a profound effect on patterns of worship in the Principality, acting also as a vigorous spur to hymn-writing. But while the words of Welsh hymns of this period are rightly revered, especially those of the Calvinistic-Methodist Williams Williams of Pantycelyn (1717–91), few tunes from this period can be found in hymn-books today. The melodies which epitomize the Welsh idiom are a product of the nineteenth century, a period when great spiritual revivals packed Methodist and Baptist chapels, especially in the industrial valleys. Many congregations developed their hymn-singing to the point where the majority could read from four-part books using Curwen's *sol-fa* notation.

The sombre and passionate quality of many Welsh tunes is typified by *Aberystwyth,* written in 1876 by Joseph Parry (1841–1903), which English congregations usually sing to the words 'Jesu, lover of my soul'. Its obsessive minor mode is briefly lightened towards the end of each verse, only to sink back to its dark-toned opening. A number of other powerful tunes follow this pattern: *Trewen* by Emlyn Evans, *Llef* by Griffiths Jones and *Ebenezer* by Thomas John Williams. There are, of course, major-key tunes of great power, such as *Hyfrydol* by R.H. Prichard, *Blaenwern* by William Penfro Williams (dating from the revival of 1904–05), and above all, *Cwm Rhondda* by John Hughes. All have a breadth and solemnity in keeping with the large and enthusiastic crowds who originally sang them.

With the gradual collapse of the communities that supported the chapels, these and other great hymns have been kept alive through the continuing tradition of *Cymanfa Ganu,* (singing meeting), a festival of local congregations similar to the German *Kirchengesängfeste*. Sadly, the *Cymanfaoedd Ganu* have largely developed a life separate from the worship of the churches from which they sprang. Like other traditions in Wales they are being preserved rather than growing and living. With few exceptions (such as Arwel Hughes' *Tydi a Roddaist*) the hymn-writing tradition has largely died out. But there are signs of change: charismatic song, sung both in Welsh and English, has rekindled a spark of Christian music in a younger generation, but it will need plenty of fanning before it resembles the roaring flames of previous generations.

PART 4

The Path Divides

1750 – 1900

Chapter 22

Music in the Courts of Europe

As the Protestant Churches struggled to create simple music that would edify their local congregations, the Roman Catholic Church continued throughout the eighteenth century to deepen its embrace of modern music. This did nothing for the common people worshipping at the parish level, but it pleased musical connoisseurs such as Charles Burney (1726–1814) who visited city churches and cathedrals not so much to worship, but to savour and to compare their music. He was particularly pleased with Vienna:

There is scarce a church or convent in Vienna, which has not every morning its mass in music: that is, a great portion of the church service of the day, set in parts, and performed with voices, accompanied by at least three or four violins, a tenor and base, besides the organ.[1]

The restless sumptuousness of eighteenth-century church architecture was matched by the frank theatricality of the worship:

Music spread its gorgeous mantle over the whole Mass, so that the other details of the rite had scarcely any significance... the liturgy was not only submerged under this ever-growing art but actually suppressed... the new age sought not the sight of the holy, but the beautiful in art and universe. And so the church became a great hall, its walls shimmering with marble and gold.[2]

In Vienna today the Michaelerkirche, Augustinerkirche and St Stephen's Cathedral among others continue to play the best of the orchestral mass settings, chiefly those of Joseph Haydn (1732–1809) and Mozart (1756–91). At the end of the eighteenth century, though, composers since eclipsed by these familiar names would have been equally well known, such as Georg Reutter, Michael Haydn (Joseph Haydn's brother) and Anton Salieri.

Such breathtaking displays of temporal and artistic riches symbolized the long-established

Francois Couperin, writing in France at the time of King Louis XIV, composed a set of sublime 'Lecons des Ténébres'('Readings from the Darkness')

alliance between the Roman Catholic Church and European courts. In France the immensely powerful régime of the Sun King, Louis XIV (reigned 1661–1715) required low Mass *(Messe basse solennelle)* to be celebrated regularly at Versailles, but with the addition of *grands motets* composed by his favourite musicians Henry Du Mont (1610–84) and Jean Baptiste Lully (1632–87).

One of the most impressive of these was Lully's 1677 setting of the *Te Deum*. Since it was performed by at least 120 musicians it was bound to overshadow the main text of Matins. Thousands of such pieces were composed during the next hundred years, by de Lalande, Charpentier and many others, the fashions of Versailles being copied elsewhere in France wherever resources permitted.

To be fair, Louis XIV did not always require music on such a scale. The intimacies of François Couperin's *Leçons de Ténèbres* for two sopranos, bass viol and organ make them among the most sublime of any music of the period. The practice of substituting organ music for sections of the Mass Proper had continued uninterrupted since the sixteenth century. Although by their very nature these organ versets deprived voices of the opportunity of singing parts of the service, French composers in particular produced fine music for the purpose, such as Louis Couperin (about 1626–61) and his nephew François (1668–1733), Nicolas de Grigny (1672–1703) and Louis-Claude Daquin (1694–1772).

Vienna was a great centre of eighteenth-century music; both Haydn and Mozart made the city their main focus. Music in the Viennese churches shared this high quality. Pictured is the Cathedral of St Stephen.

soloists that the Viennese upper classes had come to love.

In Spain, where the church was still the most powerful patron of the arts, Francisco Fajer, *maestro di capilla* of La Seo in Saragossa from 1756 to 1809, persuaded many cathedrals to return to an entirely Latin liturgy and to ban the singing of *villancicos,* recitatives and arias in the style of Italian opera.

Clamour for reform

Celebrations of temporal power became more and more of an embarrassment to an age of growing egalitarianism. For the winds of change were sweeping across Europe. In France, the Revolution of 1789 ended the commissioning of music of such lavish splendour in the Roman Catholic Church.

In Vienna, reform came from the Emperor. Joseph II, who reigned jointly with Maria Theresa from 1765 and alone from 1780–90, curbed the wealth of the Roman Church by dissolving monasteries and building parish churches and schools with the proceeds. He gave Protestants and Jews freedoms and human rights hitherto denied them. Above all, he put severe restrictions on the ceremonies that symbolized the power of the church: processions, candles, statues and the operatic settings of the Mass with orchestra and

Chapter 23

The Romantic Movement

It was in the nineteenth century that the modern 'cult of personality' emerged. Composers in the ages of patronage had certainly been praised for the magnificence or the craftmanship of their work. But they were not expected to step too far out of line. After all, they were working for patrons—church or state—who had very precise requirements of them. Too great an originality was likely to put them out of work.

The cult of the artist

In the nineteenth century, individuality was expected, even praised. The arts became for many people a means of spiritual enlightenment, even the source of revelation. Painters, poets and musicians came to be revered as vessels for these revelations, the 'supreme discerners of transcendent truth'.[1]

The adoration Wagner received during and after his lifetime epitomizes this Romantic spirit. Over 10,000 biographies of him were written before his death in 1883. People searching desperately for spiritual fulfilment tended, as literally as possible, to fall in love with his music, with all the passion and adoration that the phrase implies.

No case was more celebrated than that of King Ludwig II of Bavaria, who wrote to Wagner after a concert of his music in 1864:

Beloved and only Friend!
    Overwhelmed ... I must ... tell you how indescribable is the happiness which you have brought me. I was transported into superterrestial spheres, I breathed immeasurable bliss. But how can I begin to describe to you my ecstasy?...[2]

With such encouragement, artists became less concerned with pleasing their public than with expressing their true selves in their art, for better or worse. As a result, the nineteenth century is the first where the composers' individuality becomes a priority. It is difficult for instance to mistake a composer like Berlioz for any other, even after short acquaintance with his music.

The new middle class

The momentous changes of the industrial revolution were already deeply rooted by the beginning of the nineteenth century. While this revolution brought new wealth, it also left the vast majority of the population in a worse state. In the rapidly expanding cities (and especially in London) there was abject poverty in the appalling lifestyle of the 'climbing boys' (chimney sweeps aged as young as four, bought and sold like slaves), in the teenage prostitution and in the danger and exploitation of the factory and mine-workers as yet unprotected by unions. The benefits of the revolution were certainly not for these pitiful masses but for an increasing minority who could now afford material comforts and education.

This middle class was large enough and rich enough to create a new market for cultural entertainment. In the world of music, public concerts had been popular from the 1720s. Concert promoters became wealthy enough to be able to invite the most famous composers from abroad. It was the entrepreneur Salomon who invited Haydn to London in the 1790s. In 1813 the Philharmonic Society was formed in London, a fully professional body both able and willing to commission new music and now (as the Royal Philharmonic Society) the second oldest concert organization in the world.

One of the Philharmonic's guests of honour in 1820 was Louis Spohr, a composer in his day much better known than Beethoven. He was the first in London to take up the rôle of conducting:

I then took my stand with the score at a separate music desk, [ie not that of the leading violin, who would would at that time have led the orchestra] drew my baton from my coat-pocket and gave the signal to begin. Alarmed at such a novel procedure, some of the directors protested against it at first ...
Immediately after the first movement of the symphony, the orchestra were impressed by the new method of conducting ... In the evening the results were even more brilliant than I could have hoped.[3]

Since Spohr's first efforts, conductors have become enmeshed in the cult of personality which is as characteristic of the present as of the Romantic past.

The influence of the past

The Romantics' inspiration drew from another source too—from the past. Again, this is an attitude too familiar to make a clear perspective easy. It was only in the 1770s that the Academy of Ancient Music was formed, the first club with a specific interest in the 'music of the ancients'. For its members, 'ancient' meant the music of forty or fifty years previously, the equivalent of a present-day society unearthing the music of Schoenberg or Mahler!

Even long after the Academy's formation, musical interest generally was in the latest and most modern creations, very much more like the present-day pop culture (though even that is now making money from nostalgia). So when in 1728 Roger North discusses music of a hundred years ago, he can hardly bear to call it music:

It is a sort of harmonious murmur rather than musick; and in a time when people lived in tranquillity and at ease, the enterteinement of it was agreeable, not unlike the confused singing of birds in a grove.[4]

Josef Danhauser's painting, 'Liszt at the Piano', with its bust of Beethoven and adoring audience, shows the nineteenth century's worship of composers and performers at its peak.

The Cecilian Movement

The Romantics' rekindled interest in the past had strong resonances in the Roman Church which had so richly patronised artists, architects and musicians through the ages. The Cecilian Movement was a direct result of this new historical perspective. Its aim was to reform music in the Roman Catholic church by looking to its past glories—the sixteenth century was regarded as the 'golden age'.

It was inspired initially by Karl Proske (1794–1861), a canon and choirmaster of the cathedral at Ratisbon (now called Regensburg) but later dominated by the composer Franz Xaver Witt (1834–88). On his initiative the *Allgemeiner Deutscher Cäcelien-Verein* was founded in 1869, St Cecilia being the patron saint of music.

The society encouraged and co-ordinated reforms by establishing branches in Germany, France, the Netherlands, North America, Poland, Austria, Ireland, and finally Italy, where the *Scuola Gregoriana* of Rome was founded in 1880. These societies held meetings, published articles and issued lists of music approved for use in worship, much of it by Witt himself. They campaigned vigorously against the use of instruments apart from the organ and for the restoration of choral music.

Witt's own music was written very much under the spell of composers of the sixteenth century—but like reproduction furniture it lacks the creative touch of a master. Some musicians, like the composer Claude Debussy, were not content with mere imitation. In a letter to Prince Poniatowski, he wrote

This English painting of St Cecilia symbolizes a nineteenth-century interest in the past. This concern expressed itself in church architecture and liturgy, but above all in church music through the Cecilian Movement, which had branches in many European countries.

By way of consolation I recently had the most rewarding musical experience. This was at Saint-Gervais [in Paris], a church where an intelligent priest has the idea of reviving some beautiful ancient religious music. An unaccompanied Mass of Palestrina was a marvel. Written in a very severe style, this music is extremely pure; its feeling is not conveyed by shrieks of any kind but by melodic arabesques which combine to produce unique melodic harmonies... When one hears such music one wonders how it came about that this beautiful art developed in such an unfortunate manner.[1]

Debussy had heard this sixteenth-century music, probably for the first time, some eight years earlier in Rome. The music affected him enough for him to declare it 'the only church music I can allow. That of Gounod and company seems to me to derive from a hysterical mysticism and produces the effect of sinister farce.'[2]

Unfortunately, when the Cecilian Movement asked composers to write new music for it, it generally attracted people of small talent—especially under the editorship of Witt's successor, Franz Haberl (1840–1910). Composers of high standing amongst concert audiences (such as César Franck and Camille Saint-Saëns) suffered from the same difficulty as so many other composers of the age: in making concessions to the needs of Christian music they trivialised their musical ideas.

Two composers stand out as exceptions. One was Gabriel Fauré (1845–1924), whose few liturgical works rise head and shoulders above the efforts of all other French composers of the time. His *Requiem* (1886), *Cantique de Jean Racine* (1873) and his few other motets are among the handful of French pieces written for the liturgy whose style is inward and contemplative rather than over-persuasive and sentimental.

The other was Anton Bruckner (1824–96) who, as a deeply committed Christian, dedicated himself without compromise to God's service and to writing for the liturgy. (See main text for more on Bruckner.)

In sharp contrast, the educated public of the nineteenth century came to look on the past with new respect. The span of history lent an atmosphere of mystery to crumbling buildings and to ancient manuscripts. Scholars began in earnest to catalogue, to restore and to copy. As architects found a new interest in the Gothic style and expressed it in their buildings, musicians started to unearth the forgotten music of the past.

The decline of Christianity

For Christian music, the consequences of these attitudes were profound and by no means beneficial. The most significant was their implication that the spiritual dimension to existence was separate and distinct from everyday living.

Christianity and its music, responding little to the objective enquiries of science which were exciting so much interest, was gradually relegated to the peripheries of culture.

A number of churchmen rationalized the move by stressing the distance between the sacred and secular worlds:

Neither [Christians'] joy nor their sorrow can be expressed, with propriety, in quite the same tones as if related to things of this world. There should be a quality about them showing our consciousness of the infinite distance between us and our Maker...[5]

By the end of the nineteenth century such sentiments had become suffused with a Romantic view of the past which attributed antiquities with spiritual and numinous qualities just by reason of their age:

Our fine old cathedrals and their music ought to go together—the music should suggest worship as much as the roof and arch and window. A stranger listening at a distance and unable to catch the words, should be able to say, 'that is sacred music'.[6]

But a faith that does not inform daily living further than the occasional visit to the hallowed walls of a cathedral will command diminishing attention. In confirmation, the number of self-confessed Christians in Europe declined steadily through the century.

The Mass as performance

For composers, public concerts were now able to provide wages which were viable alternatives to commissions from church or state. Consequently the most talented composers were able to decide on more personal grounds whether they wished to write music for the liturgy. Many decided against it.

The Roman Catholic Church too, was less inclined and less able to support the sumptuous and spectacular services which had been served so well by high-art music. The operatic style of Mozart's and Haydn's liturgical music was copied well into the nineteenth century by the next generation of composers—Schubert in Vienna, Cherubini in Paris, Weber in Dresden and many others, for whose music a diminishing European royalty still provided a market:

Ecclesiastical discipline was almost a dead letter in the ducal or grand-ducal establishments for which Haydn and his successors wrote their Masses. Their princely patrons kept a stud of opera singers and players, who were turned

The Corruption and Resurrection of the Chant

The plainsong that Bruckner and his contemporaries knew had been given little respect or attention for years. He was probably unaware that it had suffered all kinds of corruptions over the previous four or five centuries. For, along with the drastic changes that music had undergone since medieval times, the chant itself had been transformed and corrupted.

A disinterest in ancient manuscripts and a desire to conform to modern tastes had created a very different kind of music, rhythmically rigid (more like a present-day hymn-tune) and with highly significant changes both to melodies and word-setting.

An idea of the corrupt musical practice then surrounding chant is provided, surprisingly enough, by Berlioz' remarks on the musical instrument called the serpent, reminiscent of its use in the west galleries of English churches:

The truly barbaric tone of this instrument would be much better suited for the bloody cult of the Druids than for that of the Roman Catholic Church, where it is still in

A corrupt printing of the Gradual 'Iustus ut Palma' published by Pustet in 1871 is here placed above the Solesmes version compiled 'after the authority of the ancient manuscripts'. The differences accumulated over hundreds of years are striking. By the nineteenth century sections had been cut from the medieval chant, the word underlay had been changed, and in particular the characteristic melismas on final syllables had been axed. To produce this edition of 'Iustus ut Palma' (published in 1908) the Solesmes scholars compared over 200 manuscripts.

loose in the church on Sundays, to perform music identical in character with that which had occupied them during the week in the Opera House... No-one in that easy-going age worried about its breaches of liturgical laws. It was a fine 'musical programme' and that was all that mattered.[7]

But these composers would hardly have made a living or be remembered today if that is all they had written, however admirably or compellingly their fulfilled their patrons' requirements.

Beethoven's two Masses—the *Mass in C* (1807) and the *Missa Solemnis* (1819-23)—were written in the same tradition, but their scale and highly personal manner (the *Missa Solemnis* in particular) has generally precluded their use in the liturgy, though when they are heard in worship, it can be a memorable experience:

His *Missa Solemnis,* heard within the context of the celebration of the Mass, as it occasionally is in Austria, does not dwarf the liturgy, even though it prolongs the service unduly, but it

use—as a monstrous symbol for the lack of understanding and the coarseness of taste and feeling which have governed the application of music in our churches since times immemorial...[1]

The so-called Medicean version of the chant was published in 1614 as a result of the revisions Palestrina had been required to make by the Council of Trent. Further alterations to the chant had been made in eighteenth-century versions, rendering the original shape of the medieval melodies barely recognizable.

Long before the Cecilians, a centre for research into the plainsong chant was already in existence. In 1833, the Benedictine monastery of St Pierre was built in Solesmes on the banks of the River Sarthe, near Le Mans. The monks there researched all the earliest manuscript versions of the chant available to them and collated them in a new edition. They hoped this would become once more the universal Christian music of the Roman Catholic Church.

The process took far longer than they had expected. It was partly slowed down

by Friederich Pustet who, in 1871 and backed by the Cecilians, republished the corrupt readings of the chant yet again. But Pius X, a pope of exceptional musical understanding and with a background of parish life, issued his *Motu Proprio* of 1903 which sanctioned the use of the Solesmes versions of the chant throughout the Church. They have been published by the Vatican ever since.

The way the chant is sung is as important as the books themselves. The received tradition of the nineteenth century encouraged a rhythmical style which did serious damage to the fluid beauty of the melodies. Worst of all, keyboard accompaniment was the palliative that made the chant acceptable to modern taste, a practice which persists nowadays.

The French composer Olivier Messiaen accompanied the chant for most of his working life and it is therefore not without a certain irony that he should have asked: 'Why is it necessary today to accompany Gregorian chant with the organ, embellishing it with a harmony which, however skilfully handled, at one stroke totally destroys its character?'

Solesmes is today an important

teaching centre for the authentic performance of the chant and its research still generates lively scholarly debate. But the aspirations of the Solesmes monks for the universality of the chant have never quite been realized, even early this century when it had many admirers. Today its future looks gloomy.

Perhaps the most significant moment for this ancient Christian music was the Eucharistic Congress of 1960 in Munich, where the chant joined together a gathering of over a million voices from across the world. Ironically enough it was also the very moment when the Second Vatican Council was initiating changes that have since destroyed the place of Gregorian chant in the Church's liturgy.

proclaims throughout a personal belief so God-centred, so enriching and sublime, that it enters into the universal and deepens the belief of the worshipping community.[8]

The striking originality of so much music of the nineteenth century makes its relationship with the liturgy one of controversy, the most flamboyant musical personalities creating the greatest tensions. Berlioz' *Grande Messe des Morts* (1837) and *Te Deum* (1849) are works of arresting individuality, of which their vast scale is only one aspect (the *Te Deum* was intended for a thousand performers). But they reflect the nature of the state occasions for which they were intended rather than a desire to write music sympathetic to liturgical needs.

Franz Liszt (1811–85) is a more complex case, for while wholeheartedly embracing Romantic ideals he was also a trained priest. In consequence perhaps, his Christian music (of which he wrote a great deal) is either startlingly akin to his dramatic works for the concert-hall (the *Christus* of 1855–67, for instance, or the *Hungarian Coronation Mass* of 1867) or it is self-effacing on the smaller scale and uneasy in its lack of character. Liszt himself was aware of the limited public success of his Christian music, and complained in a letter to a friend:

Everyone is against me. Catholics, because they find my church music profane, Protestants because to them my music is Catholic, freemasons because they think my music is clerical...[9]

There is an air of apology in Liszt's explanation of his need to write for the general public and an open admission of the gulf between the sacred and secular worlds:

Nowadays when the altar is trembling and tottering, when pulpit and religious ceremony serve as subject matter for the mockers and sceptics, art must forsake the holy of holies, expand itself, and seek a stage for its magnificent manifestation in the world outside. How often—indeed, how much more than often—music must acknowledge both people and God as its springs of life. It needs to hasten from one to the other, in order to ennoble, comfort, and chasten mankind as well as to bless and praise God.[10]

'Hastening from one to the other' also characterized the career of Charles Gounod (1818–93), though his intention to take holy orders never became reality:

Both composers wavered eternally between the secular life and the religious. The excitements of the theatre for Gounod and the easy triumphs of the concert platform for Liszt often muffled the call of the monk's cell. And then, at the height of the applause and the glory, a sudden stab of conscience would send them hurrying away... to bury themselves in pious austerity... They were alike in their religiosity, in their yearnings for the holy life and in their ambitions to write sacred music which they fondly, and vainly, believed to be greater than their other works.[11]

Charles Gounod was unlike many other well-known composers of his time in his enthusiasm in writing for the church. Following the extraordinary though short-lived success of his cantatas *Redemption* (1882) and *Mors et Vita* (1885), he turned increasingly to writing Christian music. Towards the end of his life

... religious music... was all that really interested him... Masses, prayers, motets and canticles dripped from him as the rain from heaven... There is no doubt that Gounod wrote with sincerity and belief in the religious content of his music. But sincerity is not enough to ensure a great work of art...[12]

In turn, Gounod's style became the *lingua franca* for hundreds of other composers of even more modest talent, whose efforts were confined to the specific needs of the church, needs defined more by the simple tastes of congregations and priests rather than by papal decree.

In Italy, for instance, the operatic style of liturgical music was popularized to the extent that tunes from operas (by Donizetti or Bellini for example) were adapted to the Ordinary of the Mass, a practice decried by the authorities to little avail.

Bruckner

Anton Bruckner's church music is in a class of its own. His contribution to the Cecilian Movement, in which dedicated Roman Catholics sought to reform church music by returning to the glories of the sixteenth century (see box) is unique.

Both his symphonies and the large-scale Mass-settings of the 1860s were preceded by an arduous apprenticeship, not only in musical theory but in writing for the modest talents of Upper Austrian church choirs. His obvious model should have been the operatic style—with orchestra and soloists—still to be heard in the cathedrals of Salzburg and Vienna. But it was the comparative austerity of sixteenth- and eighteenth-century music, whose techniques he had to study intensively, that led Bruckner to write with a discipline and restraint unusual for his time.

While his reputation now rests securely on the vast canvasses of his symphonies, the unaccompanied choral motets are just as valuable. Many of them are in only four parts and usually unaccompanied. Their simple and direct presentation of Latin texts central to the Christian faith show Bruckner's deep understanding of the needs of an attentive congregation.

In *Vexilla Regis,* for instance, the voice-parts almost always move together in homophony; any gentle imitation between them serving to animate the words and not to obscure them. The impressive architecture of buildings such as the cathedral at Linz, where he was organist, led him to provide silences after the frequent shouts of exultation, when the acoustic spaces are left to make their own contribution to the music.

Bruckner was well aware of the need for simplicity in Christian music and was keen to meet the challenge. In 1879 he wrote to Ignaz Traumihler, a choirmaster and supporter of Cecilian ideals, to whom he had just dedicated his motet *Os Justi:*

I should be very pleased if you found pleasure in the piece. It is written without sharps or flats, without the chord of the seventh, without a six-four chord [a three-note chord with its fifth in the bass] and without chordal combinations of four and five simultaneous notes.[13]

The Cecilian Movement published a *Pange Lingua* of Bruckner's, but autocratically and shortsightedly Witt censored some of its most poignant moments, an act which confirmed Bruckner's fears that the Society's extreme views were stifling Christian musical creativity.

Bruckner set the Ordinary of the Mass seven times, from the *Mass in C,* written when he was seventeen, to the *Mass in F minor* of 1868. Perhaps the most remarkable is the *Mass in E minor,* commissioned by the Bishop of Linz in 1866, for it avoids the usually obligatory solo singers altogether and only uses wind and brass instruments in a restrained and simple accompaniment. As in the motets, the words are the springboard for every musical idea and are never submerged by their musical surroundings. It is a rare example of how the Cecilians' ideals of a return to the 'extremely pure' Christian music of the sixteenth century could be compatible with the expressive manner of the nineteenth.

The continuity of Bruckner's music with Roman Catholic tradition is further reinforced by his respect for plainsong. His music was sung in its context and he often quoted its melodies in his own music or adapted them.

The unaccompanied motets of Austrian composer Anton Bruckner show a simplicity and a sensitivity to the words which was very different from the more grandiose compositions of some of his contemporaries.

Chapter 24

The Decline of the Lutheran Hymn

This engraving by Johann Georg Schreiber from about 1740 shows the Church of St Thomas (the Thomaskirche) with the church school alongside. The town's ability to draw good-quality musicians depended on its wealth and reputation.

In the German-speaking Lutheran Church, support for the lavish orchestral and choral music of Bach and his contemporaries had waned steadily as the nineteenth century approached. Lutheran town councils were more and more reluctant to continue to support the choir schools which were the churches' musical lifeline. The age of Pietism also heralded a backlash in the form of 'enlightened' thinking, a questioning of the fundamental tenets of Christianity. As Kant proclaimed in 1781:

Our age is the true age of criticism, to which all must be subjected.

Such attitudes led to a new emphasis on general education, alongside which the choral duties of choir schools became a nuisance. Expert choirs were run down, leaving the responsibility for the singing more with the people. This could have been a positive step, but these congregations were also left without dedicated musical leadership and the results were sometimes lamentable. Chorales were sung so slowly that 'each song of praise or thanksgiving in performance became a hymn of penitence and death'.[1]

Recovery from the poor state of Lutheran Christian music was slow. Indeed, a steady decline in church attendance precluded any return to the Church's earlier strength, for Christianity was losing its hold on people's

imagination, at parish and at diocesan level. Its music was relegated to the peripheries of cultural expression and the general public who sought some culture went instead to concert parties, to house soirées or to the opera.

Reforms

There were moves for reform, chiefly a desire to

'A Dismal Melody'

The historian Charles Burney visited the *Domkirche* in Bremen in 1772, and gives this account of the dreary and lifeless worship:

... I visited the Thomkirche or cathedral [in Bremen], belonging to the Lutherans, where I found the congregation singing a dismal melody, without the organ. When this was ended, the organist gave out the hymn tune, in the true dragging style of Sternhold and Hopkins. The instrument was large, and has a noble and well-tuned chorus, but the playing was more old-fashioned, I believe, than any thing that could have been in our country towns, during the last century. The interludes between the line[s] of the hymn were always the same.

After hearing this tune, and these interludes, repeated ten or twelve times, I went to see the town, and returning to the cathedral, two hours after, I still found the people singing all in unison, and as loud as they could, the same tune, to the same accompaniment. I went to the post-office, to make dispositions for my departure; and, rather from curiosity than the love of such music, I returned once more to this church, and, to my great astonishment, still found them, vocally and organically performing the same ditty, the duration of which seems to have exceeded that of a Scots Hymn, in the time of Charles I.[1]

It is difficult to accept that this story is not exaggerated, unless it was that several hymns were sung during the

service to the same tune. This is certainly a possibility, since the number of tunes congregations knew had very much reduced. As many as ninety hymn-texts were habitually sung to one popular tune (*Wer nur den lieben Gott*). Precentors, who often led the singing in the manner of the English parish clerk, embellished the pauses at the ends of lines with vocal ornaments. These decorations (with the slow pace of the melody) were also incorporated into the tune itself. Thus, with lack of musical (and perhaps spiritual) encouragement, many of the characteristics of English congregational singing in the eighteenth century were repeated in Germany well into the nineteenth.

This tune was noted in Charles Burney's diary to exemplify his description. As he accurately wrote: 'The interludes between the lines were all the same...' as the musical quotation shows.

return to the past and to first Lutheran principles. Logically, this required liturgies to be in German, but with unaccompanied Lutheran hymns and Gregorian chant.

The establishment in Berlin of a superb and salaried choir by King Wilhelm IV in 1843 fulfilled these Romantic ideals: it used boys and men only, they sang entirely unaccompanied and, to add to 'the distance between us and our Creator',[3] out of sight!

This move, where it was adopted elsewhere, caused much argument and trauma. It was a drastic change with which people of habit could not identify. In any case, it was only ever a compromise, as organists were unwilling to give up their central place in worship—a strict return to the mid-sixteenth century would have put a complete stop to their accompanying the congregation. Furthermore, cantors and choirs were simply not available to take an effective lead in such reforms.

Just the same, there were steady changes throughout the century. The efforts of the Cecilians to encourage unaccompanied choral singing in the Roman Church had its counterpart in the Lutheran. The music of the sixteenth-century composer Johann Eccard (1553–1611)

became popular as a German parallel to the revered Palestrina.

Church choirs were gradually re-established —though without the support of the old choir schools. A strong amateur tradition of choral music gradually evolved which still thrives today. Much of its activity was outside the routine of church worship, culminating in occasional choral festivals (*Kirchengesangfeste*), but it was bound also to have a beneficial effect on church singing.

The complexity and drama of Bach's music prevented it from playing much part in the Lutheran revival till at least half-way through the century (Mendelssohn's famous revival of Bach's *St Matthew Passion* in 1829 was not at a service, but in a concert-hall—the *Singakademie* in Berlin), but gradually Bach's organ music, chorales and last of all the cantatas began to return to Lutheran worship. Similarly, Schütz's unaccompanied music was revived at an earlier stage than his music with instruments.

By the end of the nineteenth century, a more relaxed and sympathetic attitude to the whole history of Christian music encouraged Lutheran musicians to look to anything from the past that was worshipful and excellent, even if it lay outside the traditions of their denomination.

Chapter 25

The Church of England and the Tractarians

The Church of England at the beginning of the nineteenth century reacted slowly to the desperate spiritual needs of the country at large. But it was hardly surprising. Those in high authority were simply not trained or competent to hold their offices, but still enjoyed unbelievably high salaries for being absent from their work.

The novelist Anthony Trollope memorably portrayed this 'high-and-dry' churchmanship in the character of Archbishop Grantley, a pen-portrait based on Henry Philpott, Bishop of Exeter (1778–1869). Queen Victoria was once pleased to refer to Philpott as 'that fiend, the Bishop of Exeter'.

The clamour for reform became loud in pamphlets such as *The Black Book, or Corruption Unmasked* of 1823. The Rev. John Jebb wrote a bitter exposure of the plight of the cathedrals that summarized the situation: 'The whole aspect of the Church plainly indicated the mechanical performance of a burthensome duty.'[1]

The malaise of the Anglican Church needed political as much as spiritual solutions. Parliament set up the Ecclesiastical Commissioners in 1835 which recommended that all senior cathedral posts had to be residential, limited in number and that their salaries should be reduced to release more funds for the parish clergy.

The Tractarians

These drastic changes imposed from outside were complemented by changes from within. A number of high churchmen, including John Henry Newman, John Keble and Edward Pusey expressed new ideals of integrity for the Anglican Church in a series of *Tracts for the Times*.

The first tract, by Newman, appeared in 1833 and the 90th and last (also by him) in 1841. The contents of the 90th Tract and the furore it caused led to Newman's conversion to Roman Catholicism, followed in due course by a number of others. The group have been called the 'Tractarians' or 'Puseyites' and their ideas usually termed the Oxford Movement (Keble and Pusey were Oxford professors).

The movement was the product of a Romantic age. It recommended a return to the past, to a time when the ritual and symbolic aspects of worship were fundamental. Indeed, a too-precise return to the pre-Reformation tenets of the Roman Catholic Church was the difficulty that lay behind the 90th Tract. The daily ritual of public worship, conducted in a formal and reverent fashion, was at the centre of the Tractarians' ideals for church life, just as it had been in medieval times.

At the same time the Tractarians strongly resisted the liberalism which was closing the door on a simple Christian faith. They believed firmly in the authority of the Bible and showed deep concern for individual spiritual welfare. Where they differed from the Evangelicals of the Church of England and from the dissenters was in the way they expressed those concerns.

For the Tractarians believed that (as in former times) the divinely appointed church could speak on spiritual matters with God's authority. The dissenters, on the other hand, acknowledged no authority but the Bible. The Bishop of Oxford wrote in 1840:

[The Tractarians] are forming at this moment the most remarkable movement, which, for three centuries at least, has taken place among us... The system in question, instead of being an easy comfortable form of religion, adapting itself to modern habits and luxurious

This 1852 cartoon, headed 'The Papal Invasion', conveys the hostility many felt at the practices of the Oxford Movement. The renewed Catholic emphasis of this group within the Church of England gave rise to the concern that Roman Catholicism was coming back in disguise.

tastes, is uncompromisingly stern and severe—laying the greatest stress upon self-discipline and self-denial— encouraging fasting, alms-deeds and prayer, to an extent of which the present generation, at least, know nothing—and inculcating a deference to authority which is wholly opposed to the spirit of the age.[2]

All this was symbolized by a return to the daily and timeless ritual of worship. The Tractarians took full advantage of the surviving medieval architecture by putting their choirs in the chancel with the priest, placing candelabra and symbolic silver vessels on the altar, which itself was adorned with cloths whose colours were changed with the church's year. Symbolic white robes were worn by priest, acolytes and choir, who were encouraged to process and recess before and after worship.

The choir was therefore visually associated with the priest and not with the congregation. In cathedrals, such theatrical rituals were not out of place in an architecture originally created with them in mind. But the parishioners of country churches found them disconcerting: services would sometimes be interrupted by cries of 'no popery' and even by violence. Tractarians were taken to court by fellow Christians for kneeling or prostrating themselves before the elements, for using incense or for mixing water with the wine during communion. The defection of Anglican leaders to Roman Catholicism only seemed to confirm the trend.

Nonetheless, the movement grew in influence to the point where churches were altered or newly built to a Gothic medieval plan, complete with chancel and screen, to create the English parish church of present popular imagination.

The music of the Oxford Movement

The musical consequences of the Oxford Movement were considerable. In 1841 Leeds built the first parish church whose building and worship was modelled on the cathedral tradition. Even in the country parishes there was a new desire for solemnity, in pursuit of which it was reckoned that the gallery musicians were nothing but a nuisance.

Money was raised for the purchase of organs in parish churches, many of which had probably never housed one before. Gallery musicians were almost immediately dismissed in favour of the organist, though there was often real difficulty in finding a competent player. One solution to this problem was the barrel organ:

After the construction of the organ at St Paul's Church, Walden, in 1850... a difficulty arose as to who could play it, and to get over the difficulty a dumb-organist [an automatic barrel-organ attachment] was used.[3]

After about 1850, churches unable to afford any kind of pipe organ could purchase a harmonium. They became widely used in churches and chapels throughout England and Wales. All except the rare French instruments of real quality were (and still are) hopelessly inadequate to lead congregational singing. Many are still mouldering in vestries today.

As Tractarian ideals took hold metrical psalms were gradually abandoned in England and Wales. In the reformed stronghold of Scotland, however, the singing of metrical psalms remained a deeply-ingrained national characteristic and is still a valued part of the worship of many Scottish churches today. In the remote Highlands and Islands the old style of 'lining-out' is still practised in the Free Churches (see chapter 19).

A number of alternatives were adopted in place of the metrical psalms in England. The Oxford Movement encouraged the use of Gregorian chant, but the necessity of fitting the melodies to English caused problems. Anglican chant became the solution for most parishes.

Anglican chant

Anglican chant was of course only an elaboration of Gregorian chant and had been in use since Elizabethan times in the Chapel Royal and intermittently in cathedrals. But now it was being proposed for the first time as a vehicle for corporate worship. The problem of this type of chant, unsolved to this day, is that it requires prose verses of varying length to be fitted to a musical formula that feels as if it should proceed in strict rhythm. Classical music in general creates a very clear association of chord progressions with a regular beat.

As no Western music asks for chordal progression to be set to an irregular or haphazard rhythm, to ask a humble congregation to perform the task is to require the unnatural, if not the impossible. Expert choirs can overcome the problem with rigorous training, but having arrived at perfection, they become indignant if the congregation starts to sing with them and spoil their efforts.

Other chants were eagerly revived, such as Merbecke's, (see chapter 12) but now accompanied by organ. The versicles and responses which open Morning and Evening Prayer were harmonized, as might be the intoning of the Lord's Prayer and the Creed.

Cathedral music

The composers of Anglican cathedral music were specialists, that is, they were not generally known for their compositions outside Christian liturgy. Almost all of them were deeply involved in the life of the Church, mostly as organists and choirmasters. They became excellent at providing what the casual listener would recognize as 'sacred music', but little of their work would stand up to critical listening today.

Thomas Attwood (1765–1838) was in an unusual position. He had the enviable status of having been one of Mozart's favourite pupils. On his return from study in Vienna in 1787 he was able to move into high musical circles, finally being appointed organist of St Paul's Cathedral and composer to the Chapel Royal. But even a Mozart can only stimulate and direct if his pupil has imagination. Attwood is best remembered for pieces that did not demand of him a sustained creative effort, miniatures such as *Turn thy face from my sins* or *Enter not into judgement*.

Attwood was one of the few composers of Christian music to have contact with the musical profession outside the Church. Through the rest of the century and among his successors Christian music became a closed world: John Goss (1800–80) and T.A. Walmisley (1814–56) were pupils of Attwood, J.B. Dykes (1823–76) was a pupil of Walmisley and all three worked exclusively in cathedral surroundings.

The reward of these hardworking men was to see a steady improvement in the standards of cathedral music. In turn this set an example to parish church choirs who were encouraged to emulate the musical world of the cathedral through diocesan choral festivals, the first of which was held in Lichfield Cathedral in 1865.

Some of these musicians made special contributions which easily overshadow their composing talent. Sir Frederick Ouseley (1825–89) used his considerable means to found and to staff the Church and College of St Michael at Tenbury. Its purpose was to set an example to the Anglican world at large of what could and should be done in the training of church musicians and in the reverent performance of cathedral music. John Stainer (1840–1901) was one of the first organists appointed to Tenbury (at the age of seventeen!) and his tireless work for the same cause eventually took him to St Paul's Cathedral and a knighthood.

These are only a few of the musicians whose

names still appear regularly on the service sheets of English cathedrals. Little of their music is worthy of the place it occupies today. A few pieces deserve attention simply because they are excellent, and others are sung because of their local connections. The settings of the *Magnificat and Nunc Dimittis in D minor* by Walmisley are impressive because they avoid some of the distressing general weaknesses of this music, as do some of the works of S.S. Wesley (a grandson of Charles Wesley).

As parish church choirs strengthened, cathedral works were used as yardsticks by which to measure the creation of simple and accessible music for local choirs. A huge market for anthems and canticle settings developed, fed by the ease and speed with which music could be printed. The dusty cupboards of churches and chapels throughout England and Wales are still full of mouldering copies of this musical doggerel, composed to fill a need as quickly as possible by composers of poor talent.

Tradition encourages a diminishing number of choirs to sing this music today and even to exhume some, such as J.H. Maunder's *Olivet to Calvary*. One piece, Stainer's *Crucifixion,* has never been forgotten. It is not even liturgical music, strictly speaking, but it has been used so often as an occasion for Christian contemplation that it should be considered as such. What is most remarkable is its perennial staying-power. It has been spectacularly criticized:

Sparrow-Simpson's appalling doggerel set to Stainer's squalid music is a monument to the inane. It is almost frightening that such a piece should remain so popular since it proves that most people will accept whatever they hear in church quite uncritically; indeed, they regard criticism as a form of sacrilege.[4]

The piece indicates the extent to which some church music fell short of Tractarian ideals of excellence and solemnity. Stainer regretted having written it.

HYMNS

Alongside the enormous quantities of anthem-books, canticle settings and oratorios produced for the parish church choir were equally vast quantities of hymns for the congregations. They formed important focal points in worship for Anglicans and non-conformists alike, and were shared by many denominations. While both tunes and words of many hymns were instantly forgettable (Henry Gauntlett, who wrote the tune to *Once in Royal David's City* wrote 10,000 others) a very few of them have a rightly valued place in the spiritual life of almost every English-speaking Christian.

By far the most influential hymn-book of the English-speaking world was *Hymns Ancient and Modern* published in 1861: 60 million copies had been sold by the end of the nineteenth century. The title is significant, for it reflects the Tractarians' respect for the past. One of the striking features of the collection was the inclusion of medieval Latin hymns and sequences, many translated with great imagination by J.M. Neale.

The Tractarians themselves contributed— John Keble *(Blest are the pure in heart)* and John Henry Newman *(Praise to the Holiest in the Height* and *Lead Kindly Light)* among many others.

One of the intentions behind *Hymns Ancient and Modern* was to create a collection suitable for occasions throughout the church year. Modern tunes for these new hymns were obviously plentiful, but the immense popularity of the book married tunes to words much more firmly than in the past, partnerships which in many cases are indissoluble even today (such as Sullivan's ghastly tune St Gertrude set to *Onward Christian Soldiers* or Dykes' sublime melody Nicaea to *Holy, holy, holy)*.

The Demise of the
West Gallery Players

As the Oxford Movement began to influence churches throughout England, the traditional west gallery players in country churches found themselves ousted by the 'new-fangled' organ—or a harmonium, or even a barrel organ.

Here, in Thomas Hardy's *Under the Greenwood Tree*, the west gallery players are expressing their views:[1]

'... But I don't care who hears me say it, nothing will spak to your heart wi' the sweetness o' the man of strings!'

'Strings for ever!' said little Jimmy.

'Strings alone would have held their ground against all the new comers in creation.' ('True, true!' said Bowman.) 'But clar'nets was death.' ('Death they was!' said Mr Penny.) 'And harmonions,' William continued in a louder voice, and getting excited by these signs of approval, 'harmonions and barels'organs' ('Ah!' and groans from Spinks) 'be miserable—what shall I call 'em?—miserable—'

'Sinners,' suggested Jimmy ...

'Miserable dumbledores!'

'Right, William, and so they be—miserable dumbledores!' said the whole choir with unanimity.

Chapter 26

Revival in the Nineteenth Century

D.L. Moody *(top)* and Ira Sankey *(bottom)*, the late-nineteenth century American evangelist and his director of music who published the famous 'Moody and Sankey' hymns. The title of the collection was 'Sacred Songs and Solos', and their style has influenced mission hymns ever since.

Hand in hand with North America, Britain experienced further spiritual awakening in the mid-nineteenth century. On both sides of the Atlantic the Christian gospel was proclaimed by evangelists to the huge populations of the urban areas and there were conversions by the thousand.

The meetings took place in tents, halls and in the open air as much as in churches and chapels. It was gospel songs that had the ability to reach large numbers powerfully and effectively with a simple message. The melodies were instantly memorable, their sentiments direct and their effect strong and immediate:

There is no reasoning, nor are the lines made heavy with introspection. 'Tell the story simply, as to a little child.' The feelings are touched; the stiffest of us become children again.[1]

These songs sprang partly from the increase during the century of Sunday School training amongst children and the establishment in 1844 of the Young Men's Christian Association.

Sankey and Moody

Following their first visit to England in 1872, Ira D. Sankey (formally a YMCA worker in America) and Dwight L. Moody published a pamphlet of the songs associated with their missions called *Sacred Songs and Solos.* It was expanded constantly in the following years—by 1903 it contained 1,200 items. Its sales in Britain

matched those of *Hymns Ancient and Modern* (80 million by the 1950s) and are indicative of the powerful influence of the American Evangelical movement of the time. Moody and Sankey even persuaded some Scots to reconsider the musical habits of several lifetimes. As a professor of the Free Church College in Edinburgh commented:

It is amusing to observe how entirely the latent distrust of Mr. Sankey's 'kist o'whistles' [chest of whistles, that is, an organ] has disappeared. There are different ways of using an organ. There are organs in some churches for mere display, as someone has said, 'with a devil in every pipe,' but a small harmonium designed to keep a tune right is a different matter, and is seen to be no hindrance to the devout and spiritual worship of God.[2]

The team-work of preacher (Moody) with song-leader and soloist alongside (Sankey) proved highly effective and is still being repeated to this day.

The Salvation Army

When the Salvation Army first came into being in 1878 (following a number of years' work as the Christian Mission) it followed the same pattern. Its priorities in Christian music were typical of the evangelists of the time, its first *Orders and Regulations for Field Officers* stating that, in song:

One voice alone is always much to be preferred ... because the words can be heard with so much greater distinctiveness.[3]

As the founder of the Salvation Army, General William Booth, recommended:

Let us have a real tune, that is, a melody with some distinct air in it, that one can take hold of, which people can learn, nay which makes them learn it, which takes hold of them and goes on humming in the mind ... That is the sort of tune to help you; it will preach to you, and bring you believers and converts.[4]

Booth looked on choirs with suspicion:

Merely professional music is always a curse and should you ever find a choir in

William Booth, founder of The Salvation Army, with his son and successor Bramwell. Booth used music to set the tone for his Army—rousing melodies with a martial flavour. He is credited with the famous question: 'Why should the devil have all the best tunes?'

Moody preaches to a great audience at the Agricultural Hall in Islington, London. Sankey sits at a desk beside him. Sankey's songs were geared to drawing such large numbers into the emotion of the meeting.

The music, the uniforms, the whole style of their organization—these Salvation Army cadets had been called to a campaign, to devote their lives to a serious battle to rescue people from the evils of society. The girls were popularly known as 'Hallelujah Lassies'.

connection with any hall or mission, I give you my authority to take a besom and sweep it out, promising that you do so as lovingly as possible.[5]

The fear that choirs 'confine the singing to the few, instead of making it the servant of many' kept the soloist as the sole musical leader in Salvation Army meetings till the turn of the century when the Songster Brigades developed.

The frank emotionalism of these songs and their imitation or borrowing of secular pop music for their purposes was offensive to more aesthetically-minded observers. It even caused some hesitation amongst evangelicals. But General Booth was certain of his ground:

Music is to the soul what wind is to the ship, blowing her onwards in the direction in which she is steered... Not allowed to sing that tune or this tune? Indeed! Secular music, do you say? Belongs to the devil, does it? Well, if it did, I would plunder him of it... Every note and every strain and every harmony is divine and belongs to us.[6]

The wholesale exchange of popular music between Britain and America had a profound effect on gospel song in Britain. Stephen Foster's songs served the Salvation Army well: 'Poor old Uncle Ned' became 'O what battles I've been in' and 'Poor old Joe' was transformed into 'Gone are the days of wretchedness and sin'. This is no more nor less than the principle of *contrafacta,* or text substitutions, common at many points in Christian history.

Chapter 27

The Path Divides

During the nineteenth century a problem which had beset Christian music for centuries came to a crisis. The rhetorical and forward-looking art-music of the eighteenth century had profane associations that proved too much for many Christians to tolerate.

Its most characteristic form, opera, was peopled with characters who generally made decisions about their behaviour and their relationships without reference to God or to the church's moral teaching. The clergy were therefore uneasy at the reappearance in the liturgy of this tainted secular music and enthusiastically supported the Cecilians and others in their efforts to oust such modernity. Their partial success led to a widening rift between the musical idioms of the concert hall and of the church. A writer of the time observed

the result, that Christian music became:

> **the handmaid of religion, and no longer an art which soared free, breathing alike the joys and sorrows of men, but an art which sought to shadow forth that heavenly calm which exists beyond the fever and fret of human life.**[1]

A composer's natural inclination to write for the church on the one hand and his identity as a modern and highly trained musician on the other were therefore set on a collision course. The Victorian composer Joseph Barnby (1838–96) experienced the dilemma keenly when writing Christian music:

> **You may imitate and plagiarise the old**

Pre-Raphaelite artist Edward Burne-Jones painted this diptych of choristers and musicians at the time when the Tractarian movement was gaining influence in the Church of England. The atmosphere is of timeless transcendence, evoking an unspecified age in the past, half way to heaven. His painting fits well with a ritualistic worship and a nostalgia for earlier music and liturgies.

tunes to an extent, and in all probability you will be spoken of as one who is 'thoroughly imbued with the truly devotional spirit of the old ecclesiastical writers', but you are not permitted on any account to give your natural feelings fair play; or, in short, to write spontaneously.[2]

The church's loss of contact with art-music in the nineteenth century had serious consequences for compositional standards in the Christian music of city churches and cathedrals across Europe, whether Roman Catholic, Lutheran or Anglican. Recovery from some very low points was slowed by the cartel of the cathedral organ-loft, protecting its members like a cocoon from the concerns of professional music outside.

The influence of the Tractarians

An apparent solution was offered by the Tractarians, who led the Anglicans' rediscovery of the potency of symbols in worship. The visual focus of the altar, the symbol of the cross, the priestly garments and a hundred other details all conveyed messages about the nature of worship and about the relationships of the people involved—priest, choir and congregation.

It seemed as though worship that encouraged a personal and individual response (expressed through rhetoric) was giving way once more to contemplation of universal truths (expressed through symbols). But Western culture at large was no longer medieval, no longer grounded in a profound sense of God as sustainer and synchronizer of the cosmos. In an age of industrial and social revolution the restoration of symbols could not bring back these old certainties.

The balance between the past and the present created by the Tractarians was therefore an uneasy one. In music the desire to restore the symbolic and contemplative elements was uncomfortably overridden by modern rhetorical expectations. Anglican chant makes the point. In its constant repetition of the same melody for every psalm-verse its contribution is ritualistic and impersonal, like the Gregorian psalm-tones of the Middle Ages.

The music seemed to offer the ancient and simple benefits of emphasizing the parallelism of the Hebrew text and symbolizing the unity of all believers through a song common to all. But Anglican chant contributes an additional element: it uses the powerful and rhetorical tool of harmony. Its chord progressions carry a much more modern and very different message from the unison of the plainsong chant, for they are the essential vehicle for emotional expression.

It is therefore contradictory to attempt to convey the narrative of a psalm, with its dramatic emotional contrasts, by the same rhetorical messages incessantly repeated in the music. Changing the chant in mid-psalm or the organist's changes of registration (full swell for the 'bulls of Bashan', fanfare of trumpets for 'the Lord strong and mighty') are only crude attempts to improve the expression of a psalm's emotional content. In spite of such machinations the problem remains—the music masquerades as a symbol while its true nature is rhetorical or emotional.

In all this the losers were—and to a certain extent, still are—the established Churches. Their traditions of musical excellence were deprived of the stimulus of truly inventive minds by the Churches' rejection of full-blooded Romanticism. What Christians were left with was a diluted and anodyne modern music which gained diminishing respect and attention from the educated public.

The evangelical Churches had no such difficulties. For them, music was a means of emotional persuasion like the sermon—its artistic excellence was less important. The straightforward musical rhetoric shown by the march, the drawing-room ballad and the music-hall song was already part of popular culture and evangelical Churches did not hestitate to adapt it to the Christian cause.

It is these Churches, such as the Salvation Army or the Elim Pentecostals, which were able to express their faith in music of spontaneity and enthusiasm. The striking contrast between their confidence on the one hand and the unease of the established Churches in allowing serious composers to 'write spontaneously' on the other is equally evident today.

PART FIVE

Eastern Traditions

Chapter 28

The Orthodox Churches

It is impossible not to be profoundly moved by the liturgy of our own Orthodox Church. I also love vespers. To stand on a Saturday evening in the twilight in some little country church, filled with the smoke of incense; to lose oneself in the eternal questions, whence, why and whither; to be startled from one's trance by a burst from the choir; to be carried away by the poetry of this music; to be thrilled with quiet rapture when the Royal Gates of the Iconostasis are flung open and the words ring out, 'Praise the Name of the Lord!'—all this is infinitely precious to me! One of my deepest joys![1]

So wrote Tchaikovsky in 1877. To enter an Orthodox church, to experience its music, is to enter another world. The Orthodox have a long and sometimes turbulent history, full of divisions and schisms, yet their music has a timeless quality and a changeless beauty.

Constantine and Christianity

It was the new status of Christianity as a state religion in the fourth century that first caused serious problems. The conversion of the Emperor Constantine and the spread of Christianity as a 'state religion' throughout the Roman Empire brought into focus issues of doctrine and uniformity. This led to the setting up of the Council of Nicaea (325), and further councils in the fourth and fifth centuries, eventually leading to the division of the Roman Church from the Orthodox.

Following the Emperor Constantine's adoption of Byzantium as the centre of his new Christian empire (he renamed the city Constantinople) the city quickly became the centre of Orthodox Christianity. Relations with neighbouring Armenia (whose king Tiridates III was converted to Christianity even earlier than Constantine, in 301) were good until the Chalcedon Council of 451, to which the Armenians were unable to send representatives. The Armenians disagreed with the decisions made in their absence and were thereafter branded as heretic by the Orthodox bishops. The same Council failed to reconcile the Coptic and Ethiopian Churches to orthodoxy and they also broke away.

The five patriarchs

By the fifth century authority in the Christian world was in the hands of five Patriarchs whose centres were Rome, Constantinople, Alexandria, Antioch and Jerusalem. Their jurisdiction extended to numerous districts presided over by Metropolitans. The intention was for the Patriarchs' authority to be equal, but the constant rivalry between them strengthened their frontiers, particularly between East and West. Through the turbulence in the East—the many divisions and sects, the adherence to heresy—Rome, by contrast, proved to be a centre of some stability, to whom other Patriarchs could appeal for dispassionate advice over local disagreements.

The patriarchs of Rome grew ever more aware of the importance of their apostolic succession through St Peter and believed more and more in the additional authority that this gave them over the other patriarchies. This supremacy was eventually claimed to be absolute and has never been recognized by the East.

The saddest aspect of this most serious division is the issue that lay at its heart. As before at the earlier Councils, it was a question of creed. John's Gospel states that the Holy Spirit, the third member of the Trinity, 'comes from the Father'. Western Christians were required to accept a creed which stated that the Holy Spirit proceeds from the Father 'and the Son' *(filioque)*. On this

Christian sites from the Muslims. In the First Crusade of 1095, a Christian army from the West wrested control of Jerusalem from the Muslims after great bloodshed in 1099. But the Fourth Crusade (1202–04) was disastrously directed against Constantinople—Western Christian fighting Eastern Christian. During Holy Week of 1204, Constantinople was sacked and looted by a Christian European army. Many of the spoils found their way back to Europe, where they

difference and the question of authority was built a controversy which finally (in 1054) became the chief justification of a permanent schism between the Church of Rome and the Churches of the East.

The Crusades

The incessant arguments over doctrinal matters may seem trivial, but they had very real consequences in the appalling suffering of the common people caught up with one faction or another.

The Crusades proved to be a further disaster both to the credibility and unity of the Christian faith. They began both as pilgrimages and holy wars, bent on rescuing the most precious

contributed to the fabulous wealth of such cities as Venice.

Although the reunion of East and West was discussed again, the Eastern Church was too exasperated by the forcible occupation of Constantinople to be able to negotiate.

Such carnage, based ultimately on greed, turned the gospel on its head.

The strength of Orthodoxy

Constantinople was restored as the centre of Eastern Christendom and the Byzantine Empire in 1261, but it was much weakened and gradually gave way to the Turks over the next two centuries. During the fourteenth century the

The split between Eastern and Western Christianity, which became final at the Great Schism of 1054, gained emotional intensity in the time of the Crusades. During the Fourth Crusade Byzantium was sacked, and Orthodox Christianity suffered a blow from which it never had a chance fully to recover.

emperor unsuccessfully implored the assistance of the West, hoping that the offer of reunion with Rome could be exchanged for the Western Church's help. Nothing was forthcoming. The gradual decline of the Byzantine Empire led eventually to the conquest of Constantinople by the Turks in 1453.

Curiously enough, the downfall of Constantinople temporarily increased the authority of the Orthodox Church under its patriarch, for the Turks who now ruled allowed them freedom to worship, if not to make converts or to display Christian symbols (like the cross) on their churches. And the Turks naturally identified religious leadership with national identity.

Under these conditions the patriarchs of Constantinople retained—and even gained—power and respect. But on the other hand they lived through five centuries of Turkish rule which proved to be perilous. Many patriarchs were driven from their thrones by the Turks, some abdicated, some were murdered. But the Christians clung to the faith with remarkable tenacity through their example and through the pastoral care of the country priests.

The people of the Orthodox Church have also had the advantage of a liturgy which has

St Basil's Cathedral, in Red Square, Moscow. Despite seventy years of Marxist repression, the Russian Orthodox church remained the most numerous of the Orthodox family of churches. Since communism's demise, many Russians have revealed a revitalized interest in Orthodox Christianity.

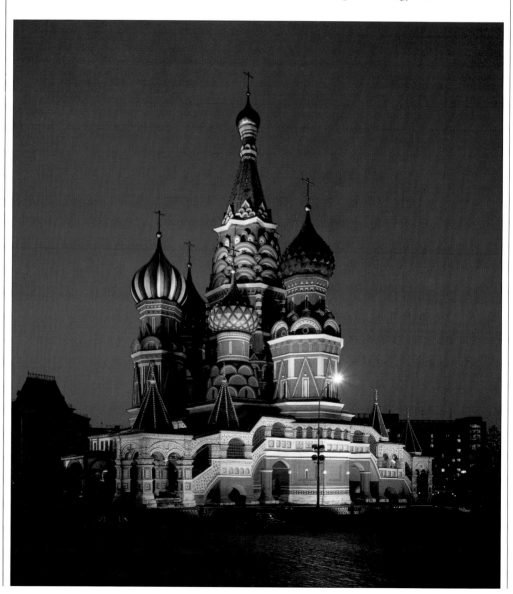

remained in a language well understood by them and of a Church in which they feel truly at home.

Orthodoxy today

Of the four ancient Orthodox patriarchies, only that of Constantinople has been discussed so far. But the other three, established at the very beginnings of the Christian faith, are still in existence, though their sphere of influence is not what it once was. The Orthodox Patriarchy of Alexandria (established by St Mark) is now small (perhaps 250,000) as most Christians in Egypt are members of the independent Coptic Church. The region of this Patriarchy also covers countries like Saudi Arabia and Libya which are nowadays almost wholly Muslim.

Antioch at the time of its conversion was an immensely important centre, politically and economically. Its Patriarchy was established at a very early stage in Christian history (earlier than AD45) but down the ages Christians in the region have become independent (such as the Church of Cyprus) or heretical (such as the Jacobites and Nestorians). Many Christians in the region are now Uniate (that is, they owe their allegiance to Rome). All this has eroded the influence of Antioch as a centre of Orthodoxy.

Jerusalem is such a vital and emotive centre for Jews, Christians and Muslims that its Orthodox Patriarchy has inevitably seen great turbulence. This is the Church whose traditions Egeria described at the start of the fifth century (see Box: *Worship in fifth-century Jerusalem* in Chapter 3). Even then the city was a centre of pilgrimage for many faiths and the Church in Jerusalem has striven to keep the peace under these most difficult circumstances.

The Orthodox Church also consists of a number of other branches, all of whom are now independent, though they use a very similar liturgy in their appropriate languages. The Church of Cyprus became independent in 431, the Church of Russia in 1589. Greece remained under Turkish rule with only one interruption (1684–1718) from the fifteenth century to the nineteenth. Modern Greece came into being in 1829, following the defeat of the Turks by Britain, France and Russia in the naval battle of Navarino. Shortly after, in 1833, the independent Orthodox Church of Greece was created, with its Metropolitan in Athens. In the later nineteenth century the Orthodox Churches of Bulgaria, Yugoslavia and Romania also became independent.

Worship in the Orthodox Church

Orthodox Christians have rich and varied musical traditions, which retain a sense of identity through the ancient liturgy.

Art historians have worked hard to introduce the West to the visual glories of Byzantine civilization. Looking at the richness of expression, it seems reasonable to suppose that the musical traditions of the Byzantine Empire must have been equally impressive.

Western traditions of early Christian music and especially those of its chant have been well documented and researched. Now the ancient Byzantine music is being studied as avidly as Western chant was a century ago. But the present-day music of the Orthodox Church is its living relative and it is not hard to find a church in most countries where the traditional music of the Orthodox liturgy is sung.

In most Christian denominations, the style of worship varies according to the type of church and local tradition. Anglican churches, for instance, may be 'high' or 'low' and resources in a cathedral differ greatly from those of a small parish church. To some degree the same is true of Orthodox churches. A monastery on Mount Athos in Greece will express the full musical heritage of the Orthodox traditions in services lasting many hours, whereas a small village church will not even be able to boast a choir. But the sense of tradition within the Eastern Churches generally is so strong that there is a close relationship between the worship of any of its member churches that is rare in the West.

To enter an Orthodox church is to be aware of a long-established and revered tradition of worship. It is a place apart. The building itself is often in the shape of a cross surmounted by a dome, creating a broad open space, the inside of which at first gives no obvious focus of attention. But however plain the exterior, the interior is richly decorated with carvings, frescoes and ikons.

Ikons may not necessarily be old, but they have been created by artists working within strict confines laid down by tradition and informed by a precise understanding of their nature. They are not religious paintings so much as 'prayers enshrined in painted wood'. Two of the ikons most prominently displayed will be to the saint after whom the church is named and to the saint who is being honoured at that particular feast, depending on the time of year.

One of the first acts of a Christian entering an Orthodox church may be to place a lighted candle in a stand, either in prayer for the living or in memory of the dead. There are few chairs in the church—most of the congregation will stand while much of the service is conducted by the priest or priests in the chancel, behind the *ikonostasis* (a word literally meaning 'picture-stand').

There are sensory experiences of all kinds: the light of candles, the rich colour of the frescoes, ikons and vestments, the scent of incense, the taste of the bread and wine perhaps, and the sound of the chant. All these are part of a worship which intends to bring heaven to earth and in which all bodily senses are caught up in a corporate and joyful experience of the love of God.

It is important not to judge these essential features of Orthodox worship by Western standards. The deep interest in ritual might, for instance, suggest an authoritarian attitude to the congregation; or that the Church exerts discipline on its congregations through its clergy; or that its firm and unerring commitment to tradition means a rigidity of thinking. In reality these are false conclusions.

Instead, the ritual and symbols encourage the worshipper to be aware not only of celebrating God's presence with the congregation, but also of the closeness of heaven (right above in the vault of the dome), of the availability of salvation (through the open doors to the chancel) and of the presence of the saints of the Church (depicted in the ikons, which are often greeted by a kiss on first entering the building).

It is vital to understand the unique place that art—and especially music—occupies here. Unlike Western Christianity today which is seeking to absorb back into the church idioms and styles in the arts which have long developed an independent life in the world outside its walls, Eastern Christians have their own unique traditions which are largely self-sustaining.

In the world of art, for example, the use of symbols in the paintings of ikons is strictly controlled, along with aspects of their design and the techniques used to create them. Orthodox Christian art sprang directly from the contemporary practice of the Middle East in the early years of the Christian church (though with important changes of emphasis) and gradually parted company with the changing fashions of secular life.

The arts of the Orthodox Churches are therefore not just a precious window onto the past, but at the same time an essential element of the Eastern Church's present-day worship. There is none of the turbulence and questioning that surround art (and particularly music) in the Christian worship of the West.

An Orthodox ceremony in a convent in Estonia shows how rich and ornate the trappings of liturgy often are. The music, too, is intensely beautiful and completely distinctive.

Chapter 29

The Greek Orthodox Church

Music is uniquely integrated into the worshipping traditions of the Eastern Churches. In the Orthodox Churches music and liturgy are interdependent. In well-endowed churches the singing is by choirs, or by the priest and people in a humble village church. Following the injunctions of the Church Fathers, musical instruments have never been accepted. The sound of the human voice raised in song is central. As Basil the Great wrote as far back as the fourth century:

A psalm is tranquillity of soul and the arbitration of peace; it settles one's tumultuous and seething thoughts... A psalm creates friendships, unites the separated and reconciles those at enmity. Who can still consider one to be a foe with whom one utters the same prayer to God! Thus psalmody provides the greatest of all goods, charity, by... joining together the people into the concord of a single chorus.[1]

The church year and its fasts, feasts and celebrations dominates national and home life in a way that is difficult for the Westerner to appreciate:

Nobody who has lived and worshipped amongst Greek Christians for any length of time but has sensed in some measure the extraordinary hold which the recurring cycle of the Church's liturgy has upon the piety of the common people. Nobody who has kept the Great Lent... who has shared in the fast which lies heavy on the nation for forty days... who has known the desolation of the holy and great Friday, when every bell in Greece tolls its lament and the body of the Saviour lies shrouded in flowers in all the village churches... who has been present at the kindling of the new fire and tasted the joy of a world released from the bondage of sin and death—none can have lived through this and not have realised that for the Greek Christian the Gospel is inseparably linked with the liturgy that is unfolded week by week in his parish church.[2]

Monastic traditions of worship are very strong in the East and the twenty monastic foundations on Mount Athos in Greece form its cornerstone. For them, life is governed by Daily Offices similar to those of the Western monastic tradition, but for churches in towns and villages only extracts from the full monastic liturgy are celebrated. The most important of these is the Divine Liturgy

A Greek Orthodox church in Cyprus dates to the twelfth century. Greek Christianity is in direct continuity with the Eastern church of Byzantium, the greatest culture and civilisation of the Middle Ages.

(that is, Mass or Communion), the central act of worship on Sundays and feast days, and the people do not receive communion without initial preparation and fasting.

The Divine Liturgy

There are three liturgies used by the Orthodox Churches today. The Liturgy of St John Chrysostom is in common use throughout the year; the Liturgy of St Basil is rather more elaborate and is used only on Christmas Eve and at Epiphany; the Liturgy of St James (the oldest of the three) is heard only rarely.

The Divine Liturgy of the Orthodox Church follows the pattern of worship that has changed little in 1,500 years. It may be interesting to compare the outline given in the box with that of Egeria's experience of Mass in fifth-century Jerusalem and the outline of the later Roman Mass.

It cannot be stressed enough how important a role music plays in the liturgy. Apart from the sermon, the silent prayers and perhaps the creed, everything is sung.

Chanting

The simplest type of chanting can be heard in the scripture readings, declaimed to a single note with deviations related to the punctuation, in a manner already described (see the music of the synagogue and the Roman Church in chapters 2 and 4). Between about the eighth and thirteenth centuries a simple but unique method was used to indicate the way in which the pitch of the reader's voice had to be raised or lowered. This *ekphonetic* (exclamatory) notation consisted of signs written above the beginnings and endings of sentences, although their meanings are still not completely understood. Today ekphonetic notations are still used in some Eastern Churches and in the Jewish synagogue.

The psalms used in the Divine Liturgy and those which also form the backbone of the Daily Office, are sung to chants belonging to one of eight modes. These modes are similar to those of Western medieval music, being scale-systems whose finals (like key-notes) are the notes D, E, F and G.

Psalm-singing is elaborated to a similar degree to Western chant. More interestingly, the eight modes are incorporated into the church's year.

For symbolic reasons buried in antiquity the modes of Byzantine chant are governed by an eight-weekly cycle, the eight modes being changed Sunday by Sunday until the cycle is begun afresh. The systematic organization of all chants into the eight modes is called the *oktoechos*.

Perhaps the most interesting feature of the modes is the tendency of music written in any one mode to develop a unique character through the use of stock melodic ideas or formulae, a practice known as centonization. This is a feature of many types of music which are created aurally rather than composed on paper.

There is evidence of centonization in Gregorian chant and it is an essential part of

Indian classical music, where a *rag* is given its character not just by the notes of the scales used, but by the melodic ideas used as the basis for improvisation. African master-drumming is based on the same principle and it is inherent in contemporary jazz.

The interior of a church on the Greek island of Aegina. The church, its liturgy and its rituals hold a stronger place in ordinary Greek life than most Western Europeans can appreciate.

Hymns

One of the most striking musical features of Orthodox worship must be its hymns, which have been composed in huge numbers from the fourth century onwards. One compilation lists at least 60,000.[3] Byzantine hymns have traditional structures which all have their proper place in the liturgy.

The simplest hymns are one verse long and called *troparia* (singular *troparion*). Originally these were short poetic prayers inserted between the verses of a psalm and set to simple music easily memorized by a congregation.

Kontakia are much more extended hymns,

being built up of many verses—it might be thirty or more. They are based on a number of traditional patterns (called *hirmoi*) which govern the numbers of lines for each verse and the number of syllables and their stresses in each line. The beginning letters of each verse make an acrostic which may spell out the name of the author, or the day and feast for which the *kontakion* was intended or perhaps the musical mode to which it was sung. Each verse has a short refrain suitable for participation by choir or congregation. Many *kontakia* were composed by Romanus in the sixth century.

Kanones became the most complex of all Byzantine hymns and replaced *kontakia* around the eighth century. In full they consist of nine

A Greek Orthodox Easter service. While the congregation 'hear' the liturgy, many will practise their own acts of devotion, kissing icons and lighting candles to symbolize particular prayers.

sections (called odes), the subject of each being based on nine biblical songs:

◆ *Exodus 15:1–19*

◆ *Deuteronomy 32:1–43*

◆ *1 Samuel 2:1–10*

◆ *Isaiah 26:9–19*

◆ *Daniel 3:26–45 and 52–56 (including the deuterocanonical section)*

◆ *Daniel 3:57–88 (ditto)*

◆ *Jonah 2:3–10*

◆ *Habakkuk 3:2–19*

◆ *Luke 1:46–55 (Magnificat)*

◆ *Luke 1:68–79 (Benedictus)*

As with the *kontakia,* the odes consist of a verse from a traditional source (the *hirmos*) followed by a number of *troparia* modelled on it.

Each ode is sung to a different melody. In practice, *kanones* in their full form are very long and are only heard nowadays at the important yearly feasts and then only in monasteries and cathedrals. They are sung during the Morning Office and split into three parts (odes 1 and 3, 4 to 6 and 7 to 9).[4] Between these parts are inserted hymns and a reading. Usually *kanones* are drastically shortened so that only the initial *hirmoi* are sung.

Stichera were a later development of the *troparia*—hymns sung after a verse of a psalm. In this respect they are similar to Western antiphons. They are divided into different categories according to their subject and the feast for which they are appropriate.

In the last few centuries of the Byzantine Empire, expert singers and composers—*maistores*—developed a highly elaborate style of *kalophonic* singing, 'beautifying' the already elaborate chant. The names and compositions of these *maistores* are known today, Joannes Koukouzeles (about 1280–1370) being the most revered (he is a saint of the Greek Orthodox Church). This unique singing tradition even had a competitive element, *maistores* rivalling each other in their spectacular elaborations of a given text. The *kalophonic* tradition lasted until the nineteenth century, when Chrysanthos of Madytos revised and simplified the chant to bring it back into closer touch with the common people.

The Byzantine chant today

How is Byzantine chant performed today? The answer of course depends on where it is performed, but under no circumstances will it be heard with musical instruments. In a village church there may very well be no choir and the chanting will be undertaken by the local priest. If the priest himself is not available, a lay-reader will be able take the role of *psaltes* (cantor), for the music will be very familiar to regular church-goers.

In a few city churches in Athens it is still

The Divine Liturgy of the Orthodox Church

Divine liturgy begins with the *prothesis* (preparation), an elaborate private ceremony preparing the bread and wine. For the participants, the service begins with the *enarxis* (opening), consisting of:

◆ An opening blessing

◆ The Greater Litany
Petitionary prayers

◆ First Antiphon
Varies according to the feast-day

◆ Short litany

◆ Second Antiphon
Ends with the *troparion* 'Only-begotten Son'

◆ Short litany and concluding prayer

This is followed by the *synaxis* (assembly), originally the part of the service where the clergy entered, but now 'upstaged' by the *enarxis*. The *synaxis* parallels the Western 'liturgy of the Word' and follows a similar pattern:

◆ The Little Entrance
During this the book of the Gospels is carried to the altar

◆ Third Antiphon

◆ *Troparia* and *Kontakia*
Hymns of the day

◆ The *Trisagion*
Hymn addressing God three times as 'holy'
Followed by a silent prayer
No Old Testament reading

◆ The *Prokeimenon*
A psalm-verse and refrain which parallels the Roman Gradual

◆ The New Testament reading

◆ Psalm-verse with Alleluia

◆ The Gospel reading

◆ The Sermon
In Greece often preceding communion but in Russia usually delivered at the end of the service

◆ Litanies of fervent prayer
For the departed and for the catechumens (candidates for baptism)

The central part of the service that follows is the Eucharist, or liturgy of the faithful:

◆ Litanies of the faithful

◆ The Great Entrance
A long private prayer of the celebrant, censing of the altar, intercessions, censing offerings and placing them on the altar, all accompanied by the singing of the *Cheroubikon,* the Cherubic Hymn

◆ The Creed

◆ The *Anaphora* (offering)
The eucharistic prayer, said silently, overlaid by the choir's sung responses

◆ The *Sanctus*
The narrative of the institution of the Eucharist at the Last Supper. Sung by the priest, with concluding 'Amens' from the choir

◆ Hymn to the *Theotokos* (Mary, of whom God was born)
Sung over silent prayers commemorating saints, prayers for the departed and for the living

◆ The Breaking of the Bread
During this a hymn is sung

◆ The Communion
During the invitation of the people to communion, the choir sings verses 26–27 of Psalm 118. During communion itself, anthems are sung, followed by a further two after communion.

◆ The Conclusion
Final prayers, the Litany of Thanksgiving, dismissal and a final blessing with responses

possible to hear Byzantine chant harmonized in a manner developed in the seventeenth and eighteenth centuries, but in most monasteries and cathedrals this is not the case. Here the music will be sung in the long-established manner by two choirs standing either side of the chancel, the left-hand choir led by the *lampadarios* and right-hand by the *protopsaltes*. The right-hand choir tends to have the more skilled singers and handles more complex music, though much of the music is antiphonal, the music moving from one choir to the other and back again. Highly skilled cantors will sing the most complex chants (such as the *prokeimenon)* as solos.

In many monastic choirs (such as that of the Monastery of Saint Simon on Mount Athos) a tradition of two-part singing is preserved. In reality the second part is not melodic but consists of held notes rather like a drone, a practice dating from about the seventeenth century. The upper part keeps to the traditional chant.

The language used by the Church for its

Notation in the Greek Orthodox Church

From the tenth century onwards a comprehensive and elaborate method of writing down Byzantine chant was developed, more sophisticated than the Roman neumatic notation and with a completely different basis.

Instead of indicating pitch by placing symbols on a grid of parallel lines, the signs indicate changes of pitch from a given starting-point. The following table lists some of the more common signs in Byzantine round notation of the thirteenth century which still form the basis of choir-books in the Greek Church today:

— stay on the same note

◡ go up one note of the scale

˒ go down one note of the scale

⌣ go up two notes

⌢ go down two notes

ᖆ go down three notes

This is a simplified explanation of a system which originally indicated the way the chant should be sung with great precision. There were, for instance, at least six different ways of descending by one note indicated by six different signs. Even the notation today can instruct cantors to execute specialized inflexions of the voice known only to singers of the East.

The modern chant often has a perceptible rhythmic pulse, probably a fairly recent development. The vertical slash in the notation is the equivalent of a bar-line. Signs also show notes of twice or half the normal length (the equivalent of minims or quavers) and of more complex durations such as triplets.

The beginning of this Troparion (one-verse hymn) has been transcribed into Western notation. It comes from the first week of the Oktoechos. The final of the mode, D, is stated in the heading (in Greek, Πα). The sign above the first syllable of 'Kyrie' indicates that the tune starts one note above the final, that is, on E. The next signs tell the singer where to move relative to the previous note. Every few bars a cautionary sign appears naming the note just sung, reassuring the singer that he is still on the right track.

traditional music is the Greek of the very earliest years of Christianity, very different from modern Greek, but nonetheless understood and revered by church-goers.

The music of course has changed since its creation in those early times. How much it still resembles the music of the ancient Byzantine Empire is a difficult question which cannot be answered easily.[5] But considering the enormous time-span from their composition to modern times the correspondence between ancient manuscripts and the present-day chant is remarkable.

This thirteenth-century manuscript of Byzantine music would be fully recognizable to the Greek Orthodox Christian today. The musical notation takes the form of signs placed above the words.

Chapter 30

The Russian Orthodox Church

The history of Christianity in Russia began properly with the baptism of Vladimir, Emperor of Kiev, into the Orthodox Christian faith in 988. As did the Roman Emperor Constantine long before him, he proclaimed:

Whosoever he be, who will not come to the river tomorrow to be baptized, be he rich or poor, will fall into disgrace with me.[1]

In the following year he married the Byzantine emperor's sister, cementing a relationship with the empire at the height of its power.

The history

For some time the Metropolitans of the Russian Church were mostly Greeks appointed by the Patriarch of Constantinople and only in the fifteenth century did the Russian Church begin to make decisions for itself.

By this time, the Byzantine liturgy was firmly established with little alteration except for its translation into Slavonic, which is the language still used by the Russian Orthodox Church today.

During the period of the Tartar occupation of Russia (1240–1461) Christianity survived, for in 1272 the Tartars embraced the Islamic faith in which—like the Turks' later occupation of Byzantium—they were tolerant of Christian 'People of the Book' (the Old Testament). A century after the fall of Constantinople and the end of the Byzantine Empire, the Russians appointed their first Patriarch in Moscow in 1589.

From that time the Russian Church had to face constant difficulties. Among them was the Time of Troubles, a civil war which followed the death of the Emperor Boris Godunov in 1605. Worse, perhaps, were the failed ambitions of Nikon (Patriarch from 1652–66) for the supremacy of the Church over the state, resulting in the Great Schism and leaving the Church under the thumb of Tsarist rule.

The most recent catastrophe was the Bolshevik Revolution of 1917. The long history of the Church's allegiance to the Tsar inevitably marked it out for special treatment by the Bolsheviks, who worked hard to diminish the Church's authority as much as possible. Sadly, they were assisted by some church leaders prepared to further the Communist cause.

The Patriarch Tikhon was arrested in 1923, and determined attempts were made to undermine the Church economically (church valuables and buildings were confiscated by the state) and spiritually (monasteries were dissolved, restrictions were placed on religious gatherings, religious teaching in schools was forbidden and more than a thousand priests were martyred in the first years of the Revolution).

The Second World War gave the Communists a short-lived awareness of the Church as a useful patriotic focus, but the Khrushchev era renewed the pressures and penalties to open confession of the Christian faith. In spite of the constant oppression, the recent collapse of Communism has revealed the churches of Russia and Eastern Europe to be very much alive and rejoicing in a new-found freedom of worship.

The music of the Russian Orthodox Church

The liturgy of Russian Orthodoxy is very closely allied to that of the Byzantine Church; many of the general remarks made about the worship of Greek Orthodox Christians in the previous chapter apply equally to the Russians.

The music, however, is very noticeably different. The story that lies behind it is complicated by the loss or corruption of early chants and by the Church's current perception of traditional or 'canonical' music, as it is termed.

The ancient chant of the Russian Church, like the Greek, was written down in a notation similar in principle to the Byzantine and manuscripts go back as far as the eleventh century. From these it is clear that the chant was a single melody just like Gregorian or Byzantine chant, and to begin with (according to the scholar Preobrazhensky) the melodies were Byzantine too. The translation of the Greek liturgy into the Slavonic language and its transplantation into a different culture rapidly changed its music to something unlike any other tradition. The name given to this collection of chant was *znamenny raspev* (chanting by signs), now known simply as *znamenny*.

Although the old books still exist in great numbers, the symbols used in the notation are ambiguous and the earliest versions of these ancient melodies cannot yet be sung with accuracy. During the seventeenth century the now-familiar Western notation was brought to Russia (together with many other Western innovations) and a few of the traditional melodies were copied out. Unfortunately, the incentive at the time was for drastic reform, imposed by the Patriarch Nikon.

The changes included the adoption of a new and Western style of music, sung in a Baroque harmonic style. This so incensed a number of Christians that they annexed themselves from the Church altogether in order to continue the old traditions.[2]

Miraculously, adherents to the old way are still worshipping today and are known as the Old Believers. Their many sects are widely distributed (with representatives in Moscow) and many of them are priestless. They have also emigrated to Canada and the United States and continue their worship there.

The Old Believers are the only Christians who still sing the *znamenny* chant in anything like its true form, reading it from a notation similar to the illustration above. Another type of chant, now even less accessible than *znamenny,* was *demestvenny,* a highly decorative chant for solo voice used for special feast-days. In its elaboration it parallelled the *kalophonic* chant of the Byzantine Church.

From the seventeenth century on, Russian church music is much more akin to the West than the East. Nikolai Diletsky (about 1630–90) was a musician from Kiev who had studied in

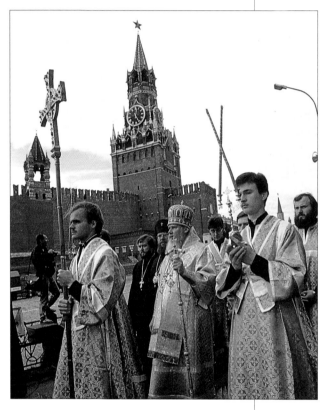

Poland (where Italian music was well known). He promoted Western styles of church music through his own compositions and text-books.

The following generation of Diletsky's pupils included Kalashnikov, who wrote sumptuous settings of texts for Vespers which he called Sacred Concertos. These are pieces for up to four choirs and in as many as twenty-four parts; their imitative effects are reminiscent of the polychoral music of Gabrieli and Monteverdi in Venice a century earlier. In such pieces all connection with the tradition of *znamenny* chant was lost.

By the close of the eighteenth century Italian

In 1990 the first Orthodox Eucharist was celebrated in Red Square during the whole time it had been called 'Red Square'. Russian Orthodoxy is set for a great revival, as people look once more for the spiritual and human dimension to life.

These two versions of ancient 'znamenny' make an interesting comparison. The lower line is taken from 'Tserkovnoje Prostopinije', 'Plainchants of the Church', published in 1906. The upper line is a transcription from the printed 'Irmologion' found in the monastery of Lviv, west of Kiev. These chant-books are almost the oldest transcribable source of 'znamenny.' The Lviv chants are quite clearly the same as those of the modern 'Prostopinije', but show the 1906 book to be a more recent tradition. No sources have been found which give more than a hazy picture of the chant of earlier centuries.

opera had been firmly established in Russia with its consequent importation of skilled and professional foreign musicians. Conversely, Russian musicians of the Court Chapel such as Berezovsky (1745–77) and Bortniansky (1751–1825) had the opportunity to study in Italy. While they did not use Italian operatic styles in their Christian music they nonetheless brought the technical skills of counterpoint and harmony to bear on it. Many of their works are settings of psalm texts and are masterpieces of concentrated economy and intensity in choral writing.

But the character of Russian church music today owes more to the nineteenth century than to any other period. It was dominated by Fyodor L'vov and his son Alexey (1798-1870 and musical director of the Court Chapel for 25 years), Pyotor Turchaninov and many others. They created the

sonorous and sometimes sentimental style of singing associated with Russian liturgical music, sometimes dubbed the 'St Petersburg style'.

The chants used in the Court Chapel were simplified and shortened versions of traditional melodies and these romantic and rhetorical harmonizations of them were published in an edition of the *Obikhod* (canticles of the Ordinary) in 1848. They were thus disseminated throughout Russia and are still the basis of Russian Orthodox music today.

It is most unfortunate that the Russian Church has come to identify its musical traditions so closely with these chants (and, even worse, with the wooden and uninspiring contributions of Bakhmetyev).

At that time Russian art-music was beginning a most exciting period of natural development, beginning with Glinka and culminating in the music of the Russian Five—Rimsky-Korsakov, Borodin, Cui, Balakirev and Mussorgsky. Tragically, none of these composers made any impact on the music of their national Church.

The difference between the sentimental harmonies of L'vov and the spectacular world of Russian symphonies and ballets must have seemed an unbridgeable gap. Only one great composer of that time made a serious and single-minded contribution to Orthodox church music, and he was taken to court for doing so.

Tchaikovsky's *Liturgy*

On 30 April 1878, Tchaikovsky wrote to his confidante Nadejda von Meck:

If the favourable mood lasts long enough, I want to do something in the way of Church music. A vast and almost untrodden field of activity lies open to composers here. I appreciate certain merits in Bortniansky, Berezovsky and others; but how little their music is in keeping with the Byzantine architecture, the ikons, and the whole spirit of the Orthodox liturgy!... It is not improbable that I shall decide to set the entire liturgy of St John Chrysostom.[3]

The Court Chapel held a monopoly on the publication of all church music (a fact that contributed greatly to its musical sterility) so, having gained approval from the Ecclesiastical Censors of his new setting of the *Liturgy of St*

1709

1906

O - braz či-sta-ho-rož dest va Tvo je - ho.

oh-ne pa-li-ma ja ku-pi-no po-ka-za ne o pal - na-ja,

i ny-ñi-na nás na-pa-stej svi-ri-pi - ju - šču-ju

u-ha-si - ti mo-lim sja pesc da Tà Bo ho - ro di-ce

ne pre-stan no ve-li - ča - jem.

John Chrysostom, Tchaikovsky published abroad. Bakhmetyev, the director of music of the Court Chapel, immediately protested and the publisher Jurgenson was taken to court. After two years, Tchaikovsky and his publisher won the case and litigation finally forced Bakhmetyev to resign.

Tchaikovsky's *Liturgy* is a work of simplicity and restraint, artistically far in advance of anything of which the Chapel composers were capable. At the same time it takes no imaginative steps outside the conventionally rhetorical world of diatonic harmony nor does anything distinctive 'in keeping with the Byzantine architecture'. Certainly Tchaikovsky used none of the old *znamenny* chant, nor showed that he was aware of its true nature.

Peter Ilyich Tchaikovsky composed a fine setting of the Liturgy of St John Chrysostom.

Rachmaninoff's *Liturgy of St John Chrysostom* and *All-Night Vigil*

Only one composer of the following generation and of similar stature to Tchaikovsky in the world of art-music made musical settings of the Orthodox liturgy—Sergei Rachmaninoff (1873-1943). This might come as a surprise, not least because his legendary reputation as a pianist and the popularity of his own music for the instrument have given a distorted impression of the breadth of his talent.

Although Rachmaninoff had expressed an interest in setting the liturgy of St John Chrysostom in 1897, it was not until 1910 that he composed his *Liturgy,* opus 31. He too, was deeply attracted to the traditions and the music of Russian Orthodox worship, a sympathy which spills over into his music for the concert hall. Like Tchaikovsky, he wanted to write music specifically for use in worship. His setting of the *Liturgy* accordingly sets all the required passages and makes due allowances for the cantillation of readings and prayers.

Like Tchaikovsky's *Liturgy,* though, the music has been ill-fated, and for similar reasons. Unaccompanied choral music lacks the dramatic rhetoric that concert-hall audiences expect and is a taste they are rarely encouraged to acquire. On the other hand, the Orthodox Church found the music too compelling, too reminiscent of opera. Early concert-hall performances of the music generated considerable enthusiasm, but for one perceptive observer of the time, the music was

absolutely wonderful, even too beautiful, but with such music it would be difficult to pray; it is not church music.[4]

Rachmaninoff seems to have recognized these unsolved (and perhaps insoluble) difficulties but was drawn once more to the liturgy, this time that of Vespers and Matins—known collectively as the *All-Night Vigil,* as they run together as a preparation for Divine Liturgy the following day. His profound respect for the old *znamenny* chant prompted him to use a number of ancient melodies as the basis for his settings and they give a unique character to the music, a flexibility that is hard to describe.

Rachmaninoff must have realized that liturgical use of his music was unlikely (it seems that the *Liturgy* was never used in worship) and perhaps wrote his *All-Night Vigil* (opus 37) more as an expression of personal faith. This puts the work (apart from extracts like *Nyne Otpushchayeshi,* the *Nunc Dimittis*) into the category of art-music. For some, its restraint effaces the composer's public identity (a hindrance to an artist in an age of individualism) and as a result its extraordinary beauties are only now beginning to be discovered.

The first performances of the *All-Night Vigil* took place in 1915, only two years before the Russian Revolution which completely overturned the world of the arts (Rachmaninoff was among many artists forced to flee to the West). As the church was forced into hiding, Christian music could no longer enjoy any creative life.

Chapter 31

The Coptic and Ethiopian Churches

The Churches of the East can be divided into three groups: first the Orthodox Churches of the four Ancient Patriarchies (Constantinople, Alexandria, Antioch and Jerusalem) already described, together with the now independent Churches still in communion with each other: Cyprus, Greece, Russia, Bulgaria, Yugoslavia and Romania. Second are the Uniate Churches, in union with the Church of Rome although following an Eastern rite. These owe their existence to Roman Catholic missionary work in the seventeenth and eighteenth centuries and are to be found in small numbers all over Eastern Europe and the Middle East, including the Melkite and Maronite Christians.

The third group of Churches are what the Orthodox Church would call heretical. That is, they broke away from the Orthodox, mostly at the time of great doctrinal struggles in about the fifth century. These are the Nestorian Church (the Church of East Syria) and the Monophysite Christians consisting of the Jacobite Church of Antioch, the Armenian Church, the Coptic Church and the Church of Ethiopia. These last two are particularly good illustrations of the wonderful riches in the Christian music of the area.

The Coptic Church

The words 'Egypt' and 'Copt' are really the same and refer to the geographical area around the Nile. The older form, Copt, has become attached to the language spoken in Egypt before Arabic became commonplace about six centuries ago. It is therefore a language that dates back, through the Bohairic dialect, to the ancient Egyptian period.

There may be as many as 7 million Coptic Christians in Egypt today, living in reasonable harmony amongst at least 40 million Muslims. Some Muslims are becoming more militant and look for an Islamic revolution as a reaction to the increasing poverty and hardship in the country. On the other hand, the Muslim and Christian communities in Egypt have lived in mutual co-operation for centuries and at present that seems set to continue.

Coptic Christians are keenly aware of their ancient ancestry. They revere the apostle Mark as the saint who established the Christian Church in Alexandria before his martyrdom there in AD68. They particularly treasure the story of Joseph and Mary's flight to Egypt with the young Jesus. Many ancient Coptic churches were built to commemorate the various resting-places of the Holy Family.

Egypt became one of the great centres of Christian monastic life from the fourth century onwards. Antony (about 251–356) is held to have been the first and finest example of a Christian following a world-renouncing life in the desert.

Many others followed. By the fifteenth century there may have been as many as 300 monasteries and nunneries in Egypt. At present there are seven, supporting some 300 monks.

When the Coptic Church separated from the Orthodox in the schism of 451, its sense of

ዘ አ መ ፡ ሐ ል የ ፡ ቅ ዱ ስ ፡ ዳ ሬ ስ ፡ ጓ ሀ ን
በ ቅ ድ መ ፡ ለ ዴ ፡ ገ ብ ረ ፡ መ አ ቀ ል ፡
ወ ል ዶ ፡ ካ ሌ ብ ፡ ን ጉ ሥ ፡ ዝ ኒ ፡ ዘ ከ ነ ፡
በ ሀ ብ ረ ፡ ጽ ዮ ን ፡
ው እ ቱ ።

This sixth-century fresco
from Tana Kirkos church in
Ethiopia is amazingly well
preserved. Below, it shows
musicians playing the
'magwamiya' (prayer stick),
'kabaro' (kettledrum) and
'sanasel' (sistrum, as found
in ancient Egypt).

161

spiritual and national identity was brought into a sharp focus which has never been lost. As a consequence, the traditions of worship have been less subject to change than in most other Eastern Churches.

A visitor to a Coptic church today is immediately aware of being put in touch with very ancient customs which words can only attempt to describe:

Perhaps nowhere in the world can you imagine yourself back in so remote an age as when you are in a Coptic Church. You go into a strange dark building; at first the European needs an effort to realise that it is a church at all, it looks so different from our usual associations... In a Coptic Church you come into low dark spaces, a labyrinth of irregular openings. There is little light from the narrow windows. Dimly you see strange rich colours and tarnished gold, all mellowed by dirt... Lamps sparkle in the gloom [and] before you is the exquisite carving, inlay and delicate patterns of the _haikal_ [chancel] screen. All around you see, dusty and confused, wonderful pieces of wood carving. Behind the screen looms the curve of the apse; on the thick columns and along the walls... are inscriptions in exquisite lettering— Coptic and Arabic.[1]

As with the Orthodox Churches, the Divine Liturgy is central to Coptic worship—even services of baptism will end with communion. The liturgy generally used is that of St Basil the Great, the liturgies of St Gregory of Nazianzus and St Mark being reserved for special occasions. There is a dramatic shape to the service which is made very evident by the involvement of everyone present. The participation is practical, too.

As in the Orthodox Church, music is an inseparable part of the liturgy and the whole service is sung from beginning to end—the music being not so much a _way_ of worshipping, but worship itself. Unlike the Orthodox however, the congregation are emotionally and vocally involved in the refrains of the litanies.

The pace of the liturgy can be very slow (depending on the priest) and the intonations have a hypnotic quality, using a very narrow range and intervals of a semitone or smaller. The responses are congregational and vocally strongly committed.

A choir, or _schola,_ will lead the singing at large gatherings. Choirs are made up of theological students, for knowledge of the music is inseparable from study of the liturgy. They accompany some chants with cymbal and triangle, a practice introduced during the Middle Ages and somewhat akin to the vocal drones of the Greek monks. The chanting is always in unison and the percussion instruments keep time with a fairly fast and syncopated beat. The _Sanctus,_ an emotional high point in the Divine Liturgy, is much enhanced by this style of accompaniment.

This very ancient liturgical music is quite different from the popular music of modern Egypt, which is often played by Western instruments such as the electric guitar and synthesizer. It can also be something of an endurance test for the younger generation—but they still attend. In Sunday School, though, there is music of a more relaxed and folk-song style. Here the children and young people sing a different collection of Christian songs, some of which may be to chants adapted from the liturgy. Instruments can be used that could never be brought into church, such as violin, flute, piano and drums. Like Middle Eastern folk-music, the melody instruments decorate and play along with the vocal melody and do not provide additional lines or harmonies.

Since most Christians attend church three times a week the liturgy and its music becomes very familiar and much treasured. It is at once one of the most ancient of all musical traditions but at the same time a vital and living force in Christian music, remarkable for its variety and richness.

The Ethiopian Church

The instruments of Musick made use of in their rites of Worship are little Drums, which they hang about their Necks, and beat with both their Hands; these are carried even by their Chief Men, and by the gravest of their Ecclesiasticks. They have sticks likewise with which they strike the Ground, accompanying the blow with a motion of their whole Bodies. They begin their Consort [that is, music-making] by Stamping their Feet on the Ground, and playing gently on their

Instruments, but when they have heated themselves by degrees, they leave off Drumming and fall to leaping, dancing, and clapping their Hands, at the same time straining their Voices to the utmost pitch, till at length they have no Regard either to the Tune, or the Pauses, and seem rather a riotous, than a religious, Assembly. For this manner of Worship they cite the Psalm of David, 'O clap your Hands, all ye Nations'.[2]

So wrote a Jesuit priest, Jerome Lobo, in 1627. By any standards, Ethiopia is an inhospitable place to live. In the last ten years or so it has been beleaguered by catastrophic famine due to repeated failures of the rains, a disastrous locust plague in 1986 followed by a malaria epidemic in 1988. The government is constantly in conflict with people fighting for independence. It is not surprising that Ethiopia is described as 'economically one of the least developed countries in the world'.

In spite of all this, it is a country of lively culture and strong spirituality, both of very long standing. The story goes that the Ethiopians adopted the Christian faith in about AD 328 as the result of the shipwreck of two Coptic Christians, Frumentius and Aedesius, on their shores. From this very early stage they have maintained strong links with the Coptic Church, siding with it in the Chalcedonian schism of 451.

The Ethiopian Church also developed a desert monastic tradition from the fifth century onwards. Many of the Ethiopian monks were highly educated and by the seventh century had translated the Bible from Syriac, Coptic and Greek into the language of Ge'ez, which is still used in the Ethiopian Church today. Like Coptic, this liturgical language is now quite different from the locally-spoken Amharic language.

In its Christian history, Ethiopia has had very little contact with the West and although it has been evangelized by Jesuits and more recently by Protestant missionaries, it is unique amongst African countries in having a Christian Church which was established before the conversion of most of Europe. That Church is strongly supported by at least 22 million members, divided amongst 20,000 parishes and led by about 250,000 priests! This represents nearly half the population, the rest being Muslims or members of traditional animist religions.

The statistics alone show a support for the Christian faith unmatched by any European country. If the number of priests suggests that their title is a nominal one, then the intensity and thoroughness of their training tells a different story. As well as priests there are deacons, monks and *dabtaras*. All of these have a knowledge of their Christian music, for it is bonded to the liturgy as closely as in other Eastern Churches. To the *dabtaras* is given the responsibility of preserving the artistic traditions of Church worship. After an elementary schooling, a *dabtara* undergoes an intense training in traditional music *(zema)*, dance *(aquaquam)*, poetry *(qene)* and perhaps in theology and church history too. The task is a huge one and may take twenty years.

In music, the *dabtara* faces a rigorous study of the traditional hymns and anthems, of which there are many hundreds. The study is sufficiently intensive for the *dabtara* to memorize them all. As part of this process he must make his own copy of the whole vast collection, manufacturing his own parchment and coloured inks, binding the books and making leather cases to preserve them. This task alone may take him seven years, during which time he must also practise the chant daily.

Then the *dabtara* must study the sacred dances and how to accompany them.

The third study, ecclesiastical poetry, is by all accounts a highly sophisticated art, resembling (and probably surpassing) the most demanding of Western disciplines. The poems first and foremost have to be a perfect fit to one of the traditional chants, for they will be heard in worship as a commentary on scripture. The poem has to be written in the ancient Church language of Ge'ez and conform to strict rules of grammar. Most important of all, the poems use a host of scriptural symbols which the congregation understand very well. The poet is judged on how subtly and cunningly he handles these symbols and all the technicalities of their expression.

Ethiopian Christians treasure their faith and its traditional expression. By this rigorous training it is handed down accurately from generation to generation, but at the same time there is room for creativity and a place for new work within its confines.

The reverence in which these traditions are held is delightfully illustrated by the legends which describe their origin. Ethiopian Orthodox Christians believe that all their sacred chant was created by Yared, a saint of the sixth century:

At this time, there were no rules for the famous zema, or liturgical chant. The offices were recited in a low voice. But when the Saviour wanted to establish sacred chant, he thought of Yared and sent three birds to him from the Garden of Eden, which spoke to him with the language of men, and carried him away to the heavenly Jerusalem, and there he learnt their chant from twenty-four heavenly priests.

Back on earth, Yared set to work composing and singing the sacred chants:

And when the king and queen heard the sound of his voice they were moved with emotion and they spent the day in

listening to him, as did the archbishop, the priests and the nobility of the kingdom. And he appointed the chants for each period of the year...for the Sundays and the festivals of the angels, prophets, martyrs and the just. He did this in three styles: in ge'ez, 'ezl and araray; and he put into these three nothing far removed from the language of men and the songs of the birds and animals.[3]

These stories are recorded in a fourteenth century *Synaxarium* (Lives of the Saints) called the *Senkessar,* but in reality the chant is likely to be even older than the time of Yared. It is probable that some direct link exists with the temple music of Jerusalem.

This connection is reinforced by some remarkable circumstantial evidence. For

A service is held in Addis Ababa to celebrate Timkat, the Orthodox Epiphany. The Ethiopian Orthodox Church has changed very little for well over a thousand years. In recent years it has had to endure repression from a Marxist regime.

instance, the characteristic shape of many of the churches is circular and inside are three sections, one inside the other. The outer passage is open to anyone and is where the *dabtara* sings. The middle section is where the baptized take communion, but the innermost chamber is only for the priests; it houses the *tabot,* an altar very much like the ark of the covenant, made of wood and draped with highly decorated cloth. Even the name of the innermost chamber *(keddusa keddusan)* is clearly connected to the Hebrew *kodesh hakkodashim*—the 'holy of holies'.

The dance is of course the most striking link with the Old Testament:

The veneration accorded to the *tabot* in Abyssinia [Ethiopia] up to the present day, its carriage in solemn procession accompanied by singing, dancing, beating of staffs or prayer-sticks, rattling

of sistra and sounding of other musical instruments remind one most forcefully of the scene in 2 Samuel 6 vv 5, 15 and 16, when David and the people dance round the ark. The entire spectacle, its substance and its atmosphere, has caused all who have witnessed it to feel transported into the times of the Old Testament.[4]

Notation in Ethiopian Music

Although the sacred music is committed to memory almost in its entirety, the Ethiopian Church has its own unique form of notation, a kind of *aide-memoire.*

A large number of traditional texts have their own music attached to them, just as the tune and words of 'Happy Birthday to You' are inseparable.

This tune is well known and so could be codified simply by the first letter of the text: H. This is the equivalent of the Ethiopian system of musical signposts, or *meleket* letters. The signpost (a single letter) is put at the beginning of a text (such as 'praise the Lord all the earth') thereby instructing the *dabtara* to sing this text to the traditional musical phrase 'H'. The melodies that the *meleket* letters represent all have to be learnt, but once that is done, there is no need for staves or neumes, crochets or quavers.

In addition, there are *meleket* signs which show the singer with great precision how the melodies should be sung. Here are a few examples:

- *(yizet)*
  stop, pause or breathe

- *(deret)*
  drop the voice to a deep chest register

- *(heedet)*
  quickly, get faster

- *(kurt)*
  cut the note short

- • • *(rikrik)*
  repeat the note several times very quickly on the same syllable[1]

Signs at the beginning of each chant indicate to which of the three distinct styles of chanting *(zema)* it belongs: the *ge'ez* (fairly unadorned and simple), *'ezl* (deep-sounding and chromatic, solemn, appropriate for fasts, vigils and funerals) or *araray* (lighter, more decorative).

Unfortunately for the *dabtara,* the alphabet used for the *meleket* letters has over 200 signs, and combinations of these are made to represent as many as 1,000 musical phrases. Memorizing them all is an amazing feat strongly reminiscent of the practice of ancient Greek and early Christian culture.

Chapter 32

Christianity East and West—
Worlds Apart?

The cult of the individual has formed the cornerstone of Western culture since the Renaissance in fifteenth-century Italy. The sanctity of personal rights, aspirations and freedom of expression are humanist ideals deeply embedded in every aspect of society—in politics, ethics, religion, social life and art.

The Western perspective

The emphasis placed on the value of the individual fits so comfortably into Western culture that it generally goes unnoticed. Occasionally it draws attention to itself by reaching absurd levels. By what yardstick, for instance, is the fabulous price on a picture by Vermeer being measured? Its value can be demolished by the news that it is a fake, even if the fake and the original are indistinguishable to any but the expert with the microscope. The breathtaking price put on such works of art does not measure their excellence, but the significance of the artist's individuality.

In the realm of music, the composers who are most revered are those with a striking identity. Beethoven epitomizes the artist-hero, at odds with society in general, fighting for his place within it without making concessions to its expectations.

But this has not always been the case. In medieval times, the priorities of Western culture were different. According to the psychiatrist Anthony Storr, the Middle Ages had

a generally agreed conception of how an individual ought to behave. The idea that anyone should pursue his personal economic ends to the limit, provided that he kept within the law, was foreign to the medieval mind, which regarded the alleviation of poverty as a duty, and the private accumulation of wealth as a danger to the soul. The Reformation made possible the growth of Calvinism, and the establishment of the Protestant work ethic. It was not long before poverty was regarded as a punishment for idleness or fecklessness, and the accumulation of wealth as a reward for the virtues of industry and thrift.[1]

In other words, before the Reformation, survival depended on conformity to a prevailing social order with rigid codes of behaviour. Expressions of individuality, whether from witches, revolutionaries or mere eccentrics, were a serious threat to medieval society, which reacted promptly and viciously against them.

The Eastern view

In the light of this, the dissimilarity of Eastern and Western Christendom is understandable, for the East has preserved attitudes overturned in the West by the European Renaissance and Reformation. For example, Eastern Churches place little emphasis on the sermon, which in Reformed Western Churches is a personal exhortation addressed to individuals. Instead, ancient ceremonial expresses continuity with the past, and with timeless truth, through the veneration of places and people associated with the great events of Christian history. Small wonder, then, that Christianity for Eastern countries provides a strong basis for collective identity and is strongly bound up with national sentiment.

Music of the East

Music contributes vitally to the Eastern Churches' sense of tradition through its great antiquity. A number of their greatest musicians are revered as saints and their music preserved with care and reverence. Change, on the whole, has been through steady evolution.

The musical dimension most important to Eastern Orthodoxy is undoubtedly that of symbol, as it was to all Christians in medieval Europe. Eastern chant does not convey the meaning of its text in a rhetorical, or emotionally expressive fashion, but symbolizes it by mode and structure. The music is a corporate gesture not only in the sense that it draws all voices and minds together in one building, but also through its simultaneous experience by worshippers throughout the land. Eastern psalmody still provides, as Basil the Great pointed out in the fourth century, 'a bond of unity ... by joining together the people into the concord of a single chorus.'[2]

When ecstatic and rhetorical music is experienced in the Eastern Church, it is a further product of tradition, in this case stretching back as far as the Old Testament. The music of the Ethiopian Christians in particular is sufficiently old to have preserved the ancient Israelites' physical dimension of dance and the heartbeat of their rhythmic accompaniment.

Symbol and rhetoric in conflict

It is rhetorical music, music that intends to persuade and to evoke feelings, that is fundamentally out of place in Orthodox worship. When in the seventeenth century Russia embraced Western culture, the Russian Orthodox Church followed suit by abandoning the old *znamenny* chant in favour of the rhetoric of harmony and polyphony. At the time, a substantial number of Christians found the new music wholly inappropriate for their worship and left the Church altogether in the Great Schism.

More recently, when composers such as Tchaikovsky and Rachmaninoff offered their outstanding gifts in the service of Russian Orthodoxy, they were turned down. The *Liturgies* they set are now their least performed works, neglected by both Church and concert-hall: too rhetorical and expressive for one and too austere for the other. Present-day composers are almost never invited to write music for the Orthodox Church. In one rare instance of such an invitation, the sympathies of the composer for

English composer John Tavener, dissatisfied with Western culture, has turned for inspiration to Eastern Orthodox Christianity and the heritage of Byzantine music.

the Eastern Church are counterbalanced by an antagonism towards Western culture.

John Tavener

Tavener is an English composer (distantly related to the sixteenth-century composer of the same name) who embraced Russian Orthodoxy in the mid-1970s. His compositions have been increasingly influenced both by Christian mysticism and by Orthodox traditions, while his attitudes to Western culture and the art it produces have become less and less sympathetic:

It sounds very extreme, but I think sacred

art has gone downhill since the Middle Ages. I feel I've come into contact with what ikon painting is, with the primordial kind of Orthodoxy that the West has never had; the fact that the Byzantine tone system is practically unchanged, the fact that Greece never had a renaissance. I think a lot of people are feeling the importance of this... however impressed I am by Michelangelo, the simple Greek peasant ikon means much, much more to me. Or to give a musical example, I'm deeply moved by the very simple harmonic music they sing at the Russian Orthodox cathedral...[3]

Arvo Pärt, an Estonian Orthodox Christian, writes reflective and deeply spiritual music.

Tavener's dissatisfaction with Western culture is expressed by his desire to compose symbolically, 'in the manner of an ikon painter'. He would also prefer the anonymity of a craftsman:

If only the Church was the wise patron she once was! I would love to have lived in Byzantine Greece at its height. I would have been part of the community of ikon painters and writers of texts, and been much more anonymous.[4]

A brief opportunity for John Tavener to join the community of Orthodox artists came from Metropolitan Anthony of Sourozh as an invitation to write music for the English Liturgy of St John Chrysostom.[5] The result, completed in 1978, is music of extreme simplicity. For the most part it avoids the sonorous harmonies typical of the Russian Church and presents the text once more as a single line, only occasionally adorned by a drone or by the simple two-part singing of the Greek monasteries.

Arvo Pärt

Arvo Pärt (born 1935) is another composer with an Orthodox background, whose music shares some of the qualities of Tavener's. Pärt comes from Estonia, although he has lived in the West since 1980. His life under a Communist régime did not prevent him from developing a profound Christian faith, and his attitude to his art produces a unique music (much of it settings of biblical texts) which is intriguing to Western musicians because it seems to differ so

profoundly in intention from their own. Rather than emotional self-expression, Pärt believes that musicians should concern themselves more with 'pauses and reflection, and evoke this reflection and this condition of stability for the people for whom we create our art'.[6]

Pärt's setting of the Ordinary of the Mass for the Western Church, *Missa Sillabica,* is informed throughout by his sense of stability and reflection. Its methodical simplicity stems from the shape of the music being governed by the syllable count of phrases, not directly by their meaning—an extension of the symbolic technique of cantillation. The result is music that can carry worship with great effectiveness and without technical difficulty.

Even these contemporary composers of the Orthodox faith show that Eastern Christianity has maintained a consistency and unanimity which were lost to the West even before the Reformation. The active presence of Eastern Orthodoxy in the Christian world today is a valuable reminder not only that culture and upbringing colour perception of the faith, but that the Western approach is not the only or even the ideal one.

PART 6

The African Genius

Chapter 33

Africa and the Influence of Western Music

The Christian ancestry of Ethiopia is unique in Africa, but in the last few decades Christianity has blossomed in many other areas of the continent, with a higher percentage of followers in some African countries than in Western Europe, the area that first evangelized them. Africa is a huge continent and a survey of its Christian music here cannot even begin to be exhaustive. Through

A deacon approaches the sanctuary in beautiful Lusaka Cathedral, Zambia. The feel of some African church buildings is very Western, and perhaps this can present an obstacle to worship in a truly African spirit. But contrast this with the picture on page 173.

brief and selective views, therefore, the following chapters trace the steady climb that Christianity is making there away from Western trappings and dogma to a faith which expresses African priorities, fully absorbed into African life. The musical consequences of this change are dramatic.

It is comparatively recently (around 150 years ago) that Western missionaries became fired with the task of converting 'pagan' Africa to the Christian faith:

> **However anxious a missionary may be to appreciate and to retain indigenous social and moral values, in the case of religion he has to be ruthless ... he has to admit and even to emphasise that the religion he teaches is opposed to the existing one and one has to cede to the other.**[1]

The traditional religions have certainly ceded. In Kenya estimates are that in 1900, 95.8 per cent of the population adhered to traditional religions and only 0.2 per cent were Christian. By 1962 the figures were respectively 37 per cent and 54 per cent; by 1972, 26.2 per cent and 66.2 per cent. Although these figures refer to one country, they reflect the general trend dramatically.

Western lifestyle

Along with these changes in religious persuasion have come imported lifestyles which have found their natural habitat in the big cities. With them come all the trappings—good and bad—of Western lifestyle: the cars, the clothes, the fast food, the ghetto-blasters. It is in such surroundings that churches with a European style of worship are to be found in great diversity, with their Western liturgies, languages and music.

But unlike Europe and North America, the majority of Africans still live in a rural setting, where traditions established over centuries, even millenia, continue to exert a powerful influence. In the cities an adapted Western culture has long been accepted and has replaced many local customs, but it is in village life that the collision of European Christianity and local customs is still an issue.

The place of music in these societies provides one indication of the cultural gulf to be bridged, for it plays a far more active part in the consciousness of Africans, penetrating deeply into traditional upbringing:

The African mother sings to her child and introduces him to many aspects of music right from the cradle. She trains the child to become aware of rhythm and movement by rocking him to music, by singing to him in nonsense syllables imitative of drum rhythms. When he is old enough to sing, he sings with his mother and learns to imitate drum rhythms by rote... Participation in children's games and stories incorporating songs enables him to learn to sing in the style of his culture, just as he learns to speak its language. His experience, even at this early stage, is not confined to children's songs, for African mothers often carry children on their backs to public ceremonies, rites and traditional dance arenas... sometimes the mothers even dance with their children on their backs...[2]

These are qualities of life, along with strong religious awareness, to which the early missionaries were blind. As the nineteenth-century missionary Robert Moffat wrote:

Satan has employed his agency with fatal success, in erasing every vestige of religious impression from the minds of the Bechuanas, Hottentots and Bushmen; leaving them without a single ray to guide them from the dark and dread futurity, or a single link to unite them with the skies.[3]

Europeans believed that the minds of Africans were empty of any sense of religion or culture and were waiting to have these instilled into them. Desmond Tutu summarizes the result:

These poor native pagans had to be clothed in Western clothes so that they could speak to the white man's God, the only God, who was obviously unable to recognise them unless they were decently clad. These poor creatures must

In Africa, daily work—in the fields, in the fishing boats, in the kitchens—is often powered by music. The rhythm of the music and of the work come together to make labour a communal activity. This has obvious implications for corporate worship.

be made to sing the white man's hymns hopelessly badly translated, they had to worship in the white man's unemotional and individualistic way, they had to think and speak of God and all the wonderful Gospel truths in the white man's well proven terms.[4]

Establishing trade with Africa was high on the European agenda in the nineteenth century and a prime reason for converting the continent to Western ways:

In the Buxton expedition of 1841... the first aim was to discover the possibilities of legitimate trade with Nigeria... But

Cameroun: African Christian Music

The Catholic Church in Cameroun began exploring the possibility of Christian music in local languages even before Vatican II. The first step was to take pre-existing Western melodies and simply to overlay them with words of the appropriate local language. This was easier said than done, for many languages in Cameroun (and in Africa generally) are tone-based, where the meaning of words is dependent on the pitch at which they are uttered. As a consequence, melodies take control of the meaning of the words set to them. The marriage of language and music of differing cultures can be an unhappy one, and in Cameroun was quite clearly a failure. So was the singing of Latin to Camerounian tunes.

The only solution was to marry Camerounian texts to Camerounian music, which has since become the life's work of Abbé Pie-Claude Ngumu. The reaction of congregations was evident in their enthusiasm and in the early 1960s the Abbé founded the choir *Maîtrise de la croix d'ébène* at Yaoundé Cathedral. The style of this music and the colour and excitement it brought to the liturgy led to further developments:

Our melodies are always rhythmic; while they are being played, those present have the greatest difficulty in stopping themselves from beating time with

head, finger, or foot. So then we asked why this movement that people had so much difficulty in restraining should not be given free rein. Yielding to our requests in this matter was the starting-point of that liturgy... that is the pride of Cameroun.[1]

The reactions of authorities and outsiders to this style of Roman Catholic worship were not always favourable:

Since it was launched, this experiment has met with a varied reception: for some it constitutes an attempt to paganize Christianity; for others it is one of the finest achievements of post-conciliar Christianity.[2]

Cameroun already boasts one of the most lively scenes in African popular music, and for the Roman Catholic Church to move towards the people's needs in that area was new.

A drummer from Cameroun in West Africa. The attempt to marry Camerouni-style music to Roman Catholic liturgy is still continuing.

the spreading of the Gospel was regarded as essential and integral to this. It was widely believed that, in order to have legitimate trade, one must have a people of developed culture, reliable and industrious habits... Christianity was confidently regarded as the foundation for all of these and all the virtues of social and commercial intercourse...[5]

The signs of a change of attitude amongst the missionary churches is evident in a hymn-book like *Africa Praise,* published in 1956 for use in English-speaking schools. It contains many of the best-loved Protestant hymns of the past two centuries, but also a large number of African songs to English words in tonic sol-fa (very few Africans have a musical training which allows them to read Western notation). The hymn-book is an indication of a desire to narrow the gap between the African and European cultures, but it was only a first step.

The Western legacy

In a few city cathedrals, resources are channelled to the provision of printed books and to musicians who know how to get the best out of them; outside their walls the music of the many churches founded by the West is in a sorry state. Without the provision of music books with stimulating contents of high quality and without the training to use such material, the Western legacy of Christian music has become a dead weight, even a millstone. Norman Warren described his experience of Christian music in Uganda after a visit in 1985:

Generally speaking, we found the life of the Church at a low ebb. All too common was the desire to ape the west...I was disappointed in coming across so little original music in worship. In most instances the music was rather formal and old-fashioned...

He noted the use of *Hymns Ancient and Modern* (standard version) at Kampala Cathedral, Moody and Sankey in a suburban church in Kusoga and *Africa Praise* at Arua Church in the north. The musical facilities available even in Mukono Cathedral were very slender:

The organ is a pedal harmonium that has

not worked for months. All the music was unaccompanied and led with great gusto by a small choir. The hymn-tunes were, without exception, Victorian... and, quite frankly, I would never want to hear them again.[6]

The language of the people

The musical legacy of the missionary churches in Africa is not wholly depressing, however. The Roman Catholic Church worldwide adopted a dramatic and new attitude to its liturgy in Vatican II (the second Vatican Council) of 1962. The abolition of Latin and the adoption of the language of the people was its most radical step.

A 'coming-of-age'

Vatican II coincided with the independence of many African countries and a powerful awareness of national identity and heritage. The feelings of Catholic African bishops were summarized in a report in 1974:

The 'coming-of-age' of the Churches signifies a turning point in the history of the Church in Africa. It is the end of the missionary period. This does not mean the end of evangelisation. But it means,

The worship in this Presbyterian church is thoroughly African. Throughout Africa, in music, liturgy and architecture, the style is beginning to express African, rather than Western, culture and feeling. Christian worship is becoming more deeply embedded in African life.

A Marriage of African and Western Music

In Nigeria, an African, Ikoli Harcourt Whyte (about 1905–77) created a unique blend of the European and African styles in his own Christian music.

Although wholly Nigerian (from Abonnema near Port Harcourt in the south) Harcourt Whyte was strongly influenced by Western culture through his contraction of leprosy at the age of fourteen.

From that time he was wholly cut off from the outside world in mission hospitals, chiefly the Uzuakoli Leprosy Hospital, a project supported jointly by the Methodists and the government. It was not until thirty years later that the drug Dapsone was discovered (through research in Uzuakoli) and through its application Harcourt Whyte was pronounced cured in 1949.

His seventeen-year-long stay at Uzuakoli brought Harcourt Whyte a resilient Christian faith:

Leprosy isolated me into a place where I could see no other books to read than the Bible and religious books. I read and read, and they transformed me... Instead of feeling bitter that all was lost, I discovered that 'all things work together for good to them that love God'.[1]

As well as a profound understanding of the language of the Ibo people and of its folk-music, he developed an acquaintance with Western music through the English missionaries at the hospital. His contact with European music was limited almost entirely to the hymns and songs of Methodist worship of the time—*Sacred Songs and Solos* of the evangelists Sankey and Moody and the *Methodist Hymnbook*.

From fairly early on Harcourt Whyte taught in the hospital school and developed his musical talents by forming choirs in the school and chapel. His self-taught musical talents became evident in the music he created for these groups and established a pattern from which he deviated very little for the rest of his life.

Apart from a few political songs, Harcourt Whyte's music is almost all Christian, consisting of hundreds of songs in Igbo, the language of the Ibo, all unaccompanied and almost all in four-part harmony. The idea of creating music for a trained group of singers, music to be listened to rather than participated in, is rare in African tradition. The harmony of his music is unusual too. It is a unique adaptation of European tradition, blinkered by Harcourt Whyte's limited knowledge of it, but coloured by African music and particularly by Igbo.

Translation difficulties

Harcourt Whyte was surrounded for most of his life by Igbo. It is a tone language, like many in Africa, and therefore poses the problems of music-setting that had caused such difficulty for European missionaries.

The Igbo word 'oke', for instance, has many meanings according to the way it is pronounced. Two syllables high in the voice give the meaning 'male of an animal', high in the voice then low would mean 'boundary', low-low means 'share' and low-high means 'rat'. Take the Igbo for 'word'—'okwu'. It must be pronounced high in the voice on both syllables—like two relatively high notes. But if the tone of the voice on the second syllable is lowered, another word altogether is created, meaning 'heap'.

Missionaries thoughtfully provided translations of Western hymns into Igbo and translated 'Thou whose Almighty Word' correctly as 'Chineke okwu Gi'. But when the phrase is put to the tune 'Moscow', the word 'okwu' receives a lowered pitch on the second syllable, which now conveys the meaning 'Thou whose almighty heap'! The crazy meanings created by subsequent verses and the entirely different melodic contours of the alto, tenor and bass lines quickly reduce the text to utter gibberish.

Harcourt Whyte addressed this problem early on. He realized that Igbo words needed melodies which (as in their folk-song) were wholly sympathetic to the language. The restrictions under which he worked were considerable, especially when he chose to set several verses to a given melody. His solution was to write his own words, but to start the creative process with a melody:

What I mostly do first is the melody. Then the words of the first verse. After this the harmony. Lastly, the words of the following verses. It is this part of the composition that takes more time due to the rise and fall of the tonal expressions of the Igbo language as one tries to bring into conformity all the verses with the melody.[2]

Although Harcourt Whyte always wrote in four parts, always used major keys, almost always tied the voice-parts together in homophony and never used chromaticism, there is plenty of variety in his songs. The words of his songs are strongly biblical, either quotations, paraphrases or commentaries and deeply moving to their hearers:

[On Good Friday, 1954 at Uzuakoli] the choir... moved into

and up the chapel in slow march to Harcourt's *E gburu Nwa Chuku (The Son of God was Crucified)*, a composition he wrote specially for... that day. By the time the choir had got to the middle and front of the chapel and taken their seats... everybody—preacher, layman, men, women and children, patients and the healthy—was already either weeping or sobbing... So powerful... are his texts and music that Sunday after Sunday people troop to that great chapel to hear him...[3]

Towards the end of his life Harcourt Whyte's music became widely known in churches where Igbo is the language of worship. As far as is known, his texts have not been translated into other languages and his music has not circulated beyond parts of southern Nigeria. This is a great shame, for his songs are a unique bridge between Western and African cultures, and they have created something new. Harcourt Whyte commented:

Just as European harmony is more developed than African harmony, so is African rhythm more developed than European rhythm.

That I do not have what you have or as much of anything you have does not make me inferior to you, or does it?... In your studies, you must try to learn both European and African musics so that you can understand better what I am driving at. I take from European music what I find good in it and use it. As rice is different from beans, so is African music different from European music... if any of them can be called superior, I think it is the product of the mixture...[4]

'Caiaphas spoke and said' is an early piece, but typical of Harcourt-Whyte's style. It dramatizes an episode in Jesus' Passion, recorded in John chapter 18 verse 4. The music interferes as little as possible with the tonal inflections of the Igbo language.

Drumming is more than entertainment in Africa; it is a form of communication. So the use of drums for dance, for music or for liturgy can be full of significance.

in the words of Pope Paul VI during his visit to Uganda: 'You Africans may become missionaries to yourselves'. In other words, the remaining task of evangelisation of Africa is primarily the responsibility of the African Church itself. This fact implies a radically changed relationship between the Church in Africa and ... the other Churches in Europe and North America.[7]

One important consequence of this new attitude is the reduction of the numbers of missionaries from the traditional societies and churches working in Africa and alongside that, the development of new styles of worship more in harmony with African culture and lifestyle.

Chapter 34

The Independent Churches

Another development in the recent history of African Christianity is the pronounced and dramatic growth of indigenous independent churches. The Kimbanguist Church of Zaire is one of hundreds founded as the result of the inability of the established missionary churches to understand African needs and aspirations in the faith. As a member of the Kimbanguist Church has written:

The arrival of the missionaries, accompanied by colonisation, obscured the new know-ledge of Christianity. The preaching of Christ was seen as another means of helping colonisation to alienate men completely from their African identity. It was in this situation that Christ turned his face towards his people and chose the prophet Simon Kimbangu as his messenger . . . [1]

Kimbanguist music

In common with many indigenous churches in Africa, the Kimbanguists value the Bible and its teachings highly and their practices are founded on biblical principles. They also denounce the traditional animist religions with vigour, but remain close to many local customs. Music is an important aid to worship, from the simple unison singing of the thrice-daily services of prayer through to the choral and instrumental sounds of Sunday worship and the colourful festivals of the church year. The beginning of the Kimbanguist musical traditions is indicative of the failure of the established missions in colonial times to understand the needs of the Christian community in Africa:

At the start of the prophet's mission at N'Kamba, the songs utilized to accomplish the work of Christ were those of Protestants. But the Protestants refused to sell their hymn-books to the followers of the prophet. Saddened, Simon Kimbangu went apart to pray, laying before God this poverty, so deeply felt by his congregation. From that was born the gift of 'catching' the songs. [2]

The musical tradition that has developed is perfectly attuned to a society where it is memory rather than the written word that provides cultural identity and continuity:

Kimbanguists catch songs in various ways: in dreams, and in visions in which they hear angels singing. As a general rule, once they have been caught, the songs are sent to an office, set up by the church called the Directorate of Kimbanguist Songs, where they are studied and to some extent modified to give them a good meaning. Other songs are deleted, if the meaning of the song is not clear. The songs have to be examined to avoid those that may be inspired by the Devil. [3]

The songs have all sorts of functions—some are songs of praise, others are 'living lessons, explaining and clarifying biblical teaching', still others are prophetic. After approval these songs are learnt by a regional choir of leaders whose members then pass them on to the local choirs. One regional choir, the Kimbanguist Theatre Group, travels round the churches using singing and drama to bring Bible stories and the church's history to life.

The True Christian Music of Africa

Christian music in Africa this century has gradually moved further and further away from the European styles of worship which were first introduced by the missionaries. Harcourt Whyte's music is a unique half-way point in that process of change and could therefore become a rich source of Christian music especially for the West, accessible because it can be written down and because the style it adopts has some Western characteristics. It only remains to be translated and published in Western notation.

But it is the indigenous churches that demonstrate most dramatically how the African musical sensibility differs from the European, above all in an emotional abandon and a delight in participation. The Westerner, after all, reads from books or newspapers, whereas the African habitually relies for cultural continuity on memory and improvization.

European music has developed relationships of counterpoint and harmony where the African thrives on a dialogue of rhythms; Western classical music is founded on narrative structures, in which the listener is taken on an emotional and dramatic journey by means of musical rhetoric. African tradition, however, has always created music of immediate and compelling physical impact, static when compared with Western expectations, ecstatic in its own right.

As Harcourt Whyte pointed out, each way is an expression of a culture, very revealing of the priorities and make-up of certain strata of their respective societies. But in the realm of Christian worship, the Western musical style that most missionaries brought to Africa sprang from nineteenth-century sub-cultures held back from the liberation of

true worship by debilitating social attitudes.

There was fear that music might become a real force in the lives of those involved in it. It was, for instance, wholly reprehensible to allow music to become rhythmic and exciting enough to invite a bodily response, so its physical dimension was banned from worship. Then, as intellectual challenge in general was threatening for evangelicals, Christian music which possessed any real rhetorical power—music that is emotionally penetrating or challenging—was not allowed any space either.

The permissible Christian music that remained was (and unhappily still is) a narrow and poverty-stricken shoot off the main cultural stem of Western culture, reflecting and tainting the Western style of Christian worship. Small wonder then, that Desmond Tutu should reject the white man's 'unemotional and individualistic' attitude to his faith and that the thriving churches in Africa are those encouraging a commitment in worship which is both spiritual and physical, wholehearted and corporate.

Westerners may find the emotionalism and the trance-like states of ecstasy disturbing, but for the many African churches they are the sign of God's presence with them. Where many missionary churches have denied the existence of demons, witches and evil spirits, indigenous churches recognize them, but exercise the power of God over them with the help of agencies like music. It is in these latter churches that the true Christian music of Africa is to be found. As an Aladura Christian has written:

A spiritual revolution was necessary... and this was promptly provided by the Aladura Churches. The Holy Spirit descended, as on Pentecost day, to proclaim afresh the Gospel message in languages which Nigerians understood and so through revelations manifested in trances, dreams, visions and prophecies, established the universality and the all-embracing, and all-saving power of Jesus Christ... the obvious conclusion that one can logically reach is that the Aladura way of worship is the true African expression of the Christian religion.[1]

Aladura Churches

The Kimbanguist Church is only one of the hundreds of indigenous Christian organizations thriving in Africa today. Because there are no Europeans involved and little sign of Western culture, they can make an impact in areas hardly touched by the older missionary churches. The Aladura Churches, for instance, which are very popular amongst the Yoruba and Ibo people in southern Nigeria, have also become established in the Muslim north of that country.

In political terms, these Churches have generally been treated in a friendly manner by emerging nationalist governments, in contrast to the previously open suspicion of the colonialists.

Among people of all walks of Nigerian life, the Aladura Churches are supported enthusiastically. Where the Kimbanguists are reminiscent of seventeenth-century Puritans in their restrictions on smoking, drinking and dancing, the Aladura celebrate their faith with hand-clapping, dancing and traditional instruments. They have incorporated other elements of traditional worship too—instantaneous healing of the sick, raising of the dead, prophecy and exorcism. As one Aladura Christian puts it, it is in their liturgy that 'the unfulfilled emotional needs in the western-oriented churches have found ample fulfillment'.[4]

An indication of the popularity of the Aladura Churches in city and country is provided by their choirs' and solo singers' great following; an American-style network of gospel music is developing fast. The guitarist Patty Obassey is one of the best known, scoring an enormous success with *Nne Galu* in 1984. Among the many choirs who have produced a number of albums are Imole Ayo and the Christian Singers, the Choir of the Eternal Sacred Order of Cherubim and Seraphim and Erasmus Jenewari and his Gospel Bells.

The balance of European and African influences on the practice of Christianity is still on the move in favour of the African, but this does not mean a wholesale eradication of Western culture. The style of vestments worn by Aladura priests is only one element borrowed from the Protestant and Catholic Churches. On the other hand, the independent churches have taught the older mission churches valuable lessons in liturgy and Christian music.

Ecstatic music

There are a growing number of indigenous churches where the style of worship is difficult to distinguish from the traditional animist religions. The African Apostolic Church, founded in 1932 by John Maranke, is an example. It is based in Eastern Zimbabwe but its influence has spread far and wide. Where the Kimbanguist Church approves and disseminates its songs in a highly organized manner, spontaneity and improvization are the most striking elements of Apostolic worship.

The main meeting of the African Apostolic Church is held on Saturday—the Sabbath—and may last several hours. Worship begins with an

invocation *'kerek! kerek!'* which is the name given to the ecstatic state the group will later experience. Then hymns are sung, which are formal not in the sense of being read out of a book, but by being commonplace amongst many churches in Africa:

Mwari Komborera Africa, Alleluia
Chisua yemina matu yedu
Mwari Baba Jesu utukomborera
Jesu, turi branda bako

Refrain: **O mueya, boanna mueya**
utukomborera

In translation, this means:

God save Africa, Alleluia
Hear our prayers

Kimbanguist Christians follow the tradition of Simon Kimbangu of Zaire; the link is similar to Methodists and John Wesley. Here a travelling choir and theatre group act out a scene as a form of biblical instruction.

God, Father, Jesus, bless us
Jesus, we are your servants

Refrain: O come Holy Spirit, bless us

The words are in Chishona, a language reserved for religious ceremony. The invocation of Father, Son and Holy Spirit (the latter is emphasized) is a sign to the people of a spiritual presence amongst them which is to become almost tangible.

The men are seated on the open ground separately from the women and all are addressed by preachers (there may be three or more) and the chief evangelist. Between them they will have agreed beforehand on the biblical topics most appropriate for the day.

After the opening hymns the preaching begins, but members are free to interrupt with songs of their own choosing at any point. They are particularly likely to jump in and lead off with a song whenever the preacher hands over to a reader. As in the Kimbanguist Church, instruments and dancing are not allowed, but their place is taken by the use of *ngoma*—vocal sounds which imitate drumming—and swaying while standing or sitting.

The call-and-response form so commonplace in African music demonstrates the relationship between a song-leader and the rest of the congregation, who respond with their refrain even before the leader's improvised verses have ended.

These songs exert a powerful emotional influence on the meeting and may very well develop into the repetitive chanting of a short refrain, such as 'God in Heaven' *(Mambo wa ku denga)*:

During chanting, the rhythmic shape of the song is transformed as worshippers put increasing emphasis on strongly accented beats...While the rhythm is accentuated, the harmonies of the chorus tighten. The loose collection of voices [of the call-and-response] becomes a tight, single unit. The overall effect is hypnotic. The rhythmic and harmonic ramifications push the singers into a state of maximum spiritual involvement. As the chant proceeds, individuals moan, yodel, and insert *ngoma*... and glossolalic utterances [the gift of tongues]. The entire congregation sways to the rhythm...[5]

It is sometimes difficult for the preacher to regain control of the service unless the chanting dies out naturally. If it does not, then he may attempt to break the spell by shouting a greeting. These songs are nevertheless regarded by the preachers as a valuable reinforcement of their message and the success of the meeting depends on the degree to which the members have experienced 'possession' by the Holy Spirit.

The congregation's sense of participation is absolute, even extending to the improvisation of songs expressing discontent—perhaps expressing disagreement with one of the church leaders or with the way in which a decision has been made. Even if problems are aired through song during the service, the sense of peace of unity after a long *kerek* is very evident.

PART 7

Music in North America

1600–Present day

Chapter 35

Christianity comes to the New World

The Pilgrim Fathers, whom many Americans look back to as their forefathers, were strongly nonconformist Christians. These origins play a strong part in forming the American soul, and help to explain the highly independent strain in their church life.

A census of citizens of North America in 1790 revealed that only 5 per cent professed any religious affiliation. Today that figure is 95 per cent, of whom nearly half worship regularly in a Christian church. These simple statistics represent a growth that might be the envy of Christians in Western Europe, whose numbers have suffered a steady decline over the same period.

The story of the development of Christian music in the United States is a complex and colourful one, additionally important for the impact that it has had on the world at large. For North Americans do not keep their faith to themselves. In 1985, Protestant Christian missionary societies alone spent more than $500m in supporting overseas missions and that figure is rising yearly. The 20,000 missionaries that the sum sends out world-wide take the hymns and songs of America with them.

The American heritage

Compared with Europe, Christianity in the United States has developed over a mere few hundred years, without the support of the wealth and traditions of an established Church. These two facts may have some bearing on the present strength of faith in the United States.

The first Christian settlement, in Jamestown, Virginia, was only established in 1607. These English settlers and the immigrants who followed them from other parts of Europe arrived with none of the resources which those they had left behind could take for granted. Their life in the New World began with the poverty and hardship that had driven them there in the first place. There was no church wealth built up over centuries, no Christian traditions of worship. They had nothing except what they carried with them, probably no more than a Bible and a metrical psalter.

Christianity in North America has grown since those times as a fire grows from a spark. But a healthy suspicion of ecclesiastical power has remained. The style of worship still valued most highly is one of directness and simplicity, without undue ceremony.

Life in North America is too easily known by its urban side, the extraordinary blend of decadence and deprivation which is supported by the technology of instant communication. For between the huge cities there are vast and sparsely-populated areas of countryside in which small communities enjoy a continuity of traditions in life and faith. Here the true Christian music of North America is to be found. It is a folk-art, which in its formative years had no chance of being influenced by music as an art-form, for classical music remained undeveloped in North America until the mid-nineteenth century. Even today it remains largely untouched by the sophistication of European traditions, a window onto the past.

Why do we mourn departed friends,

Establishing a new tradition

The Christian music sung by the early white settlers was that of the metrical psalms. Indeed, the pilgrims left their European homes with the psalm-tunes ringing in their ears:

They that stayed at Leyden feasted us that were to go at our pastor's house, being large; where we refreshed ourselves, after tears, with singing of Psalms ... and indeed it was the sweetest melody that ever mine ears heard.[1]

For the French Huguenots in Florida or the English and Dutch Puritans of New England, psalm-singing was at the heart of their musical expression of faith. Its importance to the early Christian communities is evident from the first publication of any kind in America, the *Bay Psalm Book*. Remarkably, it was published in Boston as early as 1640 and its pioneering spirit is evident from the preface:

God's altar needs not our pollishings: for wee have respected rather a plaine translation ... and so have attended Conscience rather than Elegance, fidelity rather than poetry ... that soe wee may sing in Sion the Lords songs of prayse according to his own will; untill hee take us from hence, and wipe away all our

This example of four-shape notation is from an early nineteenth-century book, 'The Easy Instructor'. Though the excerpt is in E minor, the shapes are determined by the solmization of G major. Shape-notes were a way of putting the sol-fa system onto the page.

A setting of Psalm 96 in James Lyon's 'Urania, or A Choice Collection of Psalm-Tunes, Anthems, and Hymns, From the most approv'd Authors, with some Entirely New'. When Lyon, a Princeton graduate, announced 'Urania' in the Philadelphia press, he called it the 'first Attempt of any kind to spread the Art of Psalmody in its Perfection, thro' our American Colonies'.

tears, & bid us enter into our masters joye to sing eternall Halleluiahs.

The *Bay Psalm Book* did not contain any music, but recommended the tunes of Ravenscroft's *Whole Book of Psalms* 'collected out of our chief musicians'.

The practice of 'lining out' (described in some detail in Chapter 19) was established early in America, as the Rev. John Cotton made clear in 1647:

For the present, where many in the congregation cannot read, it is convenient that the minister, or some other fit person... do read the psalm line by line before the singing thereof.[2]

The results for American psalmody were as extraordinary as for the Old World:

The same Person who sets the Tune, and guides the Congregation in Singing, commonly reads the Psalm, which is a task too few are capable of performing well, that in Singing two or three Staves, the congregation falls from a cheerful pitch to downright Grumbling, and then

some to relive themselves mount an Eighth above the rest, others perhaps a Fourth or Fifth, by which Means the Singing appears to be rather a confused noise, made up of Reading, Squecking and Grumbling...

In many places, one Man is upon this Note, while another is a Note before him, which produces something so hideous and disorderly, as is beyond Expression bad... and besides, no two Men in the Congregation quaver [decorate the tune with extra notes] alike, or together; which sounds in the Ears of a good Judge, like Five Hundred different Tunes roared out at the same time...[3]

By the early eighteenth century, some ministers were beginning to clamour for a more 'Regular' way of singing, causing 'Heats, Animosities and Contentions' amongst the old guard. Typically, it was the country areas that resisted any suggestion of change:

Tho' in the polite city of Boston this design [the new way] met with general acceptance, in the country, where they have more of the rustic, some numbers of elder and angry people bore zealous testimonies against these wicked innovations, and... not only... call the singing of these Christians a worshipping of the devil, but also they would run out of the meeting-house at the beginning of the exercise.[4]

In New England, new ways of singing eventually supplanted the old, but not in other parts of North America. Extraordinarily enough, there are still isolated parts of Appalachia and the South East where the old practice of lining-out is still practised, particularly amongst remote Baptist Churches. It is an oral tradition—just as it was 300 years ago—where the congregation relies on its memories of the tunes and sing in heterophony ('500 different tunes roared out at the same time') and at an extremely slow pace.

The singing schools

The 'New Way' of singing was really only a return to what today's church musicians would call normality; the Americans called it 'Singing by

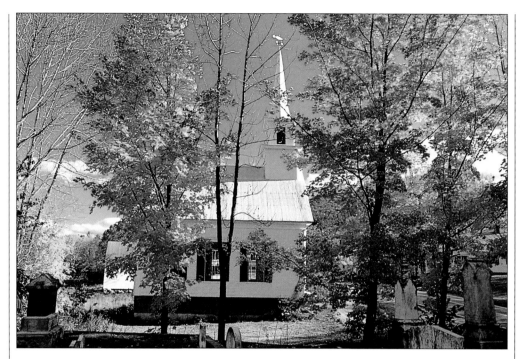

Left: **A church set amid the beauty of a New Hampshire autumn. The words of Alexis de Tocqueville could still be used today: 'There is no country in the world where the Christian religion retains a greater influence over people's souls than in America.'**

Below: **'Amazing Grace', one of the best known of all Christian songs, dates from the early nineteenth century. This is how it appears in the notation of 'Southern Harmony' (1835) where the shape of note-heads varies according to their position in the scale to assist reading. The raw harmony of fourths and fifths which surrounds the melody (middle line) has been inherited by some Western folk-traditions of the present day.**

Note'. But education had to be provided for such a change. As a minister observed as early as 1720:

> **Would it not greatly tend to promote singing of psalms if singing schools were promoted?... Where would be the difficulty, or what the disadvantages, if people who want skill in singing, would procure a person to instruct them, and meet two or three evenings in the week, from five or six o'clock to eight, and spend their time in learning to sing?[5]**

These singing schools sometimes provided more than they were originally intended, as a student at Yale revealed in a letter to a friend:

> **At present I have no inclination for anything, for I am almost sick of the World & were it not for the Hopes of going to the singing-meeting tonight & indulging myself in some of the carnal Delights of the Flesh, such as kissing, squeezing &c. &c. I should willingly leave it now.[6]**

These singing schools had their parallels in English country parishes. They were set up on a temporary basis in a schoolhouse or a tavern with the blessing of the local church, and worshippers

William Billings

Of all the singing teachers of eighteenth-century America, there was none more endearing and inspiring than William Billings (1746–1800). He was born in Boston where he himself learned music at a singing school and spent his life in incessant and enthusiastic labour for Christian music, composing, conducting and teaching.

The absence of copyright laws meant that he earned nothing from his published music, although some of it became immensely popular. Instead, he had to earn his living from time to time as a street cleaner or as a hogreeve (whose responsibility was to keep pigs off the streets). He was clearly something of an eccentric, described as:

a singular man, of moderate size, short of one leg, with one eye, without any address [ie manners], & with an uncommon negligence of person. Still he spake & sung & thought as a man above the common abilities. He died poor and neglected...[1]

Billings was convinced of music's ability to express emotion, whether of praise or supplication. In his songbook, *Continental Harmony* (1794) he wrote:

... how enraptured should we be to hear the sharp key [ie major-key music] express itself in such lofty and majestic strains as these: O come let us sing unto the Lord, let us make a joyful noise... Do I hear the voice of men, or angels! surely such angelic sound cannot yet proceed from the mouths of sinful mortals: but while we are yet warm with the thought, and ravished with the sound, the musicians change their tone, and the flat key [ie minor-key music] utters itself in strains so moving, and

pathetic, that it seems to command our attention to such mournful sounds as these: Hear my prayer O Lord, give ear to my supplication... O how these sounds thrill through my soul! how agreeably they affect my nerves! how soft, how sweet, how soothing...

Billings wrote well over 200 songs, and in an age of civil war some were strongly nationalistic:

Let tyrants shake their iron rod, And Slav'ry clank her galling chains, We fear them not, we trust in God, New England's God for ever reigns.[2]

His songs were divided into two types: 'plain', where the four parts moved together in homophony like a hymn; and 'fuging', a style of writing of which he was particularly fond. In a preface to one of his songbooks he provided his own definition of 'fuge', more enthusiastic than academic:

Notes flying after each other, altho' not always the same sound. N.B. Music is said to be Fuging, when one part comes in after another; its beauties cannot be numbered...[3]

Such a definition would not have satisfied European composers of the time, who received a strict and prolonged training in the rules to be followed when 'one part comes in after another'. Billings was refreshingly ignorant of the Baroque techniques of counterpoint.

But it is Billings' very independence of spirit that has gained him an increasing following, especially amongst modern American composers. As he wrote in the preface to *Continental Harmony:*

For my own Part, as I don't

think myself confin'd to any Rules for Composition laid down by any that went before me, neither should I think (were I to pretend to lay down Rules) that any who came after me were any ways obligated to adhere to them, any further that they should think proper: So in fact, I think it is best for every Composer to be his own Carver.[4]

Billings' music is now beginning to receive the attention it undoubtedly deserves, but largely from the music schools of universities rather than from churches. In many ways, it parallels the Christian music of the west galleries of English country parishes. That hearty but rough-hewn music was swept aside by Victorian reform, and in New England expectations and tastes were moving in a similar direction before the eighteenth century was out.

At the end of the eighteenth century ministers and their more educated congregations started to look for a more refined style in their Christian music. They were becoming aware of the difference between the music of the self-taught Yankee tunesmiths and the refined poise of European classical music. Musicians came to scorn the shape-note notation as 'dunce notes' and in New England the music printed in this way gradually fell out of favour, to be replaced by a European and 'educated' style of Christian music:

The harshness of our singing must be corrected. Our voices must be filed. Every note must be rendered smooth, persuasive and melting.[5]

The 'genteel correctness' which resulted can be sensed in the hymn-tunes of Thomas Hastings (1784–1872) and Lowell Mason (1792–1872). Mason's *Olivet* and *Missionary* (perhaps his best-known tunes in Britain) are a thousand miles from the sturdy music of Billings and his generation. In America, however, the shape-note music survived.

The vastness of the continent and the comparative isolation of country communities once again preserved a folk-like Christian music in areas of the South, whence it had spread during the eighteenth century. Thus two distinct traditions in Christian music exist today in North America, one of grammatical correctness, 'rendered smooth, persuasive and melting' and the other an uneducated and imperfect music sung at full volume and with an infectious enthusiasm which is hard to resist. Billings himself describes this in his *Continental Harmony*:

While each part is... striving for mastery, and sweetly contending for victory, the audience are most luxuriously entertained, and exceedingly delighted; in the mean time, their minds are surprizingly agitated, and extremely fluctuated; sometimes declaring in favour of one part, and sometimes another. —Now the solemn bass demands their attention, now the manly tenor, now the lofty counter [ie alto], now the volatile treble, now here, now there, now here again. —O inchanting! O ecstatic! Push on, push on ye sons of harmony... [6]

William Billings' cheerful enthusiasm shines through his music. This anthem, a setting of Psalm 108 'for Thanksgiving Day Morning', comes from his collection called 'Continental Harmony'. Trained musicians in Europe would have been horrified at the grammatical errors, such as those in bars 16 and 18.

[Allegro]

(instr)

Se - lig, Se - lig,

(instr)

Se - lig, wer in Je - su wun - den

The Dutch composer Johann Peter (1746-1813) emigrated to Pennsylvania in 1770 and became an outstanding composer for the Moravian community in North America. The style of this motet ('Blessed are they') for voices, strings and continuo is close to Joseph Haydn, Peter's contemporary. The finesse of this Christian music remained unique in America for at least the next hundred years.

were encouraged to enrol for a course of singing lessons (provided that they brought their own candles with them). The lessons were based on instruction in solmization, a system of pitching adapted from the invention of Guido d'Arezzo whereby the notes of a scale are identified by names. Where Guido used a different name for each note of the scale, the pioneers of the singing-schools used a simplified system using only four: *fa, sol, la* and *mi*. Thus an upward major scale would have been sung to the note-names *fa, sol, la, fa, sol, la, mi, fa*. Such a system might seem over-simplified to the point of confusion, but the standard of singing in many churches improved noticeably. As Samuel Sewall wrote in his diary in the early 1720s:

House was full, and the Singing extraordinarily Excellent, such as has hardly been heard before in Boston.[7]

Gradually, other systems to help people to read notation developed, from the crude system of the Rev. John Tufts, which placed letters indicating the sol-fa names in the appropriate positions on a five-line stave, to the shape-note systems of the turn of the eighteenth century, where shapes corresponded with the four sol-fa names—a triangle for *fa,* a circle for *sol,* a square, *la* and a diamond *mi.*

The many new tune-books appearing from the 1750's onward catered for the developing interest in part-singing: *Youths Entertaining Amusement* (1754), *Urania* (1761), *Royal*

Melody Complete (Boston, 1767, containing music by the British composer William Tans'ur) and others. The music of some of these books contained pieces complicated enough to be called anthems rather than psalm-tunes.

Such pieces testify to the musical ambitions and even the success of some of the singing masters who, when their course of lessons was complete, would move on to the next town to start again. Nonetheless, the instructors themselves were self-taught. There were no colleges teaching the rudiments of music, let alone the conventions of counterpoint and harmony. All that was picked up by the very imperfect example of oral tradition and through printed music.

Changing tastes in the expanding urban populations gradually ousted this rough-hewn music from city churches, but in the South and at the westward-advancing frontiers it remained popular. Nineteenth-century music collections continued to print the music of the singing-school pioneers of a century before: *Virginia Harmony, Kentucky Harmony* (1816) Knoxville Harmony (1838), *Union Harmony* (Tennessee, 1837), *Southern Harmony* (1835) and many others.

These collections also show quite clearly how folk-tunes, originally wedded to secular words, came to be accepted in church worship with Christian texts. From these sources come a number of folk-hymns whose tunes have penetrated the consciousness of the English-speaking world: in *Southern Harmony,* for instance, can be found *Wondrous Love,* and the tune to *Auld Lang Syne* put to a hymn by Isaac Watts. The best-loved of all, perhaps, is *Amazing Grace,* originally set to 'There is a land of pure delight' in *Virginia Harmony.*

A collection of 1844 called *The Sacred Harp* has a special significance, having given its name to the annual Sacred Harp Conventions which still meet today to celebrate this Christian folk-music—clear evidence that it is still known and well-loved in the Southern states.

Moravians and Shakers

Two traditions of worship established in North America in the eighteenth century created Christian music of particular richness. The cultures from which they sprang were opposites, but both for a while chose isolation rather than integration with the societies around them. Such insularity was necessary for something exceptional to grow, but it also prevented such Christian music finding its way into the worship of other denominations.

As they travelled to North America on an evangelistic mission in 1737, John and Charles Wesley found that they were sailing with a group of Moravian Brethren with the same intentions. These Moravians had come from Herrnhut, a settlement in north Germany, but the origins of their movement, the 'Unitas Fratrum', lay in the reforming zeal of Jan Hus in sixteenth-century

The Moravians had a knowledge of the European music they left behind them which was rare in eighteenth-century America. Their Christian music lay at the centre of this activity and only quite recently has the true extent of this music been uncovered. Not only did they have their own hymn-writers, but they also boasted choirs which, judging by the music composed for them, must have possessed skills quite beyond those of the New Englanders.

The Shakers, 'The United Society of Believers in Christ's Second Appearing', started life as a

Bohemia. The revival of the Moravian Church in 1722 sent missionary expeditions to the Virgin Islands, then to Greenland, South Africa, Jamaica and North America. Communities of Moravians were founded in Bethlehem in Pennsylvania and in parts of North Carolina.

For the German-speaking Moravians, as for the Lutherans, music generally held a treasured place in life. They brought instruments with them from north Germany, and there were instrument-makers among them. Thus bands were available for ceremonial occasions of all kinds—weddings, christenings and so on.

small English sect to which Ann Lee had been attracted at the age of twenty-two in 1758. She was a humble woman from the slums of Manchester, who became convinced that she was 'Ann the Word' and 'the Bride of the Lamb'. Some of her converts emigrated to North America, where, in the early years of the nineteenth century, the Society's membership grew to about 6,000, settling mostly in areas of the north-east, such as New York, Massachusetts and Connecticut.

One of her converts described Mother Ann Lee:

A group of nineteenth-century Shakers dance. Note the separation of women and men. Shaker worship was marked by great simplicity. In the words of their most lastingly famous song: 'Tis the gift to be simple, tis the gift to be free.'

Our sup-port we'll ga - ther in; For the har - vest time is come. Now to reap we will be-gin, Will you all now help us on. Twas by Christ the seed was sown; Now the har - vest does ap- pear; Now the crops are ful - ly grown. Reap, O reap, get e-ve-ry spear.

This Shaker song, called 'The Harvest', symbolizes in action the sowing, watering and reaping of spiritual seed. An eye-witness of the ceremony wrote: 'It was a most beautiful sight to see such a devoted company all moving over the ground with such simplicity and eagerness to gather a full share of blessing.' The music, with its use of a five-note scale, has the artless simplicity of folk-song.

Mother Ann Lee was sitting in a chair, and singing very melodiously, with her hands in motion; and her whole soul and body seemed to be in exercise. I felt, as it were, a stream of divine power and love flow into my soul, and was convinced at once that it came from Heaven, the source and fountain of all good. I immediately acknowledged my faith, and went and confessed my sins.[8]

The believers lived in small, exclusive and self-sustaining villages. Their very strict moral sense kept the sexes apart, even by providing separate entrances and staircases in homes and meeting-houses—though women and men had equal status. They built their own dwellings and churches, grew their own food, made their own furniture (now highly prized and much copied), everyone covenanting their wealth to a central fund.

Most Shaker songs were created as a spontaneous act of praise and under the control of the Holy Spirit, whether in a worship meeting or outside. A Shaker pamphlet of 1782 described the spontaneity of their worship, clearly related to charismatic meetings today:

One will begin to sing some odd tune, without words or rule; after a while another will strike in; and then another; and after a while they all fall in, and make a strange charm—some singing without words, and some with an unknown tongue or mutter, and some with a mixture of English ...[9]

In the earlier days these songs were passed down in oral tradition, as the Shakers initially resisted the idea of notating their music. The first printed collections of Shaker tunes did not appear till the 1830s, but surviving manuscripts and notebooks show the true scale of their creativity, containing as many as 10,000 tunes.

Shaker music is a uniquely refreshing reminder of the simplicity of much Christian music in America. In country areas around and beyond the Shaker communities, where education was even harder to come by and illiteracy was high, music was still being handed down orally from one generation to the next. It was largely a folk-art, recalled as much as read, each performer adding new flavour to an old song.

Chapter 36

Africans in America

A glance down the 'for sale' columns of eighteenth-century American newspapers would reveal dozens of small-ads such as this:

TO BE SOLD a valuable young handsome Negro Fellow about 18 or 20 years of age; has every qualification of a genteel and sensible servant and has been in many different parts of the world ... He lately came from London, and has with him two suits of new clothes, and his French horn, which the purchaser may have with him.

Slavery had begun two centuries earlier—the first slaves were brought to America by Sir John Hawkins in 1563. The plantations that developed in mid-America in the eighteenth century increased the demands for slaves enormously, bringing the number by the 1750s to 300,000. By the end of that century this figure had tripled. One estimate suggests that altogether 15 million black slaves were brought to the continent (including the West Indies and South America) before Abraham Lincoln's Proclamation of Emancipation in 1863.

The music of Africa

The wonderful musicality of Africa came with the slaves. It could be heard even in the appalling and life-threatening conditions of the slave-ship:

[the slaves on the ship] sang songs of sad lamentation ... They sang songs expressive of their fears of being beat, of their want of victuals, particularly the want of their native food, and of their

never returning to their own country.[1]

The slaves on board had to make music whether they liked it or not, being forced to dance for the entertainment of the sailors:

and if they do not, they had each of them [the boatswain and his mate] a cat to flog them and make them do it ...[2]

The many musical traditions brought over from Africa were transformed by the conditions of slavery and by the arbitrary mixing of peoples of differing cultures (this was a specific policy believed to make the slaves less rebellious) but they were not eradicated. On the contrary, music and dance remained, as in Africa, far more than a diversion from the hardship and injustice of slavery. They were vital expressions of identity occasionally permitted in a life of almost unremitting labour.

Dancing and music-making using traditional instruments were celebrated at festivals such as 'Pinkster Dagh' (a corruption of 'Pentecost Day') when white spectators could look on at a great carnival of ecstatic dancing and music lasting several days.

It was also possible to hear the musical expression—the hollers—of black slave-workers in the fields and open spaces:

Suddenly one raised such a sound as I never heard before, a long, loud, musical shout, rising and falling, and breaking into falsetto, his voice ringing through the woods in the clear, frosty night air, like a bugle call. As he finished, the melody was caught up by another, then

by several in chorus.[3]

The conversion of the blacks to the Christian faith went ahead slowly, for by no means all whites felt it appropriate for their slaves to know for themselves the privileges of their faith. But in such scraps as the slaves could pick up, they discovered the God who ignores human barriers, who delivers people from oppression and in whose sight everyone is equal. These were messages of hope and eventual liberation which came to be celebrated in music and dance of great power:

it was musicking and dancing ... with their unique power to weld into a higher

unity the contradictory experiences of sorrow, pain, joy, hope and despair, that were at the centre of their religious expression.[4]

Hymns

So when the slaves adopted Christianity and began to sing the psalms and hymns in the white churches (albeit segregated) they brought a life and vigour to the music which the whites could not fail to notice:

all breaking out in a torrent of sacred harmony, enough to bear away the whole congregation to heaven.[5]

Camp Meetings

By far the most dramatic spiritual developments in North America came with the Great Awakening at the end of the eighteenth century. The numbers of people caught up in the sweep of renewal were so great that buildings could not house them. Instead, huge throngs, black and white, would gather outdoors to worship for days on end. The scenes were sometimes so extraordinary that only eye-witness accounts can do justice to them. This scene took place in Kentucky, 1801.

The noise was like the roar of Niagara. The vast sea of human beings seemed to be agitated as if by a storm. I counted seven ministers, all preaching at one time ... Some of the people were singing. others praying, some crying for mercy in the most piteous accents, while others were shouting most vociferously ... I stepped up on to a log ... The scene ... was indescribable. At one time I saw at least five hundred swept down in a moment as if a

battery of thousands had been opened upon them, and then immediately followed shrieks and shouts that rent the heavens.[1]

By the 1830s, the camp meetings were

A nineteenth-century camp meeting in Connecticut. This is the preachers' stand; the black slaves could set up their stand behind it.

This skill and passionate sincerity in Christian music-making was brought into the homes of white Christians. In 1755 the Rev. Samuel Davies described his slaves singing from their psalters and hymn-books:

Sundry of them have lodged all night in my kitchen, and sometimes when I have awaked about two or three o'clock in the morning, a torrent of sacred harmony has poured into my chamber and carried my mind away to heaven... I cannot but observe that the Negroes, above all the Human species that I ever knew, have an Ear for Musicke, and a kind of extatic Delight in Psalmody...[6]

By now it will be evident how significant are those last few words, for through their continued celebration of 'extatic delight', the black community in America has proferred a great gift to the legacy of Christian music.

It was not until the 1770s that blacks were permitted to form their own churches.[7] The first hymnal for black churches was published in 1801, the *Collection of Spiritual Songs and Hymns Selected from Various Authors*. The hymns, with texts by Isaac Watts, Charles Wesley and others, were selected by Richard Allen, minister of one of the first independent black denominations, the African Methodist Episcopal Church (his church was in Philadelphia). The many editions of this influential hymn-book more carefully organized, though no less emotional:

About an acre and a half was surrounded on the four sides by cabins built up of rough boards; the whole area in the centre was fitted up with planks, laid about a foot from the ground, as seats. At one end... was a raised stand, which served as a pulpit for the preachers... Outside the area... were hundreds of tents pitched in every quarter... One of the preachers rose and gave out a hymn, which was sung by the congregation, amounting to about seven or eight hundred... more than twenty men and women were crying out at the highest pitch of their voices, and trying apparently to be heard above the others... When it was at its height, one of the preachers came in, and raising his voice high above the tumult, intreated the Lord to receive into his fold those who now repented and would fain return... some fell on their backs with their eyes closed, waving their hands with a slow motion, and crying out—'glory, glory, glory!'[2]

The black slaves flocked to these camp meetings and large numbers of them were converted. They were allowed to set up their tents in the area behind the preacher's stand. Their own celebrations could be enthusiastic enough even to drown out the preaching of the whites' meeting nearby. Indeed, many whites would join in the blacks' singing, picking up Christian songs which would then get sung in their own white churches, a process not always condoned by the elders. J.F. Watson wrote some *Friendly Christian Advice, to Those Methodists, Who Indulge in Extravagant Religious Emotions and Bodily Exercises*:

Here ought to be considered, too, a most exceptional error... In the blacks' quarter, the colored people get together, and sing for hours together, short songs of disjointed affirmations, pledges or prayers, lengthened out with long repetitious choruses... in the merry chorus-manner of the southern harvest field... the example has already visibly affected the religious manners of some whites.[3]

However uneasy it might have made some people feel, the final moments of camp meetings literally broke down the barriers that kept blacks and whites apart. Joint worship followed with a free exchange of Christian music in a final march round the camp, as an onlooker observed:

... accompanied with leaping, shuffling and dancing, after the order of David before the Ark when his wife thought he was crazy; accompanied by a song appropriate to the exciting occasion...[4]

A 'Shout'

Although many black Christians acknowledged secular social dancing to be sinful, they claimed it could be sanctified when it became part of worship.

Christian dance came to be known as a 'shout'. The first recorded use of the word is by an Episcopal clergyman in 1860, in terms of emphatic disapproval:

'Heathenish! quite heathenish!... Did you ever see a shout?' I responded in the negative, and inquired what it was. 'Oh, a dance of negro men and women to the accompaniment of their own voices. It's of no particular figure, and they sing to no particular tune, improvising both at pleasure, and keeping it up for an hour together.'[1]

A fuller description is given by Maria Waterbury, who observed it in the Sea Islands off Georgia, where the practice was already widespread:

It usually began when the preaching was nearly done. Aunt Chloe, or Dinah, would get blest, and seemed unable to contain the blessing, and would spring to her feet, and begin shaking hands with the nearest one to her, and in a moment the example would be contagious, and two-thirds of the congregation would rise to their feet, each shaking hands with some other, the men on one side of the church, the women on the other, and soon all would swing into the center of the church, in front of the pulpit, and shouts of some would rend the air, while those who could sing would sing as though their life depended on their making a noise, all the time swaying their bodies up and down and circling among each other, shaking hands, and moving feet as if keeping time to the music. The preachers would come down out of the pulpit, and stand ready for the hand-shaking... Perhaps after twenty minutes of such exercise, the pastor would lift his hand, when instantly the noise would cease, while he pronounced the benediction, and the worshippers would pass out of the church.[2]

(right up to recent times) are a touchstone for the changing tastes in hymn-singing of many black congregations. The early editions, for instance, contain simple, folk-like tunes popular at the revival meetings of the late eighteenth century. Subsequent editions contained the most popular spirituals of the next hundred years.

The folk-tunes of the early editions were not to everyone's taste. A Methodist Minister, J.F. Watson, wrote in 1819 of

a growing evil, in the practice of singing in our places of public and society worship, merry airs, adapted from old songs, to hymns of our [the whites'] composing: often miserable as poetry, and senseless as matter... most frequently composed and first sung by the illiterate blacks of the society.[8]

Spirituals

Camp meetings (see box) were an important basis for the growth of what are now known as spirituals. These songs, whether sung by blacks or whites, were essentially music of the countryside. The blacks brought special qualities to their spirituals, a background of field hollers (see above) and the ecstatic character of their African musical heritage.

The words of the spirituals were directly biblical, drawn especially from passages which speak of liberation (Moses, Daniel and the Book of Revelation were favourites) and perhaps adapted from popular English hymns, for example, the popular hymn by Isaac Watts:

*When I can read my title clear
to mansions in the skies,
I'll bid farewell to ev'ry fear,
And wipe my weeping eyes.*

This became the basis for several spirituals, such as the following:

Good Lord, in the mansions above,
Good Lord, in the mansions above,
My Lord, I hope to meet my Jesus
In the mansions above.

My Lord, I've had many crosses,
and trials here below;
My Lord, I hope to meet you,
In the mansions above.

The music tended to be of the call-and-response type. This simple structure, so common in African traditional music, allows great freedom: no books are needed, for the chorus is easy to pick up and the solo calls can be improvised on the spot. All this was accompanied by hand-clapping and foot-stamping, creating a Christian protest music of distilled and concentrated ecstasy.

White spirituals of the same period often adapted the texts of hymns in the same kind of way, perhaps repeating lines or adding a short refrain (like 'Glory, hallelujah!') between them, just like the blacks. The music was often borrowed or adapted from well-known folk-melodies.

Conversely, black Christians were well aware of the songs that the whites were singing in the camp meetings and were happy to sing tunes from white traditions. There were more pragmatic reasons for white ministers' disapproval of the wild conduct of black worship in the South. The words of their songs had layers of meaning which were as much earthbound as spiritual:

... no more slavery in de kingdom
no evil-doers in the kingdom
all is gladness in de kingdom[9]

There's no doubt that 'de kingdom' was as much the North, where an escape from the bondage of slavery was possible, as it was a spiritual home in 'the heavens above'.

One organization to assist slaves to flee their masters was called the Underground Railroad. A black slave, Frederick Douglass, became involved with it in 1835 in an attempted escape and later explained the coded messages embedded in spirituals:

We were, at times, remarkably buoyant, singing hymns and making joyous exclamations, almost as triumphant in their tone as if we had reached a land of freedom and safety. A keen observer might have detected in our repeated singing of 'O Canaan, sweet Canaan, I am bound for the land of Canaan,' something more than a hope of reaching heaven. We meant to reach the north—and the north was our Canaan.[10]

Many whites felt that the preaching of the Christian gospel of justice and liberty for all men was dangerous. It seems they were right.

Chapter 37

North and South

The population of the industrial areas of North America grew rapidly during the nineteenth century and with the inexorable move towards the abolition of slavery, more and more black churches were established which did not have to suffer the strict control of the white Episcopal Church. They reflected a number of traditions, from an orderliness which emulated the atmosphere of many white congregations, to an ecstatic and physical abandon characteristic of African tradition.

General Ullyses Grant and his officers ride together in 1865. They led the army of the North in the American Civil War, the aim of which was avowedly to abolish slavery from the land. The hopes of many black slaves were pinned on the northern 'yankee' troops.

African worship

Frederika Bremer visited some black churches in Cincinnati in 1850. The Episcopal Church left her with the impression of a service that was 'quiet, proper and a little tedious'. But the African Methodist Church was quite a different matter:

I found in the African Church African ardor and African life. The church was full to overflowing, and the congregation sang their own hymns. The singing ascended and poured forth like a melodious torrent, and the heads, feet and elbows of the congregation moved all in unison with it, amid evident enchantment and delight in the singing...[1]

Another report comes from William Faux who visited a black church in Philadelphia in 1820:

After sermon they began singing merrily, and continued, without stopping, one hour, till they became exhausted and breathless... While all the time they were clapping hands, shouting and jumping, and exclaiming, 'Ah Lord! Good Lord! Give me Jasus! Amen.'[2]

Such descriptions are evidence that informal dance was a central part of much black worship. Paradoxically, it was the suppression of dance by influential Puritan whites in the eighteenth century that encouraged its development when the black churches became independent.

The abolition of slavery

By the 1840s the ideological split between the Northern and Southern states was affecting every aspect of life. The white Southerners no longer holidayed in the North, nor sent their sons to be educated in the famous Northern universities of Yale, Princeton and Harvard. The issue that polarized North and South was the exercise of slavery, to which the Southerners clung as to a right.

The Northern states, better educated and more liberal than the South, had long accepted its abolition as inevitable, but the Southern states refused to comply. The issue split the church: in 1840 the Methodists in the South were unable to agree with those in the North over the morality of slavery, Baptists dividing on the same issue a year later. (The rift between the Methodists was not formally settled until 1936.)

The issue was finally settled in the Civil War of 1863, where the eventual defeat of the Southern together, but after the Civil War the deprivation and suffering of ex-slaves was very great and made worse still by the activities of white gangs such as the Ku Klux Klan, who attempted to preserve white supremacy by merciless terrorism.

The exodus of liberated slaves from the South therefore continued for the rest of the century. Gradually the spirituals of the countryside were replaced in the minds of migrant freedmen by music of the growing city churches. A

forces allowed Congress to pronounce freedom from slavery in all states in 1865. Tragically, this victory did not necessarily improve the lot of the ex-slaves, many of whom found themselves worse off than before. In an atmosphere of vengeance the South established Black Codes and 'Jim Crow' laws which made segregation almost universal. Blacks were still dependent on whites for their livelihood and given no chance to improve their position. Slavery had at least created a framework for black and white to exist

schoolteacher in Tennessee noted this change after the Civil War:

How I wish you could hear my children sing their strange, wild melodies, that bring back so vividly the old slave life with its toil and servile ignorance. Yet their old plantation songs are falling into disuse, and in their stead we hear chanted daily the hymns and psalms so familiar to Northern ears.[3]

This highly-charged painting attempts to explore the emotions of black Americans freed from slavery. Before emancipation became the dream, hopes for freedom were deferred until after death, 'beyond the Jordan', and this hope of salvation was the theme of many early spirituals.

But the spirituals were preserved in invaluable collections, the first and most important of which was *Slave Songs of the United States*. They were also popularized world-wide by black singing groups, such as the Fisk Jubilee Singers (see box) at a time when the slave culture that produced their music was rapidly disappearing.

But true folk-music (like the original spirituals) is a delicate plant. Its transportation away from its natural surroundings and the popular acclaim that follows inevitably changes and probably diminishes it. It seems that the essential qualities of the slave spiritual cannot be sensed from even the earliest collections of the music, let alone from more recently published

The Fisk Jubilee Singers

A number of organizations had been working for the cause of black emancipation; the American Missionary Association, founded in 1846, was typical. By 1871 it had acquired for the education of freedmen a number of churches, schools and a few 'institutions of learning' in the South, one of which was the Fisk University of Nashville, Tennessee. In response to a desperate need to raise money, George White, the treasurer and musical director, trained a small choir of student ex-slaves and suggested a tour of the Northern States. Their musical repertoire was varied to begin with, including anthems, ballads, patriotic and sentimental songs and a few spirituals. They sang to sophisticated and increasingly enthusiastic audiences who, by all accounts, found the spirituals moving and strange. According to a letter written to the New York Tribune, they sang:

a... collection of the most weird and plaintive bymns sung in the plantation cabins in the dark days of bondage... the very embodiment of African beart music... The barmony of these children of nature and their musical execution were beyond the reach of art.[1]

The respectful but patronizing tone of this letter emphasizes the cultural gap between the performers and their white audiences, in spite of the singers' education and musical training.

Their two American tours, in 1871

versions. Its clearest evocation may only lie in the recorded eyewitness accounts of the culture that produced it.

Far left: **The call-and-response pattern of this spiritual is rooted in African tradition. The harmonies, though, are Western. This is how the song first appeared, notated by T. F. Seward in 'Jubilee Songs'.**

Left: **The Fisk Jubilee Singers in London during their British tour.**

and 1873/4 were great financial and popular successes and led to a tour of Britain in 1874, during which the Singers raised $50,000. Their success was copied by countless other 'Jubilee Singers' across Canada and North America, introducing spirituals to audiences worldwide.

The Fisk Singers' spirituals were published in several editions, the first of which was called *Jubilee Songs*. The songs were copied down into notation by T.F. Seward, who insisted in the introduction to the collection that '... no line or phrase was introduced that did not receive full indorsement from the Singers'.

Both Seward and George White (the choir's trainer) were white and valued a European style of musical education. This gave them what they felt to be a justifiable superiority over a group that Seward reckoned were 'without culture', 'having no knowledge whatever of the rules of art' and with 'wholly untutored minds'.[2]

Probably White trained the Singers in the use of major and minor scales rather than the modes characteristic of true folk-music and corrected their harmony. And Seward was accused by Thomas Rutling, one of the original Singers, of falsifying their music:

... the musician (all due respect to him) who took down the melodies from the singing of the Jubilee Singers, made so many errors in many of them that the singers did not recognise their own songs.[3]

Chapter 38

Gospel Music: White and Black

The spirituals sung by the Fisk and other 'Jubilee' singers became immensely popular in the concert- and music-hall, but were only selectively adopted as songs for worship in the years after the Civil War. White episcopal churches would not have considered slave songs appropriate company for the hymns of Lowell Mason or the Wesleys.

Very few collections of spirituals for use in worship were published after Richard Allen's *Hymns and Spiritual Songs* of 1801. The singers of shape-note music (even in the black churches) continued to sing their traditional *Sacred Harp* songs without the invasion of spirituals.

But in the growing black congregations of city churches spirituals were adopted, but very much changed in the process. The evangelical and Pentecostal churches (especially those where instruments were welcomed as an accompaniment for singing) decorated and embellished spirituals with foot-stamping, hand-clapping and melodic improvisation. The old spontaneity was thus returned to them and the way paved for a new type of Christian music.

White Gospel Music

The first use of the term 'gospel music' in print was probably by Philip P. Bliss (1838–76) in a collection of his music published in 1874: *Gospel Songs, A Choice Collection of Hymns and Tunes, New and Old, for Gospel Meetings, Sunday School*. The title suggests the importance that popular music still held in Christian music in America. Through the

increasing influence of the Sunday School movement (The American Sunday School Union was founded in 1824), the Young Men's Christian Association (established in Boston in 1851) and many other organizations, increasingly large numbers of white Americans were experiencing conversion. From the 1870s, huge meetings were held in football stadia, tents, meeting houses and even railway depots to hear a new era of evangelists proclaim the personal significance of the Christian faith.

In 1873 Dwight L. Moody and Ira D. Sankey formed the earliest evangelistic team of preacher and musician. As one of their slogans put it: 'Mr Moody will *preach* the gospel and Mr Sankey will *sing* the gospel.' The formula was successfully taken up by many others: from John W. Chapman and the singer Charles Alexander, William A. Sunday ('Billy' Sunday) and Homer Rodeheaver, to the tele-evangelists of the present.

The 'gospel songs' of these meetings conveyed the simplest of Christian messages through music of emotional directness to huge numbers of people. The style of the music was a familiar one, closely related to the music halls and the sheet music of Tin Pan Alley. As one newspaper reported, Sankey's hymns

while written to religious words, are made attractive by many secular contrivances... a circus quickstep, a negro sentimental ballad, a college chorus, and a hymn all in one...[1]

The twentieth-century singers (Alexander

and Rodeheaver for instance) emphasized even more the informality of the meetings through the influence of ragtime and early jazz, Rodeheaver sometimes playing the trombone in meetings as well as singing.

The influence of the music of these evangelistic teams has had an equally strong impact in Britain.

Gospel song has over the years penetrated deep into the consciousness of all English-

formed the basis for 'old book singings' (Sunday evening meetings around the *Sacred Harp* book) or 'new book singings' (using the seven-shape system). Since then, sheet music has gradually taken over the circulation of songs and nowadays white gospel music reaches its public through recordings and radio.

While the gospel sound has become thoroughly commercialized (well over 1,000 radio stations are dedicated to it, promoting all

speaking countries. Much of it is still in print and available in collections such as *Sacred Songs and Solos* or *Alexander's Hymns*. As the twentieth century has progressed, the successful strategy of 'circus quickstep' and 'sentimental ballad' established by *Brighten the Corner* or George C. Stebbins' *Out of my Bondage, Sorrow and Night* was repeated with little change for fifty years, and there seemed little desire on the part of evangelists to keep pace with the rapidly changing trends in popular music.

White Southern Gospel

At the big gospel music conventions in the South today there are still traditions which go back to the shape-note singing of the early nineteenth century. Music using the shape-note system continued to be published right up to the 1940s, much of it in the form of periodicals, which

the latest albums) it still has an important base in the independent churches of the Southern states—the Baptists, Methodists and the Pentecostal and Holiness Churches.

Black Gospel

Black gospel music took on a different character from the beginning, though its identity was not fully established until the 1920s. Its roots lay much further back than those of the gospel music of the white evangelists. The Black churches had their own traditions of Christian music whose unique character was, if anything, sharpened by the Civil War and its aftermath.

The African roots of the spirituals and shouts once more found their true home in the Holiness and Sanctified movements of black churches towards the end of the nineteenthcentury. Here the intensity of Christian revival was expressed in

The soloist sings, the conductor leads and a massed choir gives the backing. Billy Graham rallies have brought this kind of mission music to most of the world's great cities. It comes straight from a longstanding tradition of such use of music to add to the emotional impact of gospel preaching.

A jazz band plays at a New Orleans funeral, as they have done for two hundred years. Such traditions on the periphery of worship have had their influence on gospel music. But it is the sound of the human voice that remains at the centre of uninhibited and ecstatic expression of the Christian faith.

moving their bodies each in his or her own idiomatic way. The level of ecstacy thus attained is a matter for each individual... but the overwhelming feeling is of a singing, dancing, praying *community*.[2]

Ancient African traditions of music-making are central to this spontaneous Christian music—a call-and-response structure between preacher and congregation is commonplace and the ecstatic qualities of music are very evident in the body-movement and hand-clapping that accompanies it. As the gospel singer Mahalia Jackson (1911–72) recalled of her childhood:

These people had no choir and no organ. They used the drum, the cymbal, the tambourine and the steel triangle. Everybody in there sang, and they clapped and stomped their feet, and sang with their whole bodies. They had a beat, a rhythm we held on to from slavery days, and their music was so strong and expressive. It used to bring tears to my eyes.[3]

the exercise of the charismatic gifts of the Spirit, particularly those of prophecy and singing in tongues. Christopher Small gives a vivid description of the inseparability of music and worship in these Pentecostal churches today:

... when the Holy Ghost descends, sometimes immediately after the ceremony begins, sometimes only after prolonged searching, the intensity of emotion has to be felt to be believed, most especially in the feeling of unity and common purpose between all present. Speech, music and dance are the tools by means of which the Holy Ghost is invoked and brought into the midst of the congregation—not as separate arts but as aspects of the one great performance art of celebration. A gifted black preacher's... performance... will grow through stages of excitement in which the sense of his words gives way to more ecstatic musicality, his often reiterated words and phrases being taken up by the congregation and thrown back to him with cries of affirmation and with Amens. Finally... the whole congregation are singing, clapping their hands, often in marvellously complex inter-locking rhythmic patterns, and

Such expressive intensity came partly through extravagant and wild colouration of the voice—moaning, growling, shouting—and the deliberate bending of pitch to create a musical scale quite different from the Western major or minor. In particular, the third, seventh and sometimes sixth and fifth degrees may be flattened by a semitone, causing ecstatically painful collisions with an accompaniment of more conventional Western harmony.

The endless expressive possibilities of these techniques were already indigenous to the blues singers, the poorest unemployed blacks, singing on street corners for their next meal. The passionate sound of these half-improvised melodies is quite distinct from the Jubilee singers' spirituals, which were influenced—even corrupted—by European traditions of harmony. The composer of the *St Louis Blues,* W.C. Handy (1873–1958) wrote of his childhood:

The Baptists had no organ in their church and no choir. They didn't need any. The lusty singers sat in the amen corner and raised the songs, raised them as they were intended to be raised, if I'm any judge. None of the dressed-up arrangements one sometimes hears on the concert stage for them. They knew a better way. Theirs was pure rhythm. While critics like to describe their numbers as shouting songs, rhythm was their basic element. And rhythm was the thing that drew me and other members of our home town quartet to attend the Baptist services.[4]

Charles A. Tindley

The essential stepping-stone to the establishment of black gospel music was Charles Tindley (about 1859–1933), a Methodist preacher and song-writer. His church in Philadelphia (East Calvary Methodist Episcopal Church—rechristened the 'Tindley Temple') developed a reputation for powerful music from its foundation at the turn of the century. Tindley wrote both the melodies and the words of his songs (like almost all gospel songs, black or white, the words and music are inseparable).

In the true tradition of the spiritual his songs give reassurance to the poor and the disadvantaged. The word 'overcome' seems especially important:

> *By and by when the morning comes,*
> *When the saints of God are gathered*
> *home,*
> *We'll tell the story how we've overcome:*
> *For we'll understand it better by and*
> *by.*[5]

The refrain of his song ('I'll overcome some day') seems to have been the inspiration for the universally known 'We shall overcome'.

Tindley was unusual in copyrighting and publishing his music (an anthology, *New Songs of Paradise* was printed in 1916). Where the gospel music of the white evangelists was published in vast quantities, black gospel songs were still a folk-art and rarely found their way into print. Not long after, the National Baptist Convention published *Gospel Pearls* (1921), a collection of traditional hymns alongside gospel songs, with a number of Tindley's among them.

Gospel music for the world

The powerful impact of Tommy Dorsey's music took black gospel into another dimension (see box). Where Tindley's songs have an immediacy and directness which spring from straightforward melodies and the simple and slow harmonic rhythms that accompany them, Dorsey's songs are linked closely to the harmonic tensions and complexities of the expressive language of the blues.

He sang with breathtaking emotional intensity, turning a simple song (such as 'Amazing Grace') into a kind of vocal sermon lasting many minutes, heightening the emotional impact of every significant word with extravagant vocal decorations. The congregation would respond to these with spontaneous applause, gasps and cries of encouragement and praise, exactly paralleled by spontaneous and wild arpeggios from the accompanying piano and Hammond organ.

The debt that secular music owes to this immensely powerful mixture—this collision of African and Western cultures—is immense. Every potent musical expression of emotion today, the very basis of rock music, seems to have its roots in gospel music.

All rock's most resilient features, the beat, the drama, the group vibrations derive from gospel. From the rock symphonies to detergent commercials, from Aretha Franklin's prototechnique to the Beatles' harmonies, gospel has simply reformed all our listening expectations. The very tension between beats, the climax we anticipate almost subliminally is straight out of the church. The dance steps that ushered in a new physical freedom were copied from the shout, the holy dance of victory. The sit-ins smoothed by hymns, the freedom marches powered by shouts, the brother and sister fraternity of revolution: the gospel church gave us all of these.[6]

But the wonderful gift of gospel music, its free expression of feeling and its invitation to an unfettered physical response, has been adapted and distorted in its secular forms. By taking the physical and emotional qualities of the music, but rejecting its spiritual basis, the worship of God through ecstatic music has been transformed into a worship of feeling and sensation itself, a change reflected by the materialist and selfish lifestyles of some of the people involved.

Mahalia Jackson made an important distinction between these two worlds, the spiritual and the secular, symbolized in her day by

A priest plays the saxophone.

Tommy Dorsey

The most influential of all black gospel singers and writers is Tommy Dorsey (born 1899). In spite of a strict Christian upbringing as the son of a travelling Baptist minister Dorsey at first sought opportunities to make music wherever he could find them, making a name for himself in his 'teens as the dance pianist 'Barrelhouse Tom'. In 1921 he heard the singing and preaching of Rev A.W. Nix at the National Baptist Convention:

He was great! He was powerful! He rocked that convention: shouts, moans, hollers, screaming... That's where I first got the gospel word, and I was converted at that meeting.[1]

The hysterical quality of Nix's preaching may be sensed from a sleeve-note to one of his most famous sermonettes, *Black Diamond Express to Hell:*

Here she comes! The Black Diamond Express to Hell, holding the throttle wide open; Pleasure is the Headlight, and the Devil is the Conductor. You can feel the roaring of the Express and the moanin' of the Drunkards, Liars, Gamblers and other folks who have got aboard. They are hell-bound and they don't want to go. The train makes eleven stops but nobody can get off...[2]

In spite of his experience at the National Baptist Convention, Dorsey continued to make his reputation in secular music. With the singer Ma Rainey and his own Wildcats Jazz Band he was the first to make blues into big business with the record companies.

In the early thirties he decided to turn wholeheartedly to writing and singing for the church; *Precious Lord,* a song written after the death of his wife and

baby daughter, was a turning point: But the expressive blues style and its secular associations caused consternation, especially with the older generation. As the singer and contemporary of Dorsey, Willie Mae Ford Smith, recalled:

They said I was bringing the blues into the church... When I first started out singing gospel they said 'We don't want that coonshine stuff in here, we don't want that ragtime singing in here,' but that didn't stop me. I kept going because that's what the Lord wanted.[3]

As well as writing nearly 1,000 songs Dorsey has also done much to promote gospel music, through his founding of the Chigaco Gospel Choral Union and the National Convention of Gospel Choirs and Chorusses. He set black gospel music firmly on the road to big business in 1932 by creating the Dorsey House of Music, the publisher of some 500 of his songs and the first business whose sole concern was the commercial cause of black gospel.

Slowly

Prec-ious Lord, take my hand, lead me on, let me stand. I am tired, I am weak, I am worn. Thru the storm, thru the night, lead me on to the light. Take my hand, Prec-ious Lord, lead me home.

On paper, the first verse of Tommy Dorsey's 'Take my Hand, Precious Lord' can only give a glimpse of the song in performance. Dorsey himself wrung passion from every word and, interrupted by a congregation's enthusiastic encouragement, the whole song of four verses might last ten minutes.

gospel music and blues. She rejected the latter, not because it did not suit her voice, but because

blues are the songs of despair, gospel songs are the songs of hope. When you are singing gospel you have a feeling there's a cure for what's wrong. When you're through with the blues you've got nothing to rest on.[7]

Many black gospel singers seem to have led

Soul was cut violently short by his murder in 1964.

To move gospel music out of the church and into the world of entertainment changes it subtly. The attractive and compelling surface of the music may conceal the very message that lies at its heart for those who are not used to Christian worship.

The group Take Six (see box) provides one example out of many. It began among students in a college in Alabama, singing very much in the

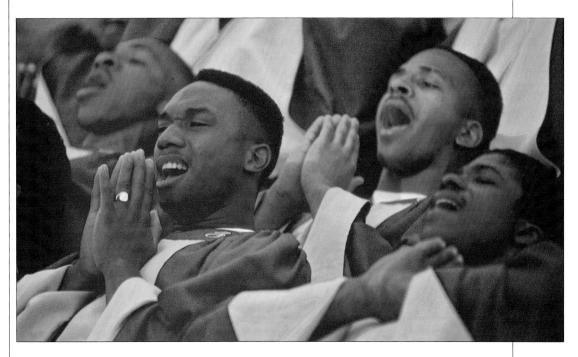

lives like Tommy Dorsey, uneasily poised between the Christian and the secular world. As the music business has become more and more interested in the commercial potential of gospel singers, its temptations have sometimes become irresistible. In the mid-fifties Sam Cooke was a lead singer with the Soul Stirrers vocal quartet:

I was happy enough on the gospel trail and making myself a nice living ... But the more I thought about the pop field the more interesting it became ... I wanted things for my family, and I wanted nice things for my own. Making a living was good enough, but what's wrong with doing better than that?[8]

His success as one of the earliest singers of

tradition of the Pentecostal black Christian music of Tindley and Dorsey. But so heavy has been the borrowing of gospel styles for commercial ends that their music is in danger of being mistaken for entertainment and its Christian message unheard and perhaps devalued.

Gospel music is now big business, even within the Christian circles in which it began. Powerful commercial forces are at work developing the business potential of gospel artists, black and white. Alongside affirmations of the truth of the gospel message and the capacity of its music to enrich, contemporary methods of promotion and the hard sell are well established.

But the true Gospel music, an inseparable part of worship in the majority of black churches and out of the glare of the media spotlight, lives still as Christian music, wholly integrated with the lives

A gospel choir, but are they in church or in performance? The intensity and musicality of black gospel has attracted the forceful attentions of the music business.

of the congregations who sing it. Like the spirituals of the previous century, if it is transplanted to the concert-hall or commercialized, it suffers a devaluation and may cease to be the Godward dialogue it once was.

Take Six

Take Six, the internationally famous group of black gospel singers, describe their music as:

gut-bucket Gospel, that down-home feeling, the traditional gospel. It's three-part harmony and a certain kind of limited improvisation which marks it out. For the black race, it's something which has been going down through the ages, where church was the place you could release those things you couldn't say in the week.[1]

For more than ten years the six singers that make up the group have developed a technical virtuosity that is truly dazzling. They sing largely without any accompaniment, or rather, they provide their own backing through vocal gymnastics, imitating the sounds of instruments—guitar, saxes, brass, rhythm section, bass—with extraordinary skill. They have claimed back to the vocal domain the instrumental dimensions of big band, jazz, rock and soul.

The songs may be spirituals *(Get Away Jordan)*, perhaps based on Bible stories *(David and Goliath, Oh, Mary don't you weep)* or reflect a Christian's encounter with Jesus.

In the concert-hall, where Take Six are now rightly received with adulation by white audiences, such lyrics are placed in a setting which makes them hard to distinguish from the conventional and infinitely cheaper text of the pop-ballad singer. In reality, the words concern God's love-relationship with mankind, beside whose radiant

intensity even the best human relationships are a mere glimmer.

Chapter 39

The United States and the European Classical Tradition

A German composer noted irritably in 1849, after an extended visit to America, that

in all departments of the fine arts—but especially in music—[the American] is behind all, and is therefore not capable of enjoying instrumental music. It is a matter of course, that only the so-called anti-classical can, in any degree, suit the taste of the American public: such as waltzes, galops, quadrilles—above all, polkas.[1]

Cultured Americans were only too aware of the low standing in which their musical education was held by Europeans and in order to improve it, any classical musician from Boston or New York was expected to go to study in Europe, if he had the means. William Mason (1829–1908), youngest son of the hymnodist Lowell Mason, John Paine (1839–1906), Dudley Buck (1839–1909), Horatio Parker (1864–1919), who was Charles Ives' teacher at Yale, George Chadwick (1854–1931)—all these composers trained in Germany or Austria and returned to America to write music in imitation of their Teutonic masters. The recognition that these composers received by critics of classical music was measured by their ability to write in the European tradition:

. . . in this work Mr Paine has shown himself strong in all the qualities which one expects to find in a great composer. In his easy mastery of the minutest details of counterpoint we recognise the devoted student of Bach. His work is distinguished by a clearness and conciseness of form which Mendelssohn has hardly surpassed . . .[2]

Paine, like most of these composers, was also an organist, and the Christian music of the episcopal churches around Boston reflected the attitudes of such men, known as the Boston classicists, who encouraged the performance of the church music of classical European composers as well as writing much of their own. Most churches were unable to find a well-trained choir to sing such music and instead made do with a paid solo quartet who also satisfied the congregations' interest in an operatic vocal style: The singers occupied a side-gallery or were placed above the pulpit, singing excerpts from 'sacred' works by Rossini or Gounod and even adaptations of opera (such as the sextet from Donizetti's *Lucia di Lammermoor* sung to 'Guide me O thou Great Jehovah'!). Dudley Buck wrote a great many anthems for such quartets in both Latin and English, easy-going music with more than a touch of sentimentality.

Opportunities to write Christian music on a much grander scale increased towards the end of the century. Both Paine and Buck showed some ability with large choral and orchestral forces, for instance Buck's *46th Psalm* (1872) and Paine's *St. Peter* (1873) but none of these compared with Horatio Parker's *Hora Novissima* (1893) which still receives an occasional performance where other pieces of the time are long forgotten.

The conservatism of these composers allowed little room for a creative approach to

Christian music. The yawning chasm between Horatio Parker's music and that of his pupil Charles Ives caused nothing but friction and unpleasantness. The problem was not only a difference of opinion, but a principled unwillingness of the teacher to understand the pupil. As Ives recalled:

He would just look at a measure or so, and hand it back with a smile, or joke about 'hogging all the keys at one meal' and then talk about something else.[3]

Such a stifling desire on the part of learned composers to write music within an approved European style did not last far into this century. Between the wars a younger generation of American composers, stimulated by the startling and colourful developments in the new music of France, Germany and Austria, were encouraged to produce music of stimulus and challenge.

Church music

For a while the music of Tin Pan Alley and jazz came to be an archetype of American-ness, not an idiom that had much application in Christian art-music of the time. With a few exceptions, therefore, the music of American composers for the concert-hall is seldom heard in a Christian context, any more than the European or British. But there is a large group of composers whose music is directed towards the white episcopal traditions of worship and to some degree follow the path of the 'Boston classicists' of the later nineteenth century.

These composers in the episcopal tradition are organists and choirmasters who have lived and worked in the surroundings of a large church, cathedral or music college. The necessity of meeting at least some of the expectations of choirs and their congregations has made their music conservative. This does not preclude the ability to speak expressively, but in such surroundings there is the temptation to become complacent and to repeat too often a formula that has proved successful.

As well as music for the American cathedrals, far greater quantities were produced for parish choirs and choirmasters who look for music which is easy on the ear, the brain and the voice. A favourite structure for such pieces is the hymn-anthem, a choral fantasy woven around a well-known hymn. Some are well-written if predictable, but many others are thrown together (and still printed) by composers lacking technique and ideas. This was the kind of music which provoked the musicologist Paul Henry Lang to write in 1946:

Only the artistically unfit continue to compose ritual music, and a more miserable, tawdry, tinsel-strewn collection than recent church music is hard to imagine.[4]

The demand for this music is immense. Even on the local level, congregations are often very large and wealthy. They are often able to support a full-time music staff and several choirs drawn from their own resources.

Hymns

Hymnals and collections of Christian music in America have been numerous since the eighteenth century—in the last hundred years they have multiplied enormously. Such a diverse society has supporters of every possible Christian sect, each of whom has established its own series of hymn- or song-books, re-edited and revised every few years.

The Episcopal Church, for example, licensed an American edition of *Hymns Ancient and Modern* in 1862. It proved much less attractive and saleable than the English edition, but it influenced Episcopalian hymn-books produced later in the century, such as *The Hymnals* with editions in 1874, 1892 and 1916. These all lacked music and several music editions were produced for each one. Only in 1918 was an Episcopalian hymn-book published with music, the *New Hymnal,* encouraging the widespread association of tune with text.

Subsequent editions of the *New Hymnal* have not simply adapted the previous ones, but reflect some rapid changes in taste in Christian music this century. The 1940 edition, for instance, drew on far more diverse sources than previous hymn-books, from plainsong on the one hand to the music of contemporary American and English composers on the other (Vaughan Williams, Holst, Geoffrey and Martin Shaw among the latter). In these respects it resembles Vaughan Williams' *English Hymnal* of 1906. The 1982 edition once again shows a considerable change with the inclusion of much new music and through the influence of the English hymnologist and writer Erik Routley.

The Methodists, the Presbyterians, the Baptists, the Congregationalists, the Lutherans, the Roman Catholics and many others have produced hymn-books and supplements in similar quantity, while other editors and publishers have produced ecumenical collections for use in all circumstances. These, such as *Ecumenical Praise* or *Faith Looking Forward,* have contained the most challenging material for congregational worship.

A large number of new hymn-tunes have been written by many American organist/composers, relatively few of which stand the test of time or the scrutiny of conservative congregations. One superb tune which shows how the concept of 'hymn' is changing is *DeTar* by Calvin Hampton. Imaginative and noble though this tune is, it has not found its way into many hymn-books.

Calvin Hampton's tune De Tar, named after a fellow American organist, hides its ingenuity under a simple exterior. In spite of its setting in chromaticism, counterpoint and an unusual symmetrical plan, the melody is easy to grasp and has been thoroughly tested by congregations. Here it is put to words, by Isaac Watts, based on Psalm 100.

Charles Ives

I *remember how the great waves of sound used to come through the trees when things like* Beulah Land, Woodworth, Nearer My God to Thee… In the Sweet Bye-and-Bye *and the like were sung by thousands of 'let-out' souls… Father, who led the singing, sometimes with his cornet or his voice, sometimes with both voice and arms, and sometimes in the quieter hymns with a violin or French horn, would always encourage the people to sing their own way. Most of them knew the words and music (their version) by heart and sang it that way. If they threw the poet or composer around a bit, so much the better for the poetry and the music. There was power and exaltation in these great conclaves of sound from humanity.[1]*

For the American composer Charles Ives (1874–1954), such childhood memories of camp meetings were vivid and enduring. His recollections are more than just a window onto a colourful past: they were also a fundamental influence on his music, which itself often recalls the fervour and passion of those 'thousands of "let-out" souls'.

The thick, swirling textures of his orchestral pieces suggest mass participation in some great emotional enterprise and are delivered with the stormy rhetoric of the preaching—ebbing and flowing between emotional extremes. Some pieces are a direct evocation of Christian worship, such as the Third Symphony (1904), subtitled 'The Camp Meeting'. Its three movements have specific associations, as their titles show: 'Old Folks Gatherin'', 'Children's Day' and 'Communion'. The music is shot through with revivalist hymn-tunes. *Woodworth* ('Just as I am, without one plea') occurs in all three movements, binding the whole work together.

Charles Ives composed the highest of art music, yet his inspiration was often the simple, moving music sung at the camp meetings he attended as a young man.

This extract from his music for Psalm 90 demonstrates the musical adventures Ives was prepared to undertake to try to capture the psalmist's breadth of vision. It was unlikely to have been accepted or understood by the New Haven choir for which it was written in 1894.

Compared with other works, Ives' Third Symphony is gentle in expression and modest in scale, but the few musicians of his time who came across it found it incomprehensible, along with most of the rest of his music. Much of the Third Symphony was arranged from organ pieces Ives had written some three years earlier and which a fellow student of his pronounced 'hideously modern...'.[2]

Indeed, Ives' visionary creativity took him into realms of modernity and experiment utterly at odds with the music and musicians of his day. Not only that, but the appearance of so much music of the common folk—not just the sentimental hymn-tunes, but Stephen Foster's parlour-songs and all that trained musicians called 'cheap trash'[3]—would have been wholly unacceptable to critics of art-music, had they even had the chance to hear it.

From the age of fourteen till 1902 when he was twenty-seven, Ives was church organist in his home town of Danbury and later in New Haven and New York. His remarkable mind must have startled his congregations from fairly early on. At seventeen, he wrote the now well-known set of organ variations on *America* (the same melody as the British National Anthem). This shows a refreshing and humorous enthusiasm for music-making; the tune is forced into all kinds of eccentric shapes over oompah accompaniments and the final variation demands a lunatic tirade of semi-quavers for the feet 'as fast as the pedals can go'.

Apart from a number of organ pieces, in every one of which there are surprises of some kind,[4] he also wrote choral music for his churches. The most moving and impressive of these are settings of psalms (24, 54, 67, 90 and 150—many more may be lost) written in 1894 for Center Church in New Haven. That any of them were performed at all is remarkable, for the directness of the texts inspired Ives to write some music of startling originality and aural challenge.

Ives drew out the spiritual implications of the psalm-texts as very few other composers have done before or since. It is a shame that such technical difficulties prevent the music from being sung by any but the most expert choirs. His settings are still rarely heard in the concert-hall, let alone in the Christian context for which he wrote them.

Chapter 40

The Charismatic Movement

In the early 1970s the traditional gospel songs of the turn of the century were suddenly ousted from some traditions of worship by a burst of creativity from Christians involved with the charismatic movement. This remarkable renewal of faith, particularly stressing the gifts of the Holy Spirit, swept through many churches in America and Britain. Unlike the Pentecostal churches, however, it grew from within the ranks of the established denominations and spoke strongly to intellectuals of the younger generation. The emphasis was on the gift of love, certainly not the free love of the sixties, but nonetheless carrying a gentle resonance of the hippy movement.

The Episcopal Church of the Redeemer in Houston, Texas, was one of the first congregations to experience a period of liberating renewal from the late sixties onwards. The musical consequences were considerable, with the habitual mould of formal Christian music being broken by the creative enthusiasm of a number of people from within the congregation. Their creative talents – in poetry, music and dance in particular – were valued as gifts of God's Holy Spirit. The atmosphere of freedom and love in which they were exercised was at once surprising and delighting:

All aspects of parish life and ministry were [by 1967] under the guidance of community-trained leaders who brought a sense of communalism to everything the Church of the Redeemer did. But somehow that integrity was intensified into a deeper unity of praise at the Sunday parish Eucharists; a unique flavour of music was giving character to the gathering together of God's people . . . It was a 'people's music', a

***Gebrauchsmusik* of high order; and there was an exciting new charism associated with it, one that clearly testified with prophetic comfort: 'This music is a gift for my praises upon this people.'[1]**

While the new songs often had the same verse-and-refrain structure of the traditional white gospel music, the best of them possessed a new and refreshing quality of quietude and meditation. The musical invention was sometimes on a higher level than in the past, and best of all, there was (and still is) a renewed awareness of the value of biblical texts.

The persuasive sound of commercial music is more evident in countless numbers of Christian musicals inspired by the renewal movement, which lack the innocence of its songs. Instead, they use the colourful and attractive surface of light orchestral rock-music to present a dozen or more songs in a loose structure which substitutes for traditional liturgy. 'Musical' is really a misnomer, for there is usually no staging, but simply spoken links provided by a minister.

The audience are encouraged to join in through singing and prayer, and the invitation to sing 'in the Spirit'. *If My People* (1973) by Carol and Jimmy Owens is typical of this wave of musicals which has given a number of songs to evangelical song-books.

Publishing houses have grown very big over the past twenty years or so, producing musicals and spiral-bound collections of songs with their associated albums. This is undoubtedly the new Christian folk-music of North America—the market-place is a vast concourse and the sellers are becoming ever more persuasive.

PART 8

Music in Twentieth-Century Europe

Chapter 41

Roman Catholic Music in Europe this Century

In the twentieth century the Roman Catholic Church has made two of the most vigorous statements on music and its role in the liturgy—the *motu proprio* of 1903 and its culmination, the *Constitution on the Sacred Liturgy,* part of the Second Vatican Council (Vatican II) of 1962. The themes of the *motu proprio*—the revision of Gregorian chant, the restoration of unaccompanied polyphonic singing (following Palestrina's example) and the encouragement of the composition of modern liturgical music—were part of the reforming spirit of the times and have had far-reaching effects. The most dramatic of these was the widespread revival of Gregorian chant, in a form drastically revised by the monks of Solesmes and closer to its origins than at any time since the fifteenth century.

The author of the *motu proprio,* Pope Pius X, had this to say about the revival of Gregorian chant:

> **Sacred music must ... possess the qualities which belong to liturgical rites, especially holiness and beauty, from which ... universality, will follow spontaneously ... These qualities are found most perfectly in Gregorian chant ... which ... the Roman Church ... insists on being used exclusively in some parts of her liturgy, and which, lastly, has been so happily restored to its original perfection and purity by recent study.[1]**

He also proposed the chant as the ideal music for restoring congregational participation at parish level, so often neglected by the Church in the past. Renewed interest in the chant provided an opportunity to redress this balance, for the chant contains a rich collection of melodies which, like the best folk-music, are tested by time and are simple and easy to learn. Although the *motu proprio* said nothing about chant accompaniment, it was quite explicit about banning the piano, along with

> **... all noisy or irreverent instruments such as drums, kettledrums, cymbals, triangles and so on ... Bands are strictly forbidden to play in church ...[2]**

An unaccompanied choral repertoire was encouraged, as well as new music for the liturgy, though the restrictions were severe:

> **... more modern music may also be allowed in churches ... nevertheless, since modern music has become chiefly a secular art, greater care must be taken, when admitting it, that nothing profane be allowed, nothing that is reminiscent of theatrical pieces, nothing based as to its form on the style of secular compositions.[3]**

Finally, Pius X recognized that none of these edicts would have the slightest effect without there being better provision and training for musicians and (the most desperate need) some education in Christian music amongst the priesthood. Theological students were therefore recommended to study the 'principles and laws of sacred music … with all diligence and love'.[4]

The French organist/composer tradition

The number of musicians in France who took advantage of the *motu proprio* formed part of a renaissance of Christian music in Europe as a whole, allowing French cathedral music to move away from the more dismal moments of the previous century.

At first the chief focus of activity was the *Schola Cantorum,* a school of liturgical chant and music founded in Paris in 1896 by Charles Bordes, Vincent d'Indy and Alexandre Guilmant. The talents of the most outstanding composers of the time, Debussy and Ravel, were lost to the cause of Christian music from the start—in spite of Debussy's appreciation of Palestrina—but the *Schola* did attract some fine artists in its early years, of whom Louis Vierne (1870–1937) is the best known amongst church musicians.

Vierne's world-wide reputation was acquired by his recital music for organ, virtuosic, highly coloured and sometimes aurally dramatic as in the finales to his organ symphonies. At the same time his *Pièces en Style Libre* for organ or harmonium significantly improved the music available to the parish church organist who did not know how to use his feet.

Vierne and Charles Marie Widor (1845-1937) were only two of a number of organist/composers working in France in the early part of this century. Between them they have provided organists with an exceptional variety and richness of music.

Charles Tournemire (1870–1939) was one of the most industrious, writing a huge cycle of organ pieces, *L'Orgue Mystique,* based on Gregorian chant appropriate for every Sunday in the church year—a kind of parallel to the cycles of cantatas by Bach or Telemann. They demonstrate the continuing Roman Catholic tradition which allows the organ to substitute for as well to support voices. The practice has continued to give French organists important positions as improvisers and composers for the liturgy. Tournemire's music has the rhythmic flexibility and the modality of an inveterate improviser on plainsong, creating a heady and numinous atmosphere wholly in keeping with its Roman Catholic tradition.

A similar quality is to be found in the music of

Jehan Alain (1911–40) but with memorable strokes of imaginative genius. His *Litanies* for organ (1937) takes only a few minutes in performance; it is wholly based on the chant but its obsessive repetition gives the piece a unique quality of excitable and desperate supplication.

In contrast to the small amount of music Alain was able to write before his untimely death in action, his teacher, Marcel Dupré (1886–1971) wrote copiously for the instrument and toured widely as a recitalist—especially playing his own music. But the interests of these composers, albeit fostered by the musical life of the great Parisian churches—Notre Dame, Ste Clotilde, St Sulpice or La Trinité—emphasize the organ at the expense of choral music.

Jean Langlais (1907–90), while working within this French organ-playing tradition and

A youth mass is prepared for performance in Westminster's Roman Catholic cathedral. Roman Catholics have experimented with modern instruments and styles of music, as well as developing higher musical forms. In this they have not been very different from Protestant churches.

travelling widely as a concert organist and composer for the instrument, had broader interests. Apart from organ works of dramatic improvisatory gestures and colourful modal reworkings of the chant (the *Te Deum* from the *Trois Paraphrases Grégoriennes* of 1934 is a deservedly often-played and typical example), he also made a lasting contribution to Christian choral music, both for choir and congregation. Here he usually chose idioms which are simple and direct.

In his *Missa Salve Regina* (first sung at Notre Dame in 1954), for example, the intricacies of choral part-writing generally give way to massive blocks of sound from voices, brass and organ,

Prelude (v.1)   Unison

Dieu, nous a-vons vu ta

gloire en ton Christ,   plein de grâce et de vé-ri-té,   en

lui fais nous vi-vre,   pleins de   cha-ri-té

et le mon-de ver-ra   les fruits de ta vic-toi - re.

Langlais' hymn 'Dieu, nous avons vu' ('Lord, we have seen your glory in your Christ') was written in 1957 and has since acted as a model for other writers. It is especially effective when sung by a large gathering and at a steady pace. The legacy of plainsong is evident in the modality and step-wise movement of the tune.

shouts of praise derived from fragments of the medieval plainsong *Salve Regina*. In this and other Mass-settings he returned to the harmonic and melodic sound-world of the fourteenth century, dominated by fifths and fourths, a compromise with outright modernity well suited to the ancient building for which the music was conceived.

Langlais is also one of the few modern French composers whose congregational music has become well-known—even outside his native country. The breadth and grandeur of his hymn *Dieu, Nous Avons Vu Ta Gloire* has acted as a model for a number of other hymn-writers, especially in America, where Langlais developed an enthusiastic following.

Olivier Messiaen

Of all the composers in this French organist tradition, none has compelled more attention than Olivier Messiaen (1908-1992). This is partly

because he wrote more copiously and more broadly than the others, but it is also due to the content of the music and the ideas that brought it into being, which have ranged very widely—far beyond the usual confines of Christian music.

Messiaen's involvement with the Church of his faith was intense, in spite of increasing demands on him as a teacher and celebrated composer. He was appointed organist at La Trinité in Paris in 1931 (at the early age of 22), playing consistently for years for the three Sunday Masses; he also taught at the *Schola Cantorum* from 1936.

Chant, which he studied and endlessly accompanied, filled much of his perspective on music, but his inquisitive mind was remarkably inclusive—of the sounds of modern Western music, of the music of nature and of the East. Such a diversity of inspiration led him to imagine sounds of startling colour and variety, but with very clear, even obsessive, trains of thought binding them together and making his work instantly recognizable.

In common with other organist/composers in Widor's tradition he was a superb and striking improvisor. But again like them he wrote almost no vocal music for the liturgy:

... for example a traditional mass with Kyrie, Gloria, Sanctus, Agnus Dei, no, that I have never written. I have only composed long organ works ... playable in whole or in part during a low mass, and which comment on the texts appropriate to each mystery, with the [prayer] that flows from them.[5]

The organ music he wrote even before his appointment to La Trinité demonstrates some extraordinary qualities. The most striking is its pace, which in terms of the conventions of Western music is painfully slow. *Le Banquet Céleste* (1928) is notated in 3/2 time but at a speed of fifty-two quavers to the minute. At this rate the first chord lasts almost seven seconds, every bar (whose contents are fairly sparse) takes almost a quarter of a minute to play and the whole piece (a mere 25 bars) at least six minutes.

It requires a special mental discipline from the player to slow his or her musical metabolism sufficiently to meet the needs of *Le banquet céleste*. Indeed, it can only be done peaceably by adopting a state of tranquil meditation and ceasing to expect anything of the music but an eternity of restful change. The player's technical difficulties at such a pace are slight, but unless one's expectations of music are profoundly rethought, such slow musical evolution can become tedious or frustrating. As in so many of his works, Messiaen is here contemplating a mystical truth, suggested both by the title and its sub-heading, which is based on the words of Jesus: 'He who eats my flesh and drinks my blood lives in me and I live in him.'

His choice of musical symbol is simplicity itself: a long melody, very gradually ascending in a series of arch-like contours to reach the upper limit of the organ keyboard, then slowly subsiding to extinction. It is a musical image to which he returned again and again, for instance in *Combat de la Mort et de la Vie* (no. 4 of *Les Corps Glorieux)* or in the motet *O Sacrum Convivium*. The underlying harmony of *Le Banquet* is based around the key of F sharp major, but the chord-changes are so infrequent that their dynamic sense of progression is very much dissipated.

Although *Le Banquet* was an early piece its composer already had a remarkably clear sense of purpose—to create music which is contemplative rather than dynamic, universal rather than personal, ecstatic and symbolic rather than rhetorical. To reinforce these characteristics, Messiaen soon moved away from using key signatures in his music and instead used scale systems of his own, which have little precedent in any music before the twentieth century.

Anyone who has struggled with scale practice knows that the distribution of their large and small intervals (the tones and semitones) is deliberately asymmetrical; it is this that allows the degrees of the scale to take on identifiable roles, such as 'tonic' (key-note) 'dominant' (the tonic's opposite pole) and so on. Because of Messiaen's choice of scales with a symmetrical plan of tones and semitones (he calls them 'modes of limited transposition') such identities are no longer clear and any music written in these modes is bound to take a big step away from a conventional harmony that stresses progression through time, so-called 'functional' harmony.

In rhythm too, Messiaen soon moved away from tradition. The regular time signatures of *Le Banquet Céleste* gave way to an unpredictable and irregular barring—in which, as often as not, he will not trouble the player with time-signatures at all. Such a rethinking of tradition is

commonplace among many Western composers since Stravinsky, the great renewer of rhythm, but Messiaen is spurred on as much by the text-governed rhythms of plainsong as by trends in modern classical music.

All these characteristics can be found in an organ piece entitled *L'Apparition de l'Eglise Eternelle* (1932). Its chord structures mostly conform to Messiaen's modes of limited transposition and begin the piece in a strange and exotic sound-world. Once again the arch-like melodic contours build culminatively to a high point, this time a long-sustained blaze of C major as the eternal church is sensed in its full glory before the vision fades to extinction.

The rhythmic contour of the melody is an unpredictable weaving of long and short notes which refuse to fit to a regular pattern—a close parallel of the freely-flowing style of plainsong performance favoured by Solesmes. It must be remembered, too, that this music was first imagined in the huge spaces of La Trinité and is best heard in similar surroundings, the music rendered impersonal both by the cavernous acoustic and by the (probably) invisible performer.

During the 1930s Messiaen wrote much more for the organ, in carefully planned sets of pieces: *L'Ascension* (1934), *La Nativité du Seigneur* (1935) and *Les Corps Glorieux* (1939). In their complete form, these collections can have no place in liturgy, but the separate movements are heard as voluntaries and occasionally as meditations during worship.

They are Christian music in the specific sense that their titles and their content draw the listeners' attention to spiritual and mystical dimensions of the faith. They do this not only by the specific images of their titles (such as 'God among us' or 'the mystery of the Holy Trinity') but also by quoting plainsong melodies which can provide associations with passages of scripture (even though the melodies are adapted to Messiaen's own special modes).

The most challenging and extraordinary developments in Messiaen's music began in about 1949. For some time he had been adorning and embellishing his basic principles of composition in a way that parallels the increasing complexity of medieval Christian music. He elaborated the melodic strands based on plainsong into streams of chords and superimposed modes on each other, sharply raising the level of dissonance. He heightened

Olivier Messiaen, who died in 1992, made an immense contribution to church music.

The central section of the 'Sortie' from Messiaen's liturgical organ work 'Messe de la Pentecôte' (1950) is a balance of medieval symbols: God's creation in nature and the cosmos are here celebrated by birdsong and by numbers. The figures (descending in the left hand, ascending in the pedals) indicate the length of chords or notes measured in semiquavers. In context, the whole effect is colourful, but static and contemplative.

further the contemplative mystical and ritual qualities of the music by incorporating rhythmic patterns drawn from Hindu musical traditions and, most of all, by emphasizing the independence of simultaneous events. Sometimes this conveys the impression that different strands of the music are evolving at differing speeds.

Then he wrote a series of keyboard pieces, some for piano, some for organ, in which his imaginative powers took a series of further leaps into unprecedented areas. The organ pieces are all the more remarkable for their new vocabulary of sounds, using combinations of stops and registers that had never before been considered musically viable. Messiaen seems here to revel in new possibilities of all kinds; and most startling of all, some of the music is intended for the liturgy.

Beyond his organ music, however, Messiaen was typical of many other French organists in showing less inclination to set texts for church use. Only his short (though beautiful) motet *O Sacrum Convivium* (1937) is really appropriate in the context of worship. His other settings of mystical texts have, on his own confession, another purpose:

… my two principal religious works played in the concert-hall are called *Trois Petites Liturgies de la Présence Divine* **and** *La Transfiguration de Notre Seigneur Jésus Christ*. **These titles are not chosen at random: I intended to accomplish a liturgical act, in other words to carry a service or some kind of praise into the concert-hall. My chief gift is to have taken the essence of the Catholic liturgy intended for the faithful out of its stone edifices and to have placed it in other buildings apparently not made to accept this kind of music, but which in the end have strongly welcomed it.[6]**

Chapter 42

The Bible in the Concert Hall

Messiaen's achievement in bringing Christian meditation into the concert-hall is really nothing new—oratorios and Mass-settings still sustain a tradition, now more than 300 years old, of bringing such music into secular surroundings. Unfortunately, the church this century has shown little inclination to support composers of high art—especially where their style is challenging or uncompromising.

An era which has enmeshed millions in two world wars and which has seen some of the worst atrocities ever committed against humanity has extracted a powerful reaction from its artists. Many musical works, while not commissioned or even recognized by the church, have a spiritual depth virtually absent from the repertoire of the previous century which did receive ecclesiastical support. On the one hand, George Bernard Shaw, writing in England in the early 1890s, could remark with partial truth that

with the exception of a few cantatas of Mendelssohn, all the Biblical music of this [nineteenth] century might be burnt without leaving the world any poorer.[1]

On the other hand, the church in the twentieth century has taken little part in what has turned out to be a renaissance in concert music of spiritual or Christian challenge. The composer John Joubert has written:

It is a pitiful comment on the musical awareness of our church authorities that only in 1958 was Benjamin Britten invited to conduct a work of his own at a Three Choirs Festival. And William Walton's oratorio *Belshazzar's Feast* had to wait

twenty-five years before being included in the same Festival programmes—long after it had been accepted everywhere else in the country.[2]

At the very beginning of the century in England, Edward Elgar (1857–1934) set to music an extended poem by the English Catholic and former Tractarian, Cardinal Newman. *The Dream of Gerontius* (1900) immediately put the artistic standards of the English oratorio onto a quite different plane from the 'religious' music that Shaw loved to hate. This was the work of which Elgar said: 'I have allowed my heart to open once'[3] and undoubtedly the emotional intensity which accompanies the spiritual journey of the poem is unprecedented in British music and has

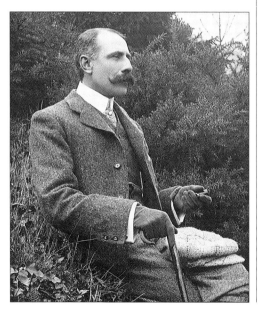

Edward Elgar in his favourite Malvern Hills. Elgar is not normally thought of as a religious composer, but his oratorio 'The Dream of Gerontius', set to a poem by John Henry Newman, is a powerful expression of Christian hope.

rarely been equalled since.

Soon after this, a younger generation of composers was acquiring new techniques and applying them to large-scale choral pieces. An early and vivid example is by the Swiss composer, Arthur Honegger (1892-1956). His *King David* (1921) is an oratorio drawing on the books of Samuel and presented by a narrator, with chorus,

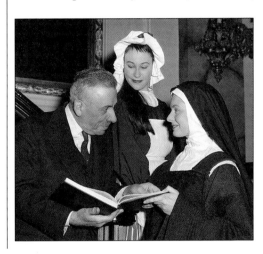

The French composer Francois Poulenc (1899-1963) at rehearsals of his opera 'The Carmelites'.

Below: Poulenc's 'Litanies à la Vierge Noire' for women's (or children's) voices and organ struck a new balance between a contemplative music reminiscent of plain-song and passionate rhetoric. By such means Poulenc escaped the tawdry sentimentality of the previous century. The Litanies stand at the head of a series of choral works which were to occupy this composer for the rest of his life.

soloists and orchestra.[4] Honegger followed it with a number of other large-scale oratorios, some requiring staging, the most spectacular of which is *Joan of Arc at the Stake* (1935). In a few of his last works, such as the *Christmas Cantata* (1953) he turned from the epic and the stressful to pastoral and quietly visionary.

The other outstanding Swiss composer of the century is Frank Martin (1890–1974). Like Honegger, his music is widely performed on the European mainland but seldom heard in Britain. He was the son of a Genevan Calvinist minister and became a convinced Christian himself. While believing that he had to express the individuality rather than the universality of his faith (which was certainly broader than Calvinism) he returned constantly to the central themes of Christianity in his work.

Martin's first and last important pieces (the *Mass for four voices* (1921–29) and the *Requiem* (1972)) draw on Roman Catholic liturgy, but perhaps his oratorios are the most compelling. The majority, apart from the war-torn *In Terra Pax* (1944), elaborate on central themes of the New Testament: *Golgotha* (1948), *The Mystery of the Nativity* (1959) and *Pilate* (1964).

For Igor Stravinsky (1882–1971), expatriate though he was for most of his life, it was Russian music that had the most enduring effect —not simply the classic and folk music of his youth, but also that of his native Orthodox Church. In 1926 he re-affirmed his Orthodox faith, celebrating a new spiritual dimension to his life over the next few years by setting some liturgical texts in Church Slavonic for unaccompanied chorus, *Otche nash'* (Our Father), *Simol' veri* (the Creed) and *Bogoroditse devo* (Hail Mary).

On a much larger scale Stravinsky designed a symphony around three psalms (39, 40 and 150). The serenity of the resulting *Symphony of Psalms* (1930), especially of its conclusion, partly stems from its reminiscences of Orthodox chant and from the pure sound of children's voices required for the upper parts of the chorus (though the latter request is seldom honoured in performance).

Stravinsky's desire to write music for the Ordinary of the Mass came some years later, in the form of the *Mass for chorus and ten wind instruments* (1948). Although Stravinsky intended this as Christian music—that is, for liturgical use—it was not commissioned by the church. Its manner is as distant as possible from the rhetoric and individualism of the Romantics, returning to the meditative universality of early Christian music, at one time so much desired by Roman Catholic reformers. Why therefore is it seldom heard in the context of the liturgy? The expense of engaging the musical expertise is doubtless one reason, but it is nevertheless another loss to the organized church that it cannot find room for Western music that symbolizes the faith so profoundly.

Since the composition of Elgar's *Gerontius* and the two large-scale oratorios that followed, *The Apostles* (1903) and *The Kingdom* (1906), British choral music has been as rich as the previous century's was poor. In particular, the threat of war or its reality has evoked some spiritually impassioned music, from Vaughan Williams' *Dona Nobis Pacem* (1936)—an uncannily prophetic piece—to Michael Tippett's *A Child of our Time* (1941)—the reaction of a courageous pacifist to war—and Benjamin Britten's *War Requiem* (1961).

More recently, Britten created further opportunities for biblical texts to be heard in concert as the result of experiencing the theatrical traditions of Japanese Noh. The result was *Curlew River* (1964), in which 'spiritual music theatre' is acted out in a setting of medieval Christendom. Britten wrote *Curlew River* as a concert piece designed for church performance and followed it by two more, *The Burning Fiery Furnace* (1966) and *The Prodigal Son* (1968).

In all these 'church parables', the influence of Noh-play and the spiritual dimension of the texts led Britten away from the emotional and expressive world of his earlier music. In doing so, he (and Stravinsky in the *Mass*) opened the way for a re-assessment of the very nature of concert music, a move which is now having an increasing effect on the way composers work and on the expectations of audiences.

New musical forms

In this century's music the grammar of 'functional' harmony, that is, the changes of harmony that are intended to convey a strong sense of journey through time, has been challenged. Generally the result has been an adaptation of this tradition rather than a complete rejection of it. Most twentieth-century music therefore expresses or evokes emotion through familiar means and by using familiar codes.

The Stravinsky Mass and the Britten 'church parables', however, suggest the possibility of music with new (or rather, much more ancient) priorities. Their music has been a cue for a number of more recent composers to distance themselves further from the rhetoric of the concert hall.

The keen interest in minimalism over the last few years—a movement which has strong connections with Eastern cultures—is a sign that composers and their audiences are rediscovering another function for music altogether, one which is contemplative and static. If there is a sense of journey in the music at all, the pace is very slow and travel is by foot rather than by air. There are strong resonances here with Messiaen.

The music of both Arvo Pärt and John Tavener, discussed in Chapter 32, cannot often be called minimalist, but its evolution is leisurely and sometimes on an epic scale. Concert audiences have found some of this music difficult. John Tavener's large-scale musical canvasses, such as *Akhmatova: Rekviem* and *Prayer for the World* (both 1980) have conveyed to some 'a feeling of

In grief at the death of a friend, Poulenc, then in his thirties, visited the Sanctuary of Rocamadour in the Dordogne. The humble chapel, cut out of the mountainside, gave him a sense of great peace, and the works which sprang from that experience have added immeasurably to a fairly thin period for French choral music.

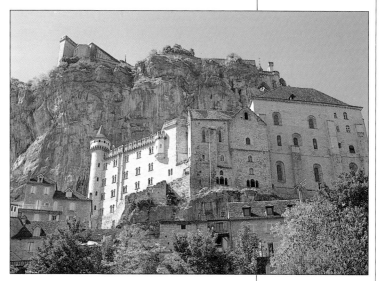

spiritual austerity rather inappropriate to the modern concert-hall.'[5]

But others have discovered a new sense of renewal in concert music which explores once more the spiritual domain. The Hilliard Ensemble, a group of four singers specializing in both early and contemporary music, has established a special relationship with Arvo Pärt which came about in a significant way.

Up until 1987 his choral music was unknown

in Britain and had received very few performances in Europe. Those few performances, given by choirs in tune with the Romantic classics (large numbers of voices, plenty of vibrato, a mass of individuals with little collective focus) dissatisfied critics and Pärt himself.

The four voices of the Hilliard Ensemble concentrate on purity of sound, perfection of tuning and exquisite blend. Their voices revealed the true nature of Pärt's music for the first time: for them and for their audiences 'every performance is a spiritual experience'.[6] The Ensemble has since toured Pärt's *St John Passion,* a setting of *Psalm 51* and other music springing from biblical texts in concert halls and cathedrals throughout Europe.

The British composer John Tavener has described concert music as a kind of outer courtyard to worship: 'Stockhausen has said that the concert hall will become the church of the future. I do not believe that this is the case, but I do think there is a kind of middle ground that deals with the sacred tradition bringing it back into the 'Temenos'. That is a Greek word that means 'the sacred area surrounding the temple' . . .'[7]

The music of many Western composers today reflects both humanity's deep need for spiritual understanding and a tacit if not overt assumption of the existence of God. However, Tavener rightly regrets that the church seems so little prepared to support artists who have a Christian message. It is a tragedy that the vision of most Christians in positions of authority—at least in Britain—is still limited to a utilitarian function for music. Surely they should be alongside composers in their desire to stake out 'sacred areas', whichever temple they choose to surround.

Chapter 43

Vatican II and the Liturgy

After the long, too long stagnation of liturgical forms, the reform decided on by the Second Vatican Council was the signal to start moving. But waters held back too long and then released sometimes look more like a destructive flood than a necessary irrigation. The tide is the bringer of both life and death. It was high time the church made an effort to adapt, just as every other living body alters. But the change in the liturgy was so sudden and so radical, that it could truly be called a crisis.[1]

So wrote the French composer and priest Joseph Gélineau, on the radical reforms brought about in the Roman Catholic Church which started in 1963 with the publication of the *Constitution on the Sacred Liturgy*. Musicians involved in Roman Catholic worship were indeed impatient for that change long before it came about, particularly in the area of congregational participation.

The tenets of the *motu proprio* of 1903 had been emphasized and amplified by other documents (such as Pope Pius XI's *Apostolic Constitution, Mediator Dei* of 1947 and the *Instruction on Sacred Music and Sacred Liturgy* of 1958). All these urged that 'the faithful . . . should not be merely detached and silent spectators, but . . . should sing alternately with the clergy or the choir . . .'[2]

But musicians like Dom Gregory Murray (1905–) did not believe this could be achieved while the liturgy remained as it was. In the firm belief that even the simpler Gregorian chants were too involved for an average parish congregation to sing effectively, Murray wrote

his *People's Mass* in 1950:

That it succeeded in achieving its aim was proved by the enormous sales the world over. Musically, as I am fully aware, it is undistinguished; but at last it made it possible for congregations to join in the singing of Mass with vigour and obvious enjoyment.[3]

Music for the people

The reforms put forward by the Second Vatican Council opened the door to drastic change. While stressing the timeless value of Gregorian chant in worship alongside other traditional aspects of Christian music, the *Constitution* emphasized the 'active participation of the people' again and again, permitting vernacular languages in worship instead of Latin. It noted:

In certain countries, especially in mission lands, there are people who have their own musical tradition, and this plays a great part in their religious and social life. For this reason their music should be held in proper esteem and a suitable place given to it . . .[4]

To allow such a breadth of musical idiom in worship, the *Constitution* had to relax its attitude to the use of instruments, with the condition that instruments should 'truly contribute to the edification of the faithful'. Composers were encouraged to write under these new circumstances, allowing the congregation to participate actively.

The effect of this on music in the Roman

Catholic Church was dramatic. In some areas the Council was only acknowledging what had already been tacitly accepted—for instance, that a great variety of styles of Christian music had developed across the world, from Africa to Latin America, and that the Church should treasure and encourage it. But a selective adoption of this legislation, especially in Europe, led to rapid and sweeping changes. These, and the subjective interpretation of Vatican II, were viewed by traditionalists with alarm.

In an eagerness to bring Christian worship in closer touch with their congregations, churches abandoned Latin very quickly (a move permitted but not required by Vatican II) and as a consequence almost all the music associated with it was dropped. Inevitably, the incomparable heritage of chant and polyphony fell into immediate disuse.

The insistent demands that music was the property of the people generated strong anti-artistic feeling: singing in harmony by experts on behalf of the congregation was out, unison singing of simple music was in. Supporters and detractors of this trend were brought into sharp conflict. Lovers of the Church's musical heritage were appalled at the erosion of valued tradition.

In the initial wave of experiment, Roman Catholic churches throughout the West echoed to sounds never heard before within their walls. A flood of Christian music of the simplest kind was produced, taking its cue from all kinds of popular sources: dance music, modern folk idioms, pop ballads, and even from rock music. An extreme was reached in the late 1960s, when a few large

L'Abbé de Silvanès

The need to foster Roman Catholic music of excellence has led to the founding of an important cultural centre at Silvanès near Albi in southern France. Its focus is a Cistercian abbey, abandoned and in ruins till about 1977. A number of artists then came together under the leadership of Père André Gouzes to re-establish it as a place of hospitality, of praise and of art.

The task of restoration is now complete and Silvanès offers a wide-ranging series of courses and spiritual activities associated with the liturgy. They include study of the history of the church and of chant, inter-faith colloquia, workshops on icon-painting, liturgical dance, calligraphy, bookbinding and even floral art, all within a Christian context.

But the main spiritual mission of Silvanès is its music, which is based on a respect for the church's liturgical heritage and can be seen as a reaction against the populist styles of worship permitted by Vatican II. Many of the courses are directed to helping choir-masters and clergy understand the nature and history of Christian music. Important feasts in the church's year are celebrated with large numbers of visitors, alongside opportunities to study voice-training, choral conducting and the theological context of chant. Père André Gouzes' *Liturgie Chorale du Peuple de Dieu*,[1] which is based on ancient chant from Western and Eastern Christendom, forms the musical basis of the centre's work, which is being taken up in other parts of France.

A candlelit service is held at Grandchamps Community in France. Candles, crosses, silence—these can be great aids to contemplation, and their use by communities such as Taizé and others has proved helpful to many for whom silence is something strange. Music for meditation can be gentle, reflective, often repeating key phrases.

liturgical events became difficult to distinguish from rock concerts.

In an attempt to clarify the dangers which they believed lay behind such musical permissiveness, a group of American Cecilians touched the heart of their problem: the reintroduction of the ecstatic and physical element of music in a tradition which had firmly resisted it since the times of the Church Fathers:

Music which is directed predominantly toward the sensitive motor responses of man is not worthy of the liturgy. This music makes its appeal ... only on the level of the purely sensual, even to the possible exclusion of the spiritual faculties ... The rhythm of this music with its primitive and uniform impulse generates in the listener a sensual, driving excitement. This monotonous, continually repeated rhythm dulls consciousness ... and dissipates into mere motor responses which serve to blot out all personal individuality. The prayer of a congregation, which ought to be vivified by the liturgy, is thus rendered impossible by music which evokes in men truly disorderly feelings and serves only to awaken essentially emotional drives ...[5]

In reality, music with the overwhelming ecstatic qualities suggested here is the exception in Roman Catholic music of recent decades in the West. Quite apart from the continued resistance to it from some quarters, fairly few churches have the means or the expertise to produce it.

In among a great deal of ephemeral material which has been published in vast quantities for use amongst parish congregations, some music is of an order of excellence which amply justifies the turmoil that brought it into existence. The most enduring are the psalm-settings.

The renewal of psalmody

It was Joseph Gélineau who gave a new impetus to psalmody. In advance of Vatican II by ten years, he published a booklet entitled *Vingt-quatre Psaumes et un Cantique,* which proposed a way of singing the psalms in translations close to the original Hebrew and yet simple and tuneful enough for congregations. Unlike Gregorian or Anglican chant, it is based on the provision of regularly accented syllables (even though the number of syllables between them may vary). The provision of antiphons allowed for the psalms to be sung responsorially. These antiphons might be sung as a preface and conclusion to the psalm, or alternated with the verses, following the time-honoured practice of interlacing psalm-verses with a refrain. The music is of extreme simplicity, requiring only the most straightforward pitch-changes from one accented syllable to the next.

Gélineau's psalms have proved immensely popular, well beyond their Roman Catholic origins. The gentle modality of his version of Psalm 23 has become a classic of its type. But his gift is not so much the settings as the method v.1   The Lord is my shepherd;

there is nothing I shall want.

Fresh and green are the pastures

where he gives   me re - pose.

Near   restful   waters he leads me,

to re- vive my droop- ing spi - rit.

Joseph Gélineau's setting of Psalm 23 (1952) closely follows the Hebrew verse-patterns, with regular stresses but varying numbers of syllables. The unused notes of the chant formula come into play in subsequent verses. In time-honoured fashion, an appropriate antiphon is sung at the beginning and end.

itself, for it encompasses so many possibilities for marrying biblical prose to music that many other composers have created their own versions of it.

In Britain, the composers Colin Mawby and Anthony Milner (among many others) have written some simple but tuneful responsorial psalm-settings for congregational use.[6] Milner's psalms alternate simple refrains for everyone with more involved settings of psalm-verses for choir; Mawby's are simple yet musically worthwhile. In Britain their example has been continued and extended by the St Thomas More Centre in London.

On another level, Joseph Gélineau has offered a valuable new perspective on the vexed disagreements over Roman Catholic liturgy. His deep spiritual awareness and firmly grounded love for God's people reads very differently from the indignation of the scholars concerning the effects of Vatican II. Writing in the late 1970s, he gave a positive view of the position in France:

... the assemblies do sing! ... much more than they did a quarter of a century ago. Then nearly all the masses celebrated on

Sundays, particularly in towns, were 'low masses', that is, without singing. The singing at high mass was generally mostly done by the choir. The Gregorian movement did succeed, with brave and persistent efforts, in getting some assemblies to join in the singing of the ordinary of the mass. But this never became general...

Today the opposite is true. There is singing at most Sunday masses, especially in towns, where it is easier to find leaders of the congregation. And the singing is essentially by the congregation. The change was not brought about by a change in the general culture, but by the ideology of the liturgical renewal: 'The ideal form of community participation in the celebration is singing.' ...It is a product of the vitality of the assemblies or at least of their organisers.[7]

Taizé

The ecumenical centre at Taizé in France at present affects not only the musical taste but the worshipping patterns of congregations all over Europe—even world-wide. The community was founded in 1949 by Brother Roger, in an area where he had sheltered Jewish refugees during the Second World War. From the 1950s, small fraternities with the same commitment to celibacy and communal life were established throughout the world, particularly in places of poverty and need.

Although the first brothers were Protestants, Taizé has maintained close and warm contacts with the Roman Catholic Church and received constant encouragement from its Popes. Indeed, in 1961 it arranged for a historic meeting of Protestant and Catholic clergy.[1] By the 1960s the Taizé community was proving increasingly attractive to young people from all parts of Europe. For them it became a centre for spiritual discovery and meditation.

The numbers that pass through the centre 'as one passes close to a spring of water'[2] is now very great and its style of worship has been carried back to Christian communities throughout the world.

The music of Taizé is characteristic, partly because it is closely bound up with the community's special dimension of peace and reconciliation, but also for the pragmatic reason that it has always had to be accessible to large numbers of people who speak many different languages. The community began by using psalmody from the sixteenth-century and by Joseph Gélineau, but the composer Jacques Berthier was invited to create new music

so that all could actively participate in the prayer of the Community . . . using simple elements . . . of real musical quality so that genuine prayer could be expressed through them . . . a solution was found in the use of

short musical phrases with singable melodic units that could be readily memorized by everybody.[3]

Latin is used quite extensively in these repeated refrains, not at all for traditional reasons, but because it is 'a foreign element for everyone, and hence neutral'. The verses sung by cantors or small groups may be in a number of languages in turn. Taizé provides evidence that the contention in the 1960s over the use or the abandonment of Latin in worship is no longer an issue for a new generation.

The excellence of the music of Taizé is not embodied in complexity or sophistication, but in orderliness. Some songs closely follow the strict balance of four parts required in the seventeenth or eighteenth century. Others use modal harmony with parallel movement more suggestive of the early twentieth. In

every case, whatever the musical style, the link between the gentle stresses of the Latin and the rhythmic patterns of the music is very close.

The flexibility of Taizé music has brought it into use in all sorts of circumstances, from a small gathering with a guitar or keyboard to a large assembly accompanied by an orchestra. In all cases, however, the music may appear empty unless it is used actively, for it is intended as a vehicle for prayer and meditation and is therefore only part of a greater Godward experience.

The tranquility of this chant by Jacques Berthier epitomizes the music of Taizé. The bass and alto lines have been composed with care to create a full and logical harmony even though the tenors and sopranos double on the tune until the final bars.

Chapter 44

Lutheran Musical Revival

One beneficial effect of the Romantics' fascination for the past was the work that scholars did for Christian music. Quantities of early music were uncovered, for instance by the scholar J.A. Philipp Spitta (1841–94) who not only wrote a monumental study of J.S. Bach, but excited musicians' interests in the wider heritage of Lutheran music.

The heritage

Johannes Brahms (1833–97) was introduced to the music of Samuel Scheidt and Heinrich Schütz by Spitta. Brahms had a life-long interest in early music, but it is partially due to Spitta that he wrote so many unaccompanied motets under its influence. The *Two Motets,* opus 74 (1877), for instance, are reanimations of the spirit of the sixteenth and seventeenth centuries dedicated to Spitta.

For a renowned composer of the time to turn his attention to this kind of music was most unusual. Compared with instrumental and solo vocal music (in the form of song or opera) there was little expertise or audience potential to draw on. Brahms' *Requiem* (1868) is in a form much more accessible to the music-loving and Christian public; it was reckoned in its day to be his greatest achievement.

Although the music of the *Requiem* adopts the accepted public manner of large chorus and symphony orchestra, its expert and pure polyphony still owes a great deal more to Christian music of the past than to the accepted conventions of the time. Brahms chose his own biblical texts for it, intending them to have a more universal application than those of the Roman Catholic liturgy. It is no coincidence that a

number of them had already been set by Schütz (in the *Cantiones Sacrae* and *Geistliche Chormusik*).

Max Reger, in the next generation (1873–1916), was equally fascinated by early music. He too wrote a number of unaccompanied motets (*Geistliche Gesänge* opus 110, *Acht Geistliche Gesänge* opus 138) which are heavily indebted to Lutheran music of the seventeenth and eighteenth centuries. Their simplicity and emotional reserve contrasts starkly with Reger's turbulent *alter ego,*—he also created music renowned for its intense emotionalism and uncompromising modernity.

The dissimilarity within Reger's music is instructive, for it points up the vast gulf between what was then believed to be suitable for the rejuvenation of Christian music and the latest artistic developments of the Romantic movement. Some of Reger's many organ pieces provide striking examples of an intriguing but uneasy alliance of the old and the new.

In response to his view that J.S. Bach was 'the beginning and end of all music' Reger created organ pieces modelled on the typical structures of the early eighteenth century. Under these circumstances, the extreme emotionalism of their content is all the more shocking. Using techniques in common with Schönberg, he presents the listener with stormy and ambivalent music, chains of ambiguous chords changing so rapidly that a sense of key is all but suppressed.

Challenging and worthwhile though it is as music, this—the true voice of Reger—does not reconcile itself with the needs of the liturgy. Such intense rhetoric, typical of the way Romanticism was then developing, only serves to worsen the collision between the universal dimension of worship and the individuality of the music. To satisfy his heart-felt desire to renew Christian choral work Reger felt he had to lean heavily on ancient styles and techniques.

But after the First World War the unbridgeable gulf perceived to exist between the modern and the ancient became less of a problem. This was partly because a significant number of musicians found the self-conscious intensity of the Romantic movement cloying and jaded. Many of them were refreshed and much more inspired by the relative simplicity of Mozart or Pergolesi and through the prime example of Stravinsky found ways of *renewing* the past rather than merely of copying it.

The opening of Max Reger's organ fantasia on the chorale 'Wachet auf, ruft uns die Stimme'(known in English as 'Wake, O wake, the night is flying'). This is as the composer wrote it, in 1900.

Hugo Distler

Distler (1908–1942) felt his relationship to Schütz particularly strongly. He laid the foundations of his own music following Schütz's example, inspired by the knowledge that, like him, his motivations were a strong faith and the desire to make it known through music. The revitalizing of word-setting was an essential part of that process of communication:

[Distler] and other composers of his generation brought to an end the undisputed reign of instrumental music... through the rediscovery of the human voice, and of its marvellous, mysterious and plastic qualities... Because the voice is bound to the word, the burden of the words assumes paramount importance... For Hugo Distler this was, first and foremost, the message of the Gospel. He wished to spread it abroad through his music as a declaration, as sermon, song of praise, and as a proclamation... One can hardly fail to be affected by the forcefulness of his musical preaching.[1]

Distler worked at a number of churches, beginning in 1931 at the Jakobikirche in Lübeck. Here it was accepted that he should write the music for the church choirs:

I have two choirs (a volunteer choir and a boys' choir) for which I compose everything myself. I already have a beautiful collection of this type of easy sacred music and hope that an entire year's repertoire will come into being from this. The children as well as the adults sing these polyphonic pieces with joy and ease.[2]

The result of this collaboration was, among much else, *Der Jahrkreis* (The year's cycle), easy three-part settings of Reformation chorales for each week of the year. This practical and edifying music sprang from the church's wholehearted encouragement of the creative gift of composition—rare outside the Lutheran community.

Distler's untimely and tragic death

left much work unfinished—the nine motets which make up *Geistliche Chormusik* (1934–41) were intended eventually to number fifty-two—again, one appropriate for each Sunday of the year. Nevertheless, they are the most beautiful of all his work and include the remarkable *Totentanz,* a large-scale piece based on medieval texts from Lübeck's Marienkirche.

A more sinister parallel between Schütz and Distler is the political turbulence and oppression in which they lived. Where the Thirty Years' War required Schütz to work with physical suffering and deprivation all around him, Distler was progressively caught up with the political oppression of the Third Reich. Soon after his move to Stuttgart in 1937, Distler was required to sit on a local examining board set up by the *Reichsmusikkammer* to 'protect the German people against the influence of undesirable and deleterious music, such as recordings by Jews and Negroes, or non-Aryan printed music'.[3]

The tension of having to take part in such a flagrantly anti-Christian exercise may be imagined. Inexorably, too, the Lutheran Church was falling into disfavour with the Nazi government, who were alarmed by its continuing spirit of renewal. Hundreds of pastors who would not swear allegiance to the Nazi régime were removed to concentration camps; choirs were disbanded and calls to military service became more insistent. In spite of his appointment to the directorship of the Berlin *Staat- und Dom-chor* in 1942, the emotional strain was too great for Distler and he took his own life.

Hugo Distler's manuscript for his 'Wir danken dir, Herr Jesu Christ', a chorale for three children's voices. Distler trained and maintained a children's choir, for which he himself wrote much of the music.

New music

While these musical changes were taking place the Lutheran Church was beginning to reap the rewards of a long campaign to restore and revitalize its own music. By the 1920s organists and cantors were expected to be musically expert and were paid a reasonable wage in return. The state founded a number of schools where church musicians could be properly

Karlheinz Stockhausen conducting. This modern and original composer has a background in Roman Catholicism, but does not now compose music for church worship.

trained. First-class organs became more widely available in churches, many built following the traditions of Baroque times. Resources available for Christian music-making began once more to resemble those of the seventeenth century.

The reward of this injection of resources into Lutheran music was in the great number of composers writing for the Church, many of them employed full-time. The list is a long one and includes such names as Arthur Mendelssohn (distantly related to Felix, 1855–1933), Johann David (1895–1977), Ernst Pepping (1901–1981), Hugo Distler (1908–42) and Siegfried Reda (1916–68). Merely to mention these composers might imply their work to be of little interest. On the contrary it is truly excellent but simply too abundant to be discussed here. It includes music in the rich variety of forms characteristic of the seventeenth and eighteenth centuries: oratorios, passions, cantatas, motets, chorales and organ works.

Most important was the rediscovery of a way of setting words to music which heightens their intensity, rather than distracting attention from them by abstract musical invention. These composers allowed the natural rhythm and contour of dramatic speech to shape the musical lines, not the other way about. In this respect they share common ground with the most outstanding opera composers of their time such as Debussy, Janáček and Britten, but the inspiration still springs from Lutheran music of the past.

The wonderful dramatizations of the Passion story by Pepping and Distler for unaccompanied voices are good examples—they are both inspired in a variety of ways by Schütz's Passion settings. In Ernst Pepping's *Passionbericht des Matthäus* (1950), the Passion story according to Matthew, the human drama is brought to life in the most compelling fashion.

The work of Hugo Distler, along with others, has added immeasurably to the stature of Christian music this century. It is a great loss that it is hardly known outside Germany. The music itself springs from a sincere faith, is inventive, skilled, accessible to its hearers and well written for choirs of all standards. Sensitive translation would certainly bring it a wider circle of admirers.

The Kirchensteuer— Church Tax

The amount of activity in Christian music in Germany today is huge. It is symptomatic of the country's support for the arts in general: the city of Stuttgart spends more on the arts in a year than does the Arts Council on the whole of the United Kingdom! For Christian music a generous scale of funding is raised by a regional income tax.

At the time of writing, *Kirchensteuer* lies between 8 per cent and 9 per cent of the total tax paid depending on the region. The money raised is divided between the Lutheran *(Evangelische)*, Roman Catholic and (interestingly) Jewish communities, according to the denominational representation of the particular region. Minority Churches, such as the Anglicans, are not included in the scheme and therefore receive nothing.

Opting out is possible: in the north it is easily and simply achieved by signing a form. In the south the regulations are tough: it might be necessary to go to court to avoid the tax. Even then there would be disadvantages in not paying, since the tax pays for a number of important facilities—such as funeral services.

The Kirchensteuer raises a large sum—well over 100 million DM every year—and is used for many purposes: to pay priests on the same level as civil servants (their salaries are perhaps four or five times those of Britain); to pay a living wage to full-time organists and choirmasters, even at parish level; to provide social welfare such as the intensive care of old people and to run many hospitals. As a result, churches remain important centres for parish life through the vital services they offer and have far-reaching opportunities for spiritual contact with the neighbourhood—which they may or may not take up.

In Lutheran Scandinavia the system is much the same. Even in a small market town the post of cantor or organist will be probably be full-time, with a salary equivalent to that of an experienced secondary school-teacher. In return he or she will be expected to provide the music for services and Bible meetings, to train local choirs (some of whom may themselves receive some pay), perhaps to give music lessons locally and to present concerts of sacred music from a yearly budget.

In Britain the Lutheran Church of St Anne and St Agnes in London is very active musically, following the German pattern, and spends nearly half of its budget on music, including the cantor's salary, fees for musicians and administration. Choral music accompanied by instruments is a regular feature of its services, including cantatas by Bach and Telemann. (Interestingly, new Lutheran music rarely features.) It also hosts an international programme of Lutheran Christian music played and sung by groups from all over the world, along with a regular series of lunchtime concerts of classical music each month.

Since the Second World War, artistic creativity in Germany has continued at a high level. Perhaps in reaction to the suppression by the Third Reich of artistic modernity of any kind, a number of composers sought to renew Christian music with the techniques developed elsewhere by Bartók, Stravinsky, Hindemith and Schönberg.

In Siegfried Reda's music, for instance, the level of dissonance is noticeably higher than that of his teachers Pepping and Distler, with a consequent lessening of the numbers of choirs able or prepared to take it on. With Helmut Bornefeld he established the *Heideheimer Tage für Neue Kirchenmusik* which ran from 1946 to 1960 as a forum for new styles in Christian music.

This more exploratory attitude to Christian music had parallels with the startling developments in modern music in Germany, in which the *Internationale Ferienkurse für Neue Musik* (International Summer Courses for New Music) in Darmstadt, also established in 1946, played a large part.

It was here that young composers like Karlheinz Stockhausen (born 1928), Pierre Boulez (born 1925) and Luciano Berio (born 1925) came under the influence of Messiaen, taking aspects of their teacher's music (such as *Messe de la Pentecôte)* several stages further. Some of this music has Christian resonances, such as Berio's orchestral *Nones* (1954) and *Allelujahs* (1954–58).

In 1956, Stockhausen wrote *Gesang der Jünglinge* (1956), music of extraordinary originality and beauty based on the *Benedicite,* the canticle sung by Shadrach, Meshach and Abednego when they were cast into the burning fiery furnace by Nebuchadnezzar.

His resources were a recording of a boy's singing voice and electronic music, the resulting multi-track tape intended for five spacially separated groups of loudspeakers in the vast spaces of Cologne Cathedral. Church authorities could not cope with such sounds in such a context and the first performance was given by the radio station West Deutsche Rundfunk. A few years later Stockhausen severed his allegiance to the Roman Catholic Church because he 'could not abide by the rules'.[1]

Among composers for the liturgy, and hardly less controversially, Heinz Werner Zimmermann (born 1930) has turned consistently to jazz as a renewing force in his Christian music. In a note to his setting of Psalm 113 he writes:

Obviously unusual in this motet is the use of the double bass. Its even pizzicato must provide a strong rhythmic foundation for the five heavily syncopated choral voices above . . . I am conscious of the fact that this rhythm has parallels in the dance music of our day— as does the harmony. This is not necessarily unfortunate. I am hoping that a new vitality . . . may thus be injected into our church music.[2]

His congregational music follows the same pattern and has the same nervous energy. A great deal more hymnody and psalmody like this has been written in the last few decades.[3] Superficially it resembles the work of the Twentieth Century Light Music Group in Britain, but the music still stands on a foundation of Lutheran traditions and has a stronger intellectual basis.

Chapter 45

Music in Britain

It must have been in 1904... when a cab drove up to the door and 'Mr Dearmer' was announced. I just knew his name vaguely as a parson who invited tramps to sleep in his drawing room... He went straight to the point and asked me to edit the music of a hymn book. I protested that I knew very little about hymns but... if I did not do the job it would be offered to a well-known Church musician with whose musical views I was much out of sympathy... the new book was being sponsored by a committee... who were dissatisfied with the new *Hymns Ancient and Modern*...

I determined to do the work thoroughly, and that, besides being a compendium of all the tunes of worth that were already in use, the book should, in addition, be a thesaurus of all the finest hymn tunes in the world—at all events all such as were compatible with the metres of the words for which I had to find tunes. Sometimes I went further, and when I found a tune for which no English words were available I took it to Dearmer... and told him he must write or get somebody else to write suitable words. This was the origin of Athelstan Riley's fine hymn *Ye Watchers and Ye Holy Ones...*[1]

In this way the composer Ralph Vaughan Williams (1872–1958) helped to create the *English Hymnal,* one of the most influential hymn-books of the century. As Ursula Vaughan Williams pointed out

The eventual value of that uncomfortable job was his discovery that for many people the music the Church gave them each week was the only music in their lives and that it was all too often unworthy both of their faith and of music itself.[2]

One of Vaughan Williams' most valuable contributions to the book was its new music, particularly the hymns by his lifelong friend Gustav Holst (1874–1934), such as *In the Bleak Midwinter,* and by himself. He made more excellent music available for use in worship through *The Oxford Book of Carols* (1928) and *Songs of Praise* (1925). In both these he collaborated with Martin Shaw (1875–1958), a composer with a similar vision for straightforward Christian music of the highest standard. Shaw's music for parish communion[3] and some of his hymns (for instance *Little Cornard)* are still sung.

The English Musical Renaissance

While the *English Hymnal* was setting new high standards in congregational hymnody and providing a welcome change from the sentimentalities of *Hymns Ancient and Modern,* Charles Villiers Stanford (1852–1924) was transforming Anglican service-music from its dismal and complacent state.

Stanford's Morning, Evening and Communion Services in G (1904) and in C (1909) are particularly fine, the first including a *Magnificat* of unusual serenity and beauty. With these settings and a number of anthems (less well-known), Stanford set standards for Christian

Third from the left in this photograph stands Ralph Vaughan Williams. To his right is Herbert Howells. Both men responded warmly to English churches and cathedrals, and wrote music to be sung in such settings.

music in Britain unknown since the days of Purcell and Handel. They have become so much the staple fare of cathedral and parish church choirs up and down the country that their continued use seems assured, in spite of recent changes to the Anglican liturgy.

Indeed, British music as a whole experienced a welcome renaissance at the beginning of the century, due not least to the inspiration and widespread influence of Stanford as a teacher. Much of the best and most enduring Christian music of this period has come from composers whose careers lay outside the Anglican Church, where financial support of the kind enjoyed by the Lutheran musicians is not forthcoming.

An insecure Christian faith does not seem to have prevented a number of composers from writing very fine music for congregation or choir. Vaughan Williams himself, happy to be known as an agnostic, saw no reason why that should prevent him from writing liturgical music.[4] His celebratory settings of psalms and canticles, such as Psalm 47: *O Clap Your Hands* (1920), *Psalm 100* (1929) and *A Festival Te Deum* (1937) are all carefully designed to give amateur singers and players opportunities to worship through music of a high standard. As well as making dozens of traditional melodies more widely available (from the many seasonal carols to his arrangement for large forces of *The Old Hundredth Psalm Tune* (1953)), he composed some exquisite settings of

words of Christian writers such as the *Five Mystical Songs* to poems by George Herbert (1911), and of scripture in the brief but unforgettable *O Taste and See* (1952).

In all this Vaughan Williams made no compromises with his creative personality in order to write Christian music. He experienced none of the problems of the Victorians as expressed by Barnby, nor did he turn, like Brahms or Reger, to a manner approved by its antiquity. The *Mass in G minor* (1921) might seem at first glance to be a loving reproduction of Tudor or Jacobean polyphony. It is certainly an expression of reverence for such music, which was then being heard for the first time since the seventeenth century, but the Mass is in the mainstream of Vaughan Williams' writing and does not copy anything. Its contemplative modality links it to his other outstanding art-works of the time—such as the *Pastoral Symphony* and *The Lark Ascending*—and in liturgical use has helped many cathedral choirs to escape from the faded sentimentality of their Victorian heritage.

John Ireland (1879–1962) contrasts sharply with Vaughan Williams in his musical contribution to the Anglican Church. Vaughan Williams was never employed by the Church, and yet did more for Christian music than any of his contemporaries. John Ireland, however, was organist at St Luke's in Chelsea from 1904 to

English church music benefits from a long and high tradition of choirs in cathedral schools and college schools, where young people are trained in musicianship. Many future cathedral organists and choristers come from this background, with church music in their bones.

embedded in the cathedral repertoire and the excellent hymn-tune *Love Unknown* is known to millions.

Herbert Howells (1892–1983), like Vaughan Williams and Ireland, was a pupil of Stanford. Again, like them, he had doubts about the Christian faith but responded with profound respect to the people and places where the Anglican liturgy is sung:

In all my music for the church, people and places have been a dual influence... Also a promise (mine) that if I made the setting of the Magnificat, the mighty should be put down from their seat without a brute force that would deny this canticle's feminine association. Equally, that in the Nunc Dimittis, the tenor's domination should characterise the gentle Simeon. Only the Gloria should raise its voice. The given promise dictated style, mood and scope.[5]

1926, but this formal relationship with Christianity inspired little music from him.

As a pagan mystic and as a humanist, most of Ireland's energies went into other areas—his deserved reputation would never have been made on the strength of his service-settings and some very dull organ music. Just the same, his fine anthem *Greater Love* (1912) is firmly

Thus Howells described his first set of Anglican canticles, called *Collegium Regale* and written for King's College Chapel Choir, Cambridge in 1944. In this and the five settings which followed[6] he adhered to these intentions sufficiently closely for them all to be instantly recognizable. Moreover, among cathedral musicians they are undoubtedly the most valued

The Royal School of Church Music

One of the best-known institutions for the encouragement of Anglican Christian music in Britain is the Royal School of Church Music, founded (originally as the School of English Church Music) by Sidney Nicholson in 1927. It was given its present title in 1945 and has been housed in Addington Palace, Croydon, since 1954. Thousands of parish church choirs are affiliated to the School, which publishes music, offers courses and holds regional festivals of Christian music. For many years the School was a bastion of conservatism, but since the 1970s its leadership and choice of teachers have given it closer contact with new thinking amongst Christian musicians. Its courses now cover such problems as arranging and writing for instrumentalists. Even so, a number of plans have been suggested for starting alternative teaching centres for Christian music, but a serious lack of funds has so far hindered them.

of the settings available. Howells' music, as he intended, seems the perfect response to the surroundings. Certainly the musicians can revel in the sensuous beauty of the opulent sounds required of them.

These canticles were written late on in Howells' career; like Vaughan Williams he made no concessions to the traditions of Christian music. They are also technically demanding. The melodies recall plainsong in their modality and rhythmic flexibility, but they are woven polyphonically around harmonies of a heady resonance that in other surroundings would delight the most hedonistic jazz enthusiast.[7]

The similarly high level of invention in Sir Michael Tippett's *Magnificat and Nunc Dimittis* (1961) unfortunately requires a level of ability which puts it beyond the reach of most choirs. Like Howells, he did not compromise his musical personality, which at the time was occupied with the new and astringent brilliance of the *Second Symphony* and the opera *King Priam*. Benjamin Britten (1913–76) wrote a great deal of choral music with a strongly Christian basis, but his choice of texts was broad and often influenced by his interest in drama and story-telling. The children's opera *Noye's Fludde* (1957) and the cantatas *Rejoice in the Lamb* (1943) and *St Nicolas* (1948) are in many senses music for worship, but they cannot often be used liturgically. Among a number of smaller choral pieces, it is the *Missa Brevis* (written in 1959 for Westminster Abbey) that has an assured place in cathedrals when the Eucharist is celebrated and a boys' choir only is available.

New music

All the above-mentioned composers are highly regarded in the world of British classical music and their contribution to liturgy is on a high artistic level. Today the standards may not be so impressive, but the quantity is as great as ever.

The Anglican tradition allows plenty of space for choral music in its sung services: anthems, two canticles, versicles and responses daily at evensong, with Communion settings and canticles for Sunday morning services in addition. Furthermore, changes to the Anglican liturgy and the two rites of the *Alternative Service Book* (1980) have created further challenges and opportunities. The quantity of music passing through a cathedral librarian's hands in a year is therefore enormous.

New pieces, however, are generally regarded (as they are in classical programming generally) as an occasional welcome diversion from the routine. With rehearsal time at a premium an unfamiliar piece must be 'user-friendly' if it is to have a chance of success. Most cathedrals and parish churches with expert choirs will commission pieces from time to time,[8] but under such pressured circumstances the music needs to conform to a house style to be successful at first use.

In this genre a convention for expressing celebration and joy consists of some modest syncopation (a distant echo of Stravinsky and

Herbert Howells' 'Like as the Hart' is one of four anthems published in 1941. This music looks back to the free part-writing of cathedral music of the earlier sixteenth century. A modal 'indecision' (here between B flat and B natural) generates much of the character of Howells' music. Such false relations are abundant in early English music.

237

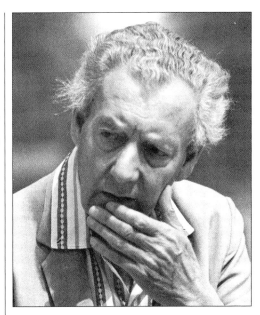

Benjamin Britten's music includes much use of Christian themes, especially his choral works for children. But their setting is more often the concert hall than the church.

Walton) to enliven the text, relatively easy part-writing achieved by doubling up sopranos with tenors, altos with basses, and a slightly tart harmonic language based on fourths rather than thirds and sevenths. William Mathias (born 1934), Bryan Kelly (born 1934) and Kenneth Leighton (1929–88) are skilled in this genre and between them have produced quantities of this type of Christian music. Leighton in particular offers greater depth. His settings of canticles are more challenging, but still widely sung and valued highly by good choirs.

Clearly, cathedrals are well supplied with new music if they choose to sing it. A small proportion of it has been briefly described and is unequivocally superb. Most of the rest is technically assured but with a standard of creative thought which will not yield much excitement on close attention. For, as the composer Jonathan Harvey recently put it:

Leaping into the Dark— Musical Innovation

In the last few years in Britain, occasional but exciting opportunities have been created for exploratory and experimental music to be heard in worship. For example, every three years since 1980, Norwich Cathedral and the University of East Anglia nearby have presented a festival of Contemporary Church Music, a week of daily services in the Cathedral interlaced with concerts. Alongside established canticles and anthems by living composers, the services give an opportunity to experience newly-commissioned music in the context of worship.

The breadth of activity is wide-ranging: not only has the festival put music by composers of an advanced style into a liturgical setting (such as Harrison Birtwhistle, Peter Maxwell Davies, Paul Patterson and Giles Swayne) but at the

opposite end of the spectrum it has provided a platform for the Christian orchestra of All Souls, Langham Place, and an evening of popular orchestral music and congregational song. Perhaps most significant of all is the organizers' willingness not only to ignore musical boundaries but denominational ones as well. The composers represent a wide spectrum of Christianity, not only Protestant and Roman Catholic: in 1989 a Vigil Service of the Orthodox Church was celebrated with music by John Tavener.

Winchester Cathedral is another centre which has established a fruitful relationship with new music, particularly through the work of Jonathan Harvey (born 1939), a composer with a high and well-deserved reputation in the world of contemporary art-music. From about 1975, poetry, art, dance, drama and music

have flourished at the Cathedral. Harvey comments:

The great building somehow both inspired and cautioned. It said: 'Do something fitting with my immensity, but woe betide anything vulgar or ordinary, because I will show it up with cruel clarity.'[1]

In music, the results were startling and remarkable. Jonathan Harvey was commissioned in 1978 to set the *Magnificat* and *Nunc Dimittis*. His musical vision for the *Nunc Dimittis* was vivid and unusual:

I imagined the dark temple and blind old Simeon: I heard his hesitant step as he felt death approach. But as his joy increases

Many fine composers in Britain today have an aesthetic in sympathy with Christianity, even if they are not strictly practising. But they are hardly ever invited by the church. The church usually invites those it is very sure of, those it knows already, those who are totally predictable.[9]

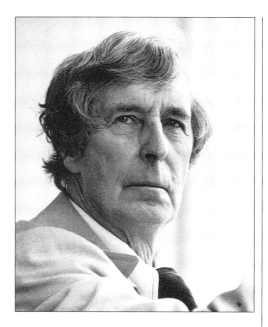

Like other leading English composers in the twentieth century, Michael Tippett has composed music for liturgy, but at a level of difficulty which takes it out of the reach of most church choirs.

to rapture, *'glory' grows to 'lighten': the whole inner world becomes illuminated by multiple repetitions—the light grows as more and more voices enter, repeating the bright vowel and final consonant 'light' until the full organ enters with a chord of universality (comprised of all 12 pitch-classes) in rich registration... In a large building this can fittingly symbolise an extreme spiritual experience.[2]*

In the *Magnificat* Harvey asks the choir not only to sing, but to express the text in all manner of ways—speaking, whispering, shouting:

We all know there's nothing difficult about speaking, but to get choirs to do it in a 'sung' Magnificat one had to ask them to make a very special effort—a change of attitude.[3]

Harvey suggests a parallel in religion:

... that is what religion often demands too—a change in

attitude. As in religion, so in art... One is excited by one's religion if the familiar texts, rituals and dogmas are recreating the world and themselves. If one hears the Sermon on the Mount for the fiftieth time, it must still change one's perceptions... Jesus'... words are resonant, renewing themselves over the centuries ceaselessly... Religion and art both use familiar things as a platform to start out from... But then from that platform they both create the new from within the old and 'coalesce' the two into a higher synthesis...

It is because of this fundamental similarity between the functions of art and religion that religious art is such an appropriate art-form... Art and religion go together perfectly: both spiral out from the familiar, both aspire to the boundless.[4]

Such a stance requires an open mind and a willingness to take risks. Harvey believes that the art which is of profound importance to religion must be

'dangerously alive' and also that:

the clergy must live dangerously, that is what religion is all about, that is what art is all about— leaping into the dark.[5]

Chapter 46

The Popular Stream

For many people, living dangerously is a frightening experience. Christianity will be for them a defence against the unknown, a place of safety and familiarity that can be constantly revisited. In that case, where some composers (see box: Leaping into the Dark) respond to the Christian faith strongly and positively with music that questions and challenges, so those who seek safety in it will respond to music which is predictable and which constantly reworks familiar ground.

So in the vast majority of parish churches up and down the country, Christian music which is exploratory is given no space. Even what seems to be new turns out to be reliving the past. John Rutter (1945–) is a composer with a deep understanding of classical music whose original pieces and arrangements are widely sung in churches and schools throughout Britain. His considerable technical ability is turned to creating music of ease, which is harmonious, tuneful, shapely, tasteful and enjoyable to sing. His contributions of original carols to *Carols for Choirs* brought his music to the attention of a very wide public. Some years later there is still delight in *The Shepherd's Pipe Carol* and its companions.

Some of Rutter's more recent pieces conform closely to the idioms of commercial music—his new settings of *All Things Bright and Beautiful* and *For the Beauty of the Earth* are examples of this trend.

With such pieces Rutter joins a type of Christian music which has run as a constant stream (even a flood-tide) for a century or more. Earlier in the twentieth century it was the song-books produced for Sunday School use that were in closest touch with popular music, for hymnals reflected the expectations of more formal worship. Even so, there has been a consistent time-lag between a musical fashion in the secular world and its adoption by Christian music. Thus the style of the three books of *Scripture Union Choruses* published between 1921 and 1939 is reminiscent of the heyday of the music-hall twenty years earlier.

In the fifties the Twentieth Century Light Music Group initiated a significant change. This group of priests, chaplains, musicians and schoolmasters suggested that:

. . . not only the great and lasting music of the past but also the ordinary and transient music of today—which is the background to the lives of so many—has a rightful place in our worship.[1]

Most of the music of the Twentieth Century Light Music Group indicates that, for them, waltzes, foxtrots and quicksteps were the 'transient music of today' just at the moment when Elvis Presley was turning popular taste in an entirely different direction. Just the same, though the best-known music of the group (by Geoffrey Beaumont and Patrick Appleford) is at best variable, it broke down a significant barrier in many churches which had always shunned music of secular styles. When finally the more relaxed worship of the Sunday School invaded the formality of Matins it was greeted with either relief or horror.

Youth Praise (1966) was the first of many song-books which attempted to reflect a balance of tastes, intending to appeal especially to the younger generation. Although the contents again betrayed the musical interests of its adult compilers and bore little relation to the secular youth music of the time (the Beatles, the Rolling Stones), it became widely used and was followed by *Youth Praise II* (1969) and *Psalm Praise* (1970).

The Charismatic Renewal

The seventies was a more fruitful period for popular Christian music. The Fountain Trust, a centre for charismatic renewal, brought with it not only a deepening of spiritual commitment, but also a correspondingly raised awareness of the contribution of the arts to worship.

The Church of the Redeemer in Houston established the 'Fisherfolk', a Christian community with a specific ministry for music in Britain. Through its influence and its publishing wing, 'Celebration Services', a great deal of new music was disseminated and adopted.[2]

Superficially the music of this charismatic movement resembles the populist Christian music of the previous decade, but there is a difference. Rather than a music imposed or recommended to a congregation by reformers from above or without, some (not all) of this music was created from within, as an expression of the intensity of the spiritual life of a Christian community. The idiom of songs created in this way has strong links with contemporary secular music, but there is a discernible move towards the contemplative, the symbolic and away from the easy rhetoric of earlier evangelical songs. The foreword to *Cry Hosanna* (1980) sets its face against

... the world's ways of romanticizing, deadening, or making frivolous the songs of God. But we will sing his praises with a pure heart, fervently ...

The musical influence of the charismatic movement of the 1970s can still be sensed today in the music of the Iona Community, a group of Christians living on the island of Iona off the north-west coast of Scotland. Like Taizé, the large numbers of visitors they receive has helped to circulate and popularize their songs, which have the simplicity and directness of folk-music and are as yet little touched by commercial pressures. However, where Taizé's songs are contemplative and symbolic and seem to benefit from extensive repetition, Iona's are in the mainstream of contemporary Christian music in their intention

to evoke feeling and are best sung in short snatches.

The Roman Catholics, too, have musical strengths in the St Thomas More Centre in London, founded in 1969 as a result of the renewal of the 1960s. Besides being a bookshop and centre for courses and discussion, it publishes new music of a high standard. The Christian music of Paul Inwood, Christopher Walker, Bernadette Farrell and others is straightforward but cast in a variety of structures arising from liturgical need, such as acclamations, litanies and responsorial psalms. This music crosses denominational boundaries freely and is therefore becoming more widely known, especially in North America.

On one Sunday in each summer, British Christians unite to march through their towns and cities as a witness to their faith. Always there is singing.

Music for all

Around Britain the speed and ease of modern music publishing has released an avalanche of spiral-bound music-books, *Mission Praise* (1983) and *Songs of Fellowship* (1985) being in wide circulation. The simplicity of their contents implies that the creation of Christian music is no longer only the province of the expert, but that it can be for all. A recent indication of this comes in the re-establishment of bands and orchestras to lead church worship.

The days of clamour against instruments in church really have gone: Bradford Cathedral has its own music group (including electric guitars) and the Organist and Master of the Choristers plays electric keyboards for it. Increasing space is being given to the musical talents of the congregation, however diverse, and (although few are as yet aware of it) this is nothing less than a return to the days of west-gallery players.

The hymns of Graham Kendrick have recently captured the imagination of many church-goers. They are finding their way into the worship of many denominations and, significantly, are better suited to instrumental accompaniment than to the organ. Their light rock or ballad style keeps them within the sound-world of commercial music, but Kendrick maintains a contact with earlier musical traditions by strongly recalling the past.

Some of Kendrick's songs have an intensity of character which may well make them more than merely transitory. *Led like a Lamb,* for instance, uses the men and women of the congregation in a simple but touching re-enactment of the dialogue between the risen Jesus and Mary Magdalene at the tomb on Easter Sunday. In verse two Mary's sudden and joyous realization that Jesus is alive is the basis for the refrain that follows: 'He's alive, he's alive, he is risen …' The dramatic contrast of contemplation and jubilant rejoicing generates the structure of the song.

Kendrick's music is distributed in as many forms as modern marketing can devise. Apart from the songbooks and the recorded music, backing tracks are available to sing along with, karaoke-fashion; the songs have been recorded in lavish arrangements for symphony orchestra ('Kendrick Gold') and videos and handbooks help local churches to learn the songs.

An offshoot of the interest in instrumental accompaniment is the increasing number of orchestras made up of Christians, playing (with or without choirs) to large and festive gatherings. The London-based *Prom Praise* events are led by the orchestra of All Souls, Langham Place, itself the centre of an extensive programme of Christian arts. The New English Orchestra concentrates on classical concerts, the Christian membership of the group being a significant further dimension. The programmes of both are usually based on well-known pieces of classical music and popular Christian songs in orchestral guise, but new and exploratory music with a Christian basis is also encouraged by the New English Orchestra.

Many churches now venture into mixed media presentations at high points in the Christian year. A project may involve dance and drama as well as music, the results depending heavily on the resources available.

The models are the musicals of Andrew Lloyd Webber, such as *Joseph and the Amazing Technicolor Dreamcoat* (1968) or his rock opera *Jesus Christ Superstar (1970)* and Christian musicals from America, such as those of Carol and Jimmy Owens.

Following these examples, hundreds of musicals are presented by churches all over the country. Roger Jones, a former music teacher in Birmingham, has devised dozens of such pieces for church use. They are not simply intended as entertainment but are often taken on as part of a ministry of spiritual encouragement and development.

Musicals are an important dimension to Christian music today: they are a clear indication of the desire of many fellowships to celebrate their faith in the most exciting way they know. The resources may be slim, the expertise to marshal them may be lacking, but the challenges involved are undoubtedly rewarding. Working on a large project of this kind can be a valuable spiritual challenge—a microcosm of life in the body of Christ, perhaps—though the artistic potential of the Christian musical has yet to be realized.

Graham Kendrick (playing guitar) has written some of the most popular hymns and songs sung in British churches over the last few years. Among his best known is 'Servant King'.

Chapter 47

Good Music—Good Worship?

The contrast between the styles of twentieth-century Christian music so briefly described in Part 8 is immense. Not only is it a contrast of quality, of sophistication and of ability, but also of intention. It therefore possesses potential for explosive dissent, framed by the vexed question of what is good and bad.

For, as the composer and critic Hugo Cole observes, what is good for music may be bad for worship and vice versa:

> **Go to King's Chapel [Cambridge] and listen to Lassus and Byrd, and the music does indeed soar aloft and is indeed glorious. Yet one understands the viewpoint of those who complain that evensong is no more than a concert in disguise. Music seems to be celebrating its own glory, which is fine for musicians. On the other hand, if we visit the church down the road where the whole congregation is singing, with genuine fervour and passion, our least favourite Dykes hymn, that is all right for the congregation but bad for musicians— and, the purist would add, 'bad for music'. In looking at church music, we are always subject to double vision: good is bad if it causes the congregation to fall apart in consternation—possibly if it is so good that (as in King's Chapel) it draws in an audience of connoisseurs and musical agnostics. Bad music is good if it fosters community spirit in the congregation and raises it collectively to higher spiritual levels.**[1]

But is it really true that only bad music will satisfy a congregation's needs? Or that good music simply turns worship into a concert? Both scenarios are being acted out daily, it is true, and in their differing ways both are undesirable. But there is plenty of evidence from this last chapter that they are not inevitable.

The music of Taizé is good by a musician's standards of compositional grammar, yet thousands know it as a self-effacing servant of deepening spiritual awareness. Indeed, it is difficult to find a bad word said about it. Some of the music arising from the charismatic movement occupies a similar position, as does some from modern Lutheran and Catholic composers. A diligent search would reveal more from a host of national and denominational backgrounds.

The quality that distinguishes this deeply spiritual music from the rest has to do with the role that music plays in worship. A danger lies in the music becoming too insistent a voice, with the possibility that it invites too much attention. It is much more likely to do this if it is rooted in rhetorical traditions. It is highly significant that the nineteenth century, the age of the most passionate expression in classical music, found Christian music so poverty-stricken that societies had to be founded to try to rescue it. The assumption behind the Western Romantic movement—that art is a unique statement from an individual about his or her inner being—is fundamentally unhelpful to a diverse congregation. The 'all sorts and conditions' of humanity that visit Taizé are not asked to identify with music that conveys a strong emotional state through the traditions of rhetoric, but are offered music which is relatively unemotional and which allows people to sense the unity that it symbolizes.

As far as Western culture is concerned, the late twentieth century is still part of the Romantic age. The emphasis in the creative arts is centred firmly on the individual's feelings and response to his or her surroundings. But some Christian artists (among the composers Arvo Pärt is one) are suggesting a new possibility, that art can express—no, not express, but perhaps inhabit or be part of—universal truths. In worship, this does not necessarily require a return to the ancient chant of the Christian church but it can only follow a rediscovery of the true nature of Christian music.

Perhaps such a reassessment will only be possible after profound changes in Western culture, which is at present so hectic, so concerned with the network of personal relationships that spiritual matters are given little space. For the present, Christians should not allow themselves simply to compromise their art with secular expectations, but through a leap of imagination (into the dark, perhaps) start once again to deal with 'the things of the spirit'.

What is Excellence?

Whereas the Orthodox Churches of the East have to this day maintained a unity of purpose immediately recognizable in the greatest basilica or in the humblest country church, the church in the West has gradually become fragmented. The fundamental split created by the Reformers of the sixteenth century itself led to several factions, each with its own interpretation of the Christian faith and its own musical style. A continuing and increasing awareness of the injustices of a class-based society led to further divisions in the eighteenth century—the establishment of Methodism in England, or the rise of Pietism among Lutherans, for example.

It is easy for trained musicians to react to the musical diversity caused by such turmoil in terms of musical 'excellence'. After all, God deserves the best sacrifice of time and talent from his creatures. But in using this yardstick, it is possible to bypass entirely the way in which God himself responds to the worship offered. Enthusiastic congregational singing, which arises from positive spiritual commitment, may be a dimension far more important than the musical idiom.

Similarly, the almost universal condemnation of the rough music of English west gallery bands may be no indication of the pleasure that God received from that worship. And where artistic musical excellence *was* assured, in the seventeenth-century English Chapel Royal and the cathedrals and court chapels of Europe, a sincerity pleasing to God would often have required a specially large camel to squeeze through the needle's eye—perhaps not quite an impossibility, but certainly a great difficulty.

The judgement of Christian music by these two distinct criteria—musical excellence or spiritual sincerity—has created ever-widening chasms between the styles of music in churches of differing denominations.

Conclusion

Christian music today is as breathtaking in its variety as the natural world, and its traditions have evolved at equally varied rates. In the Eastern Orthodox Church, change has been almost imperceptibly slow, the Copts and Ethiopians moving at a glacier-like pace. Only in the Russian Orthodox Church have revisions to the liturgy been of sufficiently disturbing rapidity to generate sectarian division. That seventeenth-century scenario may one day be repeated: present political upheavals in Russia could in time be fundamental enough to cause denominations to multiply as they have in Europe.

Western society has been turbulent far longer, with one of the many far-reaching effects of its cultural evolution being a fragmented perception of Christianity. Particularly since the Reformation, different elements in society have emphasized particular and limited aspects of the faith, splitting the white light of the gospel into a rainbow of colours. The diversity of hues has since become progressively greater, along with the segmentation of the culture that gives them expression.

A further pattern emerges from countries where Christianity has been implanted by Western Christians into a long-established culture. In Africa, for instance, European styles of worship (which include the music) are being questioned and progressively rejected in favour of patterns more in keeping with local and long-established cultural traditions. New African churches are multiplying as their indigenous presentation of the gospel captures the people's imagination. In the countryside the faith is expressed with music that is an offspring of African rather than European society; in the cities, African music has travelled full circle: across to North America with the slave trade, adopted and commercially exploited by white culture, and now returned to its homeland to be further transformed into a new gospel music.

It would be wrong to suggest that the variety of Christian music world-wide is a recent phenomenon; the picture of early Christianity was far from one of stylistic uniformity. But in spite of the early threat of schism between East and West, there was still a common understanding that music in its symbolic form was worship's most appropriate companion. Today, the archetypes of rhetoric, symbol and ecstacy can be discovered in countless interrelationships, for Christians across the world are prepared to consecrate every imaginable type of music to the worship of God.

The separation of Christians is rightly understood as a scandal. It is true that the faith's hundreds of denominations were spawned by internal disagreements and have since sustained and encouraged mistrust and strife. There are now signs, however, that mutual tolerance and respect are holding sway against sectarian confrontation and this despite the collapse of a number of plans for unity.[1] Idealistic schemes which work towards some future monolithic Church are being replaced by one which is more simple though no less ambitious: true love and acceptance of Christians in their colourful diversity.

There are clear signs from the Christian musical world that such reconciliation is in action. Disputes over style in worship no longer lead so quickly to the resignation of the organist; there is less news of churches whose singers of the older generation are at war with the instrumentalists of the next. A recent report on church music to the Archbishop of Canterbury has urged that

Musical resources must be diversified: congregations, choirs, instruments, styles, cultural and denominational variety—all need to be exploited, with a

combination of imagination and understanding of tradition...[2]

At the heart of such 'reconciled diversity' is Jesus himself and his new commandment:

You must love the Lord your God with all your heart, with all your soul, and with all your mind. This is the greatest and the first commandment. The second resembles it: You must love your neighbour as yourself...[3]

Worship that is sincere and thus pleasing to God can only spring from love. The Bible records many instances of God rejecting worship which lacks love, from the story of Cain and Abel to the Christians of Laodicea.[4] By his own example Jesus gave a lifetime's demonstration of how love for God can be expressed, and sharing in communal worship was an essential component.[5] Indeed, he visited both temple and synagogue, never favouring a particular ritual and giving absolutely no indication that God might prefer one style of worship to another. Instead, Jesus' constant challenge, then as now, is that it is the state of the heart, mind and soul that matters.

Jesus' commands have a special significance for those musicians and composers who have the responsibility for aiding worship. A necessary part of his command to love is that we should live with integrity and seek the truth: love cannot develop without this. It follows that creative artists must have this goal not just for their life but also for their work. The idea that there is a truth to be sought in art was well known in earlier times when the musics of cosmos, human soul and voice were assumed to be in subtle synchrony. But truth in art is still a reality and has all the more importance for musicians on whom depends the quality of communal worship. The Christian liturgies of the present day create so many different working conditions that it is impossible to suggest in every situation what a musician's search for truth might involve. But it will probably require a fight against artistic and intellectual laziness, against carelessness, against partial offerings of intellect or voice or body, against an unthinking contentment with gestures that have become meaningless through repetition, even against the easy and fatal hypocrisy which can make church music offensive:

... made so by the repulsive incongruity between its beauty and religious zeal and the state of things in the city slums.[6]

In all this, nothing has been said about style itself, because nothing *needs* to be said. Good music, defined as such by its truthfulness, does not have to be abstruse or highly intellectual. Mozart once wrote to his father about some concertos he was working on:

There are passages here and there from which connoisseurs alone can derive satisfaction; but these passages are written in such a way that the less learned cannot fail to be pleased, though without knowing why.[7]

Mozart recognized that good music need not alienate its audience. Even less does Christian music have to become the province of a few intellectuals in order to be profitable or edifying. But it must be honest and integral to its occasion. As Joseph Gélineau has pointed out:

A very simple tune can be dismissed as worthless if taken in isolation but makes a marvellous contribution to the spirit and beauty of the celebration, whereas a great work which is too difficult or badly done can wreck it.[8]

Whatever the colour of their coats, the responsibilities carried by musicians working in Christian worship are heavy. But as in parenthood or in any other life-challenge that God may offer, if the task is embraced wholeheartedly and in his strength then there are rich rewards. The greatest delight of all is to know that the joy travels both ways, for God takes pleasure in us. As a well-known hymn expresses it:

Lord, we know that thou rejoicest
o'er each work of thine;
thou didst ears and hands and voices
for thy praise design:
craftman's art and music's measure,
for thy pleasure all combine.

In thy house, great God, we offer
of thine own to thee,
and for thine acceptance proffer
all unworthily
hearts and minds and hands and voices
in thy choicest psalmody.

Footnotes

Biblical quotations are from *The Jerusalem Bible*, London, 1966.

Book entries in **bold** are especially helpful for further reading.

Introduction: The Power of Music

1   1 Samuel 16:14–23.

2   R. Burton, *The Anatomy of Melancholy*, edited by R. Jackson, London, 1972, volume 2, page 117, and compare with Psalm 29:6, 96:11–12, 98:7–8, 114:4.

3   M. Hood, *The Ethno-musicologist*, McGraw-Hill, 1971, page 15.

4   O. Sacks, *The Man Who Mistook his Wife for a Hat*, London, 1985, page 176.

5   O. Sacks, page 173.

6   O. Sacks, page 170.

7   2 Samuel 6:5

8   Romans 1:20.

9   R. Vaughan Williams, *National Music and Other Essays*, Oxford, 2nd edition, 1987, page 206.

10   P.M. Hamel, **Through Music to the Self**, Tisbury, Wilts, 1978, page 89.

11   Words of the composer Karlheinz Stockhausen and recorded in R. Dufallo, *Trackings*, Oxford, 1989, page 213.

12   Clement of Alexandria (about 150-215AD), *Protrepticus* 1:1–3, quoted in J. McKinnon, **Music in Early Christian Literature**, Cambridge, 1987, page 30.

13   See A. Storr, **The Dynamics of Creation**, London, 1972, page 100.

14   T.S. Eliot, *The Literary Essays of Ezra Pound*, London, 1960, pages 43 and 45.

15   This style of preaching is recorded in *The Gospel Ship*, New World Records, New York, no. NW294.

16   Quoted in B. Chatwin, *The Songlines*, London, 1987, page 302. Bruce Chatwin includes other similar observations well worth reading.

17   J. Hullah, *The History of Modern Music*, London, 1875, pages 5 and 7.

18   H. Cole, *The Changing Face of Music*, Oxford, 1978, page 92.

19   Revelation 5:9 and 7:9.

Part 1: The Birth of Christian Music

Chapter 1: Music In The Old Testament

1   Numbers 21:17–18.

2   B. Thomas, *Arabia Felix*, London, 1932, page 298.

3   Exodus 17:16.

4   Numbers 10:35–36.

5   Exodus 15:20–21.

6   1 Samuel 18:6–7.

7   2 Samuel 6:5–6, *New Jerusalem Bible*, London, 1985.

8   1 Chronicles 15.

9   1 Chronicles 16:8–36.

10   2 Chronicles 5:12–13.

11   S. Langdon, *Babylonian Liturgies*, Paris, 1913 page xii.

12   Ecclesiasticus 50:1–21.

13   Tamid VII:3.

14   Talmudian tractate Arakin II:3.

15   Quoted in W.O.E. Oesterley, **The Jews and Judaism during the Greek period**, London, 1941, page 205.

16   Psalm 18 of the Dead Sea Scrolls, quoted in A. Sendrey, **Music in Ancient Israel**, London, 1969, page 193. See also Isaiah 16:11.

The Psalms in Temple Worship

1   Tamid VII:4.

2   Psalm 119:147–148.

3   Psalm 136, Deuteronomy 27:16–26.

4   C. Sachs: **The Rise of Music in the Ancient World**, New York, 1944, page 98; Sendrey, page 438–40.

5   Foreword to the Proceedings of the 5th International Church Music Congress, 1966, and quoted in J. Overath, **Sacred Music and Liturgy Reform after Vatican II**, Rome, 1969.

Music in the Synagogue

1   Nehemiah 8, 2 Chronicles 7:7–9.

2   Acts 18:4.

3   E. Werner, **The Sacred Bridge**, London, 1959, page 24–25; A. Sendrey, page 181.

4   E. Werner, page 25.

5   Ekphonesis was a method of chanting continued in the Byzantine Church. See chapter 29.

Chapter 2: Music in the Early Church

1   Matthew 21:12.

2   See Acts 24:14–16, 26:4–8.

3   Described in Acts 15.

4   See E. Werner, **The Sacred Bridge**, London, 1959, page 79.

5   E. Werner, pages 83–94, 156–158.

6   Ephesians 5:19.

7   Augustine, *Ennarrationes in psalmos* 72:1, quoted in J. McKinnon, **Music in Early Christian Literature**, Cambridge, 1987, page 158.

8   Revelation 5:9–10, 19:1.

9   Revelation 19:6–9.

10   Luke 1:46–55, 67–79, Luke 2:29–32.

11   1 Peter 1:3–5, 1 Timothy 3:16, Philippians 2:6–11.

12   Pliny the Younger, Letter 10:16, quoted in J. McKinnon, *Music in early Christian Literature*, Cambridge, 1986, page 27.

13   Pseudo-Basil, *Commentary on Isaiah* 5:158, quoted in J. McKinnon, page 70. The passage being commented on is Isaiah 5:11–12.

14   Arnobius (d. about 330AD), *Adversus nationes* 2:42, quoted in J. McKinnon, page 49.

The spread of Christianity

1   E. Pagels, **The Gnostic Gospels**, London, 1980, page 76.

2   E. Pagels, page 99.

Chapter 3: The Beginning of the Middle Ages

1   In the *motu proprio* of 1571, Pope Pius V wrote, 'let [chants] be sung in the Spanish kingdoms according to the form of the Church of Toledo which has been handed down from a most ancient time'. See R.F. Hayburn, **Papal Legislation on Sacred Music**, Collegeville, Minnesota, 1979, page 35.

Worship in Fifth-century Jerusalem

1   Quoted in P. Weiss and R. Taruskin, *Music in the Western World*, London, 1984, page 21–23, and (in another more extensive translation) J. McKinnon, page 113.

Chapter 4: The Monastic Tradition

1   Augustine, **Confessions** translated by R.S. Pine-Coffin, London, 1961, page 191.

2   J. McKinnon, page 132.

Chapter 5: Music of the Spheres: the Medieval World-view

1   Letter to the Romans 1:20.

2   T.H. White, *The Book of Beasts*, London, 1969, page 168.

3   Pseudo-Origen, *Selecta in psalmos* 32:2–3, quoted in J. McKinnon, page 38.

4   Genesis 6:15.

5   Revelation 13:18. The books of Daniel and Revelation are closely linked and rich in number symbolism.

6   The only book of Platonic dialogue known to the Middle Ages was *Timaeus*, quoted in P. Weiss and R. Taruskin, **Music in the Western World**, London, 1984, page 9.

7   Quoted in P. Weiss and R. Taruskin, page 33. Boethius (about 480-524AD) was a Roman philosopher and a Christian whose writings on music formed the basis of the philosophy of music for hundreds of years.

8   Scientific observation on the greatest and smallest scales (astro- and sub-atomic physics) show that the cosmos has indeed a harmoniousness, but of a complexity far beyond the imaginations of medieval astronomers and philosophers. At the same time, some recent discoveries might not surprise them so much. The sun's turbulent surface has excited much interest, as it appears to be harmoniously synchronised by sound vibrations deep in the sun's interior. Its study has created a new discipline, helioseismology, dedicated in only a slightly new sense to studying the 'harmony of the spheres'.

Chapter 6: Music for the Liturgy

1   1 Corinthians 11:26.

2   See for instance G. Every, **The Mass**, Dublin, 1978.

The Development of Notation

There is ample evidence from this period onwards of the use of boys in the cathedral choirs of Medieval Europe. The assertion in Psalm 8 that the Lord's majesty was recounted by children and sucklings *[lactentium]* was an important justification for the foundation of choir-schools whose education set their inmates on the road to a career in the Church. The thoroughness of their musical training allowed them to take responsibility for some of the most complex types of the chant—including polyphony. See also J. Quasten, **Music and Worship in pagan and Christian antiquity**, Washington DC, 1983.

Chapter 7: From the Ear to the Page

1   P. Weiss and R. Taruskin, **Music in the Western World**, London, 1984, page 41.

2   The very effective techniques used in early Christian times to marshal the brain's huge potential for memorisation are described in F. Yates, **The Art of Memory**, Harmondsworth, 1969.

3   1 Corinthians 12:10.

4   Augustine, *Ennarrationes in Psalmos* 32 and 99, quoted in J. McKinnon, pages 157 and 158.

5   quoted in P. Weiss and R. Taruskin, page 46.

6   From a troped Kyrie from Salisbury Cathedral, and quoted in W.T. Marrocco and N. Sandon, **Medieval Music**, Oxford, 1977, page 29.

7   See J.E. Stevens, **Words and Music in the Middle Ages**, Cambridge, 1986, chapter 9.

8   Quoted in H. Cole, *Sounds and Signs*, Oxford, 1974, page 149.

Chapter 8: From Gregorian Chant to Polyphony

1   Anonymous IV, quoted in the **Pelican History of Music**, volume 1, London, 1982, page 224.

2   Quoted in C. Wright, **Music and Ceremony at Notre Dame of Paris, 500–1550**, Cambridge, 1989, page 339.

3   Quoted in P. Weiss and R. Taruskin, **Music in the Western World**, London, 1984, page 69.

4   The complexities of modal rhythmic notation are described in W. Apel, **The Notation of Polyphonic Music**, Cambridge, Mass., 5th edition, 1961.

5   Quoted in P. Weiss and R. Taruskin, page 62.

6   Quoted in P. Weiss and R. Taruskin, page 71.

7   Franco of Cologne, *Ars Mensurabilis Musicae*, chapter 11. Further extracts from this important treatise can be found in O. Strunk, **Source Readings in Music History**, New York, 1950, pages 139–159.

Rich Church: Poor People

1   P.B. Johnson, **A History of Christianity**, London, 1976, page 228.

2   P.B. Johnson, page 213.

3   P.B. Johnson, page 238.

Chapter 9: Wycliffe's Challenge to the Church

1   *Hoquetus* was the practice of sharing out short phrases or single notes of melody between two players or singers. The word is related to 'hiccup'.

2   J. Wycliffe, *Sermon on the Feigned Contemplative Life*, quoted in E. Routley, **The Church and Music**, London, 1967, page 105.

Part 2: Renaissance and the Reformation

Chapter 10: Luther and the Reformation

1   Quoted in O. Chadwick, *The Reformation*, Harmondsworth, 1972, page 56.

2   Quoted in F. Blume, **Protestant Church Music**, London, 1975, page 10.

3   For further details of Luther's intentions, see C. Halter and C. Schalk, **A Handbook of Church Music**, St. Louis, 1978, chapter 2.

4   Quoted in C. Halter and C. Schalk, page 64.

5   F. Blume, page 10.

6   F. Blume, footnote to page 33.

Lutheran song

1   All these have been published in facsimile this century, at Kassel (1957), Leipzig (1914), Kassel (1954), and Kessel (1929) respectively. See F. Blume, page 760.

Chapter 11: The Swiss Reformers—the Calvinist Tradition

1   See Calvin in translation in P. Weiss and R. Taruskin, **Music in the Western World**, London, 1984, pages 107–109.

The Genevan Psalter

1   Calvini, *Opera Selecta*, 2:15.

Chapter 12: The Reformation in England

1   See W.H. Frere and W.P.M. Kennedy, 'Visitation Articles and Injunctions of the Period of the Reformation', Alcuin Club Collections, 14–16.

2   These included churches and cathedrals at Arundel, Higham Ferrars, Warwick, Beverley and Ripon. See P. Le Huray, *Music and The Reformation in England*, Cambridge, 1978, page 13.

3   See the Lincoln Cathedral Injunctions of 1548, quoted in P. Le Huray, page 9.

4   J.G. Nichols, *The Diary of Henry Machyn*, Camden Society Publications, London, 1848, page 115.

5   *The praise of musicke the profit and delight it bringeth to man and other creatures of God, And the necessity of it in the service & Christian Churche of God*, British Museum MS 18B. xix, quoted more fully in M.C. Boyd, *Elizabethan Music and Musical Criticism*, Pennsylvania, 1940, page 19–20.

6   Quoted in H. Benham, **Latin Church Music c. 1460–1575**, London, 1977, page 165.

7   T. Morley, *A Plaine and Easie Introduction to Practicall Musick*, 1597, edited by R.A. Harman, London, 1963, page 293. The comment has some resonances years later with the attitude of the Tractarians of the Victorian era.

8   Quoted in C. Hogwood and R. Luckett, *Music in Eighteenth Century England*, Cambridge, 1983, page 23.

9   Letter to Peter Martyr from John Jewel, Bishop of Salisbury, 1560, in H. Robinson, *Zurich Letters, volume I*, Parker Society, 1845, page 71.

The Eton Choirbook

1 J.A. Froude, *The Life and Letters of Erasmus*, London, 1894, page 115.

Chapter 13: The Catholic Reformation

1 B. Diaz, companion to Cortes, quoted in B. Gascoigne, *The Christians*, London, 1980, page 180.

2 The Council's pronouncements on music are quoted extensively in R.F. Hayburn, **Papal Legislation on Sacred Music**, Collegeville, Minnesota, 1979, pages 25–31.

3 From A. Manuzio, *Lettere Volgari di Diversi Nobilissimi Huomini . . . Libro Terzo*, Venice, 1564, and translated by L. Lockwood in **Palestrina, Pope Marcellus Mass**, New York, 1975, page 12.

4 From the *Biblioteca Apostolica Vaticana . . . Diario Sistino*, number 7, folio 135v, translated by L. Lockwood, page 21.

5 Dedication of the Second Book of Masses, 1567.

6 Quoted in L. Lockwood, page 24.

The Golden Age of Spanish Music

1 A complete edition is published by the Institute of Medieval Music, edited by C.G. Jacobs, Brooklyn, 1967.

Organ Music

1 A. de St. Gilles (14th century) from M. Gerbet, *Scriptores Ecclesiastici de Musica*, San Blasianis, 1784, volume 3, page 316, and quoted in C. Wright, *Music, and Ceremony at Notre Dame of Paris, 500–1550*, Cambridge, 1989, page 160.

2 Published as volume I of *Musica Britannica*, London, 1952.

Chapter 14: The Power of Music

1 L. Bianconi, *Music in the Seventeenth Century*, Cambridge, 1987, page 134.

2 P. Gerhardt, *Christmas Matins in Berlin*, quoted in C. Halter and C. Schalk, **A Handbook of Church Music**, St. Louis, 1978, page 67.

Part 3: The Flowering of Christian Music

Chapter 15: The Development of Oratorio

1 T. Coryat, *Coryat's Crudities*, 1611, and quoted in T. Dart, *The Interpretation of Music*, 4th edition, London, Page 104.

2 A. Maugars (1639), quoted in P. Weiss and R. Taruskin, **Music in the Western World**, London, 1984, page 195. For details of the music, see A.F. Carver, **Cori Spezzati**, two volumes,

Cambridge, 1988.

3 See, for instance, the *Editto sopra le musiche*, (Edict on Music) of 1665, translated in L. Bianconi, pages 108–109.

4 A. Maugars, quoted in P. Weiss and R. Taruskin, page 196.

5 A. Maugars, quoted in P. Weiss and R. Taruskin, page 196.

Chapter 16: The Music of the Lutheran Church

1 L. Kruger, *Verzeichnis der Adjuvanten . . . in Beiträge zur Hamburgischen Musikgeschichte*, edited by H. Husmann, Hamburg, 1956, and quoted in H. Raynor, *A Social History of Music*, London, 1972, page 202.

2 Quoted in H. Raynor, page 203.

3 H. Raynor, pages 209–210.

4 Quoted in H. Raynor, page 203.

Christmas 1659 in the Nikolaikirche, Berlin

1 This facility, called *Zimbelstern*, is available on many German organs today. Paul Gerhardt is quoted extensively in C. Halter and C. Schalk, page 68.

Chapter 17: Heinrich Schütz

1 'Concerto' here is not used in the modern sense. See glossary.

2 Quoted in H.J. Moser, *Heinrich Schütz*, London, 1967, page 63. See also H. Raynor, page 205.

3 'Symphony' is used here in the general sense of a 'sounding together'.

Patronage

1 Quoted in H.J. Moser, *Heinrich Schütz*, London, 1967, page 80.

Chapter 18: J.S.Bach

1 The word Baroque has its origins in the Portuguese term 'barroco', meaning wild or untamed. In jewellery it referred to an uncut stone and in music to a style which used rhetorical methods to reflect the changing moods of human behaviour.

2 Constantin Bellerman, 1743, quoted in H. David and A. Mendel, editors, **The Bach Reader**, London, 1966, page 236.

3 Christian Gerber, 1732, and quoted in H. David and A. Mendel, pages 229–230.

4 The Consistory records are quoted in H. David and A. Mendel, page 52.

5 Quoted in H. David and A. Mendel, London, page 60.

6 Quoted in H. David and A. Mendel, London, page 33.

7 M. Pallis, *The Metaphysics of Musical Polyphony*, in *Studies in Comparative Religion*, volume 10, number 2, page 106.

8 Quoted in P. Weiss and R. Taruskin, page 218. For the complete work from which this extract is taken and an invaluable treatise on musical thought in Germany, see E.C. Harriss, **Johann Mattheson's Der Vollkommene Capellmeister (1739)**, Ann Arbor, Michigan, 1981.

9 *Works of Martin Luther*, volume 7, Philadelphia, 1915-32, page 284, and quoted in A.K. Swihart, **Luther and the Lutheran Church**, London, 1961, page 142.

10 H. David and A. Mendel, pages 195–196 for the complete list. Orthodoxy and Pietism in Bach's life are discussed in P. Spitta, **Johann Sebastian Bach**, London, 1884, volume 1, page 358 on, and summarized in H. Gerz, *Essays on J.S. Bach*, Ann Arbor, 1985, pages 2, 57–58.

11 W. Mellers, **Bach and the Dance of God**, London, 1980, pages 209–210.

12 The opening of the *Magnificat* or the so-called 'Air on a G-string' (the *Adagio* from Orchestral Suite No.3), are only two examples from thousands.

Bach's Cantatas

1 From E. Neumeister, *Geistlichen Cantaten statt Einer Kirchen-Musik*, 1704, and quoted in L. Schrade, **Bach, the Conflict between the Sacred and the Secular**, New York, 1973, page 60.

2 Reinhard Keiser, *Gemüts-Ergötzung*, Hamburg, 1698, and quoted in H.E. Samuel, *The Cantata in Nuremberg*, Michigan, 1982, page 72.

3 The extent to which congregations participated in the chorales of Bach's Passions anc Cantatas is unknown. See M. Boyd, **Bach**, London, 1983, page 144.

4 An introduction can be found to Bach's cantatas in J.A. Westrup, *Bach Cantatas*, BBC Music Guides, London, 1966.

The Moravian Brethren

1 The name means 'under the protection of the Lord'.

2 Quoted in F. Blume, **Protestant Church Music**, London, 1975, page 601.

3 See also page 116.

4 'Jesus, thy blood and righteousness' is an example.

Chapter 19: Turmoil in England: Commonwealth and Restoration

1 T. Mace, **Musick's Monument**, London 1676, in facsimile, Paris, 1966, part 1, chapter 10, pages 18–10.

2 Quoted in K.R. Long, **The Music of the English Church**, London, 1972, page 206.

3 From N. Temperley, **Music of the English Parish Church**,

Cambridge, 1979, volume 1, page 78.

4 From *A directory for the publicke worship of God throughout the three kingdoms of England, Scotland and Ireland*, London, 1644, in P. Hall, *Reliquiae Liturgicae*, volume III, Bath, 1847.

5 T. Mace, chapter 5, page 9.

6 Tudway (about 1716), and quoted in C. Hogwood and R. Luckett, **Music in Eighteenth Century England**, Cambridge, 1983, page 43.

7 Roger North, *Lord Keeper North*, 1676, see J.W. Wilson, *Roger North on Music*, London, 1959, page 40.

Chapter 20: The Glory of the Chapel Royal

1 Letter to Lord Harley, 1716, quoted in E.H. Fellowes, **English Cathedral Music**, London, 1969, page 133.

2 John Evelyn's diary, entry for 21 December, 1662.

3 Samuel Pepys' diary, entry for 14 October, 1660.

The Music of the Chapel Royal

1 As one scornful Puritan put it: 'In all their order of service there is no edification, according to the rule of the Apostle, but confusion; they tosse the Psalmes in most places like tennice-balles . . .' (Reverend John Field, *An Admonition to the Parliament*, 1572, quoted in M.C. Boyd, *Elizabethan Music and Musical Criticism*, Pennsylvania, 1940, page 23.

2 Quoted in E.H. Fellowes, page 31–32. For a detailed discussion of the music, see P. Phillips, **English Sacred Music 1549–1649**, Oxford, 1991.

Henry Purcell

1 J.W. Wilson, *Roger North on Music*, London, 1959, page 307.

Chapter 21: English Congregational Music: the birth of the English Hymn

1 *Hymns in Commemoration of the Sufferings of Our Blessed Saviour Jesus Christ, compos'd for the celebration of his Holy Supper*.

2 See glossary under 'psalm metre'.

3 Quoted in E. Houghton, *Christian Hymn-Writers*, Bridgend, 1982, page 57.

4 Quoted in D. Davie and R. Stevenson, **English Hymnology in the Eighteenth Century**, Los Angeles, 1980, page 10.

5 D. Davie and R. Stevenson, page 10.

6 From the London County Council's *Survey of London XXII*, London, 1950, page 103, quoted in N. Temperley, **Music of the English Parish Church**,

Cambridge, 1979, volume I, page 102.

7 See N. Temperley, volume I, page 123.

8 W. Vincent, *Considerations on parochial music*, London, 1787, page 23.

9 Preface to Thomas Billington, *The Te Deum etc, page XI* (1784), and quoted in N. Temperley, volume 1, page 161.

10 The American counterpart of this type of music is discussed in chapter 34.

11 A. Buckley, *History of the Providence Baptist Chapel, Lumb*, Rawtenstall, 1928, and see R. Elbourne, *Music and Tradition in Early Industrial Lancashire*, Wodbridge, Suffolk, 1980, Appendix 1.

12 A West Gallery Music Association exists to encourage interest in the music and social life of eighteenth-century country church musicians.

13 H. Davies, *Worship and theology in England*, Princeton, New Jersey, 1961–75, volume III, page 234.

14 J.S. Curwen, *Studies in Worship-Music*, London, 1880, page 12.

Handel and the Messiah

1 W. Millington, *Sketches of local musicians and musical societies*, Pendlebury, 1884, and quoted in N. Temperley, volume 1, page 199. See also D. Burrows, **Handel: Messiah**, Cambridge, 1991.

2 W. Mason, *Essays on English Church Music*, York, 1795, and quoted in N. Temperley, volume 1, page 200.

Part 4: The Path Divides

Chapter 22: Music in the Courts of Europe

1 C. Burney, *The Present State of Music in Germany, the Netherlands and United Provinces*, London, 1775, volume I, pages 226–227.

2 J.A. Jungman, *The Mass of the Roman Rite*, revised edition, New York, 1959, pages 111–112.

Chapter 23: The Romantic Movement

1 W.J. Gatens, **Victorian Cathedral Music in theory and practice**, Cambridge, 1986, page 49.

2 Quoted in W. Blunt, *The Dream King*, London, 1973 page 38.

3 H. Pleasants, *The Musical Journeys of Louis Spohr*, Norman, Oklahoma, 1961, page 205. Spohr was also a composer of numerous oratorios and sacred works, now largely forgotten.

4 J.W. Wilson, editor, **Roger North on Music**, London, 1959,

page 340.

5 R. Druitt, *A popular tract on church music*, London, 1845 page 36.

6 George Elvey, in M. Elvey, *Life and reminiscences of George J. Elvey*, London, 1894, page 320.

7 R.R. Terry, *The Music of the Roman Rite*, London, 1931, pages 47–48.

8 Alec Robertson, *Requiem*, London, 1967, page 30.

9 Quoted in P. Merrick, *Revolution and Religion in the Music of Liszt*, Cambridge, 1987, page 99.

10 Quoted in P. Weiss and R. Taruskin, *Music in the Western World*, London, 1984, page 367.

11 J. Harding, *Gounod*, London, 1973, page 152.

12 J. Harding, pages 213 and 211.

13 Letter to Traumihler, 25 July 1879, and quoted in H.F. Redlich, *Bruckner and Mahler*, London, 1963, page 72.

The Cecilian Movement

1 For another translation, see F. Lesure and R. Nichols, *Debussy Letters*, London, 1987, page 42.

2 Letter to Vasnier, 24 November 1885, see F. Lesure and R. Nichols, page 14.

The Corruption and Resurrection of the Chant

1 H. Berlioz, *Treatise on Instrumentation*, translated by Theodore Front, New York, 1948, page 348.

2 O. Messiaen, *Musique et Couleur (nouveaux entretiens avec Claude Samuel)*, Paris, 1986, page 30.

Chapter 24: The Decline of the Lutheran Hymn

1 J.E. Hauser, 1834, and quoted in F. Blume, *Protestant Church Music*, London, 1975, page 341.

2 The music at the Domkirche was described in great detail by the American hymn-writer Lowell Mason in April 1852. See L. Mason, *Musical Letters from Abroad*, New York, 1854, reprinted in 1967, pages 105–108 and 111–115.

'A Dismal Melody'

1 C.Burney, *An Eighteenth-century Musical Tour in Central Europe and the Netherlands*, volume 2 of P. Scholes, editor, *Dr Burney's Musical Tour in Europe*, London, 1959, pages 222–223.

Chapter 25: The Church of England and the Tractarians

1 Rev. J. Jebb, *The Choral Service of the United Church of England and Ireland*, London, 1843, page 63; much of this is challenging and readable, and

quoted *in extenso* in K.R. Long, *The Music of the English Church*, London, 1972, page 320.

2 *Charge of May 1840 to the Clergy of the Oxford Diocese on Tractarianism and Tract 90*, quoted in S. Neill, *Anglicanism*, Oxford, 1977, page 257.

3 A.T. Robinson, *Reminiscences of an Old Organist*, quoted in K.H. MacDermott, **The Old Church Gallery Minstrels**, London, 1948, page 42; see also N. Boston and L.G. Langwill, *Church and chamber barrel organs*, Edinburgh, 1967.

4 K.R. Long, page 365.

The Demise of the West Gallery Players
1 T. Hardy, *Under the Greenwood Tree*, London, 1872.

Chapter 26: Revival in the Nineteenth Century
1 J.S. Curwen, *Studies in Worship Music*, second series, London, 1885, page 40.

2 W.R. Moody, *The Life of Dwight L. Moody*, New York, 1900, page 186; there is further discussion in R.M. Stevenson, *Patterns of Protestant Church Music* Cambridge, 1953, page 151 and following.

3 Christian Mission Magazine, August, 1877, quoted in B. Boon, *Sing the Happy Song*, London, 1978, page 5.

4 William Booth, quoted in B. Boon, page 5.

5 William Booth, quoted in B. Boon, page 5.

6 William Booth, quoted in B. Boon, page 115.

Chapter 27: The Path Divides
1 F.W. Joyce, *Life of Sir F.A.G. Ouseley*, London, 1896, page 247.

2 J. Barnby, preface to his collected Hymn tunes, London, 1897, and quoted in W.J. Gatens, **Victorian Cathedral Music in Theory and practice**, 1986, page 78.

Part 5: The Glorious Liturgy

Chapter 28: The Orthodox Churches
1 Letter to Nadejda von Meck, quoted in V. Volkoff, *Tchaikovsky*, London, 1975, pages 169–170.

Chapter 29: The Greek Orthodox Church
1 J. McKinnon, *Music in Early Christian Literature*, Cambridge, 1987, pages 65 and 66.

2 R. Hammond, *The Waters of Marah*, London, 1956, pages 51–52.

3 Follieri, *Initia hymnorum*

ecclesiae graecae, quoted in the *New Grove Dictionary of Music and Musicians*, London, 1980, under 'Byzantine Rite'.

4 A glance at the subject matter of the second canticle will suggest why it is usually only included during Lent.

5 But see M.P. Dragoumis, 'The Survival of Byzantine Chant' in E. Wellesz, editor, *Studies in Eastern Chant*, Oxford, 1966, volume I, page 9.

Chapter 30: The Russian Orthodox Church
1 See N. Zernov, **Eastern Christendom**, London, 1961, page 112.

2 The transition to the new music during the seventeenth century is well documented in A.J. Swan, **Russian Music and its sources in chant and folk-song**, London, 1973, page 48 and following. For a study of *znammenny*, see J. Gardner, **Russian Church Singing**, New York, 1980 and J.L. Roccasalvo, **The Plain Chant Tradition of Southwestern Rus'**, New York, 1986.

3 R. Newmarch, editor, *The Life and Letters of P.I. Tchaikovsky*, London, 1906, pages 298–299.

4 Quoted in B. Martyn, *Rachmaninoff*, Aldershot, Hants, 1990, page 222.

Chapter 31: The Coptic and Ethiopian Churches
1 A. Fortescue, *Lesser Eastern Churches*, London, 1913, page 288.

2 Father J. Lobo, *A Voyage to Abyssinia*, translated by Samuel Johnson, London, 1735.

3 M. Powne, **Ethiopian Music**, Oxford, 1968, page 91.

4 Quoted in M. Powne, pages 98–99.

Chapter 32: Christianity, East and West ... Worlds Apart
1 A. Storr, *Solitude*, London, 1989, page 79; note also the chapter on 'The Significance of the Individual'.

2 Quoted in J. McKinnon, *Music in Early Christian Literature*, Cambridge, 1987, page 65.

3 P. Griffiths, *New Sounds, New Personalities*, London, 1985, page 106.

4 John Tavener in discussion with Basil Ramsey in *Music and Musicians*, December 1989, volume 38, number 4, page 7.

5 A recording, C IKOS 8E, is available from Ikon Records, The Cathedral of the Assumption and All Saints, Ennismore Gdns, Knightsbridge, London, SW7.

6 *Musical Times*, March 1989, page 132

Part 6: The African Genius

Chapter 33: Africa and the Influence of Western Music.
1 D. Westermann, *Africa and Christianity*, Oxford, 1937, page 94.

2 J.H. Kwabena Nketia, *The Music of Africa*, London, 1982, page 60.

3 E.W. Smith, *African Ideas of God*, London, 1961 page 83.

4 D. Tutu, 'Whither African Theology?' in *Christianity in Independent Africa*, edited by Fashole-Luke, Gray, Hastings and Tasie, London, 1978, page 365.

5 A.D. Galloway, 'Missionary Impact on Africa', in *Nigeria*, Independence issue of *Nigeria Magazine*, Lagos, October, 1960, page 60.

6 *Music in Worship* magazine, number 33, September/October 1985, page 6–7.

7 'Report on the Experiences of the Church in the Work of Evangelism in Africa'; the African Continent's report for the 1974 Synod of Bishops on 'The Evangelisation of the Modern World', page 16.

Cameroun: African Christian Music
1 P. Abega, 'Liturgical Adaptation', in *Christianity in Independent Africa*, edited by Fashole-Luke, Gray, Hastings and Tasie, London, 1978, page 599.

2 P. Abega, 'Liturgical Adaptation', page 599.

The Marriage of African and Western Music
1 A.K. Achinivu, *Ikoli Harcourt Whyte, The Man and his Music*, Number 7, Beitrage zur Ethnomusikologie, Hamburg, 1979, volume 1, page 84.

2 A.K. Achinivu, Volume 1, page 228.

3 A.K. Achinivu, Volume 1, page 322.

4 A.K. Achinivu, Volume 1, pages 50–52.

Chapter 34: The Independent Churches
1 D. Ndofunsu, 'The Role of Prayer in the Kimbanguist Church', in *Christianity in Independent Africa*, edited by Fashole-Luke, Gray, Hastings and Tasie, London, 1978, page 578.

2 D. Ndofunsu, 'The Role of Prayer in the Kimbanguist Church', page 590.

3 D. Ndofunsu, 'The Role of Prayer in the Kimbanguist Church', page 590.

4 A. Omoyajowo, 'The Aladura Churches in Nigeria since Independence', in *Christianity in Independent Africa*, page 110.

5 B. Jules-Rosette, 'Ecstatic Singing: Music and Social Integration in an African Church', in I.E. Jackson, editor, *More than Drumming*, London, 1985, page 134.

The True Christian Music of Africa
1 A. Omoyajowo, 'The Aladura Churches in Nigeria since Independence', in *Christianity in Independent Africa*, page 109.

Part 7: Music in North America

Chapter 35: Christianity comes to the New World
1 Edward Winslow, 'Hypocrisie Unmasked', and quoted in W.S. Pratt, *The Music of the Pilgrims*, Boston, 1921, page 6.

2 Cotton Mather, *Singing of Psalmes a Gospel-Ordinance*, 1647, and quoted in P. Scholes, *The Puritans in Music*, London, 1934, page 265.

3 T. Walter, *The Grounds and Rules of Music Explained*, Boston, 1721.

4 K. Silverman, *Selected Letters of Cotton Mather*, Louisiana University Press, 1971, page 376.

5 Quoted in H.W. Hitchcock, *Music in the United States*, New Jersey, 1974, page 7.

6 Quoted in I. Lowens, *Music and Musicians in Early America*, New York, 1964, page 282.

7 M.H. Thomas, editor, *The Diary of Samuel Sewall*, New York, 1973, III, page 285.

8 S.Y. Wells editor, *Testimonies Concerning the Character and Ministry of Mother Ann Lee and the First Witnesses of the Gospel*, Albany, 1827, page 101, and quoted in D.W. Patterson, **The Shaker Spiritual**, Princeton, 1979, page 18.

9 *Some Brief Hints, of a Religious Scheme, Taught and Propagated by a Number of Europeans, living in a place called Nisqueunia, in the State of New York*, Salem, 1782, quoted in E.D. Andrews, *The Gift to be Simple*, New York, 1940, page 10.

William Billings
1 W. Bentley, *The Diary of William Bentley, D.D.*, Salem, 1905–14, Volume II, page 350.

2 'Chester', from *New-England Psalm-Singer*, Boston, 1770.

3 Preface to the *Singing Master's Assistant*, 1778.

4 W. Billings, **Continental Harmony**, facsimile edited by N. Nathan, Harvard, 1961, page 28.

5 Andrew Law, *Musical Primer*, Philadelphia, 1793, page 8.

6 W. Billings, *Continental Harmony*, page 31.

Chapter 36: Africans in America
1 Ecroyd Claxton, *Minutes of the Evidence...respecting the Slave Trade*, 34, page 14–36, House of Commons, quoted in D.J. Epstein, **Sinful Tunes and Spirituals: Black Folk Music to the Civil War**, Urbana, Illinois, 1977.

2 James Towne, *Minutes of Evidence...respecting the Slave Trade*, 34, page 14–36, House of Commons, quoted in D.J. Epstein, *Sinful Tunes and Spirituals*, page 8.

3 F.L. Olmstead, *Journey in the Seaboard Slave States*, New York, 1856, volume 2, page 19, and quoted in E. Southern **The Music of Black Americans**, second edition, New York, 1983, page 156.

4 C. Small, **Music of the Common Tongue**, London, 1987, page 87.

5 S. Davies, *Letters from the Reverend Samuel Davies and Others...*, quoted in C. Hamm, *Music in the New World*, New York, 1983, page 128.

6 S. Davies, *Letters from the Reverend Samuel Davies and Others...*, quoted in C. Hamm, page 128.

7 See E. Southern, pages 73–75.

8 J.F. Watson, *Methodist Error*, Trenton, 1819.

9 Verses from the Spiritual 'Dere's No Rain' quoted in E. Southern, page 159.

10 F. Douglass, *My Bondage and My Freedom*, New York, 1855, page 87, quoted in E. Southern, 2nd edition, page 143.

Chapter 37: North and South
1 A.B. Benson, editor, *America of the Fifties: Letters of Frederika Bremer*, New York, 1924.

2 W. Faux, *Memorable Days in America...*, London, 1823, page 420.

3 L.W. Slaughter, *The Freedmen of the South*, Cincinnati, 1869, page 134.

Camp Meetings
1 Quoted in C.A. Johnson, **The Frontier Camp Meeting**, Dallas, 1955, pages 64 and 65.

2 Captain C.B. Marryat, *A Diary in America*, New York, 1839, pages 136–138.

3 J.F. Watson, *Methodist Error*, Trenton, 1819, pages 29–31.

4 Robert Todd, quoted in E. Southern, *The Music of Black Americans*, New York, 1971, page 99.

A 'Shout'
1 See E. Southern, *The Music of Black Americans*, 2nd edition, New York, 1983, page 169.

2 M. Waterbury *Seven Years Among the Freedmen*, Chicago,

second edition, 1891, pages 195–6, quoted in D.J. Epstein *Sinful Tunes and Spirituals*, Urbana, Illinois, 1977, page 287.

Fisk Jubilee Singers
1 *Tribune*, 17 Jan 1872, and quoted in L.D. Silveri, 'The Singing Tours of the Fisk Jubilee Singers', in S.V. Martin and G.R. Keck, editors, *Feel The Spirit, Studies in Nineteenth-Century Afro-American Music*, Connecticut, 1988, page 109.

2 See D.J. Epstein, 'Theodore F Seward and the Fisk Jubilee Singers', in R. Crawford, R.A. Lott, and C.J. Oja, editors, *A Celebration of American Music*, Ann Arbor, Michigan, 1990, page 40.

3 T. Rutling, *Tom: An Autobiography*, Torrington, Devon, UK, 1907, in D.J. Epstein 'Theodore F. Seward and the Fisk Jubilee Singers', page 41.

Chapter 38: Gospel Music: White and Black
1 *The Nation*, March 1876, quoted in E. Sanjek **American Popular Music and its Business**, New York, 1988, volume 2, page 251.

2 C. Small, *Music of the Common Tongue*, London, 1987, pages 103–4.

3 Quoted in V. Broughton, **Black Gospel**, Poole, 1985, page 53.

4 W.C. Handy, *Father of the Blues*, New York, 1970, page 157.

5 The music may be found in the **New Grove Dictionary of American Music**, London, 1986, volume 2, page 256.

6 A. Heilbut, *The Gospel Sound*, New York, 1971, page 10.

7 Quoted in V. Broughton, page 52.

8 Quoted in V. Broughton, page 95.

Tommy Dorsey
1 Quoted in V. Broughton, *Black Gospel*, Poole, 1985, page 36.

2 Quoted in V. Broughton, *Black Gospel*, Poole, 1985, page 37.

3 From the sound-track of the film *Say Amen Somebody*, 1982.

Take Six
1 *The Independent*, 14 November 1991, page 25.

Chapter 39: The United States and the European Classical Tradition.
1 Quoted in J.S. Dwight, *Journal of Music*, 18 December 1852, pages 83–84.

2 Critique of Paine's 1st Symphony in Atlantic Monthly, June, 1876, page 764, and quoted in B.L. Tischler, *An American*

Music, New York, 1986, page 32.

3   J. Kirkpatrick, editor, Charles E. Ives, *Memos*, New York, 1972, page 49.

4   P.H. Lang, 'Church Music—What's Left of It', in *Saturday Review of Literature*, 29 June 1946, page 30.

Charles Ives

1   Quoted in H. and S. Cowell, **Charles Ives and His Music**, Oxford, 1955, page 24.

2   See D. Wooldridge, *Charles Ives*, London, 1975, page 109.

3   'The most superficial trashy stuff that is in vogue: the negro melodies, the namby-pamby sentimental ballads, the flashy fantasias, polkas, waltzes, marches, etc., of native Americans...', in *Dwight's Music Journal*, 1850s; quoted in E. Sanjek *American Popular Music and its Business*, New York, 1988, volume 2, page 141.

4   A note at the foot of a short *Adeste Fidelis* for organ reads: 'Reverend J.B. Lee, others & Mrs Uhler said it was awful...', D. Wooldridge, *Charles Ives*, London, 1975, page 85.

Chapter 40:
The Charismatic Movement

1   W.G. Pulkingham, *They Left Their Nets*, London, 1974, page 125.

Part 8: Music in Twentieth-Century Europe

Chapter 41: Roman Catholic Music in Europe this Century

1   From the *motu proprio*, and quoted in R.F. Hayburn, **Papal Legislation on Sacred Music**, Minnesota, 1979, page 224.

2   Quoted in R.F. Hayburn, page 229.

3   Quoted in R.F. Hayburn, page 225.

4   R.F. Hayburn, page 230.

5   O. Messiaen, *Musique et Couleur (nouveaux entretiens avec Claude Samuel*, Paris, 1986, page 20.

6   O. Messiaen, *Musique et Couleur (nouveaux entretiens avec Claude Samuel*, Paris, 1986, page 22.

Chapter 42: The Bible in the Concert Hall

1   Quoted in N. Tierney, *William Walton*, London, 1984, page 64.

2   J. Joubert, 'Music and the Church' in F.J. Glendenning, editor, *The Church and the Arts*, London, 1960, page 99. The Three Choirs Festival is an annual English musical week, dating from the early eighteenth century and originally solely of sacred

works. It meets in turn at the cathedrals of Hereford, Worcester and Gloucester.

3   Elgar, letter to Jaeger, 9 October 1900.

4   *King David* is usually performed in the version for large orchestra with organ, but it can be even more effective in its original reduced version.

5   *Musical Times*, volume 129, number 1748, October 1988, page 511.

6   Music and Musicians, volume 38, 11 July 1990, page 11.

7   Music and Musicians, volume 38, number 4, December 1989, page 7.

Chapter 43: Vatican II and the Liturgy

1   J. Gélineau, **The Liturgy Today and Tomorrow**, London, 1978, page 9.

2   Pope Pius X, *Apostolic Constitution*, 1928.

3   Dom Gregory Murray, *Music and the Mass*, Leigh-on-Sea, Essex, 1977, page 73.

4   Quoted in R.F. Hayburn, **Papal Legislation on Sacred Music**, Collegeville, Minnesota, 1979, page 384.

5   'Resolution on the Use of Profane Music in Worship', quoted in J. Overath, **Sacred Music and Liturgy Reform after Vatican II**, Rome, 1969, page 182.

6   Anthony Milner (born 1925) is a fine composer of art-music—much of which is inspired by his Roman Catholic faith. He has made valuable contributions to congregational music, such as hymns and psalm-settings. Note also Colin Mawby's *Ten Psalms*, 1968.

7   J. Gélineau, page 9.

L'Abbé de Silvanès

1   Available from Atelier de Musique Liturgique, Abbaye de Silvanès, 12360 Camarès, France.

Taizé

1   As Brother Roger has written: 'never resign yourself to the scandal of the separation of Christmas, all so readily professing love for their neighbour, yet remaining divided.' *The Taizé Experience*, London, 1990, page 57.

2   A comment by Pope Paul II on a visit to Taizé in 1986.

3   *Music from Taizé* (vocal edition), London, 1982, volume I, page vii.

Chapter 44: Lutheran Music Revival

1   See R. Dufallo, *Trackings*, Oxford, 1989, page 213.

2   Foreword to Zimmermann's *Lobet, ihr Knechte des Herrn*.

3   The hymnbook of the World Council of Churches, **Cantate**

Domino, Oxford, 1980, contains Lutheran psalms and hymns by Zimmermann, Paul Rupperl (born 1913), Rolf Schweizer (b1936) and Dieter Trautwein (born 1928).

Hugo Distler

1   Oskar Söhngen, quoted in L. Palmer, **Hugo Distler and his Church Music**, London, 1967, page 104.

2   Letter from Distler to his former teacher Herrman Grabner, 17 April 1931, and quoted in L. Palmer, page 113.

3   For the musical ideology of the Nazi party, see N. Slonimsky, *Music Since 1900*, 4th edition, New York, 1971, page 1393.

Chapter 45:
Music in Britain

1   Quoted in *The First Fifty Years, A brief account of the English Hymnal, 1906-1956*, Oxford, 1956.

2   U. Vaughan Williams, *R.V.W.*, London, 1964, page 72. That discovery led to Vaughan Williams' life-long fostering of amateur music-making.

3   Martin Shaw's views on Christian music and its renewal can be found in his book *The Principles of English Church Music Composition*, London, 1921.

4   'There is no reason why an atheist could not write a good Mass' (quoted in U. Vaughan Williams, page 138).

5   Quoted in C. Palmer, **Herbert Howells**, London, 1978, page 78.

6   *Gloucester* (1946), *St. Paul's* (1954), *Collegium Sancti Johannis Cantabrigiense* (1958), *Winchester* (1968) and *Sarum* (1968).

7   There was always a certain anticipation amongst the choir of York Minster in the early 1970s when Howell's music appeared on the schedule. Amongst much musical mediocrity, everyone knew that, for a change, they were going to face a tough technical challenge which offered the chance of making some first-rate music.

8   St Matthews Church, Northampton, has an honourable reputation in its support of new Christian music.

9   J. Harvey in *Musical Times*, January 1990, page 52.

Leaping into the Dark—Musical Innovation

1   J. Harvey, page 53.

2   J. Harvey, page 53. The 'chord of universality' contains all twelve notes of the chromatic scale, one each of all the note-names.

3   J. Harvey, page 53.

4   J. Harvey, page 52.

5   J. Harvey, page 55.

Chapter 46:
The Popular Stream

1   Preface to *Thirty 20th Century Hymn Tunes*, London, 1960.

2   Particularly in *Sound of Living Waters*, London, 1974, *Fresh Sounds*, London, 1976, and *Cry Hosanna*, London, 1980.

Chapter 47:
Good Music—Good Worship?

1   H. Cole, *The Changing Face of Music*, Oxford, 1978, page 91.

Conclusion

1   In Britain in 1991 the Anglican/Methodist reunion scheme was abandoned along with the Covenant for Unity and some long-held hopes for rapprochement between the Anglicans and Roman Catholics.

2   The Royal Academy of Music's Submission to the Archbishop's Commission on Church Music, February 1990, page 23.

3   Matthew 22:36–38.

4   See for instance Genesis 4:4, Jeremiah 6:20, Revelation 3:15.

5   Luke 4:16, 6:6, John 7.

6   E. Routley, **Church Music and the Christian Faith**, Carol Stream, III, 1978, page 9.

7   Letter from W.A. Mozart to his father dated 28 December 1782, in E. Blom, *Mozart's Letters*, Harmondsworth, 1956.

8   J. Gélineau, *The Liturgy: Today and Tomorrow*, New York, 1978, page 90.

Glossary

Alleluia
At Mass, the chant between the *gradual* and the Gospel reading. It consists of a psalm verse preceded and followed by 'Alleluia'. The final syllable of the word 'Alleluia' is a long *melisma* called the *jubilus*, the rejoicing (see chapter 7).

Anabaptist
A member of a sect that did not believe in infant baptism—common in Zwickau and Munster in Germany at the time of the Reformation.

Antiphon
A chant associated with psalm-singing, usually a prose text (often though not always biblical) which begins and ends the singing of a psalm or psalm verse. A few other free-standing chants are also called antiphons. To sing or play music antiphonally is to divide music between two groups of musicians. (See box in chapter 4.)

Antiphonal, antiphoner
A compilation of antiphons and other chants, usually of the *Divine Office*.

Barrel organ
A mechanical organ operating by means of a horizontal barrel in which pins have been carefully positioned. The barrel slowly rotates and the pins push up triggers which let air into the pipes. Barrel organs became popular in the nineteenth century as replacements for church gallery players.

Basilica
Originally a palace (from the Greek *basilikos*, royal) but in Roman times a large building with aisles, nave and apse used for public meetings. Some were adapted for Christian worship; other churches were then built to the same pattern.

Breviary
Originally, any abridged or shortened book (from the latin 'brevis', short) but from the eleventh century, a liturgical book which contained a selection of items for the *Divine Office*.

Bull
An edict, from the latin *bulla*, seal.

Byzantine
From Byzantium, the centre of Eastern Christendom. The city of Byzantium was renamed Constantinople by Constantine in the fourth century and is now known as Istanbul. The traditions of Greek Orthodoxy are closely related to those of the Byzantine church.

Canon
1. An ecclesiastical law.
2. A musical structure in which identical melodies are heard out of step with each other, but which still makes logical music.
3. A fixed form of prayer at *Mass*, running from the Sanctus to the Lord's Prayer.
4. A type of *Byzantine* chant—see *kanon*.

Cantata
A musical piece for one or more voices (from the Latin *cantare*, to sing) with instrumental accompaniment. Church cantatas became a particular feature of Lutheran worship in the seventeenth and eighteenth centuries.

Canticle
The name given to hymns or other poetical texts in the Bible but outside the book of Psalms. They are often referred to by their first words in Latin translation; for example, the 'Magnificat' is the song of Mary in the Gospel of Luke which begins 'My soul doth magnify the Lord.'

Cantillation
The chanting of sacred texts. The term is usually used in connection with Jewish and Christian traditions. The equivalent term in the *Byzantine* tradition is *ekphonesis*.

Cantor
Originally a solo or principal singer (from the Latin *cantare*). Later (particularly in the seventeenth century) the term came to mean choral director or supervisor.

Cantoris
In cathedrals, the part of the choir on the cantor's side (the north). See also *decani*.

Cantus firmus (plural cantus firmi)
A melody, usually borrowed from another source, used as the basis for a more complex composition. *Cantus firmus* is Latin for 'fixed melody', *canto firmo* being the Italian form.

Cecilian Movement
A group of societies created during the nineteenth century to restore Roman Catholic music to its former glories. They were particularly interested in re-establishing *Gregorian chant* and the *polyphonic* choral style of the later sixteenth century.

Centonization
A phenomenon (from the Latin *cento* meaning patchwork) observed and analysed only this century, whereby melodies belonging to a particular *mode* tend to use the same or similar musical phrases. Centonization has been observed in Christian *chant* (Gregorian, *Byzantine* and Slavonic) and in other music with an oral tradition, such as jazz and folk-music.

Charismatic
Concerning the *charismata*, the gifts of the Spirit discussed by Paul in his first letter to the Corinthians, chapters 12, 13 and 14.

Chromatic music
Music which exploits notes which lie outside the scale-system in use at the time. If chromaticism becomes intense, an underlying scale-system may become difficult or impossible to identify.

Cistercian
A monastic order formed in France at the beginning of the twelfth century to re-establish exact observance of the Rule of St Benedict (see chapter 4).

Cithara
See *kithara*.

Clausula
In one of its many meanings, a technical term concerning early developments in western polyphony, particularly those in the *Magnus liber organi* from Notre Dame (see chapter 8). In this type of *organum*, sections of the original chant which are *melismatic* have a repetitive rhythm superimposed on them. These sections contrast strongly with their musical surroundings (where the chant is heard in very long notes) and are called clausulas. New clausulas came to be written to substitute for or to replace those already composed, giving them an independent musical identity. The addition of new text to the upper (organal) part(s) of clausulas created the medieval *motet*.

Concerto
A term which in its early use simply indicates a getting-together to make music. The Latin *concertare* means to dispute or to strive, but in the Italian *concertare*, a getting-together or an agreement is a more likely origin. Thus Schütz's *Kleine geistliche Konzerte* (little sacred concertos, 1639) are not concertos in the much later sense of soloist-with-orchestra, but simply musical opportunities for singers and players.

Conductus
Originally a piece of vocal music sung as an accompaniment to the movement of celebrants in Roman liturgy of the Middle Ages. The Latin word *conducere* means to guide or to escort. Some early references to conductus are in connection with the escorting of a reader to a lectern, but there are also examples in liturgical drama (for example the Play of Daniel). Later the term refers to a particular type of musical composition, mostly *polyphonic*.

Continuo
Short for *basso continuo*, meaning continuous bass. From about 1600 to 1760 almost all art-music was supported by a continuous presentation of the bass line and its associated harmonies. Basso continuo could be played on a wide variety of instruments, a working minimum being one bass instrument (cello, viola da gamba, bassoon) with an instrument capable of playing harmonies, for example keyboard, lute or harp.

Council of Trent
An ecclesiastical body of the Roman Catholic Church convened by Pope Paul III which met in Trento between 1542 and 1563 to pronounce on all aspects of church life (see chapter 13).

Counterpoint
A term used first in the fourteenth century to describe the combination of musical lines according to certain rules. A 'point' was a short musical phrase. When such a phrase was heard successively in two or more musical lines, then 'point' was set 'counter [against] point'. Its most common use nowadays is in describing imitative music, such as *fugue*.

Decani
A term used in medieval monasteries and cathedrals referring to the 'dean's side' of the choir (the south side, where the dean traditionally sat). The word (together with its counterpart, *cantoris*) is still used in some Protestant churches where music is sung *antiphonally*.

Diatonic music
Music which is written according to scale-systems notated by conventional key-signatures.

Discant
A general term for *polyphony*, but also with specific meanings:
1. improvised polyphony,
2. a part added to the *tenor*,
3. the top line of a *polyphonic piece* (hence also 'descant').

Divine Liturgy
The Orthodox term for the service otherwise known as Eucharist, Holy Communion or Mass.

Divine Office
The daily services set out by the Rule of St Benedict (see chapter 4).

Dumb organist
A mechanism attached to a pipe organ which played the instrument automatically with mechanical fingers. Dumb organists worked on the same principle as *barrel organs* and were used in some churches in the nineteenth century when the human variety could not be found.

Ekphonesis
A word often used over the last century to describe the *cantillation* of the *Byzantine* church. Ekphonetic notation indicates the musical equivalents of grammatical signs, such as commas, full-stops and question marks.

Friar
A member of one of the mendicant, or wandering, monastic orders, such as the Augustinians, Carmelites, Dominicans and Franciscans.

Fugue
A special case of *counterpoint*, whereby points worked on are taken up in imitation between parts, such music alternating with passages in freer style.

Gradual
An item of the *Proper* in the Latin *Mass*, sung between the readings. From as early as the fifth century graduals have been complex and demanding chants, intended for expert singers.

Graduale
A liturgical book containing graduals and other chants applicable to skilled singers.

Gregorian chant
The generic name for the Latin chant of the Western church collated during the papacy of Gregory the Great.

Heterophony
The simultaneous singing or playing of different variations of the same melody.

Hirmos (plural hirmoi)/heirmos
Part of a hymn of the *Byzantine* church, the word meaning stanza in Greek. It is used to describe the first, or model, stanza of a *kontakion* or of one of the nine odes which make up a *kanon* (see chapter 29).

Holler
Open vocal music made by African slaves in America, forming part of the complex web of music forming black *spirituals*.

Hoquetus/hocket
A device of medieval *polyphony* in which notes and rests alternate rapidly with each other in such a way that rests occur in one part at the same time as notes in another. As one fourteenth century writer described it: 'one [part] overlaps the other in the manner of roof tiles, and thus they will cut each other off continually'.

Ikonostasis
The screen on which ikons are placed in an Orthodox church.

Introit
Part of the *Proper* at Mass. It is the first musical item of the service and usually consists of an *antiphon* appropriate to the theme of the service, a psalm verse, repeat of the antiphon (perhaps omitted), the doxology (*Gloria Patri*, 'Glory to the Father…') and the antiphon again.

Jacobite Church
A church formed from followers of Jacob Baradai (died in 578). It was based in Syria and Palestine and opposed the findings of the Council of Chalcedon on the nature of Christ.

Jesuit
A member of the Society of Jesus, founded by Ignatius Loyola (1491–1556). The Society was created in order to revive the spiritual life of the Roman Catholic Church.

Jubilus
See *Alleluia*.

Kanon (plural kanones)
The most extensive and complex type of *Byzantine* hymn. A full kanon consists of nine odes, each based on a different biblical song (see chapter 29).

Kapellmeister
The German term for *precentor* or chief church musician.

Kithara
The most common stringed instrument of Old Testament times, still widespread throughout the Near East and North Africa. It is shaped like a *lyre* but the sound chest is made from wood instead of tortoise-shell.

Kontakion (plural kontakia)
An extended hymn of the *Byzantine* church. It consists of many stanzas called *oikoi*. The word means scroll.

Kyriale
A book containing chants for the *Ordinary* of the *Mass* of the Western church.

Liber usualis
Literally (from the Latin), a practical or useful book. It is the name given to the Roman Catholic collection of chant in general use until the 1960s.

Liturgy
Originally a public office or duty,

from the Greek *leitourgos* meaning public servant. The word has since come to mean a form of public worship.

Lyre

A plucked-string instrument whose strings are stretched between a soundbox and a wooden bar. The bar and soundbox are kept apart by two posts either side of the strings. The soundbox is usually made from the shell of a tortoise.

Maestro di capella

The Italian term for *precentor* or chief church musician.

Maronite Church

A church based in the Lebanon. It was founded at the time of the Crusades and is now *uniate*.

Mass

The name given by the Roman Catholic church to the most important form of Christian liturgy, otherwise known as Communion, the Eucharist, the Lord's Supper or the *Divine Liturgy*. Low Mass indicates a liturgical celebration with little ceremony (it may be without music); High Mass is very ceremonial and ornate.

Melisma

A word from the Greek for song. It means a group of several notes all sung to one syllable.

Melkites

The Christians in Egypt who did not choose to follow the *Monophysites* in the Chalcedonian Schism of 451. They were mostly state officials and were therefore nicknamed Melkites ('emperor's men') from the Syriac *malkoye*.

Mode

Literally, a manner or system of operation. In music this generates several meanings, some of which are archaic:
1. a scale-system to which the notes of a piece conform.
2. a rhythmic scheme to which a piece conforms.
3. a prevailing emotional quality to a piece (its mood).
4. the system by which long notes are divided into shorter in medieval and Renaissance times. The first meaning is the most common.

Monody/monophony

Music consisting of a single melody.

Monophysites

Christians who disagreed with the findings of the Council of Chalcedon in 451, believing that Jesus the Son of God has only one nature, which is both human and divine, instead of the orthodox formula of two natures. The Ethiopian and Coptic churches are Monophysite.

Motet

In medieval times, a sung musical item for two to four voices (most often three) built on a pre-existing melody, often a fragment of chant. See also *clausula*. Later on, the term came to mean choral music (probably unaccompanied) with a sacred text.

Motu proprio

A Latin phrase meaning 'of one's own accord'. It is applied to pronouncements from the pope made on his own initiative, independent of advice and signed by him alone.

Mutation stop

An organ stop whose pipes are tuned to reinforce a stop already drawn, thereby creating the illusion of a new timbre when both stops are heard together.

Neume

Originally a term from the Greek to denote a short musical gesture or fragment of a melody. Later (from the ninth century) the word was applied to written signs which stood for these fragments. Western neumes stood for between one and four notes and their Latin names suggest the melodic shape they represent; for example, *virga*—rod and *torculus*—twist.

Ngoma

Vocal sounds imitative of percussion instruments, a traditional part of African music.

Numerology

The study of numbers, in particular of their symbolic significance.

Obikhod

A chant-book for general use in the Russian Orthodox church.

Oktoechos

The system whereby the chants of the *Byzantine* church are organized into cycles of eight weeks, the chants for each week belonging to one of the eight *modes*.

Oratorio

An Italian word meaning 'prayer-hall'. Musical items sung in such buildings to illustrate or to comment on biblical stories became known as oratorios. (See chapter 15.)

Ordinary

The term used to describe the items in traditional Christian liturgy whose texts never alter.

Organ mass

A number of *versets* collected into book suitable for use by an organist at a particular type of service. François Couperin's *Messe pour les paroisses* (1690) is an example; its structure presumes that the singers alternate with the organ.

Organum

1. the Latin word for organ, the musical instrument.
2. a term which has no direct connection with the organ and whose derivation is obscure. From the ninth century it was used to describe the addition of a second melody to a first. Over the next three centuries it refers to a type of music where additional 'organal' voices are added to an already existing chant (see chapter 8).

Oxford Movement

See *Tractarians*

Parody Mass

A setting of texts of the *Ordinary* of the *Mass* based on a pre-existing melody, popular in the later fifteenth and sixteenth centuries. The melody might be *Gregorian chant*, love-song or battle cry (see chapter 13).

Polychoral

For many choirs.

Polyphonic

Literally 'many-sounding'; music made by combining melodies.

Precentor

Literally, 'chief singer'. The term is used in Protestant cathedrals for an important musical officer amongst the clergy, and in Scottish Presbyterian churches for a lay-person, perhaps the parish clerk, who begins the singing in the absence of any accompaniment.

Prokeimenon

The equivalent of the Roman Catholic *Gradual* in the *Byzantine Divine Liturgy*. Like Graduals, they consist of an elaborate psalm-verse with a refrain.

Proper

The term used to describe the items in traditional Christian liturgy whose texts change according to the subject of celebration. They are therefore 'proper', that is, appropriate to the occasion.

Prosaria

A liturgical book containing prosae, that is, *sequences*.

Psaltes

The *Byzantine* word for *cantor*. *Protopsaltes* is the equivalent word for *precentor* or chief singer. If a Byzantine choir is divided and positioned left and right, the protopsaltes leads the right-hand group. See *lampadarios*.

Psalm metre

The system of versification applied to metrical translations of the psalms. In order that any number of tunes might be fitted to them, the metres of English metrical psalms were largely limited to three patterns whose syllable counts per line are as follows: Short Metre (S.M.) 6.6.8.6, Common Metre (C.M.) 8.6.8.6 and Long Metre (L.M.) 8.8.8.8.

Psalter

A book containing the biblical psalms, modified to make them suitable for liturgical use.

Requiem

The *Mass* for the dead. 'Requiem' is the first word of the service, beginning the *introit: Requiem aeternam dona eis, Domine* (grant them eternal rest, O Lord).

Respond

Strictly, the response after a *versicle*, but nowadays synonymous with *responsory*.

Responsory

An elaborate chant of the Roman Catholic church, sung after the lessons at Matins. As Isidore of Seville (about 559–636) explained: 'Responsories are so called because a chorus responds... to a soloist.' As with the *gradual* and other chants, a responsory consists of a choral refrain (the respond), an elaborate psalm-verse sung by a soloist, followed by a repeat of the last part of the respond. Originally the respond was congregational.

Responsorial

The word used to describe chant in which a choir or congregation responds to or answers a soloist.

Rhetoric

In classical antiquity, one of the *trivium*, the three essential skills in the spoken arts, along with grammar and dialectic. In 1416 Quintilian's *Institutio oratoria* was rediscovered, providing a renaissance of ideas about possible connections between music and oratory, the art of persuasive speech. Since that time composers have sought rhetorical means to make music emotionally compelling. Connections between classical methods of rhetoric and musical structure were especially strong in the eighteenth century.

Schola cantorum

A school of singers, thus a choir in training and presumably expert.

Second Vatican Council

A reforming council of the Roman Catholic Church which met in 1962. It permitted some radical changes in the liturgy, notably the use of the vernacular (local languages) instead of Latin. The Council's views on music are contained in chapter 6 of the Constitution on the Sacred Liturgy, published in 1963 (see chapter 44).

Sequence

A type of Latin chant popular from about 850 to 1150. Though the style of sequences changed greatly over this period, earlier examples were composed in clearly-defined phrases, the music of each being repeated to different words. These lines of text did not rhyme, hence their common medieval name of *prosa* or prose (see chapter 7).

Sequentia

A wordless melody added to *alleluias* to which words might be added to make a prosa, or *sequence*.

Shape notes

A type of notation popular in America in the eighteenth century to help church singers to learn to read music (see chapter 35).

Shout

an informal and ecstatic assembly, with dancing, usually following a formal Black gospel service (see box in chapter 37).

Solmization

A method of indicating melodic intervals. The common Western methods in use today (tonic sol-fa, solf ge) have their origins in the solmization system of Guido (see box in chapter 7).

Spiritual

Christian song, originating in eighteenth-century North America, sung at informal gatherings by both whites and blacks (see chapter 37).

Sticheron (plural stichera)

The Greek word for 'verse'. In *Byzantine* liturgy, it refers to verses for singing immediately after a psalm verse, like the Western *antiphon*.

Stile rappresentativo

Literally, 'theatrical style'. This solo vocal style developed rapidly in the early seventeenth century as composers sought to instil into music the persuasive qualities of ancient Greek theatre.

Talmud

A collection of moral precepts and traditions (the Mishnah) and further comments on it (the Gemera), from a Hebrew word meaning instruction. The most recent parts of the Talmud were completed in the fifth century AD.

Tenebrae

The Matins and Lauds services of the Wednesday, Thursday and Friday before Easter. Following an ancient Roman Catholic tradition, candles are progressively extinguished during the psalms until finally Psalm 51 is sung in darkness, to symbolize Jesus' death.

Tenor

From the Latin 'tenere', to hold. The voice singing the chant around which medieval polyphony was constructed was called the tenor. As late as the eighteenth century it was the tenor that was given the melody in harmonized hymn-tunes.

Thoroughbass/through bass

English terms for *continuo*.

Tract

A type of chant substituted for the *gradual* at Mass in times of penitence and mourning.

Tractarians

Followers of the tenets of the *Tracts for the Times*, a series of pamphlets published in the 1830s by high-church reformers in the Church of England (see chapter 25).

Tridentine

Of the *Council of Trent*.

Troparion (plural troparia)

In the *Byzantine* tradition, originally a short prayer sung after each verse of a psalm, like a refrain. They now take the form of one-verse hymns.

Trope

An insertion of new music or words or both into an already existing chant (see chapter 7). *Polyphonic* elaborations of chant were also called tropes.

Troper

A liturgical book containing *tropes*. A well-known example, from the Old Benedictine Minster at Winchester in the tenth century, is the Winchester Troper, which contains *organum* as well as tropes for the *Ordinary*.

Uniate Churches

Eastern churches in union with Roman Catholicism, though following their own liturgy.

Vatican II

See *Second Vatican Council*

Verset

A piece of music for organ, probably based on *Gregorian chant*, substituting for a sung part of *Mass*. They were widely used in the Roman Catholic Church from the fifteenth to nineteenth centuries. It was common practice to alternate organ versets with sections of chant from the choir.

Versicle

A short verse, answered by a response. The word is also used to describe the distinct phrases that make up *sequences*.

Villancico

Spanish popular song, popular from the sixteenth to eighteenth centuries, permitted in the liturgy with appropriately sacred words at certain times of the year (see box in chapter 13). Nowadays the word means 'Christmas carol'.

Znamenny

Short for *znamenny raspev*, which means chanting by signs. It is the name given to the chief and most ancient chant of the Russian Orthodox Church, rarely sung nowadays.

Index